Literary
New York

Praise for the first edition of *Literary New York:*

"The authors have done their research well, and the engaging text is supplemented by admirable photographs and clearly drawn maps, with important literary sites numbered in such a way that even pedestrians with no bump of direction will be able to spot where Twain smoked and wrote in bed, Behan tippled, and Henry James lived 'almost back to back'—curious image!—with Herman Melville."

—Brendan Behan

"*Literary New York* is a delightful and thoroughly useful book. May it instruct the many who need to be told; New York has been a great thing for American writers, and remains so."

—Alfred Kazin

"The detail has a quietly thrilling cumulative effect. It is a lovingly conserving work, drawing together in one place the city's hopscotching literary life, and it makes the reader care about the mad poets and writer-businessmen who have stalked and strolled these streets."

—Richard R. Lingeman in the *New York Times*

"Much more than a guide, it is fascinating to anybody interested in American writing. It almost suggests that there could have been a New York without an American literature, but there could not have been an American literature without New York."

—Edwin Newman

LITERARY
NEW YORK
A History and Guide

SUSAN EDMISTON AND LINDA D. CIRINO

Introduction by
ROBERT PHILLIPS

Neighborhood walking tours revised by
PHILIP LYMAN

GIBBS·SMITH
P
PUBLISHER

PEREGRINE SMITH BOOKS

Cover design by J. Scott Knudsen, Park City, Utah
Cover illustration by Carie Henry
Maps by Rick Sweet, Square One
Walking tours revised by Philip Lyman

First revised edition
5 4 3 2 1 91 92 93 94 95

Copyright © 1976, 1991 by Susan Edmiston and
Linda D. Cirino
Introduction copyright © 1991 by Robert Phillips

Printed in the United States of America

**Library of Congress Cataloging-in-Publication
Data**

Edmiston, Susan.
         Literary New York : a history and
guide / Susan Edmiston and Linda D. Cirino ;
introduction by Robert Phillips. —Rev. ed.
                    p. cm.
         Includes bibliographical references
and index.
            ISBN 0-87905-392-5 (pbk.)
         1. American literature—New York
(N.Y.)—History and criticism. 2. Authors,
American—Homes and Haunts—New York
(N.Y.)—Guide-books. 3. Literary landmarks—
New York (N.Y.)—Guide-books. 4. New York
(N.Y.)—Description—Guide-books. 5. New York
(N.Y.)—Intellectual life. I. Cirino, Linda D. II.
Title.
PS144.N4E3 1991
810.0'97471—dc20   91-7170
                    CIP

The authors are grateful for permission to reprint from the following:
An Autobiography by Van Wyck Brooks, copyright © 1954, 1957, 1961 by Van Wyck Brooks; new edition copyright by Gladys Brooks. Published by E. P. Dutton & Co., Inc. and reprinted with their permission. *The Beat Generation* by Bruce Cook; reprinted by permission of Charles Scribner's Sons. "The Bridge" from *The Collected Poems and Selected Letters and Prose of Hart Crane*; permission of Liveright, Publishing, New York, copyright © 1933, 1958, 1966 by Liveright Publishing Corp. "y is a Well Known Athlete's Bride" from *Complete Poems 1913–1962* by E. E. Cummings; reprinted by permission of Harcourt Brace Jovanovich, Inc. *Shadow and Act* by Ralph Ellison, copyright © 1964 by Ralph Ellison; reprinted by permission of Random House, Inc. "Green Automobile" and "I Beg You Come Back & Be Cheerful" by Allen Ginsberg, from *Reality Sandwiches*, copyright © 1963 by Allen Ginsberg. "Howl," from *Howl and Other Poems* by Allen Ginsberg, copyright © 1956, 1959 by Allen Ginsberg, reprinted by permission of City Lights Books. "Dream Deferred" from *The Panther and the Lash: Poems of Our Times* by Langston Hughes, copyright 1951 by Langston Hughes; reprinted by permission of Alfred A. Knopf, Inc. "The Hotel Chelsea" by Edgar Lee Masters, reprinted by permission of Mrs. Edgar Lee Masters. "Geographical" by Ogden Nash, from *Hard Lines*, copyright 1931 by Ogden Nash, renewed © 1958; reprinted by permission of Curtis Brown, Ltd. Untitled poem on the Bronx by Ogden Nash, reprinted by permission of Curtis Brown, Ltd.; all rights reserved; appeared in the July 1964 issue of The Bronx County Historical Society Journal. "Poem" and "Weather Near St. Bridget's Steeples" from *The Collected Poems of Frank O'Hara*, edited by Donald Allen, copyright © 1971 by Maureen Granville-Smith, Administratrix of the Estate of Frank O'Hara; reprinted by permission of Alfred A. Knopf, Inc. "The Day Lady Died" from *Lunch Poems* by Frank O'Hara, copyright © 1964 by Frank O'Hara; reprinted by permission of City Lights Books. *The Autobiography of Lincoln Steffens*, copyright, 1931, by Harcourt Brace Jovanovich, Inc.; copyright, 1959 by Peter Steffens; reprinted by permission of the publisher.

Acknowledgments

THE AUTHORS would like to thank the National Endowment for the Humanities for the grant that enabled them to complete this book. Gratitude is due to Nancy Milford and Russell Lynes for their support of this project and to Lola Szladits for the continuing inspiration of her encouragement, friendship and example.

Many writers gave of themselves and their time in letters or interviews; among them were Louis Auchincloss, the late W. H. Auden, Luigi Barzini, the late Arna Bontemps, Vance Bourjaily, Paul Bowles, Susan Jenkins Brown, Curtis Cate, John Henrik Clarke, Wayne Cooper, Gregory Corso, Malcolm Cowley, James T. Farrell, Jack Gelber, Allen Ginsberg, E. Stanly Godbold, Jr., Rosa Guy, Elizabeth Hardwick, Michael Harrington, the late Hiram Haydn, Hettie Jones, Matthew Josephson, Alfred Kazin, Seymour Krim, Clay Lancaster, Julius Lester, Townsend Ludington, Dwight Macdonald, Mary McCarthy, Arthur Miller, Lewis Mumford, Larry Neal, Anaïs Nin, Ann Petry, William Phillips, Mary Pitlick, the late Ted Poston, Norman Rosten, Isidor Schneider, George S. Schuyler, Isaac Bashevis Singer, Patsy Southgate, William Styron, Ellen Tarry, Virgil Thomson, Louis Untermeyer, Dorothy Van Doren, James Sibley Watson, John Hall Wheelock, E. B. White, and Herman Wouk.

Additionally, for help and information, we are grateful to

ACKNOWLEDGMENTS

Marjorie Pearson, James Dillon and Michael Gold of the Landmarks Preservation Commission of the City of New York; Elizabeth Kray of the Academy of American Poets; Jean Hutson and Ruth Ann Stewart of the Schomburg Collection of the New York Public Library; Andreas Brown of the Gotham Book Mart; Andrew Anspach of the Algonquin Hotel; Diana Haskell of the Newberry Library; Tony Zwicker of the National Arts Club; John Lindenbusch formerly of the Long Island Historical Society; Stanley Bard of the Chelsea Hotel; Edwin Fancher and Dan Wolf, founders of the *Village Voice*; Heyward Ehrlich and Hans Bergmann of the Melvilleans; Ann Small of Arno Press; Loring McMillen of the Staten Island Historical Society; the Reverend James Harold Flye; Joseph Slade; Mary Bowling of the Butler Library of Columbia University; Lee Roberts; Marjorie Content Toomer; Pearl M. Fisher; Mrs. Rudolph Fisher; Emerson Harper; Henry Lee Moon; Carl Cowl; Ron Hobbs; Alice Davis Tibbetts; Mrs. Ralph Ellison; Ann McGovern Scheiner and Robert B. Glynn. The New York Public Library provided the authors with work space in the Frederick Lewis Allen Room and the Wertheim Study, and was invaluable for research in general. The Leonia New Jersey Public Library generously provided access to quiet work space when needed. The facilities of the Hackensack New Jersey Public Library, and in particular the assistance of Mary Otchy in locating obscure volumes, were of significant help.

For special help in locating and providing photographs we would like to thank Alice Bonnell, formerly of the Columbiana Collection; the late Poppy Cannon; Louise Dahl-Wolfe; Peter Dzwonkoski, Yale University Library; Alfred A. Knopf; Charlotte La Rue of the Museum of the City of New York; Ruth Lester, Institute of Concerned Photography; Charles Lockwood; Pack Memorial Library, Asheville, North Carolina;

ACKNOWLEDGMENTS

George Plimpton; Frances Steloff of the Gotham Book Mart; Neda M. Westlake, University of Pennsylvania Library; and Hortense Zera, American Academy of Arts and Letters.

The authors would like to thank Joyce Hartman for her patience and editorial guidance and copy editor Frances L. Apt for her dedication to detail and pursuit of perfection.

Susan Edmiston would like to thank Kathryn Paulsen and Alice K. Turner for editorial suggestions; Wendy Weil for patient and unstintingly generous help in both practical and personal matters; and Peter H. Edmiston, who trudged miles of neighborhood tours, spurred lagging inspiration with maps, books and other treasures, and, most important, shared faith and enthusiasm.

Linda Cirino feels immeasurable gratitude for the encouragement of friends and family, particularly the loyalty, tolerance and support of Antonio Cirino. Paul and Mark Cirino, though small, merit large gold medals for being remarkably respectful of the file cards and papers continually within their reach. Florence Grammerstorf deserves special personal thanks.

S. S. E.
L. D. C.

Preface

FOR THOSE OF US who live with books, what we read is as much a part of our personal history as the events we participate in. For each of us certain fictional scenes burn with a reality equal to the high points of our own experience. And the writers who created them have a special relation to us; they are sometime collaborators in our lives. Rediscovering their homes, the rooms where they gathered, the things they saw as they went from place to place, we learn something about the sources of their experience and, indirectly, ours. Such was the emotion that impelled us, two New Yorkers who love the city and its literature, to write this book.

We began with the simple motive of seeking out the houses of writers who had lived in New York and the places they wrote about. It soon became apparent that to present what we found in a readable way we should have to describe how writing developed in New York and suggest something of the city's character and style at various times, and so this book became a combined exploration in history, literature and biography. What influence the city had on the shaping of literature remains to be examined in greater depth. Over a drink at the Century Club Alfred Kazin told us, "I can't prove it but I'm sure New York is the single most important factor in American writing." He himself has written of the "aesthetic born of the extraordinary number of stimuli . . . in the modern city," exemplified in García Lorca's *The Poet in New York,* Hart Crane's *The Bridge* and Dos Passos's *Manhattan Transfer.* "The modern city," says Kazin, "has created new imperatives of literary form as well as of social thinking."

We leave it for others to delineate the esthetic impact of the city on literature. Our goal was more concrete. Exploring neighborhood by neighborhood, we have attempted to retrace the steps of the city's major writers, re-create the literary circles and currents in which they moved and pinpoint landmarks — writers' homes, haunts, gathering places and the settings of their work. We hope that others will discover, as we have, an additional dimension to the most mundane corners of the city; by association with the literary past a house, restaurant or street takes on new significance and evokes fresh emotions.

We have been hampered in our efforts by the ever changing nature of the physical city. Some buildings were demolished even as we wrote and others will have disappeared by the time this book reaches publication. By discovering and documenting those landmarks that still exist — some of them previously unknown — we hope to aid in their preservation. One other disclaimer: our reasons for including some writers and not others were sometimes complicated and arbitrary. In general, we followed the principle of emphasizing writers in proportion to their critical reputations. However, we also took into consideration how great a force the city was in their work and how much they were involved in the life of the city. Practical considerations intervened. Better biographical data exist on some past figures than on others, and some living writers preferred not to provide us with information. We also hesitated to write too extensively of those whose reputations are in the process of formation; as a general rule, we tried to include comprehensively all those who were established by the fifties. Ultimately, this book is a personal one — some writers, groups, incidents, situations and places simply aroused our interest and affections more than others.

New York has such a complex identity that it is not often characterized as a literary town. Yet the city saw the launching of a national literature with Washington Irving and James Fenimore Cooper; its coming of age with Edgar Allan Poe, Herman Melville and Walt Whitman; its exuberant development in the work of dozens of twentieth-century writers. In fact, except for the second half of the nineteenth century, when ascendancy passed to New England, New York has been and is the literary capital of America. This book, we hope, begins to bring coherence and perspective to the vast and varied history of the city's involvement in literature.

Susan Edmiston
Linda D. Cirino

New York, 1975

Publisher's Acknowledgments

THE PUBLISHER wishes thank Philip Lyman for his efforts in preparing the revised neighborhood tours. Mr. Lyman walked every step of each tour, noting which buildings still stood and which had been demolished since the first edition of this book was published in 1976. He suggested many additional sites of literary interest and provided exact information on many buildings: dates, architects, history. We were constrained by space and budget and thus unable to include all the information he provided, but hope that in future we may be able to expand this volume to match the scope of his knowledge of the city.

Robert Phillips provided an excellent introduction which gives a sense of the city's literary life in the recent past. We appreciate his enthusiasm and his suggestions for improvement.

Finally, we are grateful to Susan Edmiston and Linda D. Cirino for writing *Literary New York* in the first place. We trust the next generation of readers will take as much pleasure from this volume as has the last.

Contents

Illustrations

ILLUSTRATIONS

ILLUSTRATIONS

ILLUSTRATIONS

STREET MAPS ACCOMPANY EACH
NEIGHBORHOOD TOUR

was set upon a raised platform, prompting him to call the bathroom the "Throne Room." No entertaining detail was too small for the authors, making the book a big plum pudding. They were equally at home discussing the Lost Generation and the Beats, the Naturalists and the New York Poets. Their notes revealed they'd read everything from *The Voyages of Giovanni de Verrazano, 1524-1528* to *Henry Miller Letters to Anaïs Nin.* They also conducted interviews with many writers, including Louis Auchincloss, Arthur Miller, Larry Neal, Allen Ginsberg, and Alfred Kazin; and corresponded with others, such as Paul Bowles, W. H. Auden and Herman Wouk, to gain information and verify facts. The book was, in short, an admirable work of scholarship.

It appeared fifteen years ago. Now a new edition is being published, and I have been asked to give an accounting of what has occurred in literary New York since that time. Inasmuch as it takes fame a while to catch up with some writers, I have gone back not just fifteen, but thirty years. And my method differs from that of Edmiston and Cirino. I have not proceeded from borough to borough because, frankly, not that much has occurred on, say, Staten Island in the past three decades to shape modern literary history. The original authors were able to find literary activity in all the boroughs because they began in the 1520s rather than in the 1960s. But, I have instead proceeded from genre to genre, event to event. My aim remains the same as that of the original authors: to mirror the city's ongoing literary history in a chronological fashion.

I have been joined in this endeavor by Philip Lyman, of The Gotham Book Mart, one of New York's most knowledgeable bookmen. He has updated the walking tours, not only by adding new locations, but also by personally verifying every one of the sites to determine they are still extant. His knowledge of literary history and his architectural descriptions add considerably to the value of this new edition. In some instances he has corrected errors in the original. It is our hope that *Literary New York* will excite current readers as much as it did those of us who fell upon it when it originally appeared in the Houghton Mifflin edition.

•

Over the past three decades, New York has continued to inspire writers to create characters and plots set in and around Gotham. One such writer was James T. Farrell. Often thought of as a Chicago novelist, Farrell spent decades living in Manhattan, first in residential hotels, then at 5 Tudor City Place, and finally at 308 East 79th Street, where he died in 1979. *Judith* (1969) is about the career of a celebrated concert pianist who lives in one of the fortresslike apartment houses on Riverside Drive. During the course of the novel, she performs at Columbia University, the East Side YMCA, and Carnegie Hall. Olive, of *Olive and Mary Anne* (1977), is a millionairess who becomes a painter. The novella evokes the world of New York's 57th Street art galleries. *Sam Holman* (1983), a novel published posthumously, takes us to the world of New York intellectuals centered around Washington Square and New York University in the 1930s.

Another Chicago novelist, Saul Bellow, has also made New York the scene of some of his most important work. *Mr. Sammler's Planet* (1970) concerns an old man who lives on New York's chaotic upper West Side and spends his days in the 42nd Street New York Public Library. *Humboldt's Gift* (1975) is plainly modeled on the life and death of Delmore Schwartz, the poet and fiction writer who himself celebrated Manhattan in many works. Mental illness and creative paralysis set in during Humboldt's last years, and like Schwartz, he is "dying of unwritten poems." The novel follows Humboldt from Bedford Street in Greenwich Village to Princeton to rural New Jersey (similar to Schwartz's relocating to Baptistown, New Jersey, in the 1950s) and finally to Times Square. Schwartz died in 1966 of a heart attack suffered at the Columbia Hotel on West 46th Street near Sixth Avenue.

At the extreme opposite pole from Times Square are the settings in the novels and stories of Louis Auchincloss. Since his first novel, issued under the pseudonym of Andrew Lee, Auchincloss has written largely from his own experience about Wall Street, the legal world, and Park Avenue high society. During the period under discussion, his works have included T*he House of Five Talents* (1960), tracing one Manhattan family's history from 1873 to 1948; *Portrait in Brownstone* (1962), concerning a New York society woman; *The Dark Lady*, set in a suburban chateau very much like Caramoor in Katonah, New York; and *The Golden Calves* (1988), which explores the world of an elegant art museum on Central Park West.

Norman Mailer, who in recent years has written about Lyndon

Johnson, Egypt, the moon, convicts, and Marilyn Monroe, also produced a New York novel—*An American Dream* (1965.) One key scene occurs on top of Park Avenue's Waldorf Towers—where President Herbert Hoover lived out his last years. Richard Yates's *The Easter Parade* (1976) concerns two sisters from New York, Sarah and Emily Grimes, one of whom remains a Manhattanite living in a high, spacious apartment near Gramercy Park, while the other settles in suburbia. The novel is a variation of Arnold Bennett's city-mouse, country-mouse novel, *The Old Wives' Tale.*

Truman Capote wrote brilliantly of Manhattan and Brooklyn, perhaps nowhere better than in *Breakfast at Tiffany's* (1958), a book that has penetrated the culture to the extent that Tiffany was among the most common American girls' names of 1990. The famous jewelry emporium on Fifth Avenue figures in the plot, of course, but so does the Hamburg Heaven at 79th and Madison; Joe Bell's Bar on Lexington in the Seventies; and a row of brownstones in the East Seventies. In the unfinished novel, *Answered Prayers* (1987), Capote contrasts East Side literary salons with the human litter of West 42nd Street. Its most famous chapter, "La Côte Basque," is, of course, set in the famous restaurant of that name on East 55th Street, directly across from the St. Regis. (It originally was the site of Le Pavillon, founded in 1940.) Another landmark Manhattan restaurant, the Russian Tea Room on West 57th Street, provided the inspiration for the long section, "The Psychopathology of Everyday Life by Sigmund Freud," in Daniel Stern's *Twice Told Tales* (1989). The germ of the story was planted when a well-known New York poet checked her dog in the coatroom of the Russian Tea Room—and then forgot her. In the book Stern turns the dog into a baby.

Manhattan's high-rise offices have inspired at least four highly praised novels. William Styron's *Sophie's Choice* (1979), while set in Brooklyn with flashbacks to wartime Europe, begins in a publishing house like McGraw-Hill, where Styron briefly worked as an editor in the turquoise art nouveau building at 330 West 42nd Street. (McGraw-Hill Book Company has since moved to the Avenue of the Americas.) Also on the Avenue of the Americas is the Time-Life Building, where James Agee, Dwight Macdonald, and Joseph Heller—among others—have held jobs. The protagonist of Heller's novel *Something Happened* (1974) works in a similar space, where just about everybody is scared of somebody. Heller is especially perceptive about the psychology of New York big business:

> *In the office in which I work there are five people of whom I am afraid. Each of these five people is afraid of four people (excluding overlaps), for a total of twenty, and each of these twenty is afraid of six people, making a total of one hundred and twenty people who are feared by at least one person. Each of these one hundred and twenty people is afraid of the other one hundred and nineteen, and all of these one hundred and forty-five people are afraid of the twelve men at the top who helped found and build the company and now own and direct it.*

The office recreated in Jay McInerney's rambunctious *Bright Lights, Big City* (1984) is that of the venerable *New Yorker* magazine, where the hero works in the Department of Factual Verification as a "verificationist." In one evening he and his pet ferret, Fred, manage to make more of a shambles of that office than did the *New Yorker's* recent move across the street. Howard Lewis Russell's hilarious *Rush to Nowhere* (1988) clearly was inspired by the staff in the old offices of BBDO (Batten, Barton, Durstin and Osbourne—a name which David Ogilvy once said sounded like a log bumping down a flight of stairs!), which used to be located at the corner of Madison Avenue and 46th Street. (They, too, have moved to the Avenue of the Americas, into The Equitable Building.) Although Dancer—whose odyssey from Alabama to New York to London to Hollywood comprises the book's plot—lives in Brooklyn, he works for a giddy Manhattan advertising executive. The book has as many plot twists as *Candide*, to which it bears more than a passing resemblance. The advertising scene of the 1980s is shown to be nothing like that portrayed in Sloan Wilson's *The Man in the Grey Flannel Suit* (1955).

John Cheever's last novels—*Bullet Park* (1969), *Falconer* (1977) and *Oh What a Paradise It Seems* (1977) are set in Westchester County, a region he knew and loved well, and *Falconer* takes place in a prison much like Ossining's Sing-Sing in which Cheever did volunteer work with prisoners. Cheever not only wrote about New York—he was identified with the city. For more than thirty years the *New Yorker* was his chief market for stories and pieces of novels; the magazine published a total of 119 of his short fictions. In his now-familiar preface to *The Stories of John Cheever* (1978), the author stated, "These stories seem at times to be stories of a long-lost world when the city of New York was still filled with a river light, when you heard the Benny Goodman Quartets from a radio in the corner stationary store, and when almost everybody wore a hat . . ." That volume of 61 stories is Cheever's love letter to a city long gone in change.

While the settings of William Maxwell's novels have been varied–Chicago, a chateau in the France of 1948, a middle western college, and the fictitious small town of "Draperville, Ill."—in his first collection of stories, *Over By the River* (1977), half of the twelve pieces were set in or near New York City. The book ranks as one of the distinguished recent depictions of the lives of middle-class New Yorkers living on the Upper East Side. Their lives, despite modern accoutrements, are not altogether comfortable: signs along the River walk read,

NO DOGS

NO BICYCLES

NO THIS

NO THAT

There are intimations of impending disaster and death in these pages. Maxwell's New Yorkers live life as they feel it should be rather than as it is, and often the outside world intrudes upon that unrealistic view. Yet Maxwell's characters are capable of experiencing grace within the chaos of New York; the narrator of the final story, "The Thistle in Sweden," can conclude, "I think if it is true that we are all in the hand of God, what a capacious hand it must be."

Erica Jong is also a New York novelist who has written much about foreign places as well as her native Manhattan. *Fanny* (1980) begins in Wiltshire, England, progresses to London, then continues with an around-the-world voyage. *Serenissima* (1987) is a novel of Venice in the past as well as Venice today. But it is her New-York based novels which are most widely read. *Fear of Flying* (1973) introduced Isadora Wing, a J.A.P. (Jewish American Poet), all of whose writing "is an attempt to get love". The novel was in some ways a '60s feminine counterpart of Henry Miller's *Tropic of Cancer*. The book sold ten million copies and taught the rest of the country how a free-thinking New York woman thinks and lives (or would like to think she lives). In 1977 and 1984

Isadora made fictional comebacks in *How to Save Your Own Life* and *Parachutes & Kisses*. The former deals with problems of fame, experimentation with lesbianism and group sex, and the continual search for fulfillment; the latter addresses concerns of the 80s—the post-Feminist woman, single parenthood and the search for one's true roots. From Morningside Heights to the East Village, from assignations in glitzy discos to Alcoholics Anonymous meetings in dreary church basements, Ms. Jong has explored the life of the new New York woman—and found much of it wanting. Like Judith Rossner in the more harrowing *Looking for Mr. Goodbar* (1975), she shows us some of the terrors of the new liberation and the problems of a single woman alone in the big city.

A great cross section of New York is depicted in Tom Wolfe's *The Bonfire of the Vanities* (1989). The central figure is a young investment banker who lives in a fourteen-room apartment on Park Avenue. The plot revolves around what happens when he gets involved in an accident in the Bronx. He is suddenly thrown into contact with street people, prosecutors, politicians, the press, the police, and the clergy. Wolfe even has New York's tabloids down cold. One headline in the novel reads: SCALP GRANDMA, THEN ROB HER. The novel delivers a generous helping of the Human Comedy and is far better than the wildly miscast 1990 film version directed by Brian De Palma.

Of course New York has inspired literary works other than novels. On the stage Neil Simon has given us a series of plays based on his New York childhood, most notably *Brighton Beach Memoirs* (1983), *Broadway Bound* (1986), and *Lost in Yonkers* (1991). New York has figured importantly throughout his work. The Plaza Hotel is celebrated in *Plaza Suite* (1962) and Central Park in *Barefoot in the Park* (1963). Terrence McNally's comedies have been inspired by several New York milieus, from a steambath (*The Ritz*, 1975), to a diner (*Frankie and Johnny in the Clair de Lune*, 1987) to Broadway (*It's Only a Play*, 1986).

And poets continue to be inspired by the city. Some of the best images of New York—girls fighting on Broadway, Grant's tomb in its current disrepair, and Manhattan manhole covers—appear in *Love & Hate, Art & God* (1984) by Pulitzer Prize-winning poet Karl Shapiro. Though born in Baltimore, he now spends half of each year in an apartment overlooking the Cathedral of St. John the Divine. Louis

Simpson, born in the West Indies, also writes extensively of New York and its environs. His *Collected Poems* (1988) includes poems titled "How to Live on Long Island," "Port Jefferson," "The Psyche of Riverside Drive," "Stumpfoot on 42nd Street" and "The Union Barge on Staten Island."

But Howard Moss's anthology *New York Poems* (1980) provides the greatest compilation of modern poetic images of New York. From Ben Belitt's "Battery Park, High Noon" to Alfred Corn's "Fifty-seventh Street and Fifth," to Barbara Howes's "At 79th and Park," to Randall Jarrell's "The Subway from New Britain to the Bronx," to Al Lee's "In the Yellow Light of Brooklyn," the book allows us to see the city in fascinating and original ways. Certain subjects are repeated—Trinity Church is the focus of three poems—while Queens and Chinatown have not yet found their bards.

•

The literary and cultural cityscape of New York has not changed in a very dramatic way over the past three decades, except for a few additions and a few lamented demolitions. One of the most significant additions has been Lincoln Center for the Performing Arts, completed in 1962 at Columbus Avenue and West 64th Street. In five glittering buildings grouped around a fountain and a lagoon, it houses the Metropolitan Opera, the New York City Opera, the New York Philharmonic, the New York City Ballet, a repertory theatre company, and a library for the arts. Performances draw over four million persons a year.

Marianne Moore's poem, "Carnegie Hall: Rescued" commemorates the last-minute successful campaign to save the historic concert hall.

> *...at the fifty-ninth minute*
> *of the eleventh hour, a rescuer*
> *makes room for Mr. Carnegie's*
> *music hall, which by degrees*
> *became (becomes)*
> *our music stronghold...*

Despite picketing by a group of famous theatre people, led by the late actress Colleen Dewhurst, nothing could be done to save three jewel-like Broadway theatres–the Morosco, the Helen Hayes, and the Bijou. Part of the argument in support of demolition was that they would be replaced by a new theatre within the Marriot Marquis hotel. That theatre, in fact, is so huge that only a blockbuster musical can fill the house. Consequently it frequently is dark.

The historic Villard mansions, between 50th and 51st streets on Madison Avenue, one of which housed Random House publishers, have now lost their architectural integrity. The "Queen of Mean" Leona Helmsley, and her husband Harry Helmsley, have erected their Helmsley Palace Hotel directly atop them. It would have been far worse if they had been demolished. But the existing hotel is an anomoly.

The Biltmore Hotel, with its famous clock under which everyone was told to meet his or her date, has been stripped and rebuilt as an office building. The gold clock is gone, the Palm Court is gone, and the Biltmore Men's Bar—its very name an impossibility in today's world—is gone. It was one of the longest and most elegant mahogany bars in Manhattan. One often saw John Cheever imbibing there, waiting for the next commuter train to Ossining.

When the Algonquin was bought recently by a Japanese concern, which announced plans to "remodel," literary New York held its breath. But when the drop cloths were removed, the lobby, bar and dining room looked very much the same, almost reeking of shabby gentility. Only the rooms upstairs had been considerably changed. By contrast the Royalton—the Algonquin's neighbor directly across the street—has been gutted and now resembles a glitzy cruise ship. Before it became an ultrachic hotel, the Royalton was a favorite of pecunious British literary figures, who would book there during their New York stays, but entertain friends and contacts across the street, in the more presentable and "literary" Algonquin. It is best known as the residential hotel where George Jean Nathan and Robert Benchley maintained suites, and where theatrical agent Audrey Wood lived until she had her debilitating and ultimately fatal stroke. (Wood was Tennessee Williams's representative from 1939 until 1971.)

The New York Public Library, one of New York's finest classical buildings, designed by John Merven Carrère and Thomas Hastings

(1911), has experienced a renaissance under President Vartan Gregorian (now, no longer New York Public Library president, but president of Brown University). Under his tenure a $307 million capital campaign was launched, and the building was dramatically renovated. Arthur Rosenblatt, manager of the Metropolitan Museum's expansion, was hired to plan the physical renovation. Brooke Astor, heir to one of the fortunes that had built the library nearly a hundred years before, gave up her other philanthropies to lobby for funds for the library.

The results are breathtaking. The DeWitt Wallace Periodical Room was restored to the tune of two million dollars. Its long walls are now filled by thirteen new Richard Haas murals, each depicting a major publishing house in New York. The splendid exhibition hall on the first floor was restored with $1,250,000 from the Gottesman Foundation. Since World War II it had been partitioned off into cubicles and work spaces for an accounting office. "When we finally tore the junk away in here," said Lewis Day of Davis, Brody & Associates, the firm that restored the room, "I found myself standing in one of the most beautiful spaces I had ever seen."

Upstairs the huge central reading room on the third floor—extending the entire block-long length of the building—has been cleaned, restored, and computerized. So the library has been restored to its former elegance, while being modernized at the same time. Today it houses more than sixteen thousand public events every year, from puppet shows to chess matches to tax-help classes to book discussions. Down the street, the owners of the only other building in midtown that rivals the library in grandeur, Grand Central Terminal, have begun their own restoration program. The huge Kodak panorama advertisement on the east balcony has come down, the Newsweek clock over the 42nd Street entrance is now gone, and windows that had been painted black during World War II are now clear. There is sunshine inside the terminal where it has never shone for fifty years.

Another major institution undergoing renovation and extension is the Pierpont Morgan Library at Madison Avenue and 37th Street. Under the supervision of architects Voorsanger and Associates, the 1928 library is being linked to an adjacent, freestanding brownstone building that until recently was owned by a church organization. The roof connecting the two structures looks, rather whimsically, like a glass

French curve. No attempt has been made to match the library's Renaissance-style palazzo architecture designed by Charles F. McKim. But the roof, and the atrium beneath it, might be seen as a symbolic linking of the past with the present.

•

When I first came to Manhattan, Carl Van Vechten (1880-1964) was still holding court on Central Park West with the sophisticated artistic set, as well as stimulating interest in "Negro" culture (as it was called then). The poet Isabella Gardner (1915-1981), niece of the celebrated "Mrs. Jack" Gardner of Boston, gave lively parties in her suite at the Chelsea Hotel. Among the regulars were poets John Logan, Daniella Gioseffi, W. S. Merwin, James and Annie Wright, Ned O'Gorman, Roland Flint, myself, and Gardner's last lover, Ed Berryman. One of her parties was scheduled for September 23, 1977—when Gardner fell ill with the flu. She held it anyway, presiding over affairs from her bed in the adjacent bedroom, wearing an exquisite negligee.

The composer Virgil Thomson (1896-1989) continued the old Chelsea Hotel tradition, inhabiting and entertaining in his suite with the same Persian rugs and rosewood bookcases that had been with him for decades. As he got older, his circle of guests got smaller. He attributed this to his increasing deafness: ."..if there are more than ten people around, I don't hear."

Josephine Crane was another New York literary hostess, living at 820 Fifth Avenue. She sponsored literary lectures which she called "Monday classes." Regulars were Glenway Wescott, Monroe Wheeler, George Platt Lynes, and Cecil Beaton. Just across the Hudson, in Palisades, New York, in an eighteenth-century cottage, Horace Gregory and his wife Marya Zaturenska entertained many of New York's most substantial writers and thinkers—until the Gregorys retired to Massachusetts in 1980. Among their circle were E.E. Cummings and his wife Marion Morehouse; James T. Farrell and his companion Cleo Paturis; Norman Holmes Pearson, Dudley Fitts, Muriel Rukeyser, Joseph Campbell, Morton D. Zaubel, Arthur Gregor, and Leda and Stanley Burnshaw.

One of the most delightful New York salons was held for many years at 1230 Park Avenue, the apartment of novelist Daniel Stern and his wife, literary agent Gloria Stern. The highlight of one of their afternoons or evenings would be live chamber music—Stern is an accomplished cellist, and his wife an avid music lover. So much so, that when offered a mink coat for one of her birthdays, she told her husband she would prefer a live performance of Brahms's *Clarinet Quartet* in her home. Stern obliged.

Perhaps the most memorable of their soirées was one held in honor of Joyce Carol Oates and her husband Raymond J. Smith. Among those in attendance were: Alfred Kazin and his then-wife Ann Birstein; Wilfred and Miriam Sheed; Bernard and Ann Malamud; Dwight and Gloria Macdonald; Cynthia Ozick and husband Bernard Halot; Anne and Herman Roiphe; Ted and Virginia Solotaroff; Aaron and Linda Asher; and Philip Roth—who spent most of the evening complaining of low-back pain. At the evening's end Ozick and Oates stood by the elevator, discussing literary inspiration. Both agreed they were "dictated to" by a higher power. The featured piece that evening was a late Beethoven string quartet; the musicians were Arturo Delmonia, violin; Sylvia Rosenberg, violin; Daniel Stern, cello; Karen Phillips, viola; and Theodore Israel, viola. (The Sterns often imported performers from the New York Philharmonic to augment their musical friends.) Years later, looking back at their musicale evenings, Gloria Stern said, "The sixties were wonderful times, because there were wives then. Wives gave parties!"

Of course Isabella Gardner, Virgil Thomson, Josephine Crane, the Gregorys, even the Sterns, were not of the new generation. George Plimpton has continued to give some of the liveliest literary parties in Manhattan throughout the seventies and eighties at his home, 541 East 72nd Street, which also doubles as the offices of the *Paris Review*. The food is always arranged on the pool table, and the liquor is free flowing, as is the conversation. There is a mixture of writers, agents, publishers, and editors—by design. The median age of the young women at some of these parties seems (to me) to be twenty-one. But one can also encounter more writers per square inch at Plimpton's than perhaps anywhere else: Jay McInerny, Mona Simpson, Alan Gurganus, Harold Brodky, and Ted Hoagland are among the current regulars, as well as a woman whose face appears to be tattooed to resemble a cat's. What differentiates Plimpton's literary parties from many others is the unmistakable feeling that literary politics are being practiced. Norman

Mailer once remarked, "All those writers . . . myself included—walking rigidly through that packed room towards the drinks, our heads erect, only our eyes swiveling sideways to identify the enemy."

If a bookstore can be said to be a salon, one of the longest-running salons in Manhattan is the upstairs of The Gotham Book Mart. Frances Steloff, the proprietor, died in 1989, at the age of 101, but the store is still thriving at 41 West 47th Street with its new owner, Andreas Brown. Between 1960 and 1990, the Gotham hosted parties for—among others—W. H. Auden, Paul Bowles, Lawrence Durrell, Max Ernst, Salvador Dali, Martha Graham, Anaïs Nin, Louis Zukofsky, Tennessee Williams, Katherine Anne Porter, William Goyen, James Dickey, Marianne Moore, Stanley Kunitz, Robert Creeley, Joyce Carol Oates, James T. Farrell, John Ashbery, Allen Ginsberg, and Gary Snyder. A glittering list.

And if a restaurant can be considered a salon, Elaine's is one. Located for many years at 1703 Second Avenue at 88th Street, Elaine's Restaurant is now twice as big as it was when Nelson Aldrich and Frederick Seidel, two editors of the *Paris Review* at the time, "discovered" it. In those days it was one long, narrow room presided over by Elaine Kaufman, who used to be a ballerina. She took Aldrich and Seidel under her wing, almost protected them, and they in turn got others to frequent the place. There usually was a game of darts in progress, and Elaine once threw out Joe Fox—a Random House editor—because he never ordered a meal, but only drank milk and threw darts. She also threw out Norman Mailer for unscrewing her lamps' lightbulbs to make the place darker (he was wooing a young woman at the time). Elaine kept screwing them back in, while chanting "The fire laws! The fire laws!" Finally Elaine—who had come to resemble a Wagnerian soprano more than a ballerina—accidentally stepped on Mailer's date's foot. The young lady, more as a reflex action than anything else, slapped Elaine. Mailer roared, "Why don't you two girls go outside and settle this?" But it was Mailer and his date who ended up outside.

Over the years the phrase, "Let's go up to the fat lady's!" has meant "Let's go up to Elaine's." Among the regulars to be found in what are deemed the most desirable seats, "the row" opposite the bar in the front room, are Jack Richardson of the *New York Review of Books*, Mary Ann

Madden of the *New York Times*, Jack Gelber, Gay and Nan Talese, Norman and Norris Mailer, Adolph Green and Betty Comden, Kurt Vonnegut and Jill Krementz, Willie Morris, the former editor of *Harper's*; Bruce Jay Friedman, and of course George Plimpton and whoever currently is helping edit the *Paris Review.* The most famous table at Elaine's is, oddly enough, the one next to the kitchen door. It often has a RESERVED sign on it. When it is occupied, it is usually by Woody Allen, Mia Farrow, and their friends. No one who is anyone wants to be seated in the back room, which is called the "Paul Desmond Room" because the late saxophonist preferred the quiet there.

Some writers in the past three decades were associated not with salons, but with single, outrageous parties. One of the most glamorous was Truman Capote's "Black-and-White Dance" for five hundred of his "closest friends" in the Grand Ballroom of the Plaza Hotel on November 28, 1966. In addition to Capote's titled and socialite friends (he had not yet alienated them by publishing sections of *Answered Prayers*), literary friends who attended included Thornton Wilder, Katherine Anne Porter, Anita Loos, Janet Flanner, and Glenway Wescott. One writer who was not invited was Carson McCullers; she was so put out, she threatened to give a competitive ball of her own, one to which she'd invite Jacqueline Kennedy; the two women were not even acquainted. Capote spent sixteen thousand dollars on his party—a good sum in the 1960s.

A second party that was notorious—not for its prestige, but its politics—was the late Leonard Bernstein's January 1970 fund-raising party in his thirteen-room penthouse duplex on Park Avenue. (He later moved into the Dakota.) The funds were being raised for a group of twenty-one members of the militant Black Panther organization, who had been arrested on charges of conspiring to bomb five railroad facilities, the Bronx Botanical Garden, and a police station. At the soirée, Panthers mixed with and gave speeches to the East Side elite. The event was widely criticized, to the point where the *New York Times* published an editorial on July 16, 1970, taking Bernstein to task. Later he claimed it had been all his wife's idea. Tom Wolfe made the party subject of an article in *New York* magazine, coining the now-famous phrase "radical chic" to describe Bernstein's motives.

A third memorable, large party occurred the night that Poets &

Writers, Inc. took over the Big Apple Circus on December 15, 1985. It became a "Circus of the Literary Stars": Erica Jong rode an elephant (and was clearly scared out of her mind when the elephant stood up on its hind legs), Ken Follett juggled, Norman Mailer balanced on a bongo board, and Galen Williams and Gail Sheehy flew on the trapeze. Other participants included John Irving, E. L. Doctorow, and William Styron. Liz Smith was ringmistress. Over eight hundred attended, and not all the clowns were in the center ring.

Among the largest New York literary parties staged on a fairly regular basis are the *Paris Review* "Revels." These are enormous fund-raising gatherings of perhaps six hundred to eight hundred people, with lots of gate-crashers mixed in with the ticket holders. The Revels have been held at various locations all over town—the first three were held at The Village Gate downtown, one in a West Side disco named The Cheetah, one in a vast abandoned church on Roosevelt Island, and the most recent on a steamer at the South Street Seaport. George Plimpton recollects,

> *What many people remembered about the Revels was the use of mixed media devices—especially films, which were shown simultaneously on a multitude of screens. These were artfully spliced by Christopher Cerf of the* Review *from reels of 16mm stock purchased at cut-rate out of 42nd Street camera-shop bins—many of them old Pathé newsreels so that the revelers would look up to see on the great screens hung around the halls, or, in the case of the island Revel, set among the trees, a curious variety of images...a ping-pong match, a chimpanzee on a bicycle, the slow, writhing collapse of the suspension bridge at Yakima, Washington, a zoot-suit fashion show, a sequence of a monster grasshopper attacking a Quonset hut from a science-fiction film...all of these activities going on concurrently and silently, the projector beams criss-crossing, the screens in a constant movement of image. This kind of visual decoration was very much of an innovation then.*

•

Of course, New York writers don't always attend parties. Sometimes they actually write. And over the past thirty years, their writing has spearheaded new directions and genres in American literature. Just as the 1950s and 1960s saw the creation of "confessional poetry" and "black humor" and the "Jewish-American novel," new modes have emerged in the period from 1960 to 1990. One is the so-called nonfiction novel, which Truman Capote took credit for creating when he published *In Cold Blood* in 1966. The book was, Capote claimed "immaculately factual." *In Cold Blood* was followed by a number of books in this genre. These include Norman Mailer's *The Armies of the Night* and *The Executioner's Song*, Bob Woodward's *Veil*, and Tom Wolfe's *The Right Stuff*.

"Oral biography," in which the verbatim memories of the subject are woven into the text, emerged as an art with New Yorker Merle Miller's *Plain Speaking* (1985), about President Harry S. Truman. George Plimpton and Jean Stein made news with *Edie*, a composite oral biography of socialite Edie Sedgwick. Plimpton and Stein capitalized on its success by following it with *American Journey: The Times of Robert F. Kennedy*. Currently Plimpton is composing an oral biography of Truman Capote. Another oral biography in the works is Frances Kiernan's *Mary McCarthy*.

A much more influential genre—judging by the number of people writing in it—is either called "expansive poetry" or "the New Formalism." It allegedly began early in 1981, when Dick Allen, Frederick Feirstein, and Frederick Turner met for the first time at the Minetta Tavern in Greenwich Village. The three recognized themselves as part of a distinct literary movement, one whose practitioners were numerous. Like the Imagists before them, the Expansionists (or New Formalists) wrote a credo with six guidelines for the practice of expansionist poetry, set forth in Dick Allen's "Transcending the Self," an essay appearing in a special issue of *Crosscurrents*. Among the New York poets who are writing in the New Formalist mode are: Charles Martin, Bruce Bawer, Tom Disch, Feirstein, Dana Gioia, Rachel Hadas, Phyllis Levin, Wade Newman, Molly Peacock, Henri Cole, Karl Kirchwey, and Stephen Haven.

"The new narrative" goes hand in hand with the New Formalism, with the exception that some of the new narrative poets do not work in traditional forms. Like the New Formalists, practitioners of new narrative poetry have a manifesto of ten requirements that their work must have in order to qualify. The first such is, "A beginning, a middle, and an end." In other words, the new narrative poem must tell a story. Among New York poets now writing in this vein are Feirstein, Haven,

Gioia, Alfred Corn, Nicholas Christopher, Chase Twichell, and Brooks Haxton.

Perhaps the most controversial school of poetry since the Beats is that of the Language Poets. Though by no means confined to the New York scene, these poets subscribe to the notion that language is a set of symbols set distinctly apart from a human context. The writer is more concerned with *how* a poem makes meaning than with *what* it means—poems with no verbs, for example, or a poem composed entirely of interrogative sentences. One Language Poet, David Malnick, invents his own vocabulary lists. The poems which result, as Robert McDowell puts it, are "linguistic exercises." Still, language poetry has its advocates, including Marjorie Perloff, George Lakoff, and Jerome McGann. James Sherry's Roof Books in New York City publishes works by Language Poets, including Jean Day and Diane Ward. The group seems to have been influenced by Louis Zukofsky, Clark Coolidge, and early John Ashbery.

Part of the post-sixties New York literary scene has been the emergence of many talented women poets. When George P. Elliott's *15 Modern American Poets* was published in 1956, only three women were represented (Bishop, Rukeyser, and Miles). Donald Hall's, Robert Pack's, and Lewis Simpson's *The New Poets of England and America* (1957) included just six women. (The second selection of that anthology series in 1962 admitted seven American women, as opposed to twenty-eight men.) Today the balance would be much more equal. Women poets have asserted themselves in the context of literary tradition and have overcome decades of repression of the female voice. Their impact amounts to a virtual women's movement in American poetry. The way was paved by the publication in the early 1960s of powerful and influential volumes by Sylvia Plath, Anne Sexton, Muriel Rukeyser, and Adrienne Rich, which caused male critics (who edited the anthologies and most of the quarterlies) to admit that American women's poetry did indeed go beyond Emily Dickinson, Marianne Moore, and Elizabeth Bishop. New York poets include Siv Cedering, Helen Chasin, Jane Cooper, Sandra Gilbert, Marilyn Hacker, Judith Johnson, Rachel Hadas, Joyce Carol Oates, Erica Jong, Jana Harris, June Jordan, Audre Lord, Phyllis Levin, Robin Morgan, Sharon Olds, Katha Pollitt, Alicia Ostriker, Molly Peacock, Marie Ponsot, Cynthia Macdonald, Grace Schulman,

Jean Valentine, Karen Swenson, and the late May Swenson. Through efforts such as theirs, there has been a collective endeavor to redefine the terms "woman" and "woman poet."

While women have made immense inroads into the major anthologies, publishing lists, and reading programs, the number of Afro-American poets represented remains relatively small. But just as there was a "Harlem Renaissance" in black literature following the First World War (Claude McKay, James Weldon Johnson, Countee Cullen, Langston Hughes), and a poetics of "Black Rage" following the assassination of Malcolm X in 1965 (Bob Kaufman, LeRoi Jones, Etheridge Knight, Nikki Giovanni), black poets have received increasing attention and publication in the decade following the Vietnam War. Today's Black poetry is still very much in the oral tradition, and Rap has been an influence. Black music and musicians have influenced Michael Harper's and Quincy Troupe's poetry.

Black fiction is thriving in New York, though no author during this period has had the impact of Ralph Ellison or James Baldwin, both of whom did their most important work in the 1950s. Of special note are John A. Williams (*Sissie, The Man Who Cried I Am*), and Toni Morrison, whose *Beloved* won the Pulitzer Prize.

Other prominent black New York fiction writers include Wesley Brown, David Bradley, Gloria Naylor, Henry Van Dyke, Charles S. Wright, Paule Marshall, James Alan McPherson, Sara Wright and Terri MacMillan. While black writers are gaining larger audiences, black editors and agents have made significant inroads into publishing. Toni Morrison was an important Random House editor before stepping down to write more and to lecture. *New Yorker* writer Jamaica Kincaid now lives in Vermont. Malaika Adero is a black editor who is now an agent. And Faith Childs is another successful black literary agent.

During this same period, black theatre has been an essential element in New York's cultural life. There have been dramas, including Lorraine Hansberry's *A Raisin in the Sun* and *The Sign in Sidney Brustein's Window,* Ntozake Shange's *For Colored Girls Who Have Considered Suicide When the Rainbow Is Enuf,* Ed Bullins's *The Duplex,* Joseph A. Walker's *The River Niger,* and August Wilson's superb series of plays: *Ma Rainey's Black Bottom, Fences, Joe Turner's Come and Gone* and *The Piano Lesson.* The latter won a Pulitzer Prize. A number of rollicking black musicals have been highly visible, among them *The Wiz, Ain't Misbehaving, Black and White, Ain't Supposed to Die a Natural Death*, an off-Broadway revival of *Cabin in the Sky*, and the longest-running black musical in history, *Mama, I Want to Sing*. There have also been new productions of earlier black material, such as Langston Hughes's and Zora Neale Hurston's *Mule Bone*.

Gay literature is definitely out of the closet in New York. Some booksellers, like Three Lives in Greenwich Village and B. Dalton in Midtown, have a special section devoted to gay and lesbian literature. Some publishers, for instance St. Martin's Press, have editors devoted to accepting or soliciting gay manuscripts. *Christopher Street* magazine has gathered and published several anthologies of the best gay stories from their pages. In the past only an occasional gay or lesbian novel would get published—*The City and the Pillar, The Well of Loneliness, Giovanni's Room*—but today gay fiction is an industry. Perhaps the best gay novel to come out of New York in recent decades is Edmund White's tender *A Boy's Own Story* (1982). Excellent gay drama has also been presented, especially Harvey Feirstein's *Torch Song Trilogy* (1981), and several wrenching plays on the AIDS crisis, the best of which are *As Is* by William M. Hoffman (1985), and *Andre's Mother* by Terrence McNally (1990).

"Minimalist" fiction has come to the forefront in New York within the last ten years with its practitioners—Susan Minot, Amy Hempel, Grace Paley, the late Donald Barthelme, Elizabeth Tallent, Mark Strand, Russell Edson—who live in or have roots in New York. A number owe their discovery to one professor and editor, Gordon Lish, who has taught writing workshops at Yale and Columbia and is a senior editor at Alfred A. Knopf.

•

When New York writers aren't partying, or writing, or forging new genres, some are litigating. Among the most famous lawsuits is the one involving Lillian Hellman and Mary McCarthy. It all began on January 25 and 26, 1980, when a two-part television interview between Mary McCarthy and Dick Cavett was aired. Cavett asked Ms. McCarthy to name some overpraised writers. McCarthy replied, "The only one I can think of is a holdover like Lillian Hellman, who I think is tremendously overrated, a bad writer, and a dishonest writer."

Cavett asked what was "dishonest" about her. McCarthy replied,

"Everything...I said once in some interview that every word she writes is a lie, including 'and' and 'the'."

Lillian Hellman promptly sued McCarthy, Dick Cavett, and Channel 13 for two-and-a-quarter million dollars, "on the grounds that her reputation had been damaged—one-and-three-quarter million for pain and anguish—and half a million for punitive damages for what she charged were McCarthy's libelous remarks about her."

The lawsuit provoked a great deal of heated discussion in New York literary circles. Many defended McCarthy on the grounds that her comment had been merely a hyperbolic personal opinion, and she was exercising freedom of speech granted by the First Amendment. They felt that if Hellman won the suit, no one would feel comfortable making a critical comment on the air or in print again. There were some who felt it was not Hellman's writing which really had irked McCarthy, but rather her lifelong Stalinism. Hellman told the *New York Times* she assumed politics was at the base of the "attack": "I think she has always disliked me. It could go back to the Spanish Civil War days, in November or December of 1937, after I had returned from Spain."

Through the years of legal skirmishes McCarthy spent many thousands of dollars in her defense, as well as many hundreds of hours reading and annotating everything Hellman had written, in search of mistruths. The case ended only with Hellman's sudden death in 1984. Afterward, McCarthy remarked, "I didn't want her to die. I wanted her to lose in court..."

Truman Capote and Gore Vidal were natural rivals, since Vidal had published his first novel in 1946 at age 21 and Capote had published *Other Voices, Other Rooms* in 1948 at age 24. ("Why, he's 26 if he's a day!" Capote is supposed to have said of Vidal.) In an interview published in *Playgirl* in 1975, Capote embroidered the facts of an altercation between Vidal and Robert Kennedy at a White House party. Capote alleged that Kennedy and Arthur Schlesinger and one of the guards "just picked Gore up and carried him to the door and threw him out into Pennsylvania Avenue."

This in fact had not taken place; Vidal filed a libel suit in a New York State court. He claimed "great mental anxiety and suffering...and requested one million dollars in damages." In one of his depositions, Vidal was asked when he had last seen Capote. He replied it had been at a party.

> *Q: What occurred on that occasion?*
> *A: I sat on him.*
> *Q: What do you mean?*
> *A: I didn't have my glasses on, and I sat down on what I thought was a stool, and it was Capote.*
> *Q: Where was Capote sitting at the time you sat on him?*
> *A: On a smaller stool.*

This case dragged on for over seven years, with bizarre twists, such as Capote's friend Lee Radziwill becoming a witness for the prosecution. Capote released copies of the depositions to *New York* magazine for publication, certain they would expose Vidal as very foolish. The suit finally was settled out of court in 1983, and Capote wrote Vidal a letter of apology:

> *Dear Gore:*
>
> *I apologize for any distress, inconvenience, or expense which may have been caused you as a result of the interview with me published in the September 1975 issue of* Playgirl. *As you know, I was not present at the event about which I am quoted in that interview, and I understand from your representatives that what I am reported as saying does not accurately set forth what occurred. I can assure you that the article was not an accurate transcription of what I said, especially with regard to my remarks which might cast aspersion upon your character or behavior, and that I will avoid discussing the subject in the future.*
>
> *Best,*
>
> *Truman Capote.*

In a landmark decision, the Supreme Court ruled in 1991 that an author's alteration of quotations by a public figure can be held libelous if it significantly changes the meaning. The justices agreed that a U.S. District Court in California should allow a jury trial to be held on the merits of a libel suit brought by psychoanalyst Jeffrey Masson against author Janet Malcolm, the *New Yorker,* and Alfred Knopf for publishing Malcom's profile of Masson, *In the Freud Archives.* Two lower courts had dismissed the case "on the grounds that even if Ms. Malcolm had placed words in his mouth, as he has asserted, the misquotations provided insufficient proof of knowing or reckless falsity." Among the half-dozen passages in dispute from the forty-thousand-word article is the phrase "intellectual gigolo," which appeared in Ms. Malcolm's interview notes, but is nowhere to be heard on the forty hours of tape-recorded interviews.

•

When the Poetry Center was founded at the 92nd Street YMHA-YWHA in 1939, it was one of the few places in New York where organized readings could be found. In the words of "Y" Education Department Director Dr. William Kolodney, "The Poetry Center was started to meet the needs of the very few persons in New York to whom poetry offers the theological, the ethical and the aesthetic equivalents of traditional religion." Dr. Kolodney estimated from the outset that about 25 people would attend such readings. He was wrong. The original events averaged 50 attendees, with a maximum of 130 when W. H. Auden read. By 1950, when Dylan Thomas gave his first reading at the Poetry Center, more than a thousand people attended. Today "Poetry Center" is a misnomer—there are at least as many prose readings held there as poetry.

Presently there is a virtual explosion of readings all over New York. Poetry readings, fiction readings, drama readings...there are so many that there is a monthly New York City *Poetry Calendar* published. The calendar for December 1990 listed some 870 readings within 29 days at some 77 locations. These figures reflect the increase in literary activity nationwide. The current edition of *A Directory of American Poets and Fiction Writers* (1991-92) lists the names and addresses of 6,800 contemporary poets and fiction writers whose work has been published in the U.S. The largest concentration is in New York. What is amazing is that the 6,800 does not include playwrights, journalists, critics and authors of children's books.

There are literary reading series for every clique and school. The Poetry Project at St. Mark's Church-In-the-Bowery (Second Avenue and 10th Street) features the downtown crowd (most of them Language Poets). A Different Light (548 Hudson Street) spotlights gay writers such as David Leavitt. The Academy of American Poets' readings at the New York Historical Society (170 Central Park West) showcases readers with proven reputations. The Cornelia Street Café (29 Cornelia Street), on the other hand, is receptive to emerging faces.

To help facilitate the number of readings and workshops, a Manhattan-based organization called Poets & Writers, Inc., provides matching grants to schools, libraries, and community groups. Located at 72 Spring Street, it also serves as a clearing house of information for writers who want to teach or read, and provides lists of writing contests and programs nationwide. Poets & Writers began in 1970, as part of the Poetry Center at the 92nd Street "Y" during Galen Williams's tenure as director. When she left the "Y," she established a separate identity for Poets & Writers. Today the services and publications of Poets & Writers, Inc. are made possible in part by the literature program of the National Endowment for the Arts. The readings and workshops program is funded primarily by the literature program of the New York State Council on the Arts.

Another new Manhattan organization to help writers is Poets' House. Founded by Elizabeth Kray and Stanley Kunitz in the 1980s, Poets' House originally was located at 351 West 18th Street. In January 1991 it moved quarters to 72 Spring Street in Soho, in the same building which houses Poets & Writers. Poets' House from the beginning has been a place where poets can come to work alone or gather to hear one another read, to discuss their works-in-progress, or to find books and journals. The latter are available in abundance, since Poets' House holds the Reed Foundation Library, a collection of over twenty thousand volumes developed solely by donation, inaugurated in 1985 with a bequest from the collection of the late West Side poet and critic Paul Zweig.

If readings have exploded since the 1940s, the increase in creative-writing programs is a relatively recent phenomenon, virtually unheard of in New York four decades ago. The creative writing programs at Columbia University, New York University, The New School, Sarah Lawrence, Hofstra University, Princeton University and elsewhere have made it possible for many New York-area writers to earn a living as teachers. Many of the young writers on the New York scene in recent years are graduates of these programs.

The number of New York literary magazines has increased, though there have been some important losses as well. Among the new literary quarterlies making an appearance during this period are *Parnassus: Poetry in Review, Antaeus, Grand Street, Pequod, Night, Conjunctions,*

Manhattan Review, and the *New Criterion*. The last, under Hilton Kramer's editorship, provides a forum for dissent from the prevailing critical orthodoxies and has helped a number of young critics gain influence and reputation.

The *New York Review of Books* was founded in 1963 during a printers' strike against New York newspapers as a single-issue journal. The recent sale to new owners made unexpected millionaires of the founding editors. Critics say that the trouble with the *New York Review of Books* is it doesn't review all that many books. During the 1960s it jokingly was called "The New York Review of Vietnam." During the '70s it became known as "The New York Review of Each Other's Books." The *Village Voice Literary Supplement* is a literate, intelligent, sensible book review edited by M. Mark.

Most important in this category, of course, is the *New York Times Book Review*. The *Times Book Review* wields extraordinary power. It is sometimes perceived by editors and writers as being a tool of Publishers Row that gives too much space to books by publishers like Knopf and Farrar, Straus & Giroux (who take out ads), while not giving much space at all to small-press books, university-press books and publishers of poetry (who do not take out ads). Poets, when reviewed at all, are almost always reviewed in tandem with two other poets, which means a poet's review is two-thirds shorter than it might have been. A decade ago the then-editors tended to assign reviews to assistant professors of English at obscure, backwater colleges. Today the editors generally assign reviews of novelists to other novelists, and reviews of poets to other poets. This may be an improvement but what is wrong with assigning reviews to professional critics?

The *Hudson Review* and the *Paris Review* continue to be marked with distinction. The former, established in Manhattan after the Second World War by Joseph Bennett and Frederick Morgan, has been published continuously ever since. The *Paris Review* was founded in 1953 in Paris by Peter Matthiessen, Harold L. (Doc) Humes, and George Plimpton. In 1973 the offices were moved to Manhattan (541 East 72nd Street). After a hiatus of a year to get cranked up, the first issue to be published in Manhattan appeared. It was the magazine's twentieth anniversary issue, and contained sparkling interviews with W. H. Auden and Christopher Isherwood. Indeed, this magazine and

Plimpton's punctilious editing raised the literary interview to an art form. The names of interviewees are legendary: E. M. Forster, Ernest Hemingway, Boris Pasternak, Vladimir Nabokov, Andrei Voznesensky, William Faulkner, Dorothy Parker, Isak Dinesen.

In 1987, the *New Yorker* underwent cataclysmic changes when Robert Gottlieb, formerly editor-in-chief at Random House, took over the editorship previously held by the venerated and venerable William Shawn. Alice Quinn joined the magazine first as a fiction editor—but with the death of Howard Moss in September 1987, she became poetry editor, a post Moss had held for nearly forty years. William Maxwell, longtime fiction editor, retired on January 1, 1976. Largely edited for the "caviar sophisticates" (in the words of Harold Ross) and "not for the little old lady in Dubuque," the *New Yorker* continues to be quite vital today.

After almost sixty years' occupation of 25 West 43rd Street, the magazine moved on February 22, 1991. But not far—just across the street to 20 West 43rd. The new offices have increased the magazine's space by over two-thirds. The bright modern quarters also allow the editors for the first time to take advantage of computer technology and electronic printing. Designed by LCP Associates, a New York architectural firm, the offices are in sharp contrast to the "cherished eccentricity" of the former space. It was recently revealed that during the move 72 boxes from the magazine's archives were lost. No one is sure what was in them. But at least some important treasures will be saved: three large pencil sketches by James Thurber, which filled one wall in the old office, have been moved and given a place of honor in a central hall before a staircase in the new office. (These are not the only Thurber drawings on public view in Manhattan; others may be seen in Costello's Bar and Grill at 225 East 44th Street. They, too, were moved when Costello's left Third Avenue decades ago.)

•

In recent years the increasing political content of literary life in the city has manifested itself overtly. The 1986 International PEN Congress proved to be the most controversial since World War II. Forty foreign guests of honor from around the world joined with American writers to discuss a common theme: "The Writer's Imagination and the Imagination of the State."

Official headquarters for the congress were the St. Moritz and Essex

House hotels, and photographers stalked the lobbies in search of celebrities. American PEN Center President Norman Mailer had invited U.S. Secretary of State George Schultz to appear at the opening session, without first asking the board's approval. He later apologized, asking the board to support his invitation. The majority agreed that to withdraw the invitation at that point would create a media controversy which would detract from the goals of the congress. Later, three past PEN Presidents and others drew up a petition of protest, signed by 66 members, stating the Reagan administration had done nothing to further freedom of expression either at home or abroad, and that the administration in fact "supports governments that silence, imprison, and torture their citizens for their beliefs." When Grace Paley demanded from her place in the audience that the petition be read, Mailer allegedly replied, "I did not bring the Secretary of State here to be pussy whipped." When the Secretary of State spoke, he argued that the Reagan administration was "committed to the free expression of ideas "and that PEN and the administration had "more in common than you think." This was greeted by hisses, and two members walked out in protest.

Other controversies during the week involved the appearance of Amadou-Mahtar M'bow of Senegal, the director-general of UNESCO, who has been accused of bias against Israel and the West. Germany's Günter Grass was at least as controversial as Mailer, attacking Saul Bellow and making remarks which generally were interpreted as anti-American. Still another controversy was begun when the women present woke up to the fact that of the 117 panelists listed in the official schedule, only one out of seven was a woman. Morever, among the thirty-two writers who officially read their works that week, only eight were women. A group of women drafted a protest. It was also noted there were not enough panel participants of color—Blacks, Hispanics, and Asians.

Worse, Mailer's explanation to the *New York Times* was that "there are not many women who are intellectuals first, poets and novelists second." And one writer who is definitely both an intellectual and a novelist , Cynthia Ozick, was interrupted by honored guest Arthur Schlesinger and told she could not read her brief, typewritten statement of protest against actions by Austrian Chancellor Bruno Kreisky.

On the other hand, there were some great social evenings and readings. Imagine being able to hear, in one week, the likes of Robertson Davies, J.M. Coetzee, Donald Barthelme, Salman Rushdie, Claude Simon, Mario Vargas Llosa, Günter Grass, Amos Oz, Kurt Vonnegut, Allen Ginsberg, Nadine Gordimer, Wang Meng, and Alice Munro.

Other literary events of note during this period include the establishment of Poets' Corner at the Cathedral of St. John the Divine in 1984. The award is misnamed, since it was created to recognize and honor deceased native writers in any genre by placing their names, dates, and a quotation from their work on a stone in the cathedral floor, similar to Poets' Corner in Westminster Abbey in London. The first three writers chosen were Washington Irving, Walt Whitman, and Emily Dickinson. Since then two writers have been selected annually by a group of rotating electors and a poet-in-residence. The honored writers are: Herman Melville and Edgar Allan Poe (1985), Robert Frost and Nathaniel Hawthorne (1986), Ralph Waldo Emerson and Mark Twain (1987), Henry James and Henry David Thoreau (1988), William Faulkner and Wallace Stevens (1989), and Willa Cather and T. S. Eliot (1990). The first poet-in-residence was Daniel Haberman, followed by William Jay Smith, and then Daniel Hoffman. Haberman was from West Virginia, Smith from Manhattan, and Hoffman from Philadelphia.

Since 1966 the Mayor's Office of Film, Theatre and Broadcasting at 254 West 54th Street has helped expedite all motion picture and television production in New York City. It issues location permits, coordinates all municipal services necessary for production at no charge, cuts red tape, issues film permits, and provides information, such as which insurance requirements must be met before a permit can be issued, which hotels offer discount lodgings to film crews, and what the work rules and current rates for union day scales are. As a result a thousand films (including 139 Academy Award nominees and 63 Academy Award winners) have been made in New York City. New York's most famous film director may be Woody Allen, who shot such works as *Radio Days, Broadway Danny Rose, Hannah and Her Sisters, Zelig,* and *Alice* in and around Manhattan. But others such as Sidney Lumet, Martin Scorsese, Spike Lee, Paul Newman, Paul Mazursky, and Joan Micklin Silver also have been convinced that New York's back lot of three hundred square miles is the best back lot there is, and Astoria Studios and Silver Cup Studios in Queens are flourishing.

In contrast, the last few years have seen a trimming down of publishing houses in New York. Harcourt Brace Jovanovich has relocated to Florida and California. Vanguard was dissolved and bought by Random House purely for its backlist. Clarkson Potter and Crown Publishers also have become part of Random House. Arbor House was folded into William Morrow. E. P. Dutton is now a part of Viking/Penguin, while Viking obviously is now also part of Penguin. Scribner's and Atheneum are now merely imprints of Macmillan. Grove Press was bought by Lord Weidenfeld, who hasn't seemed to know what to do with it. Barney Rossett's attempts to buy Grove back have proved futile. And so it goes.

At the same time there has also been a marked disappearance of literary bookshops. The miles of used bookstores on Broadway have dwindled, until the Strand stands alone at 828 Broadway and 12th Street. Elsewhere in the Village, the Eighth Street Bookstore, Dauber and Pine, and the Phoenix Bookshop are gone. Last year the St. Mark's Place Bookshop nearly expired, only to be rescued in the nick. In midtown the Harcourt Brace Bookstore on Third Avenue, the Scribner's Bookstore on Fifth Avenue, one of the two Doubleday Bookshops on Fifth Avenue, and the House of Books are all history. So too is the New Yorker Bookshop on the West Side. On the other hand, good new literary bookshops have opened and flourished, including Books and Company, New York Bound, Three Lives, Bloomsbury, and Endicott Booksellers. Some of these, however, manage to exist only through subsidization.

Books are not the only literary commodity in New York. In recent years the manuscript divisions of Columbia University Library, the New York Public Library, and The Berg Collection have accumulated massive archives from publishers—such as all of Random House's and Vanguard's files, now on deposit at Columbia. Such collections make New York more than ever a center for literary research. Auction houses are dealing more and more with literary properties, too, for example the sale of Saul Bellow's manuscripts at Sotheby's.

The two largest book auctions of the past twenty years both occurred in New York in the late 1980s. The sale at Christie's of Estelle Doheny's

library, largely incunabula, between 1987 and 1989 with proceeds of
$37.4 million, set a record for private libraries. The treasures included
the Old Testament volume of a Gutenberg Bible (in original binding)
and St. Jerome's *Epistolary*, printed in 1470.

Over 10,000 books and manuscripts put up for sale by the heirs of the
late H. Bradley Martin brought $35.7 million. Martin's was a varied
collection, with splendid holdings in children's literature, Americana,
illuminated manuscripts and ornithology. Included were a bright set of
John James Audubon's *Birds of America*, which went for $3.96 million;.
George Washington's inscribed copy of the *Federalist Papers*, a first
edition of Edgar Allan Poe's first published book *Tamerlane* (one of only
about twenty copies known, and one of very few preserved in its original
binding), and a superb presentation copy of Marcel Proust's *A la
Recherche du Temps Perdu* in 13 volumes in their original printed
wrappers; and many letters from Poe, Proust, Melville and others. The
illustrated catalogues were themselves works of art: the set of ten
separate volumes bound in green cloth sold for $850.

Any overview of the past thirty years on the New York literary front
would not be complete without noting those writers and book people
who are no longer among us. The following deaths have been deeply felt
during this time: Delmore Schwartz, Philip Rahv, Dwight Macdonald, F.
W. Dupee, Lionel Trilling, Mary McCarthy, Moses Hadas, Louis Zukofsky,
James T. Farrell, E.E. Cummings, Djuna Barnes, James Jones, Nelson
Algren, John Steinbeck, Charles Jackson, S. J. Perelman, James Thurber,
Philip Horton, Léonie Adams, Louise Bogan, Marianne Moore, Anaïs
Nin, May Swenson, Babette Deutsch, Dorothy Parker, Horace Gregory,
Marya Zaturenska, Muriel Rukeyser, Norman Holmes Pearson, Isabella
Gardner, Truman Capote, Robert Lowell, John Berryman, Howard Moss,
William Goyen, Carson McCullers, Flannery O'Connor, Tennessee
Williams, Audrey Wood, John Logan, Frances Steloff, Alfred A. Knopf,
Henry Robbins, Robert Penn Warren, Malcolm Cowley, Glenway Wescott,
David Kalstone, Robert Phelps, Jean Stafford, John Cheever, Nona
Balakian, Barbara Bannon, Jerzy Kosinski, Thornton Wilder, William
Carlos Williams, Jean Garrigue, Edmund Wilson, James Baldwin, Shirley
Jackson, Stanley Edgar Hyman, W. H. Auden, Chester Kalman, William
Empson, Merle Miller, James Wright, Virgil Thomson, Aaron Copland,
Leonard Bernstein, Isaac Bashevis Singer.

Yet, as this book testifies, literary New York constantly replenishes itself. I hope new readers of *Literary New York* find the book as useful and enjoyable as has the past generation.

Robert Phillips
August 1991

I. Lower Manhattan

NEW YORK made its appearance in literature before the first white settler stepped ashore. "After a hundred leagues," Giovanni da Verrazzano wrote in 1524, "we found a very agreeable place between two small but prominent hills; between them a very wide river, deep at its mouth, flowed out into the sea." Financed by France, Verrazzano had embarked in search of a western waterway to China. Instead, he was the first explorer to sight the island the Indians called *Manhatta*. The place between "the two small but prominent hills" was the Narrows; the very wide river, the Hudson. Verrazzano noted that the natives there "dressed in birds' feathers of various colors, and they came toward us joyfully, uttering loud cries of wonderment." Because of the tides, the mariner and his crew were forced to return to their ship, though they left the land "with much regret on account of its favorable conditions and beauty."

The territory that would become New York was not settled until over a hundred years later. In 1609 Henry Hudson visited and returned to Holland with a bundle of beaver skins as evidence of the new land's potential for the fur trade. Impressed by his reports, a group of businessmen organized the Dutch West India Company to establish commerce in the New World, and in 1624 sent out a shipload of settlers, who established themselves on Governor's Island. The following year the first permanent

settlement was started on Manhattan. In its earliest years the
fledgling city must have seemed a veritable Eden, magnificent
in its natural beauty and the wealth and variety of its wild
life. Rodman Gilder, in his history of the Battery, described
the island as it was to remain for at least a century: "Safe
from the fury of ocean gales, it was washed by a great river,
and by the salt waters of a noble bay and the strait now
called the East River. For food, the Indians were not limited to
the bountiful supplies of oysters, clams, terrapin, fish, and
giant lobsters that surrounded them. There were deer, par-
tridges, turkeys, and clouds of pigeons, swans, and ducks.
Maize and tobacco were readily cultivated near the fresh-water
ponds that clotted the island; and, in season, wild strawberries
and grapes could be had for the picking."

By the middle of the seventeenth century the settlement
of New Amsterdam was well established. It stretched from the
present Greenwich Street on the west to Water Street on the
east and was bounded by Wall Street on the north. (Landfill
operations during the eighteenth and nineteenth centuries
would broaden the island and add almost the whole of Battery
Park at its tip.) The Dutch brought the flavor of their home-
land with them, building their houses gable end to the street,
as in crowded Holland, although here they had no lack of
space. They scattered windmills about the landscape, and used
an inlet that ran up Broad Street as a canal. In this setting
New Amsterdam's first poet, Jacob Steendam, made his appearance. A clerk for the Dutch West India Company, he arrived in 1653. Thanks to the Castello Plan and Nicasius de
Sille's census of New Amsterdam's houses,* we know exactly

---

* The Castello Plan, so named because it was found in the collection of the
Villa Castello near Florence in 1911, is the only known plan of New Amsterdam
to have survived from the Dutch period. It depicts the town with all its buildings
as it was in 1660. It is presumed to have been discovered in Holland by Cosimo
de' Medici on a trip he made there in 1669. De Sille's census lists all the houses

where he lived. His house stood on the north side of Pearl Street between State and Whitehall, roughly opposite where Herman Melville would be born over 150 years later. The plan shows a fair-sized house with a stable in the rear, and a trim garden with fruit trees. Here, in 1659, Steendam wrote "The Complaint of New Amsterdam to Her Mother," which he sent to Holland for publication. He followed it in 1661 with "The Praise of New Amsterdam," which included these lines:

> See, two streams my gardens bind
> From the East and North they wind
> Rivers pouring to the sea,
> Rich in fish beyond degree,
> Milk and butter; fruits to eat
> No one can enumerate,
> Every vegetable known,
> Grain the best that e'er was grown.

A glance at a map of the time shows that the two streams literally did bind Steendam's gardens; he was located at almost the very tip of the island.

In 1664 the British took over New Amsterdam. During the early days of their rule the colony's literary output increased slightly; there was an occasional history, political satire or description of the city written to attract new settlers. But literature was hardly one of New York's more vital concerns. Unlike the other colonies it had been founded for purely commercial purposes, and commercial it was to remain. William Smith, author of one of the few histories, wrote in 1757 that for a long time his own father and James De Lancey "were the only

by block in New Amsterdam on July 10, 1660. By matching the plan and the list it is possible to see just who lived in the town and where.

The Castello Plan, showing all the buildings in New Amsterdam in 1660.

A diagrammatic version of the Castello Plan superimposed on modern lower Manhattan. Jacob Steendam lived in the second house from the top of "Pearle Straet" in Block G.

academics" in the province, and that, as late as 1745, there were only thirteen more. "What a contrast," he exclaimed, "in everything respecting the cultivation of science, between this and the colonies first settled by the English!"

•

New York's literary tradition began with its journalism. In 1725 William Bradford started the first newspaper, the *New York Gazette,* in Hanover Square. The city narrowly lost having Benjamin Franklin among its literary forefathers when Bradford turned down his request for a job. "I offer'd my services to . . . old Mr. William Bradford . . ." Franklin wrote in his *Autobiography.* "He could give me no employment, having little to do, and help enough already; but says he, 'My son at Philadelphia has lately lost his principal hand . . . If you go thither, I believe he may employ you.' "

Bradford's paper was controlled by New York's Governor William Cosby, whose financial corruption had aroused public indignation. A party formed to oppose Cosby and decided to publish a paper of its own, the *New-York Weekly Journal,* with John Peter Zenger, then Bradford's apprentice, as editor. The *Journal* used satirical means to attack the government. As Edward Ellis records in *The Epic of New York City,* mock advertisements represented the sheriff as "a monkey of the larger sort, about 4 feet high," and the city recorder as "a large spaniel, of about 5 feet 5 inches high," that "has lately strayed from his kennel with his mouth full of fulsome panegyrics."

Issues of the paper were burned, and Zenger was accused of libel and thrown into jail in the City Hall at the corner of Wall and Nassau streets. He remained there nearly a year before his trial in August 1735. Andrew Hamilton, first attorney general of Pennsylvania and America's most famous lawyer, came forward for the defense. Through his efforts

Zenger was acquitted, and Hamilton's expertise was commemorated in the expression "Philadelphia lawyer."

Although the Zenger case established the crucial principle of freedom of the press, it was not until several decades had passed that the pragmatic needs of the Revolution would spur the press to produce anything of great literary interest. Thomas Paine's pamphlets and Philip Freneau's patriotic satires would stir men to passion and action; later others would sit down to thrash out in writing the principles under which the new nation would be governed. In addition to the largest Tory population of the colonies, New York had a strong faction of militant revolutionaries — the combination made the city a center of debate. As the Revolution approached, the flow of propaganda, in handbills and newspapers, quickened.

Among those who arose on the side of the rebels was Philip Freneau. Although his family home was in New Jersey, Freneau had been born on New York's Frankfort Street and had attended boarding school in the city. When he was a student at Princeton he had begun to write poetry, and with his roommate, Hugh Henry Brackenridge, produced America's first known work of fiction, a novel called *Father Bombo's Pilgrimage to Mecca in Arabia.* After several attempts at settling on a career, Freneau came to New York in 1775 and gained a reputation as a political satirist with such poems as "American Liberty" and "Libera Nos Domine." At the end of the year he left New York for St. Croix, where he sailed as a privateer and turned to the more lyrical verse on which his literary reputation rests. His life exemplifies the predicament of the writer in a time when writing was not a profession; he had no independent income and was plagued continually by the problem of how to earn a living. In a piece called "Advice to Authors," he pretended to be a Mr. Robert Slender, who supported himself by weaving stockings "on a curious loom of his own

invention." He advised his readers that "all you have to do
. . . is to graft your authorship upon some other calling, or
support drooping genius by the assistance of some mechanical
employment, in the same manner as the helpless ivy takes hold
of the vigorous oak and cleaves to it for support — I mean to
say, in plain language, that you may make something by weaving garters, or mending old sails, when an Epic poem would
be your utter destruction." Freneau's advice came from his
own experience. After being taken prisoner by the British
in 1778 when piloting his privateer, he served in the New
Jersey Militia for several years. He then edited the *Freeman's
Journal* in Philadelphia and later returned to the sea as captain
of a cargo ship that plied the waters of the Atlantic seaboard.

Meanwhile, in 1787 and 1788, two New Yorkers, Alexander
Hamilton and John Jay, joined with James Madison (who
had been a classmate of Freneau's at Princeton) in writing
what was to become America's first literary classic, *The Federalist*.* This too was in the journalistic tradition; the eighty-
five essays that composed it were originally published in several of the city's newspapers. New York's ratification of the
Constitution hung in the balance and the writers attempted
to tip the scales in its favor. Generally regarded as one of the
highest achievements in political writing, *The Federalist* thoroughly explicated the principles of the new government. The
young and brilliant Hamilton, who wrote at least fifty-one of
the essays, lived at 58 Wall Street; Jay, who wrote five, lived
nearby at 133 Broadway; and Madison, visiting from Virginia,
stayed in a boarding house at 19 Maiden Lane.

* The men who figured in the early literary history of New York were members
of a very small educated elite. There were only twelve students in Freneau
and Madison's class at Princeton. Jay was one of six awarded degrees in 1764
at King's College, later called Columbia; twenty-one were awarded degrees in
1774, the year Hamilton entered King's. (Classes were suspended at King's
from 1776 to 1784 during the Revolution and Hamilton, therefore, never graduated.)

Two short years later these men shifted their political alignment. In 1790 Hamilton backed the formation of a newspaper called the *United States Gazette,* which advocated antidemocratic policies. Madison was alarmed and wrote to Jefferson that "a free newspaper, meant for general circulation, and edited by a man of genius of republican principles would be some antidote to the doctrines and discourses circulated in favor of Monarchy and Aristocracy." Freneau, in New York again as a newspaper editor, was the "man of genius" Madison had in mind. With the approval of Jefferson, Freneau was set up as editor of a paper in Philadelphia to rival Hamilton's. He was now a thorough-going democrat, often adding to the Robert Slender pseudonym the letters O.S.M., which stood for "One of the Swinish Multitude." By contrast, Hamilton and Jay lived an aristocratic life replete with pseudo-English formal dinners, receptions and dances.

For two years the *National Gazette,* the principal advocate of Jeffersonian democracy, battled the *United States Gazette.* As a result, the editor found himself despised by many of America's influential men. George Washington referred to him as "that rascal Freneau" and Washington Irving called him "a barking cur." What was perhaps more sad, he sacrificed the development of his poetry. After the financial failure of the *Gazette,* he spun out his days in unsuccessful newspaper ventures in New York and on his family farm in Mount Pleasant.

The career of Thomas Paine paralleled that of Freneau in several respects: as author of *Common Sense* and the *Crisis,* he used his pen in the service of the Revolution; as editor of the *Pennsylvania Magazine,* he earned his living as a journalist on the side of the democrats; and as a revolutionary who out-lived his time, he ended as the object of violent hatred. "He was regarded as worse than a common felon and outlaw," says literary historian Vernon Parrington, "because more dangerous."

John Wesley Jarvis's portrait of Thomas Paine.

Paine was in New York only at the end of his life. He had
lived in America, mostly in Philadelphia, from 1774 to 1787,
but then spent sixteen years in France and England. After returning to this country, he arrived in New York in 1803 and
lived alternately in boarding houses in the city and on a farm
in New Rochelle presented to him by the state in recognition
of his services during the Revolution. But hostile neighbors

made attempts on his life, and in 1806 he gave up the farm and went to live permanently in the city. He spent his happiest months living with John Wesley Jarvis, a prominent portrait painter, at 85 Church Street. Although Paine was in his seventies and Jarvis in his thirties, the two had much in common. Paine's biographer Alfred Aldridge writes, "Both were staunch Jeffersonians; both enjoyed a somewhat Bohemian manner of life, and both were avid talkers . . ." Jarvis and Paine often sat up late discussing religion, government and the rights of man. Paine spent six months with Jarvis and then stayed briefly at several more boarding houses. Finally in July 1808, by this time requiring almost constant attention to his failing health, he moved out in the country to Greenwich Village. He died there a year later.

·

At the end of the eighteenth century, there was not one full-time professional man of letters in all of America. Washington Irving would be the first when in 1809 his brilliant satire, *A History of New York, by Diedrich Knickerbocker,* delighted Americans and Europeans alike and established his career. Irving was born in 1783 at 131 William Street, but a few weeks later his family moved across to 128, a modest two-story house of wood and brick with a garden filled with flowers, apricots, greengage plums and nectarines. As a boy Irving loved plays and often attended the nearby Park Theatre. He would run home in time for prayers and then climb out his bedroom window and go back to catch the afterpiece.

After his father's death in 1802, Irving's mother moved the family to a house on the northwest corner of Ann and William streets (marked today by a plaque), and it was here that he began to write. His first efforts were the sketches dealing with the theater that he signed Jonathan Oldstyle. Then in 1807

Irving, his brother William and his brother-in-law James K. Paulding founded the popular periodical *Salmagundi,** a series of pamphlets satirizing life in New York. The three authors, who wrote under pseudonyms in the custom of the day — Washington was Launcelot Langstaff, William was William Wizard and Paulding was Anthony Evergreen — met regularly at William's home at 17 State Street.

It was in *Salmagundi*'s pages that the city was first called Gotham, a usage that survives to this day. Richard Henry Dana, editor of the leading literary journal of the time, the *North American Review,* wrote that "it was exceedingly pleasant morning or after-dinner reading, never taking up too much of a gentleman's time from his business and pleasures nor so exalted and spiritualized as to seem mystical to his far reaching vision. It was an excellent thing in the rests between cotillions

* The word *salmagundi* referred to a hash made of minced veal, pickled herrings, anchovies and onions served with lemon juice and oil.

A view of William Street in Washington Irving's time.

and pauses between games at cards; and answered a most convenient purpose in as much as it furnished those who had none
of their own with wit enough, for sixpence, to talk out the
sitting of an evening party."

On October 27, 1809, the following item appeared in the
New York Evening Post:

DISTRESSING

Left his lodgings some time since,
and has not since been heard of, a
small elderly gentleman, dressed in
an old black coat and cocked hat,
by the name of *Knickerbocker* . . .

This was the first move in the nation's earliest literary hoax.
In answer, the *Post* printed a letter to the editor saying that a
man fitting Knickerbocker's description had been seen by passengers on the Albany stage, resting by the side of the road
above King's Bridge. He was carrying a small bundle tied in a
red bandanna and appeared "fatigued and exhausted." Ten
days later, the landlord of the Independent Columbian Hotel
in Mulberry Street published a notice saying that "a very
curious kind of a written book" had been found in the room
of one Diedrich Knickerbocker and would have to be disposed
of to satisfy the landlord for his unpaid boarding and lodging.
Then on November 28 came the finale: an advertisement for
the soon to be published *A History of New York,* "found in the
chamber of Dr. Diedrich Knickerbocker, the old gentleman
whose sudden and mysterious disappearance has been noticed."

The book, amusing even today, was a satirical history of New
York "from the Beginning of the World to the End of the
Dutch Dynasty." Although descendants of the old Dutch fami-
lies charged that Irving had defamed them, his book was an

A detail from the Ratzer Map, 1767, shows the prerevolutionary city below
Reade Street on the west and Delancey's Square on the east. The "Road to
Greenwich" (far left) and the "Road to Bloomingdale" (top center) went
to the villages that bore those names. (Edgar Allan Poe lived in Bloomingdale Village in the mid-nineteenth century.) The *"Bowry* Lane" led to the
farm of Peter Stuyvesant, marked at the right center of the island. Branch-
ing off from the lane is the "Road to King's bridge" where Diedrich
Knickerbocker was seen carrying a knapsack on his way out of the city.
Other sites of interest are Abraham Mortier's estate (center left), later
occupied by Vice President John Adams and Aaron Burr at different times;

immediate and resounding success. It was the first work by an American to be known abroad; Charles Dickens wore out a copy, and Samuel Taylor Coleridge read it at one sitting. By the end of 1810, it had brought Irving $2000, the largest amount earned by any writer to that day. The name Irving gave his quaint hero, Knickerbocker, rapidly came to characterize New Yorkers of Dutch descent, and today refers to all New Yorkers.

After the publication of the *History,* Irving fell back into the desultory life he had known before. He had studied law in a casual way for seven or eight years, was admitted to the bar in 1806 and even was listed in the 1808 city directory as "Washington Irving, attorney, 3 Wall Street." But there is no record that he ever had a client. In the absence of any more compelling interest, he became an inactive partner in his brothers' hardware business at 135 Pearl Street. He wrote little, though he managed to revise the *History* in 1811 while sharing rooms with Henry Brevoort in Mrs. Ryckman's boarding house at 16 Broadway. He alternated between periods of society, during which he was the undisputed literary lion of New York, and solitude. In 1815 he went to Europe, where he was to remain, reigning over the American literary scene in absentia, for the next seventeen years.

.

In the years following the Revolution, New York City had played a role in the early development of the novel. In 1791 *Charlotte Temple, A Tale of Truth* by Susanna Rowson, a New

Alexander Hamilton died at William Bayard's home (upper left) after dueling with Burr in Hoboken across the river. To the northeast of the Bayard residence is the estate Captain Thomas Clarke called "Chelsea," a name that survives in the neighborhood today. Other points of interest are Kip's Bay and Turtle Bay and the numerous holdings of the Delanceys, the most prominent patroons of the New York area and the family from which James Fenimore Cooper's wife, Susan, was descended.

Englander of British birth, was first published. The book, set in New York, was eventually to run through 200 editions and remain the nation's best seller until it was supplanted by *Uncle Tom's Cabin* half a century later. It was said to have been based on the true story of Charlotte Stanley. The daughter of an English clergyman, she was persuaded to elope to this country in 1774 by John Montresor, who was already married. Montresor and his wife lived on Montresor's Island, now known as Randall's Island. Charlotte died, abandoned by Montresor, after bearing his child, and was buried in Trinity churchyard. In 1793, the story goes, Susanna Rowson, who was Montresor's cousin, visited the grave while it still bore the name "Charlotte Stanley." Today, a dark slab on the north side of the church near Broadway bears the inscription "Charlotte Temple."

Although Charles Brockden Brown, the Gothic novelist, was born in Philadelphia and spent most of his life there, the years in which he tried writing were spent in New York. In 1798 he came to stay with William Dunlap, playwright, theatrical historian and manager of the Park Theatre, at 15 Park Row. The yellow fever epidemic that year provided material for his novels, particularly *Arthur Mervyn*. Around 1803 Brown became discouraged and returned to Philadelphia to publish a magazine.

Despite the efforts of Rowson and Brown, it was not until James Fenimore Cooper wrote *The Spy* in 1821 that the novel came to be firmly established in America. Six years younger than Irving, Cooper was a gentleman farmer in Scarsdale when he threw down one of the popular novels of the day and told his wife that he could write a better one. Since the name of the book Cooper vowed to surpass is unknown, we cannot judge whether his *Precaution*, published in 1820, was in fact better; we do know that it was not very good. The experience, however, made a novelist of Cooper. With hardly a pause he started on *The Spy,* inspired by a story told to him by the old Federalist John Jay, who had retired to nearby Bedford. After its publication Cooper moved his family to New York to become a literary man.

In her "Small Family Memories," Cooper's daughter Susan recalled the house they took as being "one of two recently built by the Patroon, on Broadway just above Prince Street. It was then almost 'out-of-town.' Directly opposite to us was a modest two-story house occupied by John Jacob Astor." Their house was replaced, even in Susan Cooper's time, by Niblo's Garden, an outdoor theater. The following spring the Coopers moved to a narrow three-story brick house with marble steps and oak doors at 3 Beach Street. Here Cooper wrote *The Pilot,* America's first sea novel, also undertaken as a self-imposed challenge. Cooper, who had been in the navy, maintained at a dinner party that the current best seller, Sir Walter Scott's *The Pirate,* was too error-ridden to have been written by a real sailor. On the way home he outlined a plot.

In 1825 the Coopers decided to move again. The Beach Street house was "out of repair," as Susan Cooper delicately put it. "The number of rats was really alarming; I remember distinctly their running over the bed in which I slept." On May 1, the day on which New Yorkers traditionally moved, the Coopers went to 345 Greenwich Street, "at that time a quiet dignified part of the town." They summered in Bayside or Hallett's Cove, now known as Astoria, and Cooper traveled to New York by sloop almost daily.

During this period of his life, Cooper was a highly sociable man. William Cullen Bryant compared his character to "the bark of the cinnamon, a rough and astringent rind without and an intense sweetness within. Those who penetrated below the surface found a genial temper, warm affects, and a heart with ample place for his friends . . ." Seeking out company, Cooper began to meet his friends in the Den, a small room in the bookstore on New Street belonging to his publisher, Charles Wiley. And so began New York's first literary club. Originally called the Cooper Club or the Lunch, the group was known as the Bread and Cheese when it was organized on a more formal basis. Bread signified a vote for a new member and cheese one against. The original members were Charles Wiley; William Dunlap; Henry Brevoort; the Shakespearean scholar Gulian Verplanck; the city's leading poet, Fitz-Greene Halleck; and James Kent, whose *Commentaries* were the definitive interpretation of the law. Irving, abroad in Europe, was named an honorary member. Bryant and Samuel F. B. Morse, one of the foremost painters of the day and later inventor of the telegraph, joined in 1825. The club's membership represented the literary elite of the city and embraced the most prominent writers of the Knickerbocker period.

In 1825, the entire Cooper family began studying French in preparation for going abroad the following year. Cooper's stature can be measured by the fact that, when he left, the Bread and Cheese gave him a farewell dinner, attended by Governor DeWitt Clinton, at the City Hotel. While abroad, Cooper started to write critically of America and when he returned in 1833 he found his reputation totally changed. Four days after his arrival he attended a banquet for an old friend. Many of the people he knew did not speak to him and those who did were cold and constrained. He found it impossible to sit out the dinner, and later thought it wise to decline an invitation to the obligatory City Hotel banquet honoring his return.

Disapproval soon became public as well as personal and Cooper found himself frequently vilified in the press. Rather than ignoring the attacks, he charged the publishers with libel and pleaded his own cases against them in court. These suits, which he often won, were a major contribution to the redefinition of the libel laws, establishing the illegality of public attack without supporting evidence.

Cooper's work after his return, notably *Home as Found,* criticized life in New York, with its social hypocrisies and fancy-dress balls. Among those who fell under his disapproval was the man he once had made an honorary member of his club. He now found Irving, intent on making money and gaining social esteem, the epitome of the bourgeois culture he detested. The two first titans of American literature were, therefore, never to meet during the two years they both lived in the city. Irving, who had returned from Europe in 1832, was at 3 Bridge Street with his brother Ebenezer or at John Jacob Astor's "Astoria," until he moved to Tarrytown in 1836. By this time the fashionable residential district had progressed up Broadway to Greenwich Village and Cooper and his family had taken a house on Bleecker Street. He continued to spend his winters in New York although he considered Otsego Hall in Cooperstown his home. The two men met only once, years later, in 1850, at the offices of their publisher, Putnam. They chatted pleasantly for an hour.

With Cooper and Irving retired to the country, William Cullen Bryant took the center of New York's literary stage. Having written "Thanatopsis" at seventeen, he was already known for his poetry when he arrived in New York in 1825 at the age of thirty-one. Like Irving, he had studied law, a popular profession for young men of indefinite inclination or limited means. (At the time medicine was financially unrewarding, and the ministry required a college degree.) But he found the profession uncongenial — he wrote of "the disagreeable, disgusting drudgery of the law" — and came to New York to try to earn a living as editor of the *New York Review and Athenaeum.* In 1826 he augmented his income by becoming assistant to William Coleman, editor of the *New York*

Evening Post. The magazine eventually folded and Bryant went to work on the *Evening Post* full-time. In 1829, Coleman died and Bryant became editor.

The *Evening Post* had been founded in 1801 by Alexander Hamilton and his followers, who hoped to produce a Federalist editor the equal of the great democrats, Paine and Freneau. By the time Bryant took over, however, the paper was primarily commercial. It consisted of a single sheet folded to make four pages; of these, all but page two were devoted to advertising, legal notices and other information of commercial interest.

Bryant gave the paper, which had collaborated in Irving's hoax, an increased literary flavor by printing news of writers and frequent book announcements. These were not real reviews, which were not to be found in the New York press until the days of Edgar Allan Poe and Margaret Fuller; Bryant usually did not have time to read the books. His real strength as an editor (he had only one assistant much of the time and no news staff until much later) was as a writer of eloquent, morally impeccable editorials on the issues of the day. He took controversial positions, in favor of free speech and labor unions and against slavery, that often lost the newspaper circulation and advertising. The greatest peril of his profession, he wrote in 1851, "is the strong temptation . . . it sets before men, to betray the cause of truth to public opinion, and to fall in with what are supposed to be the views held by a contemporaneous majority, which are sometimes perfectly right and sometimes grossly wrong."

As an editor Bryant combined great efficiency with great disorder. His desk was piled high with papers except for a small clear space in the middle where he worked. Like "paper-sparing Pope," he did all his writing on the backs of old letters and manuscripts. John Bigelow, an early biographer, explained his motive: "He believed that everybody in the world was made the poorer by everything that is wasted, and no one so much as he who wastes, for he experiences a waste of character as well as of property."

In personal relations, Bryant was remote with all but a very few close friends. Richard Henry Dana, who was one of his intimates, once wrote encouraging him to make the acquaintance of Poe. Bryant replied, "I do not know that I ever got acquainted with anybody, of set purpose, in my life. The three things most irksome to me in my transactions with the world are to owe money, to ask a favor, and to seek an acquaintance. The few excellent friends I have I acquired I scarcely know how — certainly by no assiduity of my own." Bryant knew Cooper but is said to have been somewhat intimidated by him. Bryant's son-in-law, Parke Godwin, described them as appearing little fitted for friendship: "Cooper, burly, brusque, and boisterous, like a bluff sailor, always bringing a breeze of a quarrel with him; Mr. Bryant, shy, modest, and delicate as a woman."

In his early years in New York, Bryant moved from boarding house to boarding house. When he first arrived he lived with a French family named Evrard on Chambers Street, where his wife and daughter joined him later in the year. Next they moved into rooms at Mrs. Meigs's at 88 Canal Street and in 1830 were on Broome Street between Hudson and Varick. Wherever Bryant lived, he followed the same regime. He rose at five-thirty and did an hour's exercises, which included chinning himself from the door frame and jumping back and forth over his bed, aided by a vaulting pole. Then, after a small breakfast, he walked to his office in lower Manhattan.

•

The great writers of the Knickerbocker period — Cooper, Irving and Bryant — made the first strides toward an American literature; they gave the country a sense of self-realization. "As Audubon 'discovered' the American birds and Catlin discovered the Indians," wrote Van Wyck Brooks, "these writers discovered, for Americans, their woods and fields, their scenery, their flowers, their rivers and prairies and mountains." But although Cooper was to survive until 1851, Irving until '59, and Bryant until 1878, their time in literature was over much sooner. By 1835, the reality of the city was clearly antithetical to their earlier vision. The grid street plan, devised for New York in 1811, probably the single most destructive influence on the city's physical character, had begun to be implemented. "The face of the island was originally diversified into hill and valley, ledge and swamp; and the more ancient parts of the city still present very nearly the same uneven surface as in the olden time," wrote Asa Greene in an 1837 guidebook to New York. "But the levelling genius of our city government has reduced to an almost entire flat the more new and recently built parts of the town. They have said emphatically, 'Stoop down ye hills! ye valleys rise!' "

With the decline of the natural and physical side of New York, in literature and in fact, came a simultaneous growth of the commercial. New York was the publishing capital of the nation. The book trade had evolved to the point where the reader, or editor, had made his appearance. Asa Greene noted, "As certain Kings and great men . . . used, in former times to keep a taster, whose business it was to see that the food was not poisoned: so do Harper & Brothers employ a reader. This course . . . not only insures the purity of the moral, and the briskness of the intellectual atmosphere, as far as the press of Harper & Brothers is concerned; but also provides effectually against the assertion that their books 'are never read.' "

Newspapers had entered a great surge of development. In

September of 1833 Benjamin H. Day began publishing the *Sun*, the first penny newspaper to survive. Until then New Yorkers had regarded a newspaper as a luxury; a year's subscription to the *Evening Post* cost eight dollars, or ten days' wages for a working man. The *Sun* did no more reporting than Bryant's *Post*, but it served the common man by bringing the newspaper within the range of his purse and printing a great many help wanted ads.

In 1835 James Gordon Bennett founded the *Herald* in a cellar at 10 Wall Street, and with it a new journalism. Bennett was the first editor to go in search of news. He started work at 5:00 A.M., and made the rounds of business offices collecting stock tables and gossip every afternoon. To be sure to get the European newspapers first, he kept a clipper ship off Montauk and ran a special train the length of Long Island. Bennett also gave the city a kind of news — the violent, vulgar and sensational — it had never known before. In 1840 he announced his own engagement with these headlines: TO THE READERS OF THE HERALD — DECLARATION OF LOVE — CAUGHT AT LAST — GOING TO BE MARRIED — NEW MOVEMENT IN CIVILIZATION.

Greatest of the newspapermen to come up in the thirties was Horace Greeley, whose *Tribune* was the first paper to be nationally distributed on a wide scale. With 250,000 readers, many of them in the frontier states, the *Tribune* was said to be second only to the Bible in influence in the emerging West. Greeley's aim was to educate his readers morally, politically and culturally. He published some of the leading writers of the day, including Poe, Dickens, and Karl Marx, then in London, who wrote a column on European politics and economics.

In the 1830s and 1840s many of the city's newspapers, magazines and book publishers gathered on Nassau Street, earning it the name "newspaper row." Going north from Fulton Street were, at various times during the forties, the *Herald* at the

Printing House Square, showing the *Times, Tribune* and *World*
buildings in 1864.

corner of Fulton, the *Sun* at 91 Nassau, the *Literary World* at 109, the *Aurora and Union* at 111, the *New York Times* at 118, the *Broadway Journal* at the corner of Beekman, the *Knickerbocker* at 139, the *Mirror* at 148 and the *Tribune* at 160.

Among the men on their staffs was Walt Whitman, who moved to Manhattan in 1841 to work for the *Aurora.* He lived in a series of boarding houses, among them a Mrs. Chipman's at 12 Centre Street. While staying there, he went home for lunch every day and then took a walk down Broadway to the Battery before returning to the office. His description of the trip back uptown re-creates the city of 1842: "Coming up Broadway, from the Bowling Green, an observer will notice, on each side, tall, quiet looking houses, with no great aspect of life or business. These are mostly boarding houses . . . After passing Trinity Church, however, the crowd thickens, and the ground stories of the buildings are principally occupied as shops." Farther on one passed what Whitman described as "that very respectable city, the Astor House," and "that most villainous specimen of architecture," the Park Theatre. "By and by, you arrive at an open space . . . In all probability your ears will be greeted with the discordant notes of the newsboys, who generally muster here in great force."

Whitman delighted in the variety of the city's people, particularly the omnibus drivers, whom he called "a strange, natural, quick-eyed and wondrous race." He often rode next to them on their rounds. Although he later lived mostly in Brooklyn, he sometimes visited the city several times a day and called himself "Manhattanese." He describes the city in several poems, including "Mannahatta":

My city's fit and noble name resumed,
Choice aboriginal name, with marvellous beauty, meaning,
*A rocky founded island — shores where ever gayly dash the coming,
    going, hurrying sea waves.*

In 1849 Whitman began frequenting Fowler and Wells's Phrenological Cabinet at 131 Nassau Street. Lorenzo Fowler charted the bumps on his head: "Leading traits of character appear to be Friendship, Sympathy, Sublimity, and Self-Esteem, and markedly among his combinations the dangerous faults of Indolence, a tendency to the pleasure of voluptuousness and alimentiveness and a certain reckless swing of animal will, too unmindful, probably, of the conviction of others." When some booksellers refused to handle the first edition of *Leaves of Grass,* which Whitman published himself, Fowler and Wells sold it in their bookstore at 308 Broadway. The phrenologists published the second edition.

•

In the 1840s New York's literati yearned for the emergence of the genius who, breaking with the English tradition represented by the Knickerbockers, would write in a way that was completely and characteristically American. Although they were unable to recognize it at the time, they got just what they wanted. Into New York came two great, incontrovertibly American originals — Herman Melville and Edgar Allan Poe.

Poe had first visited the city in 1831 when, expelled from West Point, he prepared his third book of poetry in Elam Bliss's bookstore at 111 Broadway. Later, while editing *Graham's Magazine* in Philadelphia, he used a New York event as the basis of "The Mystery of Marie Roget." After reading newspaper accounts of the murder of Mary Cecilia Rogers, who lived at 114 Liberty Street, he made the victim's name French and transferred the setting to Paris so that the story could serve as a sequel to "The Murders in the Rue Morgue." In 1844 Poe moved permanently to New York. Although he is often remembered in romantic terms — eccentric, undisciplined, ill and addicted to drugs and alcohol — he had a sound reputation as one of the country's most astute and successful critics and editors. Under his direction, the *Southern Literary Messenger* had become famous for the authority of its reviews, and he had made *Graham's* the foremost monthly in the country. During the three years of his editorship, its circulation rose from fifty-five hundred to forty thousand.

On arriving in the city, Poe became editor and part owner of the *Broadway Journal,* at the southwest corner of Beekman and Nassau streets. He published "Art-Music and Heart Music" by Walt Whitman, who described Poe as "very kindly and human, but subdued, perhaps a little jaded." The Poes lived at 130 Greenwich Street in 1844 and in the back room on the third floor of a tenement at 195 East Broadway the following year. In the few years Poe had left to live, his distaste for the city and concern for the health of his wife drove him first to the suburbs in Greenwich Village and later to the outlying countryside — the Brennan Farm near Broadway and 84th Street, the Miller Farm in Turtle Bay and finally the cottage in Fordham.

Poe's attitude toward New York was perhaps best expressed in a series of letters about the city he wrote for the *Columbia Spy* in Pottsville, Pennsylvania. He appreciated the natural setting while deploring the changes made in the name of progress. In 1844 he wrote:

> I have been roaming far and wide over this island of Manna-hatta. Some portions of its interior have a certain air of rocky sterility which may impress some imaginations as simply *dreary* — to me it conveys the sublime . . . On the eastern or "sound" face of Mannahatta are some of the most picturesque sites for villas to be found within the limits of Christendom. These localities, however, are neglected — unimproved. The only mansions upon them (principally wooden) are suffered to remain unrepaired, and present a melancholy spectacle of decrepitude. In fact, these magnificent places are doomed. The spirit of Improvement has withered them with its acrid breath. Streets are already "mapped" through them, and they are no longer suburban residences but "town-lots." In some 30 years every noble cliff will be a pier, and the whole island will be densely desecrated by buildings of brick, with portentous *façades* of brown-stone . . .

Unlike Poe, Melville was a native New Yorker — in some ways the quintessential New Yorker. He was born in 1819 at 6 Pearl Street (a plaque marks the site) with an ancestry that perfectly reflected the mixture of nationalities peculiar to New York — British, Dutch and a dash of French. His mother, Maria Gansevoort, came from a family of prominent Dutch patroons. His father, like Irving's, was a Scot, and the Melvilles had married among the French Huguenots. The elder Melville was an importer of French goods, and when his business failed the family moved to Albany. Herman taught school and in the early forties made the sea voyages that would form the background of most of his books.

Melville first entered the New York literary world in 1845 when he was arranging for an American edition of his first book, *Typee.* (Irving had helped him find a publisher in England.) He made frequent visits in connection with his books before moving to the city after his marriage in 1847. The residential district had shifted gradually uptown and the Melvilles settled down in Greenwich Village. They lived there until 1850, when Melville went to Pittsfield to write *Moby-Dick.* In June 1851 he wrote to Hawthorne, "In a week or so, I go to New York, to bury myself in a third-story room, and work & slave on my 'Whale' while it is driving thro' the press."

When *Moby-Dick* was finally published, the reaction was not what Melville had expected. Instead of recognizing it as the great American novel they had been waiting for, the New York literati responded with mixed, lukewarm reviews. Exhausted by bringing forth what Melville scholar Henry Murray called "that wild Everest of art," and bitterly disillusioned at its reception, Melville poured out his fevered emotions in *Pierre,* the book that would irrevocably damage his literary reputation. Intertwined with a theme that encompasses incest, Oedipus and the mysteries of the unconscious is the story of a young man who comes to New York and tries to earn his living as a writer in the shivering cold of a "third-story room." Not only is Pierre's masterpiece, like Melville's, ungratefully received; it is rudely condemned. In a satiric chapter entitled "Young America in Literature," Melville vented his scorn on the New York literary world.

Pierre contains many autobiographical strands and it seems likely that its third-story room is based on the one in which

Melville finished *Moby-Dick*. The fictional room is located in a building in the courtyard of one "Church of the Apostles." Murray speculates that this was modeled on the South Baptist Church at 82 Nassau Street. Melville then would have been living behind it on Dutch Street. Another scholar, Hans Bergmann, notes that the agreement between Melville and his publisher provided for the printing of *Moby-Dick* from "plates in the possession of R. Craighead." Craighead's shop was on Fulton Street between Nassau and Dutch. If Melville in fact had been involved in overseeing the stereotyping of the book, as the words "drive the book through the press" might suggest, a room on Dutch Street would have been a most convenient place to stay.

After *Pierre,* which was universally condemned as *Moby-Dick* was not, Melville might well have sunk into obscurity had it not been for C. F. Briggs, editor of the literary magazine, *Putnam's.* Over the next several years he would publish Melville's "The Encantadas," "Israel Potter" and "Bartleby the Scrivener," which re-creates the Wall Street law offices of the 1850s.

·

With the decline of Melville's reputation came the decline of New York as the nation's literary capital. The second phase of American literature had already begun in New England, where it found more hospitable soil. Unlike New York, which was cosmopolitan, commercial, anti-intellectual and fragmented by dispute, New England boasted a homogeneous people, passionately interested in learning, united in a coherent intellectual and literary movement — transcendentalism.

Later Lower Manhattan would have its literary visitors. When Henry James revisited New York in 1904, the area had already acquired the totally modern character it has today.

James observed "the multitudinous sky-scrapers standing up to the view, from the water, like extravagant pins in a cushion already overplanted." On Wall Street "the new landmarks [were] crushing the old quite as violent children stamp on snails and caterpillars." And "the special sky-scraper that over-hangs poor old Trinity to the north" was "a south face as high and wide as the mountain-wall that drops the Alpine avalanche, from time to time, upon the village, and the village spire, at its foot . . ."

In the 1920s Thomas Wolfe came to observe the activity of Washington Market and the desperation of the homeless men who spent cold nights in the public latrine opposite City Hall. E. E. Cummings visited the Aquarium, then at the Battery, and took John Dos Passos to eat at a Syrian restaurant on Washington Street. There was even an occasional resident. In 1911, after shipping out as a seaman, Eugene O'Neill came to live in a flophouse over a saloon called Jimmy the Priest's, near the waterfront at 252 Fulton Street. " 'Jimmy the Priest's' certainly was a hell hole," O'Neill said. "It was awful. One couldn't go any lower . . . The house was almost coming down and the principal housewreckers were vermin." The old red brick build-ing has been torn down but the saloon and the men O'Neill met there are depicted in his play *Anna Christie* and his story "Tomorrow." More recently, the poet and anthologist Oscar Williams and his wife, the poet Gene Derwood, lived on the top floor of an old warehouse building, now a parking lot, at 35 Water Street. But for the most part, when writers came back to the city, the city had moved uptown.

•

Lower Manhattan Tour

Virtually no literary landmarks remain in Lower Manhattan. As the financial capital of the world, its real estate value is so high that it has been rebuilt many times. Then, too, much of the early city was destroyed by fires. One fire in 1776 devastated a fourth of the area, and a second, in 1778, burned an additional sixty dwellings and numerous stores. A few buildings, however, help to re-create the times of literature's beginnings in New York.

This, then, is largely an armchair tour, to be made with a large-scale map and as many pictures of old New York as can be found. The few numbers not in parentheses are buildings or locations still there, to be seen.

(a1) 252 Fulton Street, then half a block from the waterfront, was a flophouse over a saloon where Eugene O'Neill lived in 1911. The site is now in the heart of the World Trade Center (p. 30).

1. St. Paul's Chapel, on Broadway, between Vesey and Fulton streets. Built between 1764 and 1766 by architect Thomas McBean, the tower and steeple were added in 1796 by James Crommelin Lawrence. This is Manhattan's oldest surviving pre-revolutionary public building.

(1a) 133 Broadway, on the northwest corner of Cedar Street. John Jay lived at this spot in 1787–88 (p. 8).

(1b) 114 Liberty Street. This is the site of a real-life murder which Edgar Allan Poe used as the basis for "The Mystery of Marie Roget" (p. 26).

(1c) 130 Greenwich Street, between Albany and Cedar streets. In 1844 Poe and his wife Virginia found a room with board here for seven dollars a week, "the cheapest board I ever knew" (p. 26).

(1d) 111 Broadway. The site of Elam Bliss's bookstore where Poe, in 1831, prepared his third book of poetry (p. 26).

2. Trinity Church at Wall Street and Broadway has been rebuilt twice since the fires of the 1770s, but its churchyard remains. Here can be seen the graves of William Bradford and Alexander Hamilton, and the tombstone bearing the inscription "Charlotte Temple," marking the spot where the heroine of Susanna Rowson's novel is said to be buried (p. 15–16). The exterior of the church was cleaned in 1990–91.

(2a) 16 Broadway. Mrs. Ryckman's boarding house, where Washington Irving lived in 1811, was a few yards north of the Beaver Street corner (p. 15).

3. Bowling Green. In 1771 an iron fence was erected around the green to prevent it from becoming a "receptacle of all the filth and dirt of the neighborhood." The fence still stands today, with the exception of its decorative crowns or iron balls, said to have been used as ammunition during the revolution. In the mid-nineteenth century there was a fountain on the green, which Edgar Allan Poe said looked like a "small country jail in a hard thunder shower."

(**3a**) 3 Bridge Street, on the north side, halfway between State and Whitehall streets, was Washington Irving's home from 1832 to 1836 (p. 19).

(**3b**) 6 Pearl Street, on the south side a few doors east of State Street, is the site of Herman Melville's birth in 1819 (p. 27). There is no plaque here now.

4. 7 State Street. The James Watson home is the last survivor of its time. The easterly portion, two windows wide, was built in 1793; the rest, with its curved porch and Ionic columns, was added in 1806. Additional restorations and additions were made in 1965. Attributed to architect, John McComb, it was the subject of H.C. Bunner's *The Story of a New York House,* a historical novel written in 1887.

Go east across Whitehall Street into Water Street:

(**4a**) 35 Water Street, between Broad Street and Coenties Slip. Oscar Williams and his wife Gene Derwood lived on the top floor of an old warehouse once located where this twenty-two-story building now stands (p. 30).

5. Fraunces Tavern, at the corner of Pearl and Broad streets, is a highly conjectural construction (1907) based on typical buildings of the mid-eighteenth century rather than on the actual structure that once stood here. Originally built in 1719 as a private home, it was converted into a tavern in 1762 and was later run by the celebrated West Indian innkeeper, Samuel Fraunces, who had been George Washington's steward.

(**5a**) 81 Pearl Street. William Bradford established the first printing press in the colonies at this location in 1693.

6. Hanover Square, where William Bradford started the first newspaper, the *New York Gazette,* in 1725 (p. 6). India House, at the west end of the square, was built between 1851 and 1854.

From the other end of Hanover Square, go north on Hanover Street to:

(**6a**) 58 Wall Street (then exactly opposite Hanover Street). In 1787–88 Alexander Hamilton lived at this location (p. 8).

7. Wall and Nassau streets. The structure that was once the U.S. Custom House and later the Subtreasury Building has been renamed Federal Hall National Memorial, in recognition of the fact that it stands on the site of the original Federal Hall, formerly New York City Hall. There John Peter Zenger was imprisoned until his trial in August 1735 (pp. 6–7).

(**7a**) 10 Wall Street. Melville's brother had his law office here in the 1850s, and it is described in "Bartleby the Scrivener" (pp. 29 and 23).

(**7b**) 19 Maiden Lane, now number 15, was a boarding house where James Madison stayed in 1787–88 (p. 8).

(**7c**) 131 and 128 William Street. Washington Irving was born at the first location in 1783, and spent his boyhood at the second one (p. 11).

(7d) William and Anne streets on the northwest corner. Irving's mother moved her family here in 1802; here Irving began to write (p. 11). There is no plaque now.

(7e) While overseeing the printing of *Moby Dick* on Fulton Street, Melville lived both around the corner to the east on Dutch Street, and around the corner to the west at 82 Nassau Street (p. 29).

From here north to Beekman Street there were nine newspaper offices in the 1830s; among them were those for which both Poe and Walt Whitman worked (p. 23–24).

8. Go west on Beekman Street past Theatre Alley, and on to Park Row. To the left, at numbers 21–25, was the Park Theatre. To the right, one block up, is a statue of Ben Franklin; directly behind it and across the street was the original location of:

9. Horace Greeley's statue (by John Quincy Adams Ward, 1890), which is now in the northeast quarter of City Hall Park.

(9a) 12 Centre Street, a boarding house where Whitman stayed, was at the southeast corner of Chambers Street.

(9b) 308 Broadway (second door north of Duane Street). Here was located Fowler & Wells Bookstore, where *Leaves of Grass* was sold (p. 25).

Go west on Duane Street to Church Street. Detour one block south to:

(9c) The southeast corner of Reade Street. A door or so south of this corner was 85 Church Street at the time when Thomas Paine was staying with the painter John Wesley Jarvis (p. 11).

(9d) 345 Greenwich Street, between Jay and Harrison streets, to which location James Fenimore Cooper moved his family in 1825 (p. 17).

(9e) 3 Beach Street, at the northwest corner of West Broadway was where the Coopers lived before moving to Greenwich Street.

(9f) 88 Canal Street, on the northwest corner of Greene Street. (This was the old numbering, changed in the mid-nineteenth century.) William Cullen Bryant had rooms here before moving to Broome Street (p. 21).

(9g) Broome Street between Hudson and Varick, where the Bryants were living in 1830 (p. 21).

II. Greenwich Village

No OTHER NEIGHBORHOOD in New York, perhaps in the world, has been the birthplace of more literature than Greenwich Village. Several distinct phases of literary activity correspond to stages in the Village's evolution as a community. In the 1800s, when writing was apt to be a more patrician than bohemian endeavor, the elegant residential community around Washington Square was home, meeting place and subject for New York's literary figures. After the turn of the century, when the area had entered a decline, the young, most often poor, artists and writers discovered in the rundown but still charming neighborhood cheap rents and a congenial setting. The bohemians, whose rediscovery of the neighborhood raised real estate values, were eventually replaced by middle-class academics and those writers who were sufficiently established to have respectable incomes.

The Nineteenth-Century Village: Washington Square

It has a kind of established repose which is not of frequent occurrence in other quarters of the long, shrill city; it has a riper, richer, more honorable look than any of the upper ramifications of the great longitudinal thoroughfare — the look

of having had something of a social history. It was here, as
you might have been informed on good authority, that you
had come into a world which appeared to offer a variety of
sources of interest; it was here that your grandmother lived
in venerable solitude, and dispensed a hospitality which com-
mended itself alike to the infant imagination and the infant
palate; it was here that you took your first walks abroad,
following the nursery-maid with unequal step, and sniffing
up the strange odour of the ailanthus-trees which at that
time formed the principal umbrage of the Square, and diffused
an aroma that you were not yet critical enough to dislike as it
deserved . . .

Henry James, in his description, was looking back from the
vantage point of 1881 to the 1840s, when Washington Square
was at its peak. The country village of estates and small wooden
houses where Thomas Paine had lived in 1808 had grown to
become the city's prime suburb. New York's residential center
had moved uptown in response to two forces. With each attack
of smallpox, cholera or yellow fever (there were major epidem-
ics in 1819, 1822 and 1823) the population of the city fled the
downtown area for the open country to the north. Most of the
necessary shops and businesses were hurriedly transplanted and,
as each panic subsided, a few more remained permanently behind. Simultaneously, the expansion of the business section
pressed the residential district northward. Fashionable New
York zigzagged up the island from Lower Manhattan, west to
St. John's Park, back over to Broadway and up toward Bond
Street and Astor Place.

The movements of a number of literary families in the 1820s
and 1830s reflect this pattern of migration. In 1824 the Melvilles — Herman was still a boy — moved from Cortlandt Street
to 33 Bleecker and in 1828 to 675 Broadway. William Cullen
Bryant's peregrinations traced a similar route; in 1831 he
abandoned the St. John's Park area for 4th Street and Broad-

Thomas Paine's home at 309 Bleecker Street.

way. James Fenimore Cooper, who had lived near St. John's
Park on Beach Street, took a house on Bleecker Street between
Laurens (now La Guardia Place) and Thompson when he
returned from Europe in 1833. This house, which had been
selected for the Coopers by their friend Samuel F. B. Morse,
was "too magnificent for our simple French tastes," wrote Mrs.
Cooper. Nevertheless the family settled in with French furni-

ture, four Swiss servants and a French tiger cat named Coque-
licot. The Coopers later moved to St. Mark's Place (see Chapter
III, The Lower East Side) .

One of the most elegant residential developments to result
from the northward surge was Washington Square. The park,
originally an execution ground and potter's field, was formally
dedicated in 1828, and the houses built on the south side of the
Square that year made the area fashionable. In the spring of
1831 several prominent New Yorkers agreed to construct an
even more distinguished row on the north side. The houses,
many of which remain today, had elegant architectural features.
Inside there were Italian carved marble mantels and gilt-bronze
chandeliers. Walks laid in alternating black and white marble
squares led up to the white marble steps. Behind, there were
gardens with flower borders and white grape-covered trellises.

In the 1840s, when Henry James was just opening his eyes to
the world, literary gatherings were taking place regularly around
Washington Square. The most scholarly were held at Evert
Duyckinck's house at 20 Clinton Place. Duyckinck was then an
editor for the publishers Wiley and Putnam and for a critical
magazine called the *Literary World*. He was said to know the
field of English and American literature as "seamen know the
sea," and, as author of the *Cyclopaedia of American Literature,*
he chronicled the development of the nation's writing. He was
a thoughtful and generous friend, bringing writers into congenial company, midwiving their works into being and lending
them money and books from the eighteen thousand-volume
library that lined the rooms of his house.

Among those who gathered regularly in Duyckinck's basement study was Melville, who lived at 103 Fourth Avenue from
1847 to 1850 while writing *Mardi, Redburn* and *White-Jacket*.
It was here that Melville began his literary education — meeting
Irving and Bryant, reading voraciously in Duyckinck's library

and engaging in the spirited conversation that would be reflected in *Mardi*. In 1851, after moving to Pittsfield, Melville was writing nostalgically to Duyckinck:

> "I suppose the Knights of the Round Table still assemble over their cigars and punch, and I know that once every week the 'Literary World' revolves upon its axis. I should like to hear again the old tinkle of glasses in your basement, and may do so, before many months."

More social evenings were held by Anne Charlotte Lynch, a poet and teacher of English composition sometimes credited with having had the first salon in America. Miss Lynch lived first at 116 Waverly Place, where she entertained in a large double parlor with fires burning at either end. Her guests included Bryant, Melville, Margaret Fuller, Fitz-Greene Halleck, Bayard Taylor, Catharine Sedgwick and, most notably, Edgar Allan Poe, who is said to have read "The Raven" there.

Poe lived nearby at 18 Amity Street in 1844 and 85 Amity in 1845 while editing the *Broadway Journal*. Earlier, when he had come to the city penniless in 1837, he had lived in the older section of the Village, first in a red brick house on the corner of Sixth Avenue and Waverly Place and later in a frame house with a high-pitched roof and shuttered windows at 113½ Carmine Street.

In 1843 the man who was to set Washington Square in the public mind was born at 21 Washington Place. Henry James, revisiting the site of his birth when he came home in 1904 from a long residence in England, was shocked to find that the house had been "suppressed," as he called it, because of the construction of a new building by New York University. The interloper, which had taken the place of the old Gothic university building as well as the house where James was born, was "a high square, impersonal structure" that so blocked his view of the past that

he felt he had been "amputated of half his history." In the
convoluted prose that had become characteristic of him, James
noted:

> The grey and more or less "hallowed" University building —
> wasn't it somehow, with a desperate bravery, both castellated
> and gabled? — has vanished from the earth, and vanished with
> it the two or three adjacent houses, of which the birthplace
> was one. This was the snub . . . that, whereas the inner
> sense had positively erected there for its private contempla-
> tion a commemorative mural tablet, the very wall that should
> have borne this inscription had been smashed as for demon-
> stration that tablets, in New York, are unthinkable . . .
> Where, in fact, is the point of inserting a mural tablet, at any
> legible height, in a building certain to be destroyed to make
> room for a sky-scraper?

Today there is a tablet commemorating James, but he would
doubtless consider it ironic that it is in the wrong place — on
the NYU Brown Building half a block from his birthplace.

James lived at the Washington Place house only six months
before his parents took him to Europe. His family did not
return to New York until 1847, when they stopped briefly at 11
Fifth Avenue and then moved to 58 West 14th Street, the house
from which most of the author's childhood memories date.
Here he met Thackeray and remembered the occasional presence of "the great and urbane" Emerson, in addition to lesser
literary figures: Parke Godwin, Charles Dana, Rufus Griswold
and N. P. Willis. Here James's brother, William, told him
Poe's stories, "The Gold-Bug" and "The Pit and the Pendu-
lum," and recited "The Raven," "Lenore" and " 'Annabel*lee.*' "
From this house he went to school, first in Waverly Place, where
his teacher was "a stout red-faced lady with grey hair and a
large apron, the latter convenience somehow suggesting . . .
that she viewed her little pupils as so many slices cut from the

Henry James's grandmother's home, third house from the right,
19 Washington Square North.

loaf of life and on which she was to dab the butter of arithmetic
and spelling, accompanied by way of jam with a light applica-
tion of the practice of prize-giving." Later, when he went to
school on East 23rd Street, he took great pleasure in the walk
home past the "country-place," a big brown house on the northeast corner of 18th Street "in 'grounds' peopled with animal
life . . . two or three elegant little cows of refined form and
colour, two or three nibbling fawns and a larger company, above
all, of peacocks and guineafowl . . ."

During these years James also spent many hours at 19 Washington Square North in the "maternal parlours" of his grandmother Elizabeth Walsh. Here he absorbed the atmosphere he
would later re-create in *Washington Square*. James transformed
an anecdote told to him by the English actress Fanny Kemble
into a study of the interplay of wills between Dr. John Sloper and
his daughter, Catherine, and set it in the scene of his boyhood.

"The ideal of quiet and genteel retirement, in 1835," James wrote in the opening pages, "was found in Washington Square, where the Doctor built himself a handsome, modern, wide-fronted house, with a big balcony before the drawing-room windows, and a flight of marble steps ascending to a portal which was also faced with white marble. This structure, and so many of its neighbours, which it exactly resembled, were supposed . . . to embody the last results of architectural science, and they remain to this day very solid and honourable dwellings."

In later years when James revisited New York, he was to write that, after experiencing the congestion of uptown, getting back to Washington Square "was as if the wine of life had been poured for you, in advance, into some pleasant old punch-bowl . . . To come and go where East 11th Street, where West 10th opened their kind short arms was at least to keep clear of the awful hug of the serpent." Coming back to America in 1904 after an absence of twenty years, he found some points of reference in the midst of change. One was the home of Mary Cadwalader Jones at 21 East 11th Street, still very much as it must have been in James's time. Minnie Jones, as she was known, was a friend of James's from his youth and had been married to Edith Wharton's brother, though the two writers did not meet until 1888. Her house, where Brooks and Henry Adams, Theodore Roosevelt, Augustus Saint-Gaudens and John Singer Sargent often came to Sunday lunch, was known as something of a salon. On James's visit, he was given rooms on the first floor, where he stayed whenever his travels that year brought him back to New York.

Edith Wharton, like Henry James, is linked to Washington Square, although the two knew somewhat different sides of it. As Edith Wharton — Edith Jones before her marriage — was to become painfully aware, the writers and thinkers who found their way so frequently to the Jameses' house would have been out of place in the drawing rooms she frequented as a young woman. Years later she ruefully remarked, "I was a failure in Boston . . . because they thought I was too fashionable to be intelligent, and a failure in New York because they were afraid I was too intelligent to be fashionable." As Louis Auchincloss has observed: "The Jameses were more like the English Arnolds or Darwins, a deeply congenial family of inherited means and large ideas whose generations were united by a love of the arts and sciences. Young Henry was encouraged from the beginning to become a writer. Not so Edith Jones." Wharton belonged to a much more fashionable set.

She was able, however, to use the values and mores of her world as material for her art, and she described the concrete details of life in fashionable New York with incomparable vividness. The stories in *Old New York* trace society's uptown progress. In "False Dawn," subtitled "The 'Forties," the Raycie family has a town house in Canal Street and a country house on the Sound, as the upper portion of the East River was then called. By the 1850s, the period in which "The Old Maid" takes place, society has progressed several miles uptown. Delia Lovell, whose parents' house is in Mercer Street, marries James Ralston and goes to live in Gramercy Park. By "New Year's Day (the 'Seventies)'" the residential area has reached 31st Street.

Edith Wharton's family's geography closely parallels that of her stories. Her grandparents and aunt lived in Mercer Street and when her parents were married they set up a house in Gramercy Park, "then just within the built-on limits of New York." By the time Edith was born in 1862 they were living on 23rd Street. Despite the northward movement of younger generations, the older patriarchs stayed in Washington Square and so, in a sense, old New York society remained grounded there. (Their

Edith Wharton: "too fashionable to be intelligent
. . . too intelligent to be fashionable."

tenacity in holding on to their houses was one of the factors
that enabled the Old Row on the north side of the Square to
remain uninterruptedly aristocratic; some of the houses were
kept by the original families until 1935 and 1936.) Thus the
spirit of Washington Square and its passing dominates Wharton's greatest novel, *The Age of Innocence,* even though it is

set in the 1870s. It is the values of the venerable old family homes in University Place and lower Fifth Avenue — " 'purest 1830,' with a grim harmony of cabbage-rose-garlanded carpets, rosewood consoles, round-arched fireplaces with black marble mantels and immense glazed book-cases of mahogany" — that are the central concern of the book. Although Wharton was to live in Washington Square only a short time (when she returned from Europe in 1882 after her father's death), the fashionable society it symbolized was her artistic territory.

.

In the second half of the nineteenth century, when New England dominated the national literary scene, only a few writers were connected with the Village. In the sixties a tavern named Pfaff's at 653 Broadway became a center for those associated with the *Saturday Press,* New York's liveliest and most important literary publication. The *Press* printed Whitman's poetry, then considered unpublishable elsewhere, and introduced Mark Twain to readers with "The Jumping Frog of Calaveras County," later the title story in his first book. William Dean Howells had also appeared in the *Press's* pages, and when he came to New York looking for a job he stopped by Pfaff's to meet Whitman. The group associated with the magazine was considered bohemian because, as Howells wrote, it was violently opposed to "all existing forms of respectability." Emerson was introduced to the Pfaff's crowd by Whitman and found them "noisy and rowdy firemen."

A few other writers were scattered here and there. Melville, his literary career virtually over, had returned from Massachusetts in 1866 and was working as a customs inspector on the piers near Gansevoort Street. In 1870 Bret Harte came east and stayed at his sister's home at 16 Fifth Avenue. Around 1875 he took an apartment at 713 Broadway.

Mark Twain at the billiard table, where he spent
many hours while living at 21 Fifth Avenue.

In 1900, at the height of his popularity, Mark Twain came to live in New York and chose the still fashionable precincts of Washington Square. The Clemens family spent the winter in a furnished house at 14 West 10th Street, which suddenly became one of the most "conspicuous" residences in New York. Clemens's daughter Clara recalled: "One could never begin to describe in words the atmosphere of adulation that swept across the threshold. Every day was like some great festive occasion. One felt that a large party was going on and that by and by the guests would be leaving. But there was no leaving. More and more came." The following year Clemens moved his family to Riverdale, where his wife became seriously ill. After her death in 1904 he again returned to the Village, this time to a house at 21 Fifth Avenue designed by James Renwick, Jr., the architect of St. Patrick's Cathedral and Grace Church.

Clemens spent most of his days lying in a huge Italian carved bed — pillows placed at the foot so that he could enjoy the ornate headboard — receiving visitors, dictating and smoking eternally. Each evening he had his secretary play for him on the Aeolian Orchestrelle, an immense player organ that performed sixty selections of classical music. During this time he worked on *The Mysterious Stranger* and *2,000 Years Among the Microbes*. In 1906 Clemens accepted Albert Bigelow Paine's suggestion that the latter become his biographer. Paine moved in, acting as companion and editor as well as the stimulus for Clemens's intensified autobiographical dictations.

William Dean Howells, who was living in New York at this time, recalled Clemens's residence on Fifth Avenue as the period of "his efflorescence in white serge." Howells noted in *My Mark Twain*: "Until he imagined the suit of white serge, he wore always a suit of black serge, truly deplorable in the cut of the sagging frock . . . But the white serge was an inspiration which few men would have had the courage to act upon." Clemens

loved to walk up and down Fifth Avenue, glorying in the recognition of the crowds. When John Dos Passos was just a boy, his
father introduced him to Clemens on Fifth Avenue one day.
"But all I remember," Dos Passos wrote, "was his flowing hair
and white suit, which seemed incongruous on such a cold day,
and the fact that his name wasn't really Mark Twain at all."

Clemens's last two years at the Fifth Avenue house were
primarily played out at a billiard table he had received for
Christmas in 1906. The table displaced his bed, which was
moved into the study, and Clemens enlisted Paine in long
sessions, often lasting into the early morning hours. In 1908
Clemens moved to Redding, Connecticut, where he died in
April of 1910. His body was placed on view at the Brick Presbyterian Church, then on Fifth Avenue and 37th Street. Van Wyck
Brooks, who had never seen him alive, was one of the viewers
and remembered Clemens "with his white hair spread loose,
dressed for the last time in his white flannels."

The Birth of Bohemia

Mark Twain was the last in the gentlemanly tradition of Washington Square. By the turn of the century Greenwich Village,
as a symbol of the artists' bohemia, had begun to take shape.
In the early 1900s it would become what Max Eastman, editor
of the *Masses,* called "a self-conscious entity, an American
Bohemia or Gipsy-minded Latin Quarter." For most of the
nineteenth century the neighborhood, known as the "American
Ward" for its lack of immigrants, had remained undisturbed by
the classic progression of city development from residential area
to business district to slum. But in the 1890s tenements began
to creep toward the center of the Village. The area south of
Washington Square had been predominantly Negro during the

nineteenth century* but in the 1890s and 1900s the Negroes were supplanted by Italians as the old houses were replaced with six- and seven-story stacks of railroad flats. Simultaneously, tenements spread from the waterfront through the old West Village.

The pattern of migration of young artists, writers and political rebels followed the decline in real estate values; they settled in the western and southern sections of Greenwich Village. One of the most desirable locations was the south side of Washington Square, where the once elegant brick homes, affected by the pressure of the tenements at their backs, had been converted into rooming houses. (The houses on the north side, buffered by the park, remained private homes.) In the prewar period the center of Village literary life was Washington Square South and MacDougal Street.

"Of all the ambitions of the Great Unpublished, the one that is strongest, the most abiding, is the ambition to get to New York," Frank Norris wrote in *Blix*. "For these, New York is the *point de départ,* the pedestal, the niche, the indispensable vantage ground." Writers came to New York, which had become the country's publishing center, to find publishers for their work; editors and publishers looked to the West for talent to staff their newspapers and magazines. Norris was a case in point. S. S. McClure had discovered his work in a San Francisco literary magazine and asked him to come to New York to write for *McClure's Magazine.* Norris arrived in 1898, first living on 33rd Street and later settling in the Village. He took a small front bedroom at 61 Washington Square,† where his San Francisco

---

* In 1865 one fourth of the city's black population concentrated in the area around Bleecker, Sullivan, Thompson and MacDougal streets, which was known as "Little Africa." The first Negro newspaper in the country, *Freedom Journal,* was published here in 1827, and the first Negro theater, the African Grove, opened on Mercer Street in 1821. Whites were segregated into the back seats because, according to a handbill, they "do not know how to conduct themselves at entertainments for ladies and gentlemen of color."

† Sixty-one Washington Square was known as Mme. Katharine Branchard's

friend Gelett Burgess had stayed, and ate his meals at the
Judson Hotel at 63 Washington Square.

Edwin Arlington Robinson had moved to New York from
Maine in 1899. After several years in Chelsea, he took a room
in the Judson Hotel in 1906. President Roosevelt had gotten
him a sinecure in the U.S. Customs House and he slept late each
day, appearing at his office in the afternoon, if at all. When
Roosevelt left the White House in 1909, Robinson found himself out of a job. Fortunately, he almost immediately acquired
another patron, Mrs. Clara Potter Davidge, who built a studio
for him behind her house at 121 Washington Place. He moved
there in December 1909 and stayed off and on for several years.
From 1913 to 1922 he lived in other parts of the city. Then,
temporarily lacking a place to stay, he knocked at the door of his
friends James and Laura Fraser at 28 West 8th Street (Fraser, a
sculptor, designed the buffalo nickel) ; they not only gave him
a room for the night but asked him to stay permanently in the
skylighted studio on the top floor of their house. Here Robinson wrote his most popular work, *Tristram*.

Next to arrive, also brought by McClure, who had discovered
her teaching school in Pittsburgh, was Willa Cather. In 1906
she took a studio at 60 Washington Square, where Edith Lewis,
who was to be her lifetime friend, also had a room. "In 1906,"
Lewis wrote in her biography, *Willa Cather Living*, "Washington Square was one of the most charming places in New York.
On the north side the long row of houses of rose-red brick,
residences of aristocratic old New York families, gave it an aura
of gentility and dignity. On the south side, writers and artists

---

"House of Genius" because, in addition to Norris, Stephen Crane, Theodore
Dreiser, O. Henry, Eugene O'Neill, John Reed, Lincoln Steffens, Willa Cather,
John Dos Passos and Allan Seeger were said to have lived there. There is no
evidence, however, that any of these writers did, with the exception of Seeger
and Norris. Cather, Reed, O'Neill, Steffens and Dos Passos lived on the Square,
but at different addresses.

lived. But it was a very sedate Bohemia; most of the artists were poor and hard-working." During her first years in the city, Cather became managing editor of *McClure's,* but eventually she left to devote all her time to writing. Years later she drew on her days in Washington Square for her story "Coming, Aphrodite!" which deals with the relationship between a painter who has a big room on the top floor of an old house on the Square and a young woman who comes to live in the rooms next to his. Cather was here for two years before moving to the six-story apartment house at 82 Washington Place and finally to her long-time Village residence at 5 Bank Street in 1913.

In 1911, John Reed, a young Harvard graduate, came to live in an apartment at 42 Washington Square South with several classmates. Handsome and high-spirited, Reed rapidly became a central Village figure. He plunged zestfully into his new life, which he described in a poem called "Forty-Two Washington Square":

> But nobody questions your morals,
> And nobody asks for the rent —
> There's no one to pry if we're tight, you and I,
> Or demand how our evenings are spent.
> The furniture's ancient but plenty,
> The linen is spotless and fair,
> O life is a joy to a broth of a boy
> At Forty-two Washington Square!

Reed dedicated this bit of doggerel to Lincoln Steffens, who had found him a job on the *American Magazine.* Steffens had been a friend of Reed's father, who had asked him to keep an eye on his son, an occupation from which the veteran muckraker derived much pleasure. In 1912, after his wife died, Steffens went to live at 42 Washington Square in the room below Jack Reed's. "I used to go early to bed and to sleep," he wrote, "but I liked it when Jack, a big, growing, happy being, would slam into my room and wake me up to tell me about the 'most wonderful thing in the world' that he had seen, been, or done that night. Girls, plays, bums, I.W.W.'s, strikers — each experience was vivid in him . . ."

One night in 1913, in a Village apartment, John Reed heard the I.W.W. leader Bill Haywood describe the plight of silk weavers striking for an eight-hour day in Paterson, New Jersey. One of them had been killed by the police but the press had refused to cover the strike. Mabel Dodge, who had a brief but memorable salon in 1913 at 23 Fifth Avenue, was present and suggested, "Why don't you hire a great hall and re-enact the strike over here?" John Reed sprang up and said, "I'll do it!" And he did. The strike — killing, funeral, graveside speeches by Haywood and Elizabeth Gurley Flynn — was re-enacted by a thousand people on the stage of Madison Square Garden. Thus began the radicalization of John Reed and his affair with Mabel Dodge. The affair was relatively short-lived but the radicalization was to last until his early death in Moscow in 1920.

Mabel Dodge had come to New York after a sojourn in Florence and made the acquaintance of a number of talented New Yorkers, including Jo Davidson, Carl Van Vechten, Lincoln Steffens, Hutchins Hapgood and Walter Lippmann. Soon they were visiting frequently and bringing others. The salon that developed was very much a collaboration between Mabel Dodge and her friends. She credited Steffens with the idea that she set aside a particular evening for her callers, and Lippmann with the suggestion that each evening be organized around a theme. She provided the setting; her apartment was decorated with white paper-covered walls and windows draped with white linen. In the front room a white bearskin rug lay before a white marble fireplace, and a large porcelain chandelier covered with colorful birds and flowers hung from the ceiling. Against the white background, she placed gray French chairs and chaises

John Reed, left, before leaving to cover the First World War, with
Fannie Hurst and Boardman Robinson in Washington Square Park.

upholstered in light gray blues and pale yellows. On her "evenings," according to Steffens,

> she sat quietly in a great armchair and rarely said a word: her
> guests did the talking, and with such a variety of guests, her
> success was amazing . . . Her secret, I think, was to start the
> talk going with a living theme. She would seize a time when
> there was an I.W.W. strike to invite, say, Bill Haywood especially. He would sit or stand near her and strike out, in the
> hot, harsh spirit of his organization, some challenging idea,
> answer brutally a few questions, and — that evening everybody talked I.W.W. Emma Goldman said something about
> anarchism one evening when the anarchists were in the news,
> and that night we discussed anarchism. It was there and thus
> that some of us first heard of psychoanalysis and the new
> psychology of Freud and Jung . . .

The affair between Mabel Dodge and John Reed dissolved toward the end of 1913, and with it the salon. Reed's story, "War in Paterson," which only the *Masses* would publish, led the *Metropolitan* to send him to Mexico to cover the uprising of Pancho Villa, and the dispatches he sent back established him, at the age of twenty-seven, as the country's leading war correspondent. Next he went to Europe to cover the beginning of the First World War. His interviews with French soldiers convinced him that the war was a clash between "traders," not a struggle for democracy and liberty. Each of the dispatches he sent the *Masses* ended with the words "This is not our war." On a trip home to Oregon in 1915, Reed met a young woman named Louise Bryant and brought her to live with him at Washington Square.

·

As the new Villagers arrived in the area around Washington Square South, the stage was set for the development of several institutions that would influence American culture. Two strains

WHEN LIFE IS VERY STRENUOUS AND SPIRITS ARE WAY DOWN
YOU'D BETTER GO TO POLLY'S IN LITTLE GREENWICH TOWN
FOR THERE THE CLANS ARE GATHERED - ITS THERE YOU'L FIND 'EM ALL
THE ARTISTS AND THE WRITERS RANGED ALONG THE WALL
MISS POLLY TAKES THE MONEY AND MIKE SAYS HE JUST CAN'T
WAIT ANY FASTER ON THE FOLKS IN POLLY'S RES-TAU-RANT
J.T.B.
GREENWICH VILLAGE - NEW YORK
© JESSIE TARBOX BEALS

Polly's Restaurant at 137 MacDougal Street, downstairs from the
Liberal Club and next door to the Washington Square Book Shop.

— the political and the artistic — were present from the beginning. The Liberal Club was organized in the early teens as "A
Meeting Place for Those Interested in New Ideas," in rooms on
the second floor of a house at 137 MacDougal Street — two large
parlors and a sunroom with high ceilings, fireplaces, mahogany
doors and cubist and futurist art on the walls. Conveniently
located downstairs was Polly's, a restaurant run by Paula Holliday with Hippolyte Havel as cook and waiter. Havel was an
anarchist who was fond of calling the patrons "Bourgeois pigs!"
The Liberal Club, with Polly's, was important not for anything
it did, but because it provided a gathering place for the exchange
of ideas. Among those who frequented it were Theodore
Dreiser, Upton Sinclair, Vachel Lindsay, Lincoln Steffens, Sin-

clair Lewis, Sherwood Anderson, Louis Untermeyer and Max Eastman.

Next to develop was the *Masses*, a magazine organized in 1911 by an anarchist named Piet Vlag. Vlag apparently conceived the endeavor as an artists' and writers' cooperative, but he quickly tired of his role as amateur editor and publisher and left the magazine, without funds, in the hands of its contributors, a group that included the painter John Sloan and his wife, Dolly, Louis Untermeyer and the artist Art Young. They in turn decided that Max Eastman, a young man from Elmira, New York, who was teaching philosophy at Columbia, would be the ideal editor and fund-raiser. They sent him a note in Connecticut, where he was spending the summer, saying, "You are elected editor of the *Masses*. No pay."

Under Eastman, the *Masses* became an invigorating mixture of politics, art, literature and humor. The magazine generally defended all causes on the left but was open to a wide range of socialist opinion rather than committed to one point of view, a policy that eventually led to serious disagreement among the contributors. In literature and criticism it published the early work of Untermeyer, Carl Sandburg, Harry Kemp, Randolph Bourne and William Rose Benét. The text was broken by political drawings and cartoons, and several professional humorists were prominent among the contributors. The artists were represented by Sloan, Young and Glenn O. Coleman, and the political thinkers by Reed, Eastman and a young poet named Floyd Dell. Dell, who later became managing editor, listed the magazine's causes as "Fun, Truth, Beauty, Realism, Peace, Feminism, and Revolution."

The *Masses* quickly became a focus of Village intellectual life, both at its offices at 91 Greenwich Avenue and at the monthly meetings held in the roomy studios of Sloan or Young, where contributors met to vote on material that had been submitted for publication. "We had a custom," said Eastman "of inviting our friends to these meetings — a good part of New York's intelligentsia turned up at one time or another — and we always urged them to join the voting." The crowd included everyone from John Reed to Hippolyte Havel, who would protest that voting was bourgeois. "Voting! . . . Poetry is something from the soul! You can't vote on poetry!" The crowd's fund-raising costume balls, held at Webster Hall on 11th Street near Third Avenue, became a Village tradition.

The playful atmosphere around the *Masses* darkened as the country became increasingly involved in the First World War and the magazine became a spearhead for the resistance to it. In the summer of 1917 the *Masses* lost its mailing privileges, which deprived it of its subscription income; simultaneously its large contributors withdrew their financial support. In November the Department of Justice charged Eastman, Reed, Dell and several others with "conspiracy against the government" and "interfering with enlistment," and the magazine closed its offices.

Two trials were held, one in April and one in October of 1918. Both resulted in hung juries. John Reed, who had been covering the Russian revolution, returned to stand trial with the others. He and Louise Bryant took an apartment in Patchin Place and he wrote the articles that comprised *Ten Days That Shook the World* in an upstairs room at Polly Holliday's new restaurant at 147 West 4th Street.

In order to publish Reed's articles, Eastman started a new magazine, the *Liberator,* at 138 West 13th Street. He continued to print art and writing by those connected with the *Masses* and added the work of Edna St. Vincent Millay, William Carlos Williams, Elinor Wylie, E. E. Cummings, John Dos Passos and Ernest Hemingway. Where the *Masses* had been fascinated by the "Russian experiment" as only one facet of its interest in socialism, the *Liberator* became more fully committed to the

Communist line. In 1922 Eastman resigned because of political disagreements, and left the magazine in the hands of Michael Gold. It merged in 1924 with two smaller magazines and became a Communist party organ.

.

Many of those involved in the Liberal Club and the *Masses* were also involved in the formation of the Provincetown Players, which, through its connection with Eugene O'Neill, was to be responsible for changing playwrighting in America. "Before O'Neill, the United States had theater," wrote one magazine. "After O'Neill, it had drama."

Eugene O'Neill had arrived in the Village in 1915 and lived in a room he called "the garbage flat" at 38 Washington Square. He wrote six or seven hours a day and spent his evenings at the Golden Swan, a saloon at the corner of Sixth Avenue and 4th Street, popularly known as the Hell Hole. The saloon had a mixed crowd — thugs, writers, artists, coachmen and streetwalkers — and a proprietor named Tom Wallace, who, it was said, had never ventured outside in twenty years. Here O'Neill met Hippolyte Havel and another anarchist named Terry Karlin. Years later the playwright used the Hell Hole and the people he knew there in *The Iceman Cometh*. Harry Hope, the fictional saloon's owner, is modeled on Wallace; Larry Slade is based on Karlin; and Hugo Kalmar bears a strong resemblance to Havel. The philosophy of the play, perhaps learned in his Hell Hole days, is, in O'Neill's words, "that there is always one dream left, one final dream, no matter how low you have fallen, down there at the bottom of the bottle. I know because I saw it."

In the summer of 1916 O'Neill went off to Provincetown with Terry Karlin. The previous year a group of Villagers vacationing there had started a summer theater led by a Chicagoan named George Cram "Jig" Cook. Cook met Karlin one day

The Provincetown Playhouse, 133 MacDougal Street, around 1920.

and asked him if he had any plays. He said he hadn't but that O'Neill had a trunkful. The production that season of O'Neill's *Bound East for Cardiff* was such a success that it inspired John Reed to broach the idea of continuing the theater during the winter. A constitution was drawn up, Jig Cook was elected president and the Provincetown Players was born. Back in the Village, Cook opened the theater on the parlor floor of a house at 139 MacDougal Street, next door to Polly's first restaurant and the Liberal Club. The following year the players moved to larger quarters nearby at 133 MacDougal, where they were to remain for ten years. During the summer O'Neill had fallen in love with Louise Bryant and in the fall he took a room at 42

Washington Square to be near her. (Jack Reed was then ill in the Johns Hopkins Hospital in Baltimore.) The affair formed the basis for *Strange Interlude*.

The actors and writers in the Provincetown Players gathered in a number of homes, restaurants and taverns. In addition to the Cooks' on Milligan Place, they met at the home of James and Susan Light (he was an actor, director and stage manager of the Provincetown) at 86 Greenwich Avenue, called Maison Clemenceau because the French statesman had once lived there. The Lights had a seven-room apartment and at various times rented rooms to Matthew Josephson, Djuna Barnes and Kenneth Burke. Other meeting places included Polly's; the Hell Hole; a speakeasy called the Black Knight, across the street from the playhouse and Luke O'Connor's, better known as the Working Girls' Home, at the corner of Christopher and Greenwich. (John Masefield had worked there as a janitor in 1895.) A series of tearooms, primarily operated for tourists, began to flourish during Prohibition but the only one frequented by authentic Villagers was Romany Marie's, on the southeast corner of Thompson and Washington Square South. (In 1929 Romany Marie moved to a spot on the site of 40 West 8th Street and Buckminster Fuller decorated her new restaurant. In return, she said he could eat one meal a day there for the rest of his life.) The only tearoom or saloon to survive from this era is the Jumble Shop, at 176 MacDougal Street, in recent years renamed Shakespeare's.

When the Villagers were feeling flush, they patronized two other establishments that were to play host to literary New Yorkers for several decades. Special occasions were celebrated at the Brevoort Hotel, on the northeast corner of Fifth Avenue and 8th Street, diagonally across from the site of Henry Brevoort's home, where Washington Irving had often visited. There was a basement café, reminiscent of those in Paris, divided into small rooms with mirrored partitions and marble-topped tables. Steffens, O'Neill, Edna St. Vincent Millay, Isadora Duncan, Dreiser, Lippmann, Reed, Dodge and Eastman could often be found here in the early days. John Dos Passos wrote to a friend about sitting at the table next to Emma Goldman's in 1917: "It was wonderful," he said. "She's a Bronxy fattish little old woman who looks like a rather good cook. She has a charmingly munchy fashion of eating sandwiches and pats her myrmidons on the head and kisses them in a motherly fashion."

The Lafayette Hotel, on the southeast corner of University Place and 9th Street, also had a European-style café with marble tables and newspapers on racks. Villagers came here for more informal occasions to drink and talk. Although, according to Matthew Josephson, the drinks were bad and cost twice as much as anyplace else and the waiters were surly, the Lafayette was the unrivaled meeting place of high bohemia during the twenties.

As new people arrived in the Village, they in turn created their own institutions, particularly a spate of "little magazines" that explored new ground in poetry and fiction. Next door to Polly's and the Liberal Club was Albert and Charles Boni's Washington Square Book Shop, which would serve as a seedbed for American publishing with the founding of Boni and Liveright and the Modern Library. In 1913 the Bonis agreed to finance a publication edited by Alfred Kreymborg, soon to become a perennial founder of little magazines. The magazine was called *Glebe,* an Old English word meaning "soil" or "field." Each issue was to be devoted to one person's work — "one-man shows on an intimate scale" said Kreymborg. After six issues Kreymborg resigned when the Bonis pressured him to include translations of European work. Undaunted, he started another magazine called *Others.* The contributors began gathering every Sunday at Kreymborg's home in Grantwood, New Jersey, but in the fall of 1915 he moved to Bank Street and the meetings

continued there. Among the regulars were Maxwell Bodenheim, William Carlos Williams, Wallace Stevens and Marianne
Moore.

In 1917 the *Little Review,* which had begun publication in
Chicago, joined *Others* in New York. The editor was a volatile
and inventive original named Margaret Anderson, who had
camped out on the shore of Lake Michigan when she had no
house, lived in an apartment furnished only with a grand piano
when she had no furniture and kept the *Little Review* going by
ingenuity when it had no financial support. She arrived in New
York with Jane Heap, the assistant editor, who always spelled
her name lower case, and found a basement studio at 31 West
14th Street to use as an office. She and Jane lived at 24 West
16th Street in the house that had once belonged to William
Cullen Bryant. "We bought gold Chinese paper at a Japanese
paper shop, in long oblong strips," she wrote. "Papering the
walls with these required Chinese patience, as they were disposed to tear under the most delicate touch. The woodwork
was pale cream, the floor dark plum, the furniture old mahogany. The feature of the room was a large divan hung from the
ceiling by heavy black chains. It was covered with dull-toned
blue and on it were four silk cushions — emerald green, ma-
genta, royal purple, tilleul . . . Here the poets, writers, painters came to see us . . ." Among those who came was Hart
Crane, who was living in a room on the top floor of the same
house, and Djuna Barnes, whose *A Night Among the Horses*
had been published in the magazine.

While in Chicago, the *Little Review* was devoted primarily to
criticism, but in New York it turned to experimental fiction and
poetry. The printing of Joyce's *Ulysses* in installments from
1918 through 1920 — its first publication anywhere — was possibly the magazine's most significant achievement. The editors
were convicted of obscenity and fined $100.

The last important Village magazine of the prewar period was *Seven Arts*. The magazine owed its existence, at least indirectly, to the burgeoning influence of psychoanalysis; the editor, James Oppenheim, and the patron, Mrs. A. K. Rankine, were both patients of an analyst who suggested it as a therapeutic project. With Waldo Frank and Van Wyck Brooks as associate editors, the magazine published Sherwood Anderson's *Winesburg* stories, Eugene O'Neill's first short story, "Tomorrow," and the work of many other fine writers, including D. H. Lawrence, S. N. Behrman, Robert Frost, Carl Sandburg, Amy Lowell, Stephen Vincent Benét and John Dos Passos. The magazine lasted only a year; Oppenheim's violent opposition to America's participation in the war caused the sponsor to withdraw her support.

.

In addition to providing a community for poets, editors, dramatists and political intellectuals, the prewar Village was home to two major twentieth-century novelists. Although Willa Cather and Theodore Dreiser were not recluses, they spent their working time in solitude and were not involved in the communal activities that occupied many of the early Villagers. In 1913 Cather had moved from Washington Place to 5 Bank Street, where she would write six novels, including *My Antonia*. The apartment, which she took with Edith Lewis, was seven high-ceilinged rooms on the second floor of a large brick house. (In later years, she also rented the apartment above, keeping it empty so that she would not be disturbed by noise.) The front three rooms were used as one huge living room. "At auction rooms on University Place," Edith Lewis recalls in her biography of Cather, "we bought mahogany chests and a round mahogany dining-room table for a few dollars. Among our possessions were a number of large oriental rugs; and we got some comfortable chairs." In the living room there were low open bookshelves and, over the mantel, a "large etching by Couture of George Sand — not because she [Cather] particularly admired George Sand, but because she liked the etching."

Visitors remember that there was always the scent of flowers at 5 Bank Street: in winter, the smell of orange blossoms, camellias, violets, freesias; in spring, jonquils, narcissuses, lilacs and dogwood. Each day Cather followed the same routine. Early in the morning she did the shopping at nearby Jefferson Market, hunting for red raspberries or perfect leaf lettuce, to be served with a dressing of olive oil, wine vinegar and tarragon. Then she went home to do her stint of work before the French maid came in to fix lunch.

In 1917 Cather began a Bank Street tradition of Fridays at home. People dropped in for tea but seldom were they the people involved in the *Masses,* the Provincetown Players or any of the little magazines. Cather was more allied to the older set associated with *McClure's,* and even refused to see the Provincetown's productions of O'Neill's plays. Nevertheless the Friday afternoons were popular, "so popular, in fact," writes Edith Lewis, "that eventually she had to give them up; instead of half-a-dozen or so of her friends dropping in for tea, it became at last too much of a responsibility." Among the literary people who visited were the D. H. Lawrences, who came in 1924 after having spent the summer in Ceylon. Edith Lewis remembers Lawrence imitating "the sounds the leopards made, when they leaped on the roof of the bungalow at night, hunting for mice in the thatch." In 1927, 5 Bank Street was demolished when the IND-Sixth Avenue subway was built. Willa Cather and Edith Lewis moved to the Grosvenor Hotel at 35 Fifth Avenue, where they lived for five years before going uptown to 570 Park Avenue.

While Cather was pioneering the literature of the mid-

Willa Cather in the early 1930s.

western prairie, Dreiser was breaking other ground. He had first come to live in New York in 1895, when he stayed at the Mills Hotel (now the Greenwich Hotel) on Bleecker Street, paying twenty-five cents a night for a bed. By 1897 he was earning enough from writing popular magazine stories to move to the Salmagundi Club at 14 West 12th Street and then to his own apartment at 232 West 15th. Dreiser had grown up in rural Indiana, and the city—first Chicago, then St. Louis and Pittsburgh and finally New York — had a tremendous impact on him. With *Sister Carrie,* published in 1900, he created the "city novel," announcing the themes — alienation, the breakdown of tradition, the impact of mechanization, materialism, the conflict between the artist and society — that would occupy twentieth-century novelists from Dos Passos and Wolfe to the social realists of the forties. The city would be seen as a powerful force, sometimes as protagonist, as in Dos Passos's *Manhattan Transfer,* but usually as a disillusioning and destructive antagonist. And New York, in which all the qualities of urban life were writ large, was the ultimate city. Here even a world traveler as sophisticated as Howells felt the impact of the city anew, and Dreiser observed that not even Chicago had prepared him for Manhattan. "The thing that interested me . . . about New York," he wrote in *Color of a Great City,* ". . . was the sharp, and at the same time immense, contrast it showed between the dull and the shrewd, the strong and the weak, the rich and the poor, the wise and the ignorant."

But Dreiser did more than introduce a new subject. As Dos Passos was to remark, "the ponderous battering ram of his novels opened the way through the genteel reticences of American fiction." Not that the struggle was easy: *Sister Carrie* had been accepted for publication at Doubleday, Page and Company by Frank Norris and other editors there while Frank N. Doubleday and his wife were abroad. When they read the galleys, the Doubledays were horrified by Dreiser's realism and tried to get out of publishing the book. Dreiser forced them to proceed, only to find that critics branded the book immoral, bookstores refused to handle it and his friends slighted him on the street.

Dreiser was to have similar problems with *The "Genius,"* a book he finished while living at 165 West 10th Street. The autobiographically inspired novel tells the story of Eugene Witla, a painter who comes from Chicago to live in the area around Washington Square. Dreiser hired Floyd Dell to help him edit the book. Dell took large chunks of manuscript home and penciled out what he thought could be eliminated, only to find Dreiser, "with a large eraser, rescuing from oblivion such pages, paragraphs and sentences as he felt could not be spared." Again it was what Dreiser chose unflinchingly to include — his hero's infidelities and multiple sexual alliances — that got him into trouble. After the book was published in 1915, John S. Sumner, the head of the Society for the Suppression of Vice who later brought charges against the *Little Review* for its publication of *Ulysses,* threatened to arrest any bookdealer who dared to sell *The "Genius."* Despite the efforts of Mencken and other writers, the publisher withdrew the novel for ten years.

During his years in the Village, Dreiser kept to himself and spent little time in neighborhood haunts, with the occasional exception of Polly Holliday's. His few friends, among them Hutchins Hapgood and Waldo Frank, knew that he worked from nine to four and was not to be disturbed. In 1915 Dreiser and Kirah Markham, an actress he was living with at the time, announced that they would be "at home" on Sunday evenings between November and March. Friends, including Mencken when he was in town, came to listen to phonograph records and play the Ouija board. Once, at a special party in his honor, Edgar Lee Masters read from *Spoon River.*

In 1922, after three years in Los Angeles, Dreiser came back to the Village and rented the parlor floor at 16 St. Luke's Place.

Theodore Dreiser at 16 St. Luke's Place. The desk at rear was
made from his brother's piano.

This, like his other apartments, was furnished simply, except for
the desk he had made from his brother's piano. Sherwood
Anderson lived two doors away, at 12 St. Luke's Place. He
wrote:

> I decided I would go and call upon Dreiser . . . I went up the
> stairs and there was his name, on a little white card, and there
> was a bell to punch. My fingers trembled above the bell but
> I did not ring it. I turned and hurried away. "But how do I
> know he will want to see me?" I asked myself. To me he was

and has always remained a great man, one of the few really great ones of America. "He may be at work on a book," I said to myself. On several occasions I climbed the several steps to his door, my finger hovered over the bell but I did not ring it. And then, one morning, I did . . . And then the door opened and there he was . . .

"I am Sherwood Anderson. I thought I would come to see you."

"Oh, hello," he said. He shut the door in my face.

So there I was on the Dreiser's doorstep, facing the blank door. I was shocked. Then I was furious.

"The beast," I said. "The son of a bitch" . . .

I went along a street, muttering this against the Dreiser. I went into a saloon and had drinks. I got half drunk. And then later in the day, I went home to my apartment and there was a note from him. The man had simply been embarrassed, as I was, when we stood facing each other . . ."

In September 1923, Dreiser moved to 118 West 11th Street, one of the houses in Rhinelander Gardens, a once elegant row with a New Orleans-style ironwork balcony. Here he wrote *An American Tragedy.* Its great success enabled him to move uptown to 200 West 57th Street, his last New York address.

The Lost Generation

Around 1916 and 1917 a new younger crop of men and women, members of what Gertrude Stein was to characterize as the Lost Generation, began arriving in the Village. In the vanguard were Hart Crane, Edmund Wilson, Matthew Josephson and E. E. Cummings. Wilson and Cummings left in April 1917 for the war in France. When they returned, many others came with them. "After college and the war," Malcolm Cowley wrote in *Exile's Return,* "most of us drifted to Manhattan, to the crooked streets south of Fourteenth, where you could rent a furnished hall-bedroom for two or three dollars weekly or the top floor of a rickety house for 30 dollars a month . . . We came because living was cheap, because friends of ours had come already . . . because it seemed that New York was the only city where a young writer could be published." Around 1919 and '20 the ranks were swelled by Cowley, Mark Van Doren and William Slater Brown. But in 1921 many of the writers, disillusioned with the situation of the artist in America, exiled themselves to Europe. The Village chapter of this group (the more famous exiles — Hemingway, Pound, Eliot, Stein — were not associated with the Village) included Cowley, Cummings, Josephson and Dos Passos. Their "exile" was short-lived, however — they found European artists and intellectuals more defeated and demoralized than those at home — and all of them were back in the Village by 1923.

Village literary life in the twenties was dominated by critics and poets. Many of the Lost Generation's Greenwich Village branch were to become "literary men," perhaps producing a play, a few short stories, some poetry or even a novel, but ultimately establishing their reputations as critics or editors.

Among the poets were Marianne Moore, Edna St. Vincent Millay, Hart Crane and E. E. Cummings. Moore, one of the central members of the *Others* crowd, had moved to the Village from New Jersey in 1918. She and her mother took a ground-floor apartment at 14 St. Luke's Place, across the street from the Hudson Park branch of the New York Public Library, where she worked from 1921 to 1925. Moore is most familiar to us with her gray hair and three-cornered hat, but William Carlos Williams described how she looked as a young woman: "Marianne had two cords, cables rather, of red hair coiled around her rather small cranium . . . and was straight up and down like the two-by-fours of a building under construction." Alfred Kreymborg said that she was "an astonishing person with Titian hair, a brilliant complexion and a mellifluous flow of polysyllables which held every man in awe." She was famous for knowing about everything, but Kreymborg once proposed to Williams that he could stump her. He took her to a Cubs and Giants game at the Polo Grounds (before her interest in baseball was known) and was stupefied to find that she knew all about Christy Mathewson.

Moore was the first of the *Others* group to be published in the *Dial,* the most important cultural magazine of the twenties. At first her poems were rejected. Then, she recalled, "Lola Ridge had a party . . . and much to my disgust, we were induced to read something we had written. And Scofield Thayer said of my piece, 'Would you send that to us at the *Dial?*'

" 'I did send it,' I said.

"And he said, 'Well, send it again.' "

In 1924 Marianne Moore received the Dial Award and in 1925 she became editor of the magazine.

Edna St. Vincent Millay had been known around the Village since 1912, when her poem "Renascence" was published in an anthology of the best poetry of that year. In 1917, after four years at Vassar, Millay arrived in person, intending to support herself by working as an actress. After a brief and discouraging experience with the Theatre Guild, she got a part in Floyd Dell's "The Angel Intrudes" at the Provincetown Playhouse. Dell helped her and her sister Norma find an unheated room with a fireplace at 139 Waverly Place. "She lived in that gay poverty," he wrote, "which is traditional of the village, and one may find vivid reminiscences of that life in her poetry." In the spring of 1918 Millay and her sister moved to a charming brick house at 25 Charlton Street, where another sister and her mother joined them. For the next several years she was active in the Provincetown Players, acting in and directing her own *Aria da Capo* and *The Princess Marries the Page*.

During these years Millay acquired a legendary reputation in the Village. To begin with, she and her sisters were extremely beautiful. "One cannot really write about Edna Millay," Edmund Wilson commented, "without bringing to the foreground of the picture her intoxicating effect on people . . . She was one of those women whose features are not perfect and who in their moments of dimness may not seem even pretty, but who, excited by the blood or the spirit, become almost supernaturally beautiful. She was small, but her figure was full, though she did not appear plump. She had a lovely and very long throat that gave her the look of a muse, and her reading of her poetry was thrilling." She apparently rejected the double standard, as did many other women of her day, and reserved to herself the right to take lovers on her own terms. Finally, her poetry, as Wilson wrote, "was her real overmastering passion," to which she subordinated everything, including the men in her life.

It was through Wilson, who fell in love with Millay upon meeting her in 1920, that she gained her immense popularity. He was then working at *Vanity Fair* and brought her to the attention of his editor, Frank Crowninshield. The magazine began publishing a great deal of her poetry as well as satirical dialogues and sketches that she wrote under the pen name Nancy Boyd. During the same year, her volume *Figs and Thistles* appeared. The "First Fig," which begins, "My candle burns at both ends," became the motto of a generation.

In 1921 Millay went to Paris on assignment for *Vanity Fair*. She returned in 1923, the year she won a Pulitzer Prize, and married Eugen Boissevain. They lived for a short time at $75\frac{1}{2}$ Bedford Street before moving to Steepletop, the farm in Austerlitz, New York, where she spent the rest of her life.

One of the youngest members of the Lost Generation and yet the one longest connected with the Village was Hart

Crane, who arrived from Cleveland in 1916 and took a room at 139 East 15th Street. His first poem, "C 33" (the number of Oscar Wilde's cell in Reading Gaol), had been published the previous year, when Crane was only fifteen years old, in a precursor of the Village literary magazines called *Bruno's Bohemia*. In 1917 Crane was living in the Village proper, first in a six-dollars-a-week room at 54 West 10th Street, then at 25 East 11th Street. Both structures, in Crane's day cheap rooming houses, have been restored to their former elegance. Crane moved several times every year and never had a permanent address until he went to Brooklyn Heights in 1925. In 1919 he took a room on the top floor of the building where Margaret Anderson lived. Despite the fact that she was "never a great fan of his poetry," the *Little Review* did more than any other magazine to establish his reputation.

Late in 1919 Crane went home to Cleveland for four years. When he returned, he sublet a room he particularly liked in an old house at 45 Grove Street. There was a good writing table and no "inquisitive landlady always looking through the keyhole." When the original tenant returned, Crane moved to 15 Van Nest Place.

E. E. Cummings was in the Village briefly in 1917, living at 21 East 15th Street and working at P. F. Collier, a mail order book company. When the war began he joined the ambulance service in France. There he met William Slater Brown, who was later imprisoned because his letters did not pass the censor. Cummings refused to abandon him and was imprisoned also, an experience he described in *The Enormous Room*. (Brown is the "B" of the novel.) When they were released in January 1918, they shared an apartment at 11 Christopher Street until Cummings was drafted and stationed in Massachusetts for the remainder of the war. Then they took a top-floor studio at 9 West 14th Street. Cummings accompanied the Lost Generation to Europe in 1921 and when he returned in 1923 found a studio on the top floor of 4 Patchin Place.

According to John Dos Passos, Cummings was the "hub" of a group of literary friends from Harvard that included Dr. James Sibley Watson, Scofield Thayer and Stewart Mitchell of the *Dial* and Dos Passos when he was in town. Cummings was briefly married to Thayer's former wife, Elaine Orr, whom Dos Passos described as "the poet's dream." Dos Passos and Cummings sometimes lunched at a Syrian restaurant on Washington Street and then wandered through the Washington Market stalls or walked to the Aquarium at the Battery. After an afternoon of work they would meet for tea at Elaine's apartment at 3 Washington Square North. Usually other friends would appear and they would all go to their "Italian speakeasy of the moment — as I remember they were all named Maria's — for supper." Dos Passos continued: "After a couple of brandies on top of the wine Cummings would deliver himself of geysers of talk. I've never heard anything that remotely approached it. It was comical ironical learned brilliantlycolored intricatelycadenced damnably poetic and sometimes just naughty. It was as if he were spouting pages of prose and verse from an unwritten volume. Then suddenly he would go off to Patchin Place to put some of it down before the fountain ceased to flow."

Cummings and his third wife, Marion Morehouse, gradually acquired most of the house at 4 Patchin Place except for the third-floor front room, which was occupied by a couple he called "radioactive" because they played the radio a lot. Cummings described the house:

"4" signifies a delapidated [sic] house perhaps 100 years young, perhaps younger. If asked "why" I live here,I'd answer "because" here's friendly,unscientific,private,human. Actually I live here in 2 places:away up & away down. The larger(ground-

E. E. Cummings outside 4 Patchin Place.

floor)"apartment" is really Marion's;but she shares it with me &
we both share it with the socalled world—& sometimes entertain
(more often are entertained by)our few friends. The smaller(top-
floor)"studio" is where I go to be alone & do my work

Other poets visited at Patchin Place. Allen Tate brought
T. S. Eliot; Ezra Pound came in 1939 when he made his first
visit to the United States in twenty-five years; and Dylan
Thomas, drinking in a bar on Christopher Street in 1950, pre-
vailed upon John Malcolm Brinnin to take him to meet Cummings.

•

Among those who would distinguish themselves primarily as
critics was Edmund Wilson, who first came to the Village after
graduating from Princeton in 1916. He got a job as reporter
for the *New York Evening Sun* and took an apartment on 8th
Street between Fifth and Sixth avenues with three friends from
Yale. The four roommates kept a Chinese servant and often
had people in for dinner. From 1917 to 1919 Wilson was
away serving in the army. When he returned he found an
apartment at 114 West 16th Street and a job as managing editor of *Vanity Fair*. In 1920 he met Edna Millay and, although
his relationship with her lasted only a year, allusions to her
appear in the writing he did during the next two decades.
Characters based on Millay appear in two plays, *The Crime in
the Whistler Room* and *This Room and This Gin and These
Sandwiches,* and in Wilson's novel *I Thought of Daisy,* where
she is represented as a poet named Rita. Rita leaves the Village, ending her affairs, among them one with the narrator.
In anger he rejects his love for her and turns to Daisy, a
chorus girl who exemplifies the popular culture.

Around 1921 Wilson, now managing editor of the *New Republic,* moved to 3 Washington Square North. In 1923 he

married the actress Mary Blair and at the end of the year, with their new baby, they moved a few doors away to 1 University Place. At this time Wilson seemed to many a very serious, even pompous, young man, dressed in what Fitzgerald called his "inevitable brown get-up." At the same time, the critic had a witty, whimsical side. He and Elinor Wylie often played practical jokes on people. At other times his wife was his co-conspirator. Burton Rascoe reported in *A Bookman's Day-book:*

> About nine o'clock tonight a taxi drove up and there came trooping up the stairs Mary Blair, Wilson's wife, dressed in pajamas, house slippers and raincoat; Tallulah Bankhead in bathing suit and cutaway coat; and Edmund Wilson, Jr., in a brown dressing gown and top hat. They gave us forthwith a superb vaudeville performance. Tallulah imitated . . . Sarah Bernhardt. Mary recited "The Little Tin Soldier Is Covered With Dust" . . . and Bunny [Wilson] performed some feats of legerdemain and conjuring. It was all refreshing and amusing and I pondered the happy circumstances which allows [sic] so serious and studious a young man as Bunny to forget himself in a riot of giddy nonsense and absurdity. True enough, he did spoil it to a slight extent by becoming grave later on and reciting Anatole France's forlorn and pessimistic comment on the life of Racine . . .

John Dos Passos recalled the first time he met Wilson: "There appeared a slight sandyheaded young man with a handsome clear profile. He wore a formal dark business suit. The moment we had been introduced, while we were waiting for the elevator, Bunny gave an accent to the occasion by turning, with a perfectly straight face, a neat somersault."

Another of the critics, Malcolm Cowley, was living after the war at 16 Dominick Street in what he called the most battered and primitive lodging to be found in New York. According to

Matthew Josephson, Cowley's wife, Peggy Johns (she had previously been married to the poet Orrick Johns), often held all-night poker games. Cowley worked through it all in a corner, where he kept his typewriter, books and papers neatly arranged on a table. The Cowleys moved in a circle that included Hart Crane, William Slater Brown, Susan and James Light, Kenneth Burke, Allen Tate and Matthew Josephson. The group gathered often at the Lights's apartment at 30 Jones Street. Here Crane met Emil Opffer, a young ship's steward, who gave the poet a room in his Brooklyn Heights home. (Susan Light later married William Slater Brown, and Crane later became engaged to Peggy Johns Cowley.) They ate frequently at John Squarcialupi's restaurant, a speakeasy located first at 30 Perry Street and later on Waverly Place. It was there Tate had been introduced to the group one night when Hart Crane appeared, "accompanied by a wispy, blond young man with an enormous cranium and diminutive and delicate features." Tate, who had been a member of the "Fugitives" at Nashville's Vanderbilt University, came to New York in 1924 in search of the avant-garde. By the following year he was "disenchanted with the avant-garde and disgusted by the filth and confusion of the city" and moved to upstate New York. In 1927 he was back, living in a basement apartment at 27 Bank Street, where he worked as janitor in lieu of rent while writing his biography of Stonewall Jackson.

Cowley recalled the evenings at Squarcialupi's: "We were all writing poems then and, sitting after dinner around the long table in the back room, we used to read them . . . Kenneth Burke would wipe his spectacles with a napkin and give an affirmative 'mhmmm.' — 'That's good enough to read again,' Allen Tate might say; 'I'd like to catch the rhyme scheme.' John Squarcialupi would stand in the kitchen doorway listening, with a bottle of red wine in each hand . . .

We were all about 26, a good age, and looked no older; we were interested only in writing and in keeping alive while we wrote, and we had the feeling of being invulnerable . . ."

Susan Light Brown remembers that Cowley's job was to compute everyone's share of the check and that Crane often played popular songs by ear on the upright piano, "a foot on the loud pedal, accentuating the pronounced rhythms, shaking his head with its bristly, brush-cut stand of hair in time to the music." Cowley, Burke, the Lights and Mary Blair Wilson had all gone to Peabody High School in Pittsburgh and sometimes they would sing the school song, accompanied by Crane on the piano.

The group was involved with several literary magazines. While in Europe, Josephson, unofficially aided by Cowley, had been editor of *Secession*. Gorham Munson had started the magazine but after several issues returned to New York, where, assisted by Kenneth Burke, he tried to control its content. He and Josephson fell out, whereupon Josephson was fired. When Josephson and Cowley returned to New York in 1923, they went to work for *Broom,* an international magazine of the arts started by Alfred Kreymborg and Harold Loeb. (Loeb, proprietor of the Sunrise Turn Bookshop at 51 East 44th Street, was the model for Robert Cohn in Hemingway's *The Sun Also Rises.*) *Broom* had been publishing in Europe but moved to an office at 3 East 9th Street with Josephson as editor, Cowley as coeditor and William Slater Brown as associate editor.

Foremost among the little magazines of the twenties was the *Dial.* As Marianne Moore noted, it had gone through several metamorphoses. It was founded in 1840 in Cambridge, Massachusetts, as an organ for the transcendentalists, with Margaret Fuller and later Ralph Waldo Emerson as editor, but was discontinued after four years. In 1880 it was revived in Chicago and published until 1916 as "a sedate, critical fortnightly review." In 1917 it moved to New York under new ownership and became a fortnightly with a socially analytical and humanitarian emphasis. During this period Conrad Aiken, Randolph Bourne, Van Wyck Brooks and Scofield Thayer were associated with it. In 1920 it sold out to Scofield Thayer and Dr. J. Sibley Watson, Jr., who made it a non-political monthly of arts and letters. It was in this incarnation that the *Dial* gained its greatest distinction. Its aim was to present "the best of European and American art, experimental and conventional," and it fulfilled this intention with greater taste and knowledgeability than any other literary magazine of its day. Three quarters of its pages were devoted to criticism of the arts; the remaining fourth was given to stories, poems and reproductions of paintings and sculpture.

Although the *Dial* drew criticism from all quarters, it was simply the best there was. William Carlos Williams attacked it over the reproduction of a Chagall in 1921: "If there is a loonier pack of nitwits in the world than you fellows who are making *The Dial,* they are not advertising it to the world as you are. This is the brazenest kind of prostitution, because it is colossal affectation. The Greenwich Village brand of moral and spiritual and artistic degeneracy. You are not discovering new worlds, but only helping to ruin the beauty in this." But Williams changed his mind. He accepted the Dial Award in 1926; "an epoch making event for me, it put me on my feet." T. S. Eliot wrote that the *Dial* competed in dullness with the *Atlantic Monthly* and that "there is far too much in it, and it is all second rate and exceedingly solemn," yet chose it for the first publication of *The Waste Land.* Although Cowley attacked it, his ultimate assessment was that "it was the best magazine of the arts that we have had in this country."

The *Dial*'s offices were in a brick house at 152 West 13th Street. Marianne Moore, who edited it from 1925 until it closed in 1929, wrote: "I think of the compacted pleasantness of those days . . . and the three story brick building with carpeted stairs, fireplace and white mantelpiece rooms, business office in the first storey front parlour, and of the plain gold-leaf block letters, The Dial, on the windows to the right of the brown stone steps leading to the front door . . . There was for us of the staff a constant atmosphere of excited triumph — interiorly, whatever the impression outside; and from Editor or Publisher a natural firework of little parenthetic wit too good to print — implying that efflatus [sic] is not chary of surplus."

.

During the twenties two major novelists, John Dos Passos and Thomas Wolfe, were closely associated with the Village. Dos Passos was in the city only intermittently because, as he noted, "at the slightest excuse, and particularly upon the occasion of the publication of a book, I bolted for foreign parts. It was during these years that I lost track of the number of times I crossed the Atlantic . . . Young women I met at cocktail parties liked to tell me I was running away from myself."

His sporadic residence in New York notwithstanding, he managed to absorb enough of the city to make it the subject of his second book, *Manhattan Transfer*. The novel draws its detail, like the Syrian restaurant on Washington Street, directly from his own experience. The character most like Dos Passos, a journalist named Jimmy Herf, lives first in a "small square bleak room on the south side of Washington Square" and later at 190 West 12th Street. Dos Passos himself had a room on the Square in 1922, in the studio building behind 3 Washington Square, which he rented from Elaine Cummings.

Thomas Wolfe arrived from Harvard late in 1923 to write plays and teach at New York University. (His classes were held in the Brown Building.) He drew an unflattering picture of the college, his students and his colleagues in *Of Time and the River*. During this period, he lived in Room 2220 at the Hotel Albert (the Hotel Leopold in the novel) on University Place. He was totally unknown and uninvolved in the Village literary scene.

In 1925 Wolfe met Aline Bernstein, the stage designer, who was to become his mistress and exert a strong influence on his artistic life. She rented a loft for thirty-five dollars a month at 13 East 8th Street. The address had once been an elegant one; in 1888 Richard Watson Gilder, editor of the *Century Magazine,* had made the house, with its high front stoop and climbing wisteria, a gathering place for artists and writers. In Wolfe's time it had changed radically. "I am living in a dilapidated old building over a pressing club down in Eighth Street," he wrote his mother. "I have no bath, but cold water, toilet, and a huge room with skylights — the whole floor, formerly a sweatshop, I believe." Aline Bernstein used the room as her studio and Wolfe lived there, getting his mail and his baths at the Harvard Club. It was here that Wolfe began *Look Homeward, Angel.* He later described the house, transposed to Waverly Place, in *The Web and the Rock,* the autobiographical novel dealing with this period of his life. It had, he said, "the sag and lean of an old house, the worn modeling of time from which all sharp new edges and all solid holds have been worn away."

Wolfe next moved to 263 West 11th Street, where he and Aline Bernstein split the $135-a-month rent. She used the front room as a studio and place to receive clients and he wrote in the one in the rear. He again described his home to his mother: "It is a magnificent place in an old New York house . . . I have a garden behind, and a quiet old New York street — one of the few remaining — in front. It is

one of the old parts of town, 8 minutes from the University."
A similar house — this time transposed to 12th Street — appears in the opening pages of *You Can't Go Home Again*.
Wolfe wrote:

> He loved this old house on Twelfth Street, its red brick walls,
> its rooms of noble height and spaciousness, its old dark woods
> and floors that creaked; and in the magic of the moment it
> seemed to be enriched and given a profound and lonely
> dignity by all the human beings it had sheltered in its ninety
> years. The house became like a living presence. Every ob-
> ject seemed to have an animate vitality of its own — walls, rooms,
> chairs, tables, even a half-wet bath towel hanging from the
> shower ring above the tub, a coat thrown down upon a chair,
> and his papers, manuscripts, and books scattered about the room
> in wild confusion.

After a trip to Europe, his fourth since 1924, Wolfe moved
to a second-floor rear room at 27 West 15th Street in December
1928. (The house, haphazardly remodeled, is still there.) In
1930 he again left for Europe and when he returned in March
of 1931 he moved to Brooklyn Heights to elude Aline Bernstein and escape from the public he had acquired with the publication of *Look Homeward, Angel* in 1929.

All his subsequent books were set in New York, which he
used as much more than a background. The city is a force
against whose values and meanings the hero, always a new-
comer, is tested. Speaking of the thirties, Wolfe later wrote:
"The life of the great city fascinated me as it had always done,
but also aroused all the old feelings of naked homelessness, root-
lessness, and loneliness which I have always felt there. It was,
and has always remained for me, at least, the most homesick
city in the world; the place where I have felt mostly an alien
and a stranger."

•

"About the year 1924," Malcolm Cowley has noted, "there began a great exodus toward Connecticut, the Catskills, northern New Jersey and Bucks County, Pennsylvania." Some left because they preferred the country; others simply because the rents were too high. The decline in Village real estate values had been reversed; the progress of the tenements had stopped and there was now a residential backflow to the Village. Young professionals and members of the middle class came back; old houses were restored; rooming houses were reconverted to apartments and single residences; apartment houses were built. The rents were driven up and the artists and writers were driven out. In 1927 the *Christian Science Monitor* ran a headline: GREENWICH VILLAGE TOO COSTLY NOW FOR ARTISTS TO LIVE THERE: VALUES INCREASE SO THAT ONLY THOSE WHO CAN WRITE FLUENTLY IN CHECK BOOKS CAN AFFORD IT: ONE ROOM AND BATH COST $65. Some few writers remained and some who had already made their reputations or had secure jobs within the literary establishment chose this time to return.

Among them were William Rose Benét, a former editor of the *Century* who was associated with the *Literary Review* (the progenitor of the *Saturday Review of Literature*) from its inception in 1920, and his wife, Elinor Wylie. Wylie had originally arrived in the Village from Washington, D.C., in 1921, preceded by her reputation. She had married at twenty, but left her husband and child five years later for Horace Wylie, who was also married. They lived abroad for five years as "Mr. and Mrs. Waring." When they returned, Horace Wylie got a divorce — Elinor's husband had killed himself — and in 1916 they were married. In Washington Elinor was not forgiven and had few friends. However, as Carl Van Doren wrote, "What in Washington had seemed shocking, in New York seemed dramatic. Almost nobody knew exactly what her story was, but everybody knew she had a story and thought of her as some kind of heroine." Doubtless her great beauty helped. Louis Untermeyer said she looked like Nefertiti: "the same imperious brows; the high cheekbones and the scooped-out cheeks; the proud and narrow nose; the small taut mouth; the carved and resolute chin; the long smooth column of the throat." Carl Van Doren said she was like "iced chalk," a description she liked. "White faced . . . she had no color but in her lustrous eyes and her bronze hair."

In 1921, after Harcourt, Brace and Howe decided to publish a book of her poetry, Elinor began coming to New York for a few days every two weeks. The following year she left Wylie, whom she divorced two years later, and found a large high-ceilinged room on the entrance floor of 1 University Place, "then still one of the great old houses facing the Square." Like Margaret Anderson, Wylie had the ability to create a great deal of style out of very little. "That one room," her sister Nancy Hoyt remembered, "looked like a mixture of Horace Walpole, Lady Mary Wortley Montague and Miss Austen . . . In the dusk of early spring the lamps and candles glowed under the high ceiling of a drawing room which would have been suitable as one of a lady's 20 rooms but seemed slightly ridiculous and almost unbelievable as the only dwelling place of a human being." Elinor was able to conceal all the practicalities — cooking utensils, dressing table accoutrements and such — in the bathroom. To this apartment came Benét, Wilson, Dos Passos (the young woman who prepares endless cups of coffee in her bathroom-kitchen in his *Most Likely to Succeed* may have been inspired by Wylie), John Peale Bishop and others. They often went to Marta's, at 75 Washington Place. During this period Elinor was employed by *Vanity Fair* as poetry editor at fifty dollars a week.

In 1923 Elinor married William Rose Benét, who had been at Yale with her brother. They first lived near Sheridan Square in "a tiny, cheerful apartment on a short, sunny rather messy side street," but soon moved to 142 East 18th Street. After a winter there, they bought a house in New Canaan, Connecticut. By 1926, however, they were back in the Village at 36 West 9th Street. Both names, BENÉT and WYLIE, were on the bell. The apartment took up the whole second floor of the house. "The front room was the formal sitting-room and dining-room, with a little study off it crowded with Bill's books and pictures. White shelves of books, gay and leather bound . . . lined the walls. There were high windows onto 9th Street." The living room was furnished with the blue velveteen sofa, the Wedgwood lamp, the eighteenth-century Sheffield silver mirror and the beautifully shaped chairs Elinor had had at 1 University Place. There was a kitchen and a double bedroom and a room where Elinor worked on "an enormous deal table unpainted and unvarnished." She used greenish blue pencils and typed on blue bond paper with a bluish green typewriter ribbon.

In August 1928, shortly before Elinor Wylie's untimely death in December at the age of forty-three, the Benéts' old friend Sinclair Lewis came to live a block away at 37 West 10th Street with his new wife, the journalist Dorothy Thompson. (Lewis had, in 1910, lived briefly at 10 Van Nest Place, now 69 Charles Street, in the same row of houses Hart Crane later inhabited.) Dorothy Thompson used the second floor as a studio. Lewis was at this time America's most famous writer and Dorothy must have expected, as Vincent Sheean has written, that life "in the largest of American cities, on an income which even for the United States was really large, would have some elements of variety, glitter, change and excitement. Not at all." Lewis did not like to go out to the theater or to other people's homes, refused to make plans in advance, yet would invite any number of guests to his own home on the spur of the moment. "Red's hospitality was incorrigible," wrote Sheean. "He always asked everybody to come and never wanted anybody to go. If he felt the need of solitude, or even of sleep, he would abandon the company and retire for an hour, almost always with the solemn injunction that nobody was to go away . . . Dorothy was also extremely hospitable but she did have the habits of civilization; she could tell lunch from dinner; if she asked you for cocktails she did not expect you to stay all night; and furthermore she always recognized that other people had other things to do, which Red treated as a chimerical notion." Thus began the dissolution of the Lewis marriage. They were at 10th Street only a year.

Toward the end of the decade, what Allen Churchill has called "the most exclusive — not to say respectable — literary group in the Village" gathered around Bleecker and West 11th streets. Mark Van Doren bought a house at 393 Bleecker and with his neighbors on Perry and West 11th "demolished back fences and outbuildings at one stroke, paved the space thus opened up, planted the edges of it with shrubs and trees, and there was Bleecker Gardens." Although the Van Dorens moved to Connecticut in 1959, the families on Bleecker between 11th and Perry still contribute to a common fund for the maintenance of the Gardens. Van Doren had first lived in the Village in 1920, when he and Joseph Wood Krutch took an apartment at 43 Barrow Street. Krutch lived in the back room, which was heated by a gas radiator, and Van Doren had the front room, with a potbellied stove that burned hard coal. During this period Van Doren, who was to win a Pulitzer Prize for poetry in 1939, was literary editor of the *Nation* and taught English at Columbia. His brother, Carl, who was also teaching at Columbia and who had preceded Mark as literary editor of the *Nation*, was literary editor of the *Century Magazine* from 1922 to 1925 and of the Literary Guild from 1926 to 1934. "What first made me want to live in Greenwich Village," he wrote in *Three Worlds,* "was the houses I looked down on as I passed over them in the elevated on the way between my flat near Columbia and my office at the *Nation* in Vesey Street: picturesque, small, weathered houses excitingly unlike the piled-up tiers of flats on Morningside . . . The Canbys [Henry Seidel Canby had founded the *Literary Review*] had a house in Charlton Street, which architecturally belonged in the American wing of the Metropolitan Museum and which stood on ground which Aaron Burr had once leased from Trinity." Carl Van Doren took this house, 47 Charlton Street, in 1922, and five years later moved to a house at 123 West 11th Street.

Among Mark Van Doren's close friends was James Thurber, who was living in the same building as E. B. White on West 13th Street. Thurber had a furnished room and White had an apartment with three other Cornell alumni. Later in the year, Thurber moved to a basement apartment on Horatio Street near the Ninth Avenue El. "I used to walk quickly past the house in W. 13th Street between 6th and 7th where F. P. A. [Franklin P. Adams] lived, and the block seemed to tremble under my feet," White wrote in *Here Is New York.*

Perhaps drawn partly by his distinguished colleagues, Lionel Trilling, then an instructor at Columbia, moved downtown in 1929. "I signalized my solidarity with the intellectual life by taking an apartment in Greenwich Village," he wrote.

I was under no illusion that the Village was any longer in its great days — I knew that in the matter of residential preference I was a mere epigone. So much so, indeed, that my apartment was not in a brownstone house or in a more-or-less reconditioned tenement, but in a brand-new, yellow-brick, jerry-built six-story apartment building, exactly like the apartment buildings that were going up all over the Bronx and Brooklyn. Still, the Village was the Village, there seemed no other place in New York where a right-thinking person might live . . .

What is more, my address was Bank Street, which, of all the
famous streets of the Village, seemed to me at the time to
have had the most distinguished literary past . . .

After the Twenties

As Lionel Trilling noted, by 1929 the great days of the Village
were over. A period of relative inactivity followed, a literary
hibernation from which the area would not emerge until after
the Second World War. By the thirties most of the major figures
had gone: Dreiser and Cather, now successful, lived uptown;
Crane, Wolfe and Marianne Moore had moved to Brooklyn;
Djuna Barnes and Margaret Anderson had gone to Europe.
There remained only a few of those who had made the late teens
and twenties a vital literary period. Cummings stayed in the
Village until his death in 1962; the Mark Van Dorens remained
until 1959; their friend Joseph Wood Krutch lived at 144 West
12th Street and then 11 West 11th until he moved to Arizona in
1958.

Sherwood Anderson was living on his farm, Ripshin, in Trout-
dale, Virginia, but when he came into New York during the
thirties he stayed at the home of his good friend Mary Emmett
at 54 Washington Mews. She was the widow of Burton Emmett,
who had been Anderson's patron. Anderson found himself unable to work in Mary's house. "There is too much ringing of
phones," he wrote. "And besides, Mary is too rich. There are
too many rare books and art objects about. There is something
of the monk in me. I like bare walls." So Anderson went to a
neighborhood hotel, where he got a room at half price because
the proprietor had read his books. He came to work one
morning and found the chambermaid reading his manuscript.

The proprietor and chambermaid were both Jewish and Anderson took their interest in writing to be a racial characteristic. "Is it not an amazing race?" he wrote.

James Agee in his apartment at 172 Bleecker Street during the 1940s.

Other writers came for brief periods. Sara Teasdale moved to 1 Fifth Avenue in 1932, and in the midst of a depression committed suicide there in 1933 by taking all the barbiturates she had been prescribed to help her sleep. Nathanael West lived at the Brevoort during the winter of 1935 and the spring of 1936 while James T. Farrell was also in residence. Farrell came to West's room to read him parts of the *Studs Lonigan* trilogy, which he was finishing at the time.

One of the few new arrivals was James Agee, who moved into a basement apartment at 38 Perry Street in 1932. Agee had just been at Harvard, where he had worked on a parody of *Time* magazine that had landed him a job with *Fortune,* another Time-Life publication. He wrote his Tennessee friend Reverend James H. Flye that he was living in two large rooms in "a nice and unusually old house" that had "a broad and sheltered back porch, and a large yard with pool, large trees, incipient grass, flower beds and ivy." Later Agee moved to 121 Leroy Street. Then, during the summer of 1936, he and the photographer Walker Evans went south to do a study of tenant farmers. *Fortune* considered the article too liberal for its readers so Agee decided to turn it into the book that would be called *Let Us Now Praise Famous Men.* He retired to New Jersey to work on it, returning to the city late in 1939 to take a job at *Time.* His main address during this period was 172 Bleecker Street, where four flights up (or 172 steps, according to Father Flye) he had a floor-through apartment, which he occupied from 1941 to 1951. He also kept a studio at 33 Cornelia Street, where he did his writing. He was reviewing the same movies, often differently, for both *Time* and the *Nation.*

Agee was a familiar Village figure. A heavy but solitary drinker, he could often be seen at the San Remo, which became the hub of Village literary life in the late forties and fifties. After suffering a heart attack in 1951 he abandoned the Bleecker

Street walkup and bought a house at 17 King Street, where he lived until his death in 1955.

As the clouds of war gathered, some of the expatriates began returning home. Djuna Barnes came back to 5 Patchin Place. The publication of her extraordinary novel, *Nightwood,* in Paris in 1936 had made her reputation legendary. T. S. Eliot called it "so good a novel that only sensibilities trained in poetry can wholly appreciate it." But in New York she lived the life of a recluse.

Anaïs Nin, who had grown up on the West Side but spent the thirties in Europe, returned in January 1940. After living at several temporary addresses, she found an apartment at 215 West 13th Street for sixty dollars a month. It was a skylight studio on the top floor — one room, a kitchen and bathroom — with a terrace overlooking the backyard. "I bought the simplest of unpainted furniture, beds and large tables," she wrote in her *Diary.* "The tenants left a brown wall-to-wall carpet, and I covered this with American Indian serapes." In 1942, intending to publish her own work, Nin bought a press and rented an attic studio at 144 MacDougal Street for thirty-five dollars a month. Her first project was her novel, *Winter of Artifice;* she set the type herself and the book was published in May 1942. Next came a book of drawings by Max Ernst and, in January 1944, *Under a Glass Bell,* a collection of Nin's stories that drew the praise of Edmund Wilson. In 1944 the press moved to "more businesslike quarters," an office in a small green two-story house at 17 East 13th Street.

Several others arrived before the postwar period blossomed. Tennessee Williams came to New York in 1939 after winning a Rockefeller Fellowship and took a course in play-writing at the New School. At the end of 1941 he shared an apartment with an abstract painter in the warehouse district of the West Village and worked, waiting on tables and reciting poetry, in the Beggar's Bar. In 1942, when he was eighteen, James Baldwin left Harlem for Greenwich Village. His first apartment was twenty-five dollars a month and had two toilets and a roof garden. Baldwin also worked as a waiter to earn his living; he found a job in a basement restaurant on Sullivan Street called the Calypso. Richard Wright, whom Baldwin had already sought out in Brooklyn, was a frequent patron. The restaurant was run by a West Indian woman who, Wright said, "would tolerate no ill manners from bigots." In November 1945, Wright and his family moved to a four-room apartment on the third floor of 82 Washington Place, the same building in which Willa Cather had lived thirty-five years earlier. Later Wright bought a brownstone, replaced now by an apartment building, at 13 Charles Street.

Baldwin was a familiar figure around the Village until he went to Paris in 1948. "By the time I was 24," he told his biographer, Fern Eckman, "— since I was not stupid, I realized there was no point in my staying in the country at all. If I'd been born in Mississippi, I might have come to New York. But, being born in New York, there's no place that you can go. You have to go *out. Out* of the country."

The major literary institution of the late thirties and forties was the *Partisan Review,* which had its offices slightly east of the Village at 45 Astor Place. It had begun in 1934 as a publication of the New York City John Reed Club — one of many established throughout the country by the Communist party as forums for the discussion of Marxist-Leninist doctrine as it applied to art and literature. The earlier Village hero, Reed, was considered the exemplary radical intellectual for having immersed his life and art in revolutionary journalism. Founding editors of *PR* were Philip Rahv and William Phillips, and the first issue featured an excerpt from James T. Farrell's *Studs Lonigan.* In 1937 the magazine announced its independence from any organized political group, and Dwight Macdonald and F. W. Dupee joined its staff. Mary McCarthy met the editors at Farrell's apartment when she was living at 18 Gay Street after separating from her first husband, and became *PR*'s drama critic. "It was a period of intense happiness," she recalled. ". . . I moved into a one-room apartment on a crooked street in Greenwich Village and exulted in being poor and alone." The crowd associated with *PR* often met at Farrell's, at Macdonald's on East 10th Street, or in the forties at Phillip's on West 11th Street or Rahv's on West 10th. William Barrett, who joined the staff in 1945, wrote of Phillip's apartment:

> For some of us it was a kind of home away from home, and no doubt we abused his amiability and patience. Nevertheless, his apartment continued during the late 40's as a center for whatever currents were alive at the time. "Salon" is too stuffy a word for it. It was always informal, sometimes rowdy in argument, but open in its ideas and attitudes. All kinds of people flowed through it, and visiting foreigners — like Camus and Merleau-Ponty — entered easily into the general verbal melee . . .
>
> By contrast an evening at the Rahv's was a much more sedate, careful, and measured affair; and one had sometimes, depending on the guests, to tread warily. The late Isaac Rosenfeld, who was a sometime guest until Philip decided he was no longer a "winner," once described a typical evening very well: "It was like throwing darts."

Such excitement surrounded the magazine that it overflowed into the streets. "There was a ceaseless flow of dialogue," Elizabeth Hardwick recalled. "Harold Rosenberg, Meyer Schapiro, William Phillips, Lionel Abel, Philip Rahv — you could always see these people in the Village, talking on the streets." Simone de Beauvoir, who visited New York in 1947, took away another impression. She described a party given for her by

Dwight Macdonald: "I found myself surrounded by the staff of a review which called itself Left-wing and *avant-garde* and whose aggressiveness surprised me . . . To like the American literature we admired at home was to insult the intelligentsia of the U.S.A. They treasured Faulkner, but they tore to pieces Hemingway, Dos Passos, Caldwell, and, above all, Steinbeck, their *bête noire*. I was bewildered; I did not know their review at all well."

After World War II a period of renewed literary activity began in the Village. In a number of ways, this period was similar to the one that had followed the First World War. Again there was an influx of young writers, many of them veterans studying on the G.I. Bill. Again there was an interest in psychoanalysis — this time focused on Wilhelm Reich rather than on Sigmund Freud. Again there was a social life centered on bars — this time the San Remo, Minetta's, Louis' and later the White Horse.

For a time in the late forties many writers frequented the San Remo, an Italian restaurant at the corner of Bleecker and MacDougal streets. Baldwin had often been there earlier, Agee was still a habitué, as was Maxwell Bodenheim, a relic from the earlier bohemian period. The socialist writer Michael Harrington, who went there every night after arriving from Chicago in 1949, remembered that there were "bad, yellowed paintings over the bar and the Entr'Acte from Wolf-Ferrari's *Jewels of the Madonna* on the jukebox." The regular crowd included seamen on the beach, "heterosexuals on the make; homosexuals who preferred erotic integration to the exclusively gay bars then on Eighth Street; Communists, Socialists and Trotskyists; potheads . . . and innovators of the future . . ." In the last category were William Burroughs, Allen Ginsberg, Gregory Corso and Jack Kerouac. Although Ginsberg and Kerouac lived on the Lower East Side, or the East

William Burroughs
outside the San Remo in
the early 1950s.

Village, as it came to be known, they still came to the San Remo to do their drinking. Corso had been born in 1930 at 190 Bleecker, across the street from the San Remo, when "all it was was an Italian neighborhood with people running around taking bets." In 1950 he met Ginsberg in a Lesbian bar on West 4th Street called the Pony Stable and so began his career as a poet. Ginsberg told him, "I want you to meet a Chinaman — a Wise One," and took him to see Mark Van Doren on Bleecker Street.

The San Remo reigned as the social center of the Village, its overflow pouring into Minetta's up the street, until about 1950, when it was the subject of what *Village Voice* publisher Ed Fancher called "an incredible social phenomenon." The Remo's tough bartenders would occasionally beat up the Village crowd and after one incident everybody left and moved to a bar called Louis' near Sheridan Square. "Before the incident, there would be four hundred people in the Remo; after that there were five." Though the San Remo regained some of is clientele, "it was never quite the same again," said Fancher.

Among those who frequented the Remo and Louis' was William Styron, who came to New York in 1947 to work as a junior editor at McGraw-Hill. He took "a horrible single room ($11 a week) at a fleabag elegantly known as the University Residence Club on West 11th Street between 5th and 6th Avenues." He "was very lonely, had a bout of hepatitis, and did not know any girls." His take-home pay after taxes was thirty-four dollars a week.

In the fall, after being fired from McGraw-Hill (reportedly for flying a paper airplane into a superior's office), Styron enrolled in the first writing class given by a Bobbs-Merrill editor named Hiram Haydn at the New School. After reading the first twenty pages of *Lie Down in Darkness,* Haydn told Styron it was a waste of time for him to stay in the class and took an option on the novel for his company. The start of the novel, as Dorothy Parker later remarked, "took your heart and flung it over there." Styron found the rest of the book did not come as easily, however, and went home to North Carolina for a year. In 1949 he was back, living in Rockland County, where he finished the first half of the novel that fall and the following spring. He then commuted between a brownstone apartment at 314 West 88th Street and the home of a young woman with whom he was "keeping company," who lived in a five-floor walkup on the east side of 6th Avenue below Prince Street. The last 15 or 20 pages of the novel were written there.

Styron's precocious achievement — he started *Lie Down in Darkness* when he was twenty-three and finished it when he was just twenty-six — doubtless helped Hiram Haydn's class acquire its legendary reputation. The class was limited to twelve students each year, who, throughout the twelve years Haydn taught it, included Mario Puzo, Bel Kaufman and three Prix de Rome winners.

After finishing his book, Styron went into the Marines, returning in time for its publication in 1951. That fall and winter he had "a tiny but rather nice (my first nice) apartment at 45 Greenwich Avenue." He was a Village celebrity and young women, impressed by the understanding of their sex evinced in his novel, would ring his doorbell.

Another late forties arrival was Edward Albee, who left home at the age of twenty for an apartment on lower Fifth Avenue. Albee, the adopted son of the heirs to the Keith-Albee vaudeville chain, was the beneficiary of a $100,000 trust fund set up by his grandmother. For the next ten years he supplemented his income with a succession of odd jobs as record salesman, waiter, copy boy, counterman and Western Union messenger, and lived in a series of inexpensive apartments in the Village, Chelsea and Little Italy. His evenings were spent in literary and philosophical discussions in MacDougal Street coffee houses or Village bars. Nine years after leaving home, Albee wrote *The Zoo Story* "on a wobbly table" in the kitchen of the apartment where he was living at the time — 238 West 4th Street. "I did a draft, made pencil revisions, and typed a second script, and that's the way I've been doing my plays since," he recalled in an interview. "I finished *The Zoo Story* in three weeks." The play, set in a crumbling apartment house on Columbus Avenue inhabited by a black homosexual, a Puerto Rican and a woman who cries all day behind a locked door, was presented at the Provincetown Playhouse on January 14, 1960. It is fitting that O'Neill's successor as the major innovative force in American theater should have had his first play produced by O'Neill's playhouse. In 1961 Albee moved to a six-room, ground-floor apartment on West 12th Street. Here he wrote his greatest commercial success, *Who's Afraid of Virginia Woolf?* In a *Paris Review* interview, Albee recalled the genesis of the title:

> There was a saloon — it's changed its name now — on Tenth Street, between Greenwich Avenue and Waverly Place . . . and they had a big mirror on the downstairs bar in this saloon where people used to scrawl graffiti. At one point back in about . . . 1954 I think it was — long before any of us started doing much of anything — I was in there having a beer one night, and I saw "Who's Afraid of Virginia Woolf?" scrawled in soap, I suppose, on this mirror. When I started to write the play it cropped up in my mind again. And of course, Who's afraid of Virginia Woolf means who's afraid of the big *bad* wolf . . . who's afraid of living life without false illusions.

Albee became a member, with Richard Barr and Clinton Wilder, of a group called Theater 1964, which produced plays, including the works of Beckett and Pinter, at the Cherry Lane Theater. He reinvested part of the profits from *Who's Afraid of Virginia Woolf?* to found a playwrights' school, called the New Playwrights Unit Workshop, that supported the work of LeRoi Jones and others.

In the fifties, the White Horse Tavern at Hudson and 11th streets succeeded the San Remo as the favorite Village literary hangout. Norman Mailer, who was living in the East Village in 1951, became the center of a group that gathered there. Dan Wolf, who founded the *Village Voice* in 1955 with Mailer and Ed Fancher, suggested that Mailer make it a Sunday afternoon tradition to go to the White Horse. "Norman found that if you invited people to your house it was not that easy to get rid of them," Wolf recalled. The White Horse was the perfect alternative. "It had a pleasant atmosphere; it was in the right setting — the 'real' Village; it was an old bar and had a quiet neighborhood quality." Wolf went only once but Mailer went regularly and a group of young writers gathered around him. Some time later Dylan Thomas began telling people he drank there, and as Michael Harrington recalled, "every English major in the Northeast corridor began to make a pilgrimage to the White Horse." Thomas died in the Village in 1953 at St. Vincent's Hospital on Seventh Avenue and 12th Street.

For more than ten years Harrington himself went to the White Horse every night when he was in New York. "As the people of Königsberg were said to set their clocks by Immanuel Kant's walks, you would see me, punctually dissolute, appear on week nights at midnight and on weekends at one o'clock." When the White Horse closed early, the regulars would go across the street to a bar called the Ideal, which was nicknamed the Ordeal because of confrontations there between bohemia and square America.

Another group, which gathered at the home of Vance Bourjaily at 49 Grove Street, included Merle Miller, Louis Auchincloss, Gore Vidal, Hortense Calisher, William Styron and Calder Willingham. At one party, Bourjaily recalled, James Jones met Montgomery Clift and "they decided then and there that he should play Pruitt [in *From Here to Eternity*]."

Since the fifties the Village has lost most of its literary residents. There are a few exceptions: Djuna Barnes still lives in Patchin Place, Anaïs Nin spends part of the year in Washington Square Village and Michael Harrington now owns a house on Perry Street. In the sixties Edward Albee owned a carriage house at 50 West 10th Street and Marianne Moore returned from Brooklyn and lived at 35 West 9th Street until her death in 1971. In the seventies Westbeth, a special housing project

Dylan Thomas at the White Horse Tavern,
where he held court in the early 1950s.

for artists in all fields, provides reasonably priced housing for
young writers. But in general the Village has become too expensive for those just starting out and does not offer the large
apartments required by those with families. For the most part,
writers have had to turn to other parts of the city to find living
space.

The Village has such a great concentration of literary landmarks that only buildings still standing or sites marked by

plaques are noted in the tours. Most other sites of former buildings are omitted. Tour 1 covers the area east of Sixth Avenue and Tour 2 the area west of Sixth.

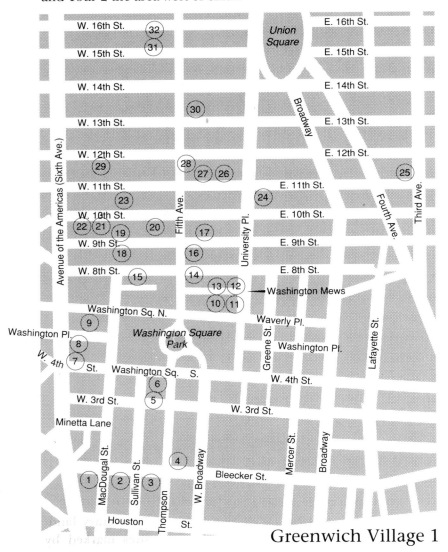

Greenwich Village 1

Greenwich Village Tour 1

1. 190 Bleecker Street, just west of MacDougal. The birthplace of Beat poet Gregory Corso (p. 96).

(1a) 189 Bleecker, on the northwest corner of MacDougal was the San Remo bar (pp. 91 and 95), frequented by Corso and others. It is now Carpo's Cafe.

2. 172 Bleecker. James Agee lived here on the top floor from 1941 to 1951 (p. 91).

3. 160 Bleecker. Mills House number one. Theodore Dreiser's first address when he came to New York in 1895 (p. 65). He paid twenty-five cents a night for a bed. Designed in 1895 by Ernest Flagg, since 1976 it has housed the Atrium apartments.

4. 145 Bleecker. This house was occupied by James Fenimore Cooper in 1833 (p. 37). When Cooper lived here, this block of Bleecker was called Carroll Place.

(4a) 647 Broadway (three doors north of Bleecker) Pfaff's Tavern (a literary center in the 1860s) was in the basement here (perhaps in this very building) from 1855 to about 1864, when it moved to 653 Broadway (p. 45).

5. 85 West 3rd Street (originally Amity Place). Poe lived here in two rooms on the second floor in 1845 (p. 39). The two lower stories have been remodeled.

6. 53 Washington Square South. This was the Judson Hotel when Edwin Arlington Robinson stayed here from 1906 to 1909 (p. 50).

(6a) 133 MacDougal. This was the home of the Provincetown Players from 1917–27. The theatre is still here, in back, with an entrance in the present, later building (p. 59).

7. 147 West 4th Street. Polly Halliday's second restaurant opened here in 1918 (p. 57). John Reed wrote the articles which became *Ten Days That Shook the World* in an upstairs room. The building, now Ristorante Volare, dates from 1849–50.

8. 82 Washington Place. Willa Cather lived here 1908–13 (p. 51) and it was home to Richard Wright in 1945 (p. 93). This Beaux-Arts-style apartment building was constructed in 1903 by architects Horenburger & Straub.

9. 75 Washington Place. Marta's, a favorite eating place for Elinor Wylie, William Rose Benét, John Dos Passos, and others, around 1921 (p. 85) is still here. The building dates from 1847.

(9a) 19 Washington Square North. (Today it would be number 18 if it

Part of James Fenimore Cooper's block on Bleecker Street
as it looked in the 1890s.

were standing.) The home of Henry James's maternal grandmother. Other houses (1835–36) still here suggest what hers must have looked like (p. 41).

10. 7 Washington Square North. Edith Wharton lived here with her mother in 1882 (p. 45).

11. 3 Washington Square North. This was the home of Elaine Orr, and a meeting place of writers (p. 74). Edmund Wilson lived here 1921–23 (pp. 76–77); others lived in the studio at back in Washington Mews. (see number 12). The new façade and studio tower were added in 1884 by architect J. E. Terhune. In the twenties this was the only building on this block of early nineteenth-century houses (the Old Row) to have been remodeled.

(11a) 21 Washington Place, on the northeast corner of Greene Street.

This was the site of Henry James's birthplace—not 27 Washington Place, where there was once a plaque in commemoration (pp. 39–40).

12. 14A Washington Mews, the studio for 3 Washington Square North. Five high floors, which housed, at various times, John Dos Passos, Edward Hopper, William Glackens, and Rockwell Kent (p. 81).

13. 54 Washington Mews. The building dates to 1834 and was remodeled in 1916. In the 1930s, Sherwood Anderson often stayed here with friend and patron Mary Emmett (p. 89).

14. 1 Fifth Avenue on the southeast corner of 8th Street. Sara Teasdale moved here in 1932, and here she committed suicide the following year (p. 91).

15. 28 West 8th Street. The Jumble Shop Tea Rooms, which had opened about 1922 at 21 West 8th Street, moved here in 1934, into space which had been converted to a restaurant in 1926. It extended through the block to 3 MacDougal Alley, and then into the former stable at 176 MacDougal Street (p. 60). About 1968 the 8th Street rooms closed, and a few years later the name was changed to Shakespeare's Pub, which closed about 1983. At present there is a hole-in-the-wall and sidewalk restaurant at 182 MacDougal Street called Shakespeare's Hamburger. E. A. Robinson lived at this address in the 1920s with his friends, the Frasers (pp. 50 and 60).

16. 21 Fifth Avenue, on the southeast corner of 9th Street. Mark Twain lived here 1904–08. There is a plaque on the 9th Street side (p. 47–48).

17. 3 East 9th Street. Harold Loeb's *Broom* magazine had its offices here, in the basement, around 1923 (p. 79). The building dates from 1840–41.

18. 36 West 9th Street. Elinor Wylie and William Rose Benét, her husband, were living here in 1926. They had the entire second floor (p. 86). This house was originally three stories, built in 1845.

19. 35 West 9th Street. Marianne Moore lived on the seventh floor of this house until her death in 1971 (p. 100).

20. 14 West 10th Street This grand mansion, built 1855–56, was rented furnished by Mark Twain in the winter of 1900–01. There is a plaque (p. 47). Originally it must have had an entrance stoop like number 16, its twin next door, whose façade has been flattened.

21. 50 West 10th Street. Edward Albee occupied this carriage house in the 1960s (p. 100). It was built between 1863 and 1879; the stable doors are original.

22. 54 West 10th Street. Hart Crane lived here in 1917 in a six-dollar-a-week room (p. 73). Built in 1839, this house was originally three stories.

23. 37 West 10th Street. Sinclair Lewis and Dorothy Thompson, his wife at the time, lived here for a year in 1928–29 (p. 86). Two floors were added to this 1830s building in the 1920s.

24. University Place and 11th Street, on the southeast corner. Once Hotel Albert, now Albert Apartments, the building was designed in 1893 by Henry Hardenbergh. Thomas Wolfe lived here in room 2220, when he first moved to New York in 1923 to teach at NYU (pp. 81–82).

If you have time, detour east on 10th Street to Fourth Avenue, then to:

25. 119 East 11th Street, near Third Avenue is Webster Hall. The liberal crowd held their fund-raising costume balls here (p. 57). Until 1989, it housed the Ritz Rock & Roll Club, which then moved to Studio 54. The building, with its seventy-foot façade lavishly decorated with white plaster ornament, dates from 1866; the architect was Charles Rentz.

Go back via 12th Street to:

26. 25 East 11th Street. Hart Crane lived here in 1917 (p. 73). Then a cheap rooming house, it is one of a row of five lovely houses dating 1842–45.

27. 21 East 11th Street. Built in 1848, this was the home of Mary Cadwalader Jones. Henry James stayed here when he visited America in 1904 (p. 42).

28. 47 Fifth Avenue, between 11th and 12th streets. The Salmagundi Club, formed in 1871 for "the promotion of social intercourse among artists," was named for Washington Irving's satirical magazine. Since 1917, the club has occupied this last of the brownstone mansions (built in 1853) that once lined Fifth Avenue. The original location of the club was 14 West 12th Street. Dreiser moved there in 1897 (p. 66). The building was a twin to number 16 next door, which is still standing.

29. 66 West 12th Street. The New School for Social Research, which was built in 1930 by architect Joseph Urban (p. 97).

30. 17 East 13th Street. Anaïs Nin moved her Gemor Press to an office in this small two-story building in 1944 (p. 92).

31. 27 West 15th Street. Thomas Wolfe moved to a second-floor rear room in this five-story house (now renovated) in 1928 (p. 83).

32. 24 West 16th Street; there is an interesting plaque. William Cullen Bryant lived here from 1867 to 1878; Margaret Anderson, the editor of the *Little Review*, had a floor here in 1917; Hart Crane rented a room on the top floor. The washed-out façade has been further defaced by a brick excrescence at the street level (pp. 73 and 62).

Greenwich Village Tour 2

At the southwest corner of the Village lies the Charlton-King-Vandam Historic District. The elegant mansion known as Richmond Hill once stood near the present intersection of Charlton and Varick streets. George Washington used the house as his headquarters in 1776; John Adams

Greenwich Village 2

occupied it when he was vice-president; and in 1797 Aaron Burr acquired it as an entertainment center for those who might further his political career. John Jacob Astor bought much of the land in 1817, leveled the hills, and divided it into lots. Meanwhile the house itself lost its glamour, was moved across the street, served as a theater and amusement garden, and was finally demolished in 1849. Many houses built in the 1820s are still standing in this part of the Village.

1. 25 Charlton Street, between Sixth Avenue and Varick. Edna St. Vincent Millay lived in this house for six months in 1918 with her mother and two sisters (p. 71).

2. 17 King Street (one block below Houston Street). James Agee bought this house, now run-down, in 1951 and lived here until his death in 1955 (pp. 91–92).

3. 12 St. Luke's Place. In 1923 Sherwood Anderson lived in a basement apartment here, in this row of lovely Italianate houses built between 1852 and 1854 (p. 68).

4. 14 St. Luke's Place. Marianne Moore and her mother lived in the basement apartment here from 1918 to 1929. Across the way at 66 Leroy Street is the Hudson Park Branch of the New York Public Library, where Moore worked part-time from 1921 to 1925 (p. 70).

5. 16 St. Luke's Place. Theodore Dreiser rented the parlor floor for a year in 1922–23 (pp. 67–69).

6. 75 ½ Bedford Street. Edna St. Vincent Millay lived in this 9 ½ -foot-wide house from November of 1923 to June of 1925 (p. 72).

7. 38 Commerce Street (around the corner left from Bedford Street). Built in 1836 as a brewery, this has been the Cherry Lane Theater since 1924 (p. 99).

8. 43 Barrow Street. Mark Van Doren and Joseph Wood Krutch shared an apartment here in 1920 (p. 87). The third floor of this 1828 house was added in the 1870s. (Numbers 41 and 51 in the row are in their original condition.)

9. 45 Grove Street. Hart Crane sublet a room he particularly liked in this house, described by the Landmarks Commission as "undoubtedly one of the finest and largest Federal residences in Greenwich Village." The house was originally surrounded by spacious grounds and had its own hothouse and stables (p. 73).

10. 49 Grove Street (on the northeast corner). Vance Bourjaily lived in this orange brick apartment house in the 1950s. Here he was visited by many writers (p. 100).

(10a) 59 Grove Street. In 1809, during the last months of his life,

Thomas Paine was totally confined to his bed and begged his old friend Madame Bonneville to take care of him. She rented a house on this site (then in the middle of farm property) just a few yards away from his own on Herring (now Bleecker) Street. Paine was carried there in an armchair, and died a month later in a back room.

11. 121 Washington Place. Behind the house in the garden, Mrs. Clara Potter Davidge built a studio, one large room with a sleeping loft, for Edwin Arlington Robinson in 1909. The poet lived there on and off for several years. When he was in residence, breakfast was brought to him each morning. The house, built in 1831, was completely remodeled in 1925; floor levels were changed, and a new brick front was added.

12. 139 Waverly Place. Edna St. Vincent Millay and her sister Norma found an unheated room with a fireplace here in 1931 (p. 71).

13. 14 Gay Street. Ruth McKenney, whose sister Eileen married Nathanael West in 1940, portrayed this picturesque block in the popular comedy *My Sister Eileen.*

14. 18 Gay Street. Mary McCarthy, exulting in being "poor and alone," lived here in a one-room apartment, in the 1940s (p. 94).

15. 4 Patchin Place. E. E. Cummings lived here from 1923 until his death in 1962 (pp. 74–76).

16. 5 Patchin Place. Djuna Barnes lived here, in a one-room apartment, from the early 1940s until her death in 1982 (p. 92).

(16a) 118 West 11th Street. Theodore Dreiser lived here from 1923 to 1927, when he was writing *An American Tragedy.* Dreiser's house, one of a row of elegant townhouses set back 40 feet from the street, was exactly opposite number 117 on the other side of the street. The row was razed in 1955 (p. 69).

17. 123 West 11th Street. Carl Van Doren, in 1927, lived here in one of the row of five houses built in 1849 which retain something close to their original shape.

18. 43 Greenwich Avenue (halfway between Perry and Charles). William Styron, after publication of *Lie Down in Darkness* had his first "nice" apartment here. Numbers 43–49 are four houses built in 1848 and remodeled, with uniform façade, in 1930.

(18a) 13 Charles Street. Richard Wright owned a brownstone house here from 1945 to 1947 (p. 93). This was a row of nine houses built in 1847–48. Number 9, similar to Wright's house, is largely original.

19. 139 West 10th Street. This saloon, now called The Ninth Circle, was the place where Edward Albee saw "Who's Afraid Of Virginia Woolf" scrawled in soap on a mirror over the downstairs bar (p. 99).

(19a) 165 West 10th Street. Dreiser lived at this site from 1914 to 1920 while finishing *The Genius* (p. 67).

20. 238 West 4th Street. Albee wrote his first play, *The Zoo Story*, in an apartment in this tenement building (pp. 98–99).

21. 79 Charles Street was number 15 on Van Nest Place when Hart Crane lived here in 1920.

22. 69 Charles Street. Sinclair Lewis rented a small room here (then 10 Van Nest) from 1910 to 1913 (p. 86).

23. 38 Perry Street. James Agee's first New York apartment was in the basement here from 1932 to 1937 (p. 91).

24. 30 Perry Street. John Squarcialupi's restaurant, a meeting place for writers (p. 78).

25. 393 Bleecker Street. Mark Van Doren lived here (in "Bleecker Gardens") from 1929 to 1959 (p. 87).

26. 567 Hudson Street (on the southwest corner of West 11th). The White Horse Tavern, a hangout of Norman Mailer and Dylan Thomas in the early 1950s (pp. 99–100) is still here.

27. 155 Bank Street (between Washington and West). In 1969 the former Bell Telephone Labs was converted into artists' housing, called Westbeth. Muriel Rukeyser lived here until her death in 1980, and Galway Kinnell lived here for a time.

28. 263 West 11th Street. Thomas Wolfe and Aline Bernstein lived here in 1927–28 (pp. 82–83). A similar house is described in the opening pages of *You Can't Go Home Again*.

29. 27 Bank Street. Allen Tate lived in a basement apartment here in 1927 (p. 78), where he served as janitor in lieu of paying rent.

(29a) 5 Bank Street. Willa Cather lived on the second floor of a house at this location from 1913 until it was torn down in 1927 (pp. 51, 63–64).

(29b) 91 Greenwich Avenue. Offices of The Masses, an intellectual focus of Village life (pp. 56–57), were located at this address.

(29c) 86 Greenwich Avenue. James Light's apartment was a meeting place for actors and writers (p. 60). The Sheridan Theater, now gone, was built here in 1920–21.

30. Seventh Avenue, on the east side, between 11th and 12th streets is St. Vincent's Hospital where Dylan Thomas died in 1953. The hospital is now mostly new buildings.

31. 215 West 13th Street. Anaïs Nin had a skylight studio here from 1940 to 1948 (p. 92).

32. 152 West 13th Street. Offices of The *Dial* were here until it ceased publication in 1929 (pp. 80–81).

33. 138 West 13th Street. Max Eastman was editing the *Liberator* magazine here in the early 1920s (pp. 57–58).

III. The Lower East Side

The Immigrants' City

In 1890 a Danish immigrant named Jacob Riis drew the attention of America to the section of New York then known as the "East Side." Riis was a reporter for the *New York Sun* and his classic work of journalism, *How the Other Half Lives*, described trenchantly the city's immigrant neighborhoods. Each morning at 2:00 A.M. Riis walked through them from his office on Mulberry Street near Houston on his way home to Brooklyn. First came the Italian section, culminating in "the Bend," where Mulberry Street "crooks like an elbow." Here, in what Riis called the "foul core of New York's slums," was a vast marketplace with two rows of hucksters' and peddlers' booths against a background of tenements. East of Mulberry were the streets of Chinatown, their opium dens jammed "with these hapless victims of a passion which, once acquired, demands the sacrifice of every instinct of decency to its insatiate desire." A little farther on, where Baxter Street runs into Worth Street today, was Five Points, historically one of the worst slums in the world. Charles Dickens had visited it in 1842 and written, "all that is loathsome, drooping, and decayed is here . . ." And across the Bowery to the east was the Jewish district, according to Riis "picketed from end to end with the outposts of Israel . . . Hebrew faces, Hebrew signs, and incessant chatter in . . . Hebrew."

Jacob A. Riis's photograph of Mulberry Bend, "the foul core of New York's slums," about 1888.

Like all New York's old neighborhoods, the East Side had once been fashionable. On his walk Riis would have passed the Mulberry Street house that had once belonged to Stephen Van Rensselaer, member of one of New York's wealthiest Dutch families. Still farther on, close to Five Points, he would have come to the former home of Edward Mooney, a wholesale meat merchant. And perhaps he occasionally would have passed the house at 1 Cherry Street where George Washington had lived during the brief year when New York was the nation's capital. Riis himself remarked the changes that were particularly apparent in the President's old neighborhood: "We stand upon the domain of the tenement. In the shadow of the great stone abutments, the old Knickerbocker houses linger like ghosts of a departed day. Down the winding slope of Cherry Street — proud and fashionable Cherry Hill that was — their broad steps, sloping roofs, and dormer windows are easily made out; all the more easily for the contrast with the ugly barracks that elbow them right and left . . ."

The changes Riis documented had begun as early as the 1840s, when Walt Whitman, then a young Manhattan newspaperman, described the area as "the region of Jews, jewelry, and second-hand clothing." Chatham Square was filled with dray carts, coaches and cabs. "On the right loom up small hills of furniture, of every quality," wrote Whitman, "with here and there an auctioneer, standing on a table or barreltop, and crying out to the crowd around him, the merits of the articles and the bids made for them." (During the same decade the ever impoverished Edgar Allan Poe had lived for a short time in a tenement at 195 East Broadway.) The area east of the Bowery had been the home of Irish and German immigrants, among them many German Jews, since the 1840s. But between 1880 and 1910 successive waves of immigrants from Eastern Europe, spurred by pogroms in Russia and Poland, swelled the neighborhood and gave it what was to be its most enduring ethnic quality. Riis was writing at the peak of the immigration. In all, one third of Eastern European Jews came to America, and in 1892 75 per cent of them were to be found on the Lower East Side. By 1900 the area bounded by Cherry Street, the East River, the Bowery and 10th Street was called "the great ghetto" and was known throughout Europe. (There were three other New York ghettos: Brownsville and Williamsburg in Brooklyn and an area between 98th and 116th streets east of Central Park.) In 1886 the words of Emma

Lazarus, herself a New York Jew whose father had been a founder of the aristocratic Knickerbocker Club, were inscribed on the Statue of Liberty, welcoming "the huddled masses yearning to breathe free." But on the Lower East Side the tenements were packed tightly together, with light and air available only to the apartments at the end of the row. In between the streets were crevices several feet wide with names like Blind Man's Alley, Penitentiary Row and Jews' Alley, where the most indigent lived in squalid conditions.

Jacob Riis, who himself had slept in Bowery doorways when he first arrived in 1870, was already known as a pioneering journalist when *How the Other Half Lives* was published. As a reporter, he found the deeper story behind the daily spate of crimes to lie in the social conditions that produced it. Lincoln Steffens, who studied Riis's methods when he first became a newspaperman, credited him with "the wiping out of whole blocks of rookeries, the making of small parks, and the regulation of the tenements." He said that Riis "not only got the news; he cared about the news."

Among those who were profoundly influenced by Riis's book was a young writer named Stephen Crane. Crane, who was to write *The Red Badge of Courage* before he had ever seen war, composed the first version of *Maggie: A Girl of the Streets* before he had ever experienced life on the Bowery. The first draft was written while he was a student at Syracuse University. The following summer Crane began frequenting the Lower East Side, staying in hotels or returning home at night to New Jersey. His experiences filled out the next three revisions of the book.

Crane later remarked that "it was on the Bowery that I got my artistic education." It was not that the Bowery showed him things he had never seen before, but that it taught him a new way of seeing. In one inscription of *Maggie,* Crane wrote, "It is inevitable that you be greatly shocked by this book, but continue, please, with all possible courage to the end. For it tries to show that environment is a tremendous thing in the world and frequently shapes lives regardless." *Maggie* is the story of a young woman in love with a Bowery bartender who offers her relief from the harshness of her life. When Maggie is seduced by her lover, her hypocritical family, condemning the victim rather than the seducer, throws her out of the house. Her lover abandons her and she is driven to prostitution and, finally, suicide. The story is set against the slum background, which Crane described vividly:

> Eventually they entered a dark region where, from a careening building, a dozen gruesome doorways gave up loads of babies to the street and the gutter . . . A wind of early autumn raised yellow dust from cobbles and swirled it against a hundred windows. Long streamers of garments fluttered from fire-escapes. On all unhandy places there were buckets, brooms, rags, and bottles. In the street infants played or fought with other infants or sat stupidly in the way of vehicles. Formidable women, with uncombed hair and disordered dress, gossiped while leaning on railings or screamed in frantic quarrels. Withered persons, in curious postures of submission to something, sat smoking pipes in obscure corners. A thousand odors of cooking food came forth to the street. The building quivered and creaked from the weight of humanity stamping about in its bowels.

In Crane's day the Bowery, which he called "the only interesting street in New York," had a total of eighty-two bars along its fourteen-block length, an average of six per block. Today the bars are still there and the Bowery remains New York's skid row, but the upper floors of many of the tenement buildings have been converted into artists' lofts.

Crane's characters were Irish, but by the time his book was

published in 1893 the area behind the Bowery to the east had become the center of a separate Yiddish culture, which was developing its own distinctive journalism, literature and politics. For many decades the central figure in this community was to be Abraham Cahan, who arrived from Vilna, Poland, as a young man in 1882. He got a job stripping tobacco and after learning English began teaching it to other immigrants at the local YMHA. He moved to a different address in the East Broadway area every few years but considered "the best years of my life in America" the ones he spent at 213 Clinton Street, a two-story private house where he had a slant-roofed attic room. In 1892 Cahan went to work on the *Arbeiter Zeitung,* a Yiddish labor weekly. William Dean Howells, who had written in passing about the Lower East Side in *A Hazard of New Fortunes,* sought out Cahan there to ask for information on labor unions for his book *A Traveler from Altruria.* Howells encouraged Cahan to write about the life he knew on the Lower East Side. Cahan took his advice and in 1894 finished *Yekl,* a novel about the problems between a "greenhorn," as a new immigrant was called, and her already Americanized husband. Through Howells's influence the book was published by D. Appleton in 1896. Despite good reviews, including praise from Howells, it sold poorly, and Cahan was not to achieve success as a fiction writer until 1917, when he published *The Rise of David Levinsky.*

In the meantime, Cahan founded a newspaper called the *Jewish Daily Forward* in 1897. He left briefly because of disputes among the paper's various socialist factions and worked for Lincoln Steffens on the *Commercial Adverstiser,* but returned in 1899 as editor, a position he held until his death in 1951. Under his leadership the paper became the single most important cultural institution of the Lower East Side. It educated the immigrant to adapt and survive in his new home, acted as spokesman for the Jewish community to the English-speaking world, organized its readers to attack neighborhood problems by political means and served as a center and stimulus for the creation of Yiddish-American literature.

As Samuel Niger, Yiddish cultural historian, noted: "In other languages journalism was at best a branch of literature; in Yiddish all literature stemmed from journalism." Between 1885 and 1914 there were over 150 newspapers in Yiddish, English and other languages on the Lower East Side. The Yiddish press devoted a large share of its columns to literature. There were essays on all subjects — science, philosophy, economics — as well as poetry, short stories and serialized novels. Book publishing was almost superfluous; almost all Yiddish literature originally appeared in newspapers.

As a literary vehicle, the *Jewish Daily Forward* was preeminent. Sholom Aleichem began sending his humorous stories about rural Russia to the *Forward* long before he came to America in 1905. Sholem Asch sent stories from Poland before he arrived in 1914. Although he lived elsewhere in the city, he wrote a novel, *The Mother,* about a Polish family that settles on the Lower East Side. I. J. (Israel Joshua) Singer, whose work had been serialized in the *Forward,* arrived from Poland in 1933. Two years later he brought over his younger brother, Isaac Bashevis Singer, and got him a job on the *Forward,* where he has worked ever since. He first wrote book reviews and human interest stories as a free lance and in 1944 became a staff writer on a regular salary. His introduction to the English-speaking public came in 1953, when Saul Bellow translated his story "Gimpel the Fool" for the *Partisan Review.* Since then Singer has won a series of major literary awards and has become a grand old man of American letters. He always writes in Yiddish and all of his work is first published in the *Forward* and later translated into English with his collaboration. Singer has never written about the Lower East Side and has never lived there, although he sometimes eats at the Garden Cafeteria on East Broadway. Until recently his stories were about Eastern Europe, but they now deal with Yiddish-speaking people on the upper West Side, where he has lived for more than thirty years (see Chapter VIII, The West Side).

Singer was one of the few Yiddish writers to become known outside the Jewish community and his recognition, of course, was directly tied to his publication in English. Another was Morris Rosenfeld, one of a group known as "the sweatshop poets," writers who worked twelve or fourteen hours a day sewing and ironing in the Lower East Side's omnipresent clothing industry. Riis had written that "before you have traveled the length of a single block in any of the East Side streets" you hear "the whir of a thousand sewing machines, worked at high pressure from earliest dawn till mind and muscle give out together." Rosenfeld's most popular poem, "My Boy," told how a child, who rarely saw his father because he worked such long hours, failed to recognize him. Rosenfeld's poems were "discovered" by a Semitic scholar who translated them and had them published as a book, *Songs of the Ghetto*. The success of the book enabled the poet to move to Yonkers, ending a dozen years of work in the sweatshops.

There were many others — journalists, poets, Hebrew scholars — who are unknown today but who, in their time, created a thriving cultural and intellectual life on the Lower East Side. This life was centered in the cafés, a tradition transplanted from Europe; in these meeting places all would gather over the favored beverage, "a glass tea," drunk authentically through a piece of lump sugar held between the teeth. By 1905 there were some 250 to 300 coffee houses dotted all over the area. In his history of Russian Jewish immigration, Moses Rischin describes the function the cafés had in Lower East Side life:

. . . Over steaming Russian tea and lemon, thin slices of cake, and Russian cigarettes, 'confused minds,' disturbed by life's complexities, found respite and tonic in talk. On Rutgers Street and East Broadway, cafés entertained through the night as the journalists of Yiddish Newspaper Row defended their signed columns against the sallies of their challengers . . . Here the admirers of Marx and Kropotkin, Zola and Tolstoy, debated abstruse turns in philosophy and political economy, the purposes of art, and the standards of the theater. Even elderly Talmudists with untrimmed beards and long black coats drank honey cider, chewed lima beans, and disputed the finer points of the Law in their favorite cafés.

The cafés where the newspapermen met clustered around Rutgers Square, which today is Straus Square. The *Forward* Building overlooked the square directly at 175 East Broadway, the *Tageblatt* was at 187, and the *Day* was at 183, in a building still marked by a decaying sign. The *Forward* staff favored a café called Herrick's at 141 Division Street, now replaced by the Seward Park housing project.

It was in Sachs's Café nearby on Suffolk Street that Emma Goldman, who would play a literary as well as political role with her journal, *Mother Earth*, met Alexander Berkman on the first day she arrived in New York in 1889. Berkman, an anarchist most famous for his attempt to assassinate Pittsburgh industrialist Henry Clay Frick, became her lover and lifelong friend. Goldman continued her political education at Justus Schwab's saloon, an anarchist hangout at 50 First Avenue, and lived with Berkman at the upper limits of the Lower East Side at 210 East 13th Street. The apartment, called "the home for lost dogs" because those who had no money and no place to stay often ended up there, became an intellectual gathering place. One room, decorated with a picture of Prince Kropotkin, served as an all-purpose living room, dining room, bedroom and office for *Mother Earth*. The journal was the first to publish the work of Strindberg and Ibsen in this country and it was in its pages that Eugene O'Neill, then a high school student, discovered their work. The other room was a kitchen with a stove that provided the apartment's only heat. The crumbling brown brick building is still standing today.

The animated intellectual life around the cafés was brought to the attention of the larger community by Hutchins Hapgood, a reporter for the *Commercial Advertiser,* who, between 1898 and 1902, wrote a series of articles on the Lower East Side. Hapgood had become acquainted with the intellectual side of Lower East Side life through Abraham Cahan during Cahan's period on the same paper. Hapgood talked with the sweatshop poets and the Hebrew scholars and investigated the Yiddish theater and Jewish customs and family life. He joined the discussions in the cafés and discovered both the intellectual vigor of the immigrants and the difficulties they faced in preserving their ancient customs in the new world. Cahan said that Hapgood was "the only Gentile who knows and understands the spirit of the ghetto."

Hapgood's articles were published as a book, *The Spirit of the Ghetto,* in 1902, with illustrations by a nineteen-year-old immigrant named Jacob Epstein. Epstein, who was to become one of the world's greatest sculptors, lived in a tumbledown building at 102 Hester Street. "When my parents moved to a more respectable and duller part of the city," Epstein wrote in his autobiography, "it held no interest whatever for me. I hired a room in Hester Street in a wooden, ramshackle building that seemed to date back at least a hundred years and, from my window overlooking the market, made drawings daily." The market Epstein sketched, called the "Pig-market," had been described by Riis in 1890. "The name was given to it probably in derision, for pork is the one ware that is not on sale in the Pig-market. There is scarcely anything else that

The Hester Street market, which Jacob Epstein sketched around 1888.

can be hawked from a wagon that is not to be found, and at ridiculously low prices." Today a descendant of this great market, crowded with sidewalk stalls filled primarily with clothing, can be found in the several blocks of Orchard Street stretching south of Delancey Street.

Hapgood was not the first to be drawn to the Lower East Side. His editor, Lincoln Steffens, had written of a slightly earlier period: "I at that time was almost a Jew. I had become as infatuated with the Ghetto as eastern boys were with the wild west, and nailed a mazuza on my office door . . ."

Nor would Hapgood be the last. Van Wyck Brooks often "spent the whole of a Sunday at a café on East Houston Street, reading and writing at one of the marble-topped tables. I was surrounded there by the real mysteries of the ghetto and by Yiddish actors and newspapermen playing chess and drinking tea like figures from the Russian novels I was greedily absorbing." Later, in the twenties, the Lower East Side drew other writers. E. E. Cummings recorded the pleasures he found there in a poem that begins "My eyes are fond of the east side." He wrote of the peddlers of "smooth fruits of eager colours" and "little, huddling nuts" and the pleasant torture of the "L's" roar.

On Saturday nights, John Dos Passos and his friends gathered at Moscowitz's "Rumanian Broilings" near Second Avenue. The restaurant had originally been located on Rivington Street, where it was a wine cellar popular with the Rumanians. Moscowitz played the gypsy cymbalon in a long narrow basement painted with scenes of Rumanian life. At one end, under the American flag, was a picture of Theodore Roosevelt at San Juan Hill; at the other, a Zionist flag draping a picture of Theodor Herzl. Steaks were grilled on a spit over an open charcoal fire. The Café Royale, at 12th Street and Second Avenue, where Cummings and Dos Passos also went, attracted an uptown crowd that mixed with the actors and playwrights who participated in the Yiddish theater, then thriving on Second Avenue.

In the thirties, books written by those who had grown up in the ghetto began to appear. Michael Gold, who was the leading spokesman of the Communist party in this country during that decade, opened his book, *Jews Without Money,* with a description of the street where he had lived: "A tenement canyon hung with fire-escapes, bed-clothing, and faces. Always these faces at the tenement windows. The street never failed them. It was an immense excitement. It never slept. It roared like a sea. It exploded like fireworks." One of the books became a classic. Henry Roth's *Call It Sleep,* a novel that portrays the experience of a six-year-old immigrant boy named David, was first published in 1934 but was ignored until it was reissued in 1960. Through the child's perceptions, the East Side neighborhood at 9th Street and Avenue D, where his family comes to live, is seen as "an avalanche of sound" — the conglomerate noises of beer wagons, garbage carts, coal trucks and boat horns.

Roth wrote the one novel and began a second, which he destroyed unfinished even though Maxwell Perkins of Scribner's had approved its opening pages. In the years since, he has worked as a substitute teacher, a precision metal grinder, a state hospital attendant, a tutor in mathematics and Latin and, finally, a farmer of ducks and geese in Augusta, Maine. Asked in 1971 why he had stopped writing, he answered, speaking of himself in the third person, in an article for the *New York Times:*

Continuity was destroyed when his family moved from snug, orthodox 9th Street, from the homogeneous East Side to rowdy, heterogeneous Harlem . . . That which informed him, connective tissue of his people, inculcated by *cheder,* countenanced by the street, sanctioned by God, all that dissolved when his parents moved from the East Side to Mick Harlem. The struts

went and the staves. It would have to follow that the personality became amorphous, ambiguous, at once mystical and
soiled, at once unbridled, inquisitive, shrinking. No longer at
home. I guess that's the word, after this smother of words.
No longer at home.

Roth's experience — moving out of and up from the ghetto
— was a typical one for the great majority of families on the
Lower East Side. With time, those who could leave did until,
by the fifties, the neighborhood's characteristic Jewish accent
was almost entirely silenced. In 1974 the *Forward* Building,
perhaps the most significant landmark of the Jewish Lower
East Side, was sold to a Chinese-American organization, sym-
bolically marking the changes already long established in the
neighborhood. Meanwhile, however, a new character had
come to the section of the Lower East Side above Houston
Street. Instead of the cafés where the immigrant intellectuals
had gathered, there were now coffee houses where young
avant-garde poets read their work. The Yiddish theater, which
once had flourished on Second Avenue, was replaced by a
burgeoning of experimental playhouses. Even painters, lured
by inexpensive studio and gallery space, came to inhabit the
area. Once again the Lower East Side had an artistic life.

The East Village

In the early fifties, as rents rose ever higher in Greenwich
Village, writers began to find homes on the Lower East Side.
Although Allen Ginsberg, Jack Kerouac and Norman Mailer
drank in the San Remo on Bleecker Street or the White Horse
on Hudson, they went home to the region east of Third Avenue. Gradually the migration into the area north of Houston

and south of 14th Street swelled until the neighborhood came to be known as the East Village. Its tenement-lined streets, where rents were among the cheapest in the city, provided an incubating ground for the writers of the "Beat Generation." Later, in an outcast tradition exemplified by these writers, the East Village became the center of the counterculture of the sixties, producing its most avant-garde poetry and theater and representing its lifestyle at its most extreme.

Much of the East Village was originally the farm of Peter Stuyvesant, which stretched from Broadway to the river and from 5th to 17th streets. In the early nineteenth century the land was broken into lots, and prosperous New Yorkers lived in the brick houses that still stand on 10th Street, Stuyvesant Street, St. Mark's Place and other blocks on the area's western edge. Washington Irving lived in historic Colonnade Row at 428 to 434 Lafayette Street (the Astor Place Theatre now occupies 434), in 1836; and James Fenimore Cooper rented 6 St. Mark's Place in 1834. Later the tenements Henry Roth described were built farther to the east. More recently the area has been a patchwork of ethnic enclaves — Poles, Ukrainians, Italians, Puerto Ricans and Jews living in clusters side by side — and it was not until the arrival of the Beats that it began to take on the literary dimension it has today.

The Beat Generation is sometimes said to have been made up of four people — Allen Ginsberg, Jack Kerouac, William Burroughs and Gregory Corso. Although Ginsberg, Kerouac and Burroughs had met around Columbia University and Ginsberg traces the birth of the Beat sensibility to an apartment on 115th Street and Morningside Drive (see Chapter VIII, The West Side), they came to be most strongly associated with the Lower East Side. It is tempting to link the "beatness" of the movement with the current desolation of the neighborhood, but Ginsberg says there is no connection.

Allen Ginsberg's photograph of Jack Kerouac on the fire
escape of Ginsberg's East 7th Street apartment, 1953.

"New York was Charlie Chaplin-land then," he said. "You'd walk around the city hearing 'Rhapsody in Blue' in your head."

The term *Beat* referred to a certain sensibility rather than a physical state or surroundings. It was Kerouac who gave it a name. In an article called "The Origins of the Beat Generation," he wrote, "John Clellon Holmes . . . and I were sitting around trying to think up the meaning of the Lost Generation and the subsequent existentialism and I said, 'You know, this is really a beat generation' and he leapt up and said 'That's it, that's right.' " According to Holmes, who also wrote an article on the subject, Kerouac described Beat as meaning "being right down to it, to ourselves, because we all *really* know where we are — and a weariness with all the forms, all the conventions of the world." Whatever Beat may have meant exactly — Kerouac later said it was "beatific"; Holmes likened it to Kierkegaardian rather than Sartrean existentialism; and Ginsberg and Kerouac had originally heard the term from a Times Square junkie named Herbert Huncke — it came to represent a revolt against both the political and literary establishments in favor of a glorification of spontaneous, personal and mystical, rather than academic, experience.

Ginsberg was the first of the Beats to move to the Lower East Side. He had been hanging out in Village bars since 1948 and in 1951 took an apartment at 206 East 7th Street, which rapidly became an outpost for his friends. Here he regularly received letters from Burroughs, who was in South America and Mexico. In 1953, two years after Burroughs accidentally killed his wife (he tried to shoot a glass off her head in an imitation of William Tell), he came back to New York and moved in with Ginsberg. Burroughs assembled his letters as two books — *The Yage Letters* and *Queer* — and Ginsberg, in one of the first of his endless activities as agent, publicist, promoter, mediator and exchange bureau for poets and writers,

set out to get them published. Earlier, he had been successful
with *Junkie,* which he sold to his friend Carl Solomon at Ace
Books. (Ginsberg had met Solomon, to whom he later dedicated *Howl,* when both were patients at Columbia Psychiatric
Institute.) *Junkie,* set in part in a tenement apartment on
the Lower East Side, told the story of Burroughs's addiction
to morphine and heroin. It was originally published as *Junkie*
by "William Lee." Meanwhile, Ginsberg was writing the
first three poems of *Reality Sandwiches.*

Jack Kerouac often stayed at the 7th Street apartment and
it was there that he met the woman he would depict as Mardou
Fox in *The Subterraneans.* The relationship that ensued was
more intense than his generally superficial affairs with women.
For two months he spent a great deal of time in her apartment
at 501 East 11th Street, a glorified tenement building with an
inner courtyard known to the Beats as "Paradise Alley." After
the affair was over, Kerouac went home to Queens and wrote
The Subterraneans in "three full moon nights" of October
1953, typing at his mother's kitchen table.

Like all of Kerouac's books, *The Subterraneans* is a barely
disguised retelling of his own experience. Kerouac is Leo
Percepied, Allen Ginsberg is Adam Moorad, William Burroughs is Frank Carmody and Gregory Corso is Uri Gligoric.
Kerouac shifts the scene from Paradise Alley to a fictional
Heavenly Lane in San Francisco. But the novel is an exact
description of the Lower East Side scene of the time, with its
parties, jazz and drugs. He describes

the Pierre-of-Melville goof and wonder of it, the dark little
beat burlap dresses, the stories you'd hear about great tenormen
shooting junk by broken windows and starting at their horns, or
great young pads with beats lying high in Rouault-like saintly ob-
scurities, Heavenly Lane the famous Heavenly Lane where
they'd all at one time or another the beat subterraneans lived

. . . seeing it for the first time . . . the wash hung over the court, actually the back courtyard of a big 20-family tenement with bay windows, the wash hung out and in the afternoon the great symphony of Italian mothers, children, fathers BeFinneganing and yelling from stepladders, smells, cats mewing, Mexicans, the music from all the radios whether bolero of Mexican or Italian tenor of spaghetti eaters or loud suddenly turned-up KPFA symphonies of Vivaldi harpischord intellectuals performances boom blam the tremendous sound of it . . .

In invoking the "Pierre-of-Melville" comparison, Kerouac makes the link the Beats frequently did between themselves and other writers once outcast and in disrepute like Melville and Whitman. John Clellon Holmes, in an essay on Kerouac called "The Great Rememberer," draws a direct parallel: "Melville, armed with the manuscript of *Typee*, must have struck the Boston Brahmins in much the same way. Stocky, medium-tall, Kerouac had the tendoned forearms, heavily muscled thighs and broad neck of a man who exults in his physical life." And Ginsberg, like Kerouac, compares life on the Lower East Side in the fifties with the society of poets and outcasts Melville had depicted in *Pierre* a hundred years earlier. "Like *The Subterraneans*," said Ginsberg, "*Pierre* depicts the gnostic, garbage culture of its time." With the Lower East Side experience, Beat broadened its dimensions. Said Ginsberg: "This was the loam or soil out of which a lot of it grew . . . the apocalyptic sensibility, the interest in the mystic arts, the marginal leavings, the garbage of society . . . the beginning of Department of Sanitation culture."

Beat, therefore, was a social stance first — an attitude of protest against the establishment. It was a protest, again, as a literary movement — the Beats stood in opposition to the writing and criticism of the academy in favor of the literature drawn from their own spontaneous experience. Seymour Krim reduces it to the simplest terms: "The real thing to remember is that they were people . . . who had respect for their own experience and wanted to write from it."

Technically, William Carlos Williams was the Beats' major poetic influence. They took his dictum, "No ideas but in things," as a starting point ("Williams' precise real images are such a relief after affected iambics," said Ginsberg) and learned from his use of the natural breath in the poetic line. But they went on from there to develop a kind of prosody that Ginsberg has sometimes compared to jazz and called "spontaneous bop prosody," the syntax and rhythms arising out of the attempt to "transcribe the thought all at once so that its ramifications appear on the page."

And there was always the extraliterary influence of drugs. Burroughs's *Naked Lunch* was written on cannabis; Kerouac did virtually all his work on benzedrine; Ginsberg wrote *Howl* on peyote for visions. Later, there would come experimentation with the altered states of consciousness, which Ginsberg recorded in a series of poems named for the drugs under which they were produced, like "Lysergic Acid" and "Mescaline."

In the third poem in *Reality Sandwiches,* "The Green Automobile," Ginsberg wrote: "If I had a Green Automobile/I'd go find my old companion/in his house on the Western ocean." The poem was addressed to Neal Cassady, who had been Ginsberg's lover and who was the hero of Kerouac's *On the Road.* Cassady occupied a rather mythic position in the Beat pantheon, both as hero and as muse, and it was he rather than any literary scene that drew Ginsberg and Kerouac to California. There were, however, a number of poets living in the San Francisco area — Michael McClure, Gary Snyder, Philip Whalen, Philip Lamantia and, from an older generation, Kenneth Rexroth — and Ginsberg's great organizational energies and publicity instincts catalyzed what was to be called the San Francisco Renaissance. In 1955, two years after arriving in California, Ginsberg organized a reading of six poets and there first read *Howl*. The poem, which launched the Beat poets in the public mind, recalled the Lower East Side experience of those

> who ate fire in paint hotels or drank turpentine in Paradise
> Alley, death, or purgatoried their torsos night after night
> with dreams, with drugs, with waking nightmares, alcohol and
> cock and endless balls . . .

While the Beats were in California, Norman Mailer was living out another Lower East Side experience. In 1951, after returning to New York from Hollywood, he had moved to a simple, cold water flat on Pitt Street, "way over on the Lower East Side beneath the Williamsburg Bridge, a grim apartment, renovated in battle-ship gray," as he described it in *Advertisements for Myself*. He was trying to write stories for magazines, without much success, and at the same time thinking disconnectedly about a long novel. One morning he woke with the plan in his mind for a prologue and eight-book work concerning the adventures of a mythical hero named Sergius O'Shaughnessy. Mailer plunged into part one, *The Deer Park*, and when he finished the first draft decided to forget the eight-novel concept. *The Deer Park*, said to be about Mailer's second wife, Adele Morales, draws on his experience in Hollywood and ends with its protagonist living in a "hole in New York, a cold-water flat outside the boundary of the Village."

Mailer's next address was 39 First Avenue, the top floor of a five-story red brick tenement. Dan Wolf, who later founded the *Village Voice* with Mailer and Ed Fancher, lived on the top floor of the house next door and would walk over the roof to visit. "There was a kosher brewery or winery on the ground floor and its odor permeated the building," recalled Wolf.

Mailer's next address was a huge loft on Monroe Street — "you needed a bicycle to go from one end to another," says Wolf. Here Mailer held enormous parties attended by hundreds of people, some of them celebrities. "It was a very rough neighborhood, and at one of the parties — I remember Montgomery Clift was there that night," said Dan Wolf, "a bunch of toughs came in. They began hitting Norman over the head with a hammer. It was the stunned and silent fifties and nobody rose to the occasion and helped him." After this experience Mailer left the Lower East Side for the more civilized East Fifties.

In 1957, with his essays "The White Negro" and "Reflections on Hip," Mailer charted his own variant of Beat, which he called "hip." Later he differentiated between the two attitudes in "Hipster and Beatnik." "The Beat Generation," he wrote, "is probably best used to include hipsters and beatniks . . . Still, it must be said that the differences between hipsters and beatniks may be more important than their similarities, even if they share the following general characteristics: Marijuana, jazz, not much money, and a community of feeling that society is the prison of the nervous system." Mailer went on to distinguish between the hipster as coming out of "a muted rebellion of the proletariat" and the beatnik as coming from the middle class and choosing not to work as a "sentence against the conformity of his parents." While hipster and beatnik agreed on "the first tenet of the faith: that one's orgasm is the clue to how well one is living," their bodies were not the same: the hipster moves like a cat and dresses with chic while the beatnik is slovenly and has less body with which to lift himself by his sexual bootstraps. For a time, Mailer allied himself with the hipsters and classified Ginsberg and Kerouac in a hybrid group, the "hipniks and beatsters."

In 1957 Allen Ginsberg and Jack Kerouac came back east and found, like prophets who leave their own countries and achieve recognition, that California had made them famous. Strangely, they were now referred to as "San Francisco poets," which both they and the true San Franciscans found insulting. But succcess was finally theirs. *Evergreen Review* published a special issue on the San Francisco Renaissance, which included *Howl* and a piece by Kerouac. Malcolm Cowley, one of Kerouac's early supporters, had finally aroused enough enthusiasm at the Viking Press for the publication of *On the Road,* and *The Subterraneans* was scheduled for publication by Grove Press. *Howl* was sold out at the Eighth Street Bookshop and the Gotham Book Mart. The *Village Voice* heralded the writers' arrival with an article headlined WITLESS MADCAPS COME HOME TO ROOST. But they did not roost long. Kerouac, Ginsberg, Corso and Peter Orlovsky, whom Ginsberg had met in San Francisco, all left for Tangier to visit William Burroughs.

Kerouac was back in New York within three months but Ginsberg and Orlovsky spent two years in Europe. In 1959 they returned to the Lower East Side and moved into Apartment 16 at 170 East 2nd Street, a red brick building with white stone trim one notch above a tenement. The apartment is the setting for Ginsberg's "I beg you come back & be cheerful," which captures the mixed Spanish-Jewish quality of the neighborhood.

> Tonite I got hi in the window of my apartment
> chair at 3 : AM
> gazing at Blue incandescent torches
> bright-lit street below
> clotted shadows loomin on a new laid pave
> — as last week Medieval rabbiz
> plodded thru the brown raw
> dirt turned over — sticks
> & cans
> and tired ladies sitting on spanish
> garbage pails — in the deadly heat . . .

Here Ginsberg wrote "Kaddish" and edited Burroughs's *Naked Lunch* (the title was originally *Naked Lust* but Kerouac misread it and Burroughs liked his version better). Ginsberg found himself at the center of the scene, which had expanded to include such writers as Diane di Prima, Tuli Kupferberg, Seymour Krim, LeRoi Jones and Hubert Selby. The Cedar Street Tavern at 24 University Place between 8th and 9th streets,* which had been a hangout for abstract expressionist painters like Jackson Pollock, Franz Kline and Willem de Kooning, who had studios and galleries on the Lower East Side, also became the watering place of the Beats. "Who was there?" asked Seymour Krim. "Well, everybody you might expect — Holmes, Ginsberg, Corso and occasionally Kerouac and then others that might be thought of more as the Black Mountain crowd — [Hubert] Selby, Gilbert Sorrentino, and for a while Robert Creeley."

Also "there" was the poet Frank O'Hara, who linked painters and writers through his work as an associate curator of the Museum of Modern Art. "John Ashbery, Barbara Guest, Kenneth Koch and I, being poets," he wrote, "divided our time between the literary bar, the San Remo, and the artists' bar, the Cedar Tavern. In the San Remo we argued and gossiped: in the Cedar we often wrote poems while listening to the painters argue and gossip. So far as I know nobody painted in the San Remo while they listened to the writers argue." In 1957 O'Hara moved downtown to 90 University Place, an old three-story gray brick building. The apartment appears in one of what he called his " 'I do this I do that' poems":

> I live above a dyke bar and I'm happy.
> The police car is always near the door
>   in case they cry

* The Cedar, its original building torn down to make way for an apartment house, moved up the street to 82 University Place.

Allen Ginsberg and Frank O'Hara at 791 Broadway during a party
for the Italian poet Giuseppe Ungaretti, May 1964.

or the key doesn't work in the lock. But
         he can't open it either. So we go to Joan's
and sleep over,
             Bridget and Joe and I.
I meet Mike for a beer in the Cedar as
the wind flops up the Place, pushing the leaves
against the streetlights . . .

In 1959 O'Hara moved deep into the East Side to 441 East 9th Street. This apartment was "a tenement dump, a two-room flat," said Patsy Southgate, poet, translator and close friend of O'Hara's. "Frank preferred to spend his money on cabs, restaurants, liquor, cigarettes, rather than living quarters." Among O'Hara's close friends were Ginsberg, Koch and LeRoi Jones. "People just dropped by," said Southgate. "They drank at his house and then went out to a restaurant to eat — Il Bambino, El Charro, John's on East Tenth Street and Second Avenue, Joe's, Angelina's or the Cedar bar. Once at Ninth Street and Avenue A I spent a whole evening trying to convince LeRoi than James Baldwin had a point and wasn't really so radical. LeRoi had nothing but white friends."

In 1964 O'Hara moved to 791 Broadway, across from Grace Church. "The apartment was a sort of elegant big loft facing the rose window of the church. It was all painted white, including the floor," said Patsy Southgate. "There were paintings by De Kooning, Frankenthaler, Motherwell, Franz Kline, Mike Goldberg and Joan Mitchell. It was his first sort of 'grand lodgings.' Usually the TV set would be on and Frank would be on the phone and probably the record player would be on and the icebox would be empty. I never saw anything in it except orange juice for making screwdrivers and maybe a prune whip yoghurt."

One night O'Hara, Jones and the painter Larry Rivers were to be on a television panel together. "LeRoi turned up at Frank's with a lot of blacks and all of a sudden fought with Frank over a glass," remembered Southgate. "When we got to the TV program he gave his famous speech in which he said 'the only good white man is a dead white man.' Then he moved up to Harlem."

LeRoi Jones, now known as Amiri Baraka, had lived first in a one-and-a-half-room apartment on the top floor of 7 Morton

Street in the West Village, where he and his wife, Hettie, put out a magazine called *Yugen,* financed on her salary as manager of the *Partisan Review.* The magazine, which published many of the Beat writers, was named for a Zen term that meant "flower of the miraculous." Hettie prepared the magazine on an old IBM electric typewriter. "The people in San Francisco said 'Oh, it's such a messy thing,' " she recalled. "No one had considered amateurism before. We didn't have any money but we thought these things were valuable to put out." At one point a controversy regarding the nature of poetry between those Hettie Jones called "the crazy faction — Allen, Gregory, Peter and Jack" and "the Black Mountain plus New York people — Frank, Kenneth Koch, John Ashbery" raged over several issues. During its course O'Hara wrote "Personism: A Manifesto" in which he stated that the poem should be "between two persons instead of two pages." In writing, "you just go on your nerve. If someone's chasing you down the street with a knife you just run, you don't turn around and shout, 'Give it up! I was a track star for Mineola Prep' . . . As for measure and other technical apparatus, that's just common sense: if you're going to buy a pair of pants you want them to be tight enough so everyone will want to go to bed with you."

At this time the Joneses also published books in collaboration with Eli Wilentz of the Eighth Street Book Shop under the imprint of Totem Books. The most important of these was Charles Olson's *Projective Verse,* in which he outlined the concepts that would dominate the poetry of the sixties. There were three main principles: "A poem is energy transferred from where the poet got it . . . by way of the poem itself to, all the way over to, the reader. FORM IS NEVER MORE THAN AN EXTENSION OF CONTENT. And, ONE PERCEPTION MUST IMMEDIATELY AND DIRECTLY LEAD TO A FURTHER PERCEPTION."

In the fall of 1958, the Joneses moved to 402 West 20th Street and then in 1960 to 324 East 14th Street — the parlor floor of a Victorian house that has since been radically remodeled. "It was huge, baronial and a bitch to clean," said Hettie. "This home soon became a center for people who would stay overnight, like Joel Oppenheimer who lived in the Bronx and Gilbert Sorrentino who lived in Brooklyn or those like John Wieners and Gary Snyder who came from out west and stayed longer." There were immense parties: "I could feed hundreds on one pot of spaghetti."

By the sixties, said Hettie, "the Lower East Side had become a 'scene.' There was the Cedar bar, happenings and the beginning of black bohemia." The writers also hung out at the Five Spot, where owner Iggy Tormini let musicians like Billie Holiday perform without cabaret cards, and writers and artists listen without paying. On July 17, 1959, on reading of the death of Billie Holiday in the newspaper, O'Hara wrote "The Day Lady Died," which ended with the lines:

> then I go back where I came from 6th Avenue
> and the tobacconist in the Ziegfeld Theatre and
> casually ask for a carton of Gauloises and a carton
> of Picayunes, and a NEW YORK POST with her face on it
> and I am sweating a lot by now and thinking of
> leaning on the john door in the 5 SPOT
> while she whispered a song along the keyboard
> to Mal Waldron and everyone and I stopped breathing . . .

In the winter of 1962 the Joneses moved again, this time to 27 Cooper Square. They installed heating in what had previously been a "cold-water flophouse for bums with upward mobility" and here LeRoi wrote *Blues People* before moving uptown to Harlem.

Unaffiliated with Beat, hip or any of their variants, W. H. Auden lived quietly on the Lower East Side from 1953 to 1972 at 77 St. Mark's Place, where Trotsky had printed *Novy Mir* in

Christopher Isherwood and W. H. Auden in Central Park, 1938.

the basement. Auden's ties were with the academics and West Side intellectuals whom the Beats opposed. In fact, one evening at the Trillings', Auden chided Diana Trilling for having been moved by a Ginsberg reading. A visitor described Auden's second-floor walkup as it was in 1971: "Auden writes on a new portable typewriter ('the best money can buy') in his small, windowless living room, which is cluttered with books, phonograph records and manuscripts. Off the living room are a sleeping alcove with a rumpled bed, a kitchen where he cooks gourmet meals . . . for himself and his friends and another room, also cluttered, which overlooks St. Mark's Place." Although not a presence on the neighborhood poetry scene, Auden was a parishioner at his local church, the historic St. Mark's-in-the-Bouwerie, and a familiar figure to local shopkeepers.

In 1963, when Allen Ginsberg and Peter Orlovsky returned after traveling in South America, Europe and India, they found the Lower East Side in full swing. The media had discovered the area's intense poetic activity and made it the subject of a publicity explosion. Poetry readings had begun in 1960 at the 10th Street Coffee-House, owned by Mickey Ruskin. On Mondays there were open readings and on Wednesdays a guest poet was invited. In 1961 Ruskin bought Les Deux Megots [sic] Coffeehouse on East 7th Street and the poetry readings moved there. At the end of '62 Ruskin gave up Les Deux Megots and the readings were re-established in the winter of 1963 at the Café Le Metro. Generally 125 people would be allowed in and another twenty-five or fifty waited outside. During 1964, readings held on radio, in bars, theaters, art galleries and churches diversified and proliferated.

There were many little magazines and a number of important subcommunities. One of these was a group of black poets called the Society of Umbra, which set up its own workshop and magazine. Among those originally involved were Calvin Hernton and David Henderson. *Umbra* was still publishing as recently as 1970–71, when Larry Neal, Ishmael Reed, Toni Cade, LeRoi Jones, Langston Hughes and Nikki Giovanni were among the writers represented in an issue edited by David Henderson.

Another group formed around Diane di Prima and Alan Marlowe's American Theatre for Poets, which presented happenings, dance programs and a series of new one-act plays, including works by Diane di Prima, Robert Duncan, LeRoi Jones, Frank O'Hara, and Michael McClure. Di Prima, who lived at 31 Cooper Square, also published a large and varied selection of books through the Poet's Press, which she founded, and *The Floating Bear,* a magazine that she had cofounded with LeRoi Jones in February 1961.

Although he was not involved with the East Village scene, one of the most important figures in the experimental theater lived for several years on the Lower East Side. Jack Gelber had come to New York from San Francisco in 1955 and found a "rundown smelly apartment" at 435 East 5th Street. He paid $11.20 a month for the place, which he shared with a saxophone player whose acquaintances were constantly coming and going. Next he went to live at 11 Pitt Street, where he wrote the *Connection,* based mostly on San Francisco experiences but set in a "shooting gallery" that had something of the atmosphere of his 5th Street apartment.

After the Le Metro poetry readings ended in 1965, the Lower East Side "community climate," as poet and editor Allen de Loach called it, began to ebb. Strangely enough, it was only after it was all over that one of the foremost Beats, Gregory Corso, came to live in the area. In 1967 he lived on 5th Street and Avenue C, "right in the heart of the horror," as he described it. "Oh how oppressive it was!" In the late sixties, in a mass fulfillment of the Beat ethos, the Lower East Side became New York headquarters of the psychedelic counterculture. For a brief period the East Village was a colorful center of rock music and hippie life; ethnic dance halls became discotheques and Yiddish theaters were transformed into rock auditoriums. But the runaways who flocked to the area from all over the country were unprepared for the harshness of tenement life. Today many of the poets, of necessity, still live on the Lower East Side — many others have moved to Westbeth in the West Village — and regular poetry readings at St. Mark's-in-the-Bouwerie maintain the tradition. But the increasing viciousness of the neighborhood has created an atmosphere inhospitable to the vital communal scene that existed in the sixties. Of the major figures only Ginsberg, truly indifferent to material comfort, has remained in the neighborhood. He and Peter Orlovsky lived in the East 10th Street apartment they took in 1965 until 1975 and then moved several blocks away.

Lower East Side Tour 1

Starting at Houston and Mulberry, one can retrace Jacob Riis's route through the Immigrants' City. The area above Grand Street is still "Little Italy" as it was in his day.

1. 149 Mulberry Street at Grand. This 1816 house once belonged to Stephen Van Rensselaer. Originally at 153 Mulberry, it was moved to its

The Lower East Side 1

present location in 1841, and is now Paolucci's Restaurant (p. 111-12).

2. The street still curves at "Mulberry Bend" between Bayard and Park streets, although the pushcarts and most of the tenements are gone (p. 112).

3. 18 Bowery, on the southwest corner of Pell Street. This is the oldest surviving row house in Manhattan. Built about 1785 by Edward Mooney, it was remodeled in 1807 and restored in 1971 (p. 112).

(3a) Straight south at Franklin Square, where Pearl Street passes under the Brooklyn Bridge roadway, was 3 Cherry Street; George Washington lived here for a year, in 1789, when New York was the nation's capital (p. 112). Cherry Street extended northeast, through what is now the Governor Al Smith Houses (p. 113).

(3b) To the north the Bowery extends fourteen blocks to Cooper Square. Today between Chatham Square and Houston Street, there are only two bars (p. 115).

Across Chatham Square, East Broadway leads into what was "the great ghetto" (pp. 113–14). Very little of the Jewish neighborhood survives.

4. 165 East Broadway, on the southeast corner of Rutgers Street. This is the site of the Garden Cafeteria, once frequented by writers from the *Jewish Daily Forward,* and now the Wing Shing Restaurant (p. 118).

5. 175 East Broadway. The *Forward* building, twelve stories high, was built in 1912 by architect George A. Boehm (p. 119). Sold in 1974, it is now New York Ling Liang Church. Before 1912 the Forward offices were in a store across the street facing the present building (pp. 116–17).

6. 183 East Broadway is the former home of the *Day;* and 187 East Broadway is where the *Tageblatt* was published (p. 119).

(6a) 102 Hester Street, between Eldridge and Forsythe streets. Jacob Epstein lived here at age nineteen, overlooking the "Pig Market" (p. 120).

7. Orchard Street from Delancey to Houston streets is an outdoor market reminiscent of the Hester Street market that existed in Jacob Riis's time (pp. 120–22).

Lower East Side Tour 2

The square mile or so of the East Village is a study in ethnic diversity. At its northern end, the neighborhood is strongly Spanish, and now has

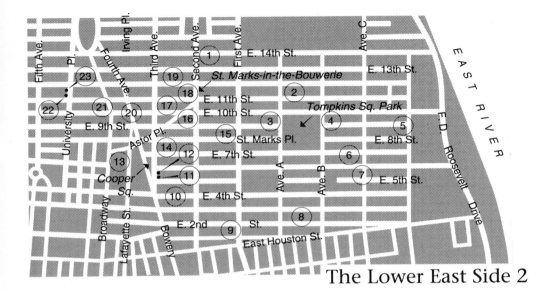

The Lower East Side 2

many East Indian shop owners. Walking toward the south and east, one sees vestiges of the Italian culture Jack Kerouac described in *The Subterraneans* in 1953. Farther south the neighborhood is Eastern European—Ukrainian and Polish—in flavor.

1. 324 East 14th Street. LeRoi and Hettie Jones lived on the parlor floor of this Victorian house in 1960–62, before it was radically remodeled (p. 138).

2. 501 East 11th Street. Kerouac's "Paradise Alley" is now a parking lot (p. 128).

3. 441 East 9th Street. Frank O'Hara lived here from 1959 to 1964 in a "tenement dump" (p. 136). From his window he could see St. Brigid's Church, diagonally across Tompkins Square Park, and described it in his poem, "Weather Near St. Bridget's Steeples."

> You are so beautiful and trusting
> lying there on the sky
> > through the leaves
> you seem to be breathing softly
> you look slightly nude, as if the clouds had parted

4. 151 Avenue B, between 9th and 10th streets. Charlie Parker lived here from 1950 to 1954. His residence in the neighborhood, along with Allen Ginsberg's on East 7th Street, inspired artists, musicians, and writers to move to the Lower East Side.

5. 9th Street and Avenue D is the setting of Henry Roth's *Call It Sleep* (1960). Roth might not recognize it now, with its towers of a housing development on one side and mixture of abandoned and torn-down buildings on the other. In the empty lots is an odd resurrection of vegetable gardens, little shanties, and chickens wandering around. His next book (1987) was called *Shifting Landscape* (pp. 123–24).

6. 206 East 7th Street. Allen Ginsberg moved here in 1951 (pp. 127–28) and William Burroughs came to stay in 1953. This tenement must look just as it did then, with its high stoop and ten-foot-high double doors.

7. Avenue C and 5th Street. Gregory Corso moved here in 1967, when this area was at its most desolate, and the Beat movement was largely over (p. 141). The neighborhood is now somewhat upbeat, with block-long, pink three-story housing, and active street life. In 1986 Avenue C was officially given an additional name, Loisaida Avenue (pronounced low-ees-SIDE-a), the Puerto Rican version of Lower East Side.

8. 170 East 2nd Street, where Allen Ginsberg and Peter Orlovsky moved in 1959, and where he wrote "Kaddish" (pp. 133–34).

9. 39 First Avenue. Norman Mailer lived here on the top floor when there was a kosher brewery in the basement (pp. 131–32).

10. 4th Street, between Second Avenue and the Bowery, was the heart of Off-Off-Broadway. The Café LaMama at 74A East 4th is still here; The Truck and Warehouse at 79 East 4th is now called the Fourth Wall Political Theatre, but Diane di Prima's East End Theatre at 85 East 4th is now a Ukrainian news store.

11. 27 Cooper Square, where LeRoi Jones lived before moving up to Harlem (pp. 138, 136).

12. 31 Cooper Square, where Diane di Prima lived (p. 140-41).

In this stretch of the Bowery, south to Houston Street, there is not a single bar these days; but a few doors east on 7th Street is McSorley's, immortalized by Joseph Mitchell in *McSorley's Wonderful Saloon*.

13. 434 Lafayette St. The Astor Place Theater occupies part of historic Colonnade Row, which includes numbers 428–434. With its Corinthian columns, the row is considered one of the finest examples of the treatment of a series of houses as a single architectural unit (p. 125). Four of the original nine houses are still standing.

14. 4 St. Mark's Place. In 1834 James Fenimore Cooper rented a town house here which included two drawing rooms, a dining room, and eight bedrooms (p. 125).

15. 77 St. Mark's Place. W.H. Auden spent his winters here from 1953 to 1972 (pp. 138–40).

16. 149 Second Avenue. Home of the Café Le Metro from 1963 to 1965, where numerous poetry readings took place (p. 140). For a while it was the Beautiful Way, a vegetarian restaurant; now it is Telephone, a coffeehouse.

17. 117 East 10th Street, between Second and Third avenues. Dwight Macdonald lived in this red-brick row house, where many gatherings of the *Partisan Review* staff were held.

18. 10th Street and Second Avenue. St. Mark's-in-the-Bouwerie, where Auden was a parishioner. The building was constructed in 1799, and the steeple was added in 1828, It has been for some years a leading center for poetry readings.

19. 210 East 13th Street. While Emma Goldman resided on the top floor of one of these twin buildings, from 1904 to 1913, she published the journal *Mother Earth* (pp. 119–20). The buildings were erected in 1903. Goldman probably lived in the east building, now numbered 212.

20. Fourth Avenue from 9th Street to 14th Street. Today there is not one bookstore left on the famous old Booksellers' Row; the last survivor is Pageant, around the corner at 109 East 9th Street.

21. 791 Broadway, between 10th and 11th streets. An old four-story building, where Frank O'Hara had his white-painted loft in 1964 (p. 136).

(21a) 24 University Place. The original Cedar Street Tavern was a storefront three doors north of 8th Street in a six-story loft building (p. 134).

22. 82 University Place. The new Cedar Street Tavern is here, owned by the same family, with the same pictures on the walls.

23. 90 University Place. In 1957 Frank O'Hara moved to this old three-story building, which has been refaced in antique red brick. The "dyke bar" is now a Japanese restaurant (p. 134).

IV. Gramercy Park

IN THE 1850s, Edith Wharton records, "the pioneers of the younger set were just beginning to affect" the area around Gramercy Park. By "younger set" Wharton meant the aristocratic younger set, of course, and descendants of the old Knickerbocker families were to be found in the new neighborhood. Theodore Roosevelt was born in 1858 in a black-shuttered brownstone at 28 East 20th Street, and Washington Irving's nephew John Treat Irving, Jr., lived in another brownstone at 46 East 21st Street. Among the new residents were some with literary connections. Horace Greeley had bought a three-story brick house at 35 East 19th Street in the early fifties. More accustomed to the wilds of Turtle Bay, where he had lived earlier, Greeley found the row unfamiliar and often tried his key at other doors in his block. Perhaps to preserve a little of the country atmosphere he was used to, he kept a goat in the backyard. Encouraged by Greeley, the Cary sisters, Alice and Phoebe, came to New York from Cincinnati and established something of a salon at their house at 52 East 20th Street. The

The Cary sisters' house
at 52 East 20th Street.

sisters were poets (the 1850 city directory lists "Alice Cary, authoress"), and for over fifteen years they held Sunday evening receptions attended by literary New Yorkers.

Although the Roosevelt, Irving and Greeley houses survive, they are overwhelmed by the warehouses and tall commercial buildings that now crowd around Fifth Avenue and Broadway. Scarcely noticeable, they are anomalies in an area given over to manufacture and shipping. One must go east to Irving Place and the region immediately surrounding Gramercy Park to recapture the quality of the neighborhood as it was in the nineteenth century. Lazy and residential, Gramercy Park and, even farther east, Stuyvesant Square have given literature little in the way of subject matter but they occasionally have provided writers with homes.

Among the writers who might have been found at the Cary sisters' for a time was Herman Melville, by birth a New Yorker qualified to move in Wharton's set. Melville had moved into the area in 1862 and was briefly at 150 East 18th Street before buying the house at 104 East 26th that was his residence until his death in 1891. In this period of his life Melville's fortunes were in decline. The public had not appreciated *Moby-Dick* or *Pierre* after the simpler South Sea adventure tales that had made his early reputation. He was largely forgotten and was unable to earn a living by his art. "If I wrote the Gospels in this century I should die in the gutter," he lamented, and was forced to earn his living working as a customs inspector, a job he had described in *Redburn* as "a most inglorious one; indeed worse than driving geese to water."

The house in which Melville lived, replaced by the Armory that would house the famous 1913 Armory Show of postimpressionist art, was yellow-painted brick with brownstone trim. "Our home," wrote Melville's granddaughter Frances Thomas Osborne, "was one of a long row of houses on East 26th Street,

each exactly alike except for the number on the door, or perhaps
for the tawny color of the cat walking on the iron fence in
front." There was mahogany furniture in the parlor and a
print of the Bay of Naples hanging in the front hall. Lewis
Mumford, one of the critics who began the rediscovery of
Melville in the 1920s, noted in his biography that the house
had "a quiet interior of its own, an interior like Herman Melville's, acquired before the débâcle of the Civil War. The
brown wallpaper and the black iron bed in the wan north light
of Herman Melville's room almost alone indicate that a day has
dawned that is somewhat darker than a starless night."

Melville customarily took walks to Madison Square with his
granddaughter, but on days that were stormy they used the
"dusty, chill back porch" instead.

> Grandpa would walk back and forth, I trotting alongside in
> this uninteresting sport until I suppose enough energy had
> been worked off to warrant going inside again. One of the
> redeeming features of the piazza walks was the sight of a blue
> and red china butterfly . . . It was high in one corner and,
> looking very life-like to me, I always hoped it would fly
> lower one day so that we could touch it. The other intriguing
> thing was the music of the Aeolian harp on the windowsill.
> The wind blowing through it must have reminded grandpa
> of the wind in the rigging at sea. In *White Jacket* he men-
> tions an Aeolian harp as a cure for the blues.

Finally, in 1885, Melville's wife came into an inheritance and
he was able to retire from the customs house and devote his
days to writing again. Here, at the end of his life, he produced
one last masterpiece, *Billy Budd.*

While Melville was at East 26th Street, Henry James, who
had been abroad, came to live almost back to back at 111 East
25th. James had decided to try New York to see whether it
would allay his craving for Europe. He spent six busy months

in the city completing *Roderick Hudson,* which was running
in the *Atlantic Monthly,* and reviewing books, drama and art
for the *Nation.* He decided that New York had turned him into
a literary hack and confirmed for himself that it was better to
live in Europe. In 1881, when he returned again briefly for a
visit, he stayed at 115 East 25th Street with Edwin Godkin, his
former editor at the *Nation.* Like Melville's house, both of
James's addresses have been swallowed up by the Armory.

While Henry James was explaining the American to Europe,
as Van Wyck Brooks expressed it, William Dean Howells was
explaining the American to America. For about three years,
from late 1888 to 1892, Howells was living on Stuyvesant
Square, first in a two-floor apartment in a huge old house
overlooking the park at 330 East 17th Street and later in a
handsome brownstone at 241 East 17th Street. Howells had
begun to work at Harper's, and the area was convenient to his
office at Franklin Square. He could take the elevated straight
down Third Avenue, an experience he described in *A Hazard
of New Fortunes.* His hero, Basil March, finds "the variety of
people in the car as unfailingly entertaining as ever." Howells
wrote: "New York is still popularly supposed to be in the
control of the Irish, but March noticed in these East Side travels
of his what must strike every observer returning to the city
after a prolonged absence: the numerical subordination of the
dominant race. If they do not outvote them, the people of
Germanic, of Slavonic, of Pelasgic, of Mongolian stock out-
number the prepotent Celts . . .."

Howells wrote *A Hazard of New Fortunes* in the "uppermost
room" of the house at 330 East 17th Street. The novel, which
deals with a gentle, middle-class couple based on Howells and
his wife, documents the author's growth in social consciousness.
March comes to New York from Boston to become the editor of
a literary publication whose offices are on West 11th Street.

Exposed to the anticapitalist ideas of his old tutor, whom he encounters again in the city, the editor moves from a position of complacent liberalism to guarded sympathy. The climax of the book is a confrontation in Union Square based on the Haymarket Square riots in Chicago, where members of labor organizations clashed with the police. As the headquarters of the periodical that March edits could not have been located anywhere else (its publisher says, "There's only one city that belongs to the whole country, and that's New York"), so *A Hazard of New Fortunes* could not have been set in any other place. New York as a wide-open city — a place of opportunity where the poor and the rich, the capitalist and the revolutionary, mingle and clash — is essential to Howells's purposes. As such, *A Hazard of New Fortunes* is the first novel to deal with the city's characteristics in a significant way. The novel stands firmly in the tradition of realism Howells advocated, a revolt against romanticism with an emphasis on the didactic rather than the emotional. "If a novel flatters the passions, and exalts them above the principles, it is poisonous," he stated. "It may not kill, but it will certainly injure." Howells wanted to be realistic in both the presentation of physical details and lives as they were really lived. "We must ask ourselves before we ask anything else, is the novel true? — true to the motives, the impulses, the principles that shape the life of actual men and women?"

In 1893 a young man named Stephen Crane had paid for the publication of his first novel, *Maggie: A Girl of the Streets*, under the pseudonym Johnston Smith. Crane sent a copy of the book to Hamlin Garland, then living on 105th Street in Harlem (in 1897 he would be at 23 Gramercy Park), and Garland suggested he send a copy to Howells. Howells, who had moved uptown to 59th Street, read the novel — it was just the realism he had been waiting for — and invited Crane to

Stephen Crane in a friend's studio, 1893.

tea. Meanwhile, Crane had moved into Howells's old neighborhood and was living with three friends in a studio in the building at 143 East 23rd Street that had housed the Art Students League. Crane's roommates were painters and he described their life in his novel *The Third Violet,* the story of a poor artist who falls in love with an aristocratic young woman. "Occasionally one could hear the tramp of feet in the intricate corridors of the begrimed building which squatted, slumbering and old, between two exalted commercial structures which would have had to bend afar down to perceive it. The northward march of the city's progress had happened not to overturn this aged structure, and it huddled there, lost and forgotten, while the cloud-veering towers strode on." When the gas was lit in the room, "the flood of orange light showed clearly the dull walls lined with sketches, the tousled bed in one corner, the masses of boxes and trunks in another, a little dead stove, and the wonderful table. Moreover there were wine-coloured draperies flung in some places, and on a shelf, high up, there were plaster casts, with dust in the creases . . ." Three of the young men slept in the "tousled" double bed, taking turns in the middle, and the fourth used a cot. They bought their food at a delicatessen named Boeuf-à-la-Mode, nicknamed the Buffalo-Mud. Here Crane completed *The Third Violet*. Almost concurrently, Howells was publishing *The Coast of Bohemia*, set in the same 23rd Street Art Students League. In his notebook Crane wrote an Emerson quotation he had seen chalked in the "topmost and remotest" studio in the building: "Congratulate yourselves if you have done something strange and extravagant and broken the monotony of a decorous age." It was a motto Crane would amply fulfill. Although he left the studio in May 1893, he returned periodically for brief stays and it was here that he finished *The Red Badge of Courage*. One of his roommates, R. G. Vosburgh, recorded that "Every incident and phase of character in *The Red Badge* was discussed fully and completely before being incorporated in the story."

The literary figure most strongly associated with the Gramercy Park area is William Sydney Porter, who went to live at 55 Irving Place in 1903, a year after he arrived in the city. He had signed a contract to produce a story a week for $100 under his pen name, O. Henry, for the *Sunday World,* and his new-found financial security enabled him to take a spacious, comfortable room there. He had a large bay window, in which he would sit for hours watching the people go by along the street, and his room had a white marble fireplace and an old-fashioned chandelier with glass beads and prisms, under which stood a long library table.

Porter turned all the characteristics of his new neighborhood to account. Diagonally across Irving Place was Healy's Café, also known as the Club, which he described in a story called "The Lost Blend." Wearing a slouch hat and a black bow tie, Porter would arrive every night about midnight at the red brick café (today called Pete's Tavern) and stand alone at the end of the bar. Never speaking to anyone, he would drink a few beers and then be gone. A German beer hall and restaurant at Third Avenue and 17th Street was the locale of his story "The Halberdier of the Little Rheinschloss." Called in Porter's time Scheffel Hall, the restaurant is now named Tuesday's; in the story Porter called it the Old Munich. "The big hall with its smoky rafters, rows of imported steins, portrait of Goethe, and verses painted on the walls — translated into German from the original of the Cincinnati poets — seems atmospherically correct when viewed through the bottom of the glass," he wrote. The restaurant still has the smoky rafters, the imported steins and the verses painted on the walls.

Near Fourth Avenue at 15th Street was the Hotel America, and Porter found the Latin Americans who frequented it good inspiration for the characters of his stories. In "The Gold That Glittered," the hotel appears as the Hotel Español. Porter was told that Washington Irving had lived in a yellow house at 17th Street and Irving Place, and he was proud to live "three doors from Irving's old home." Unfortunately, Porter, like many others, was mistaken. The house on 17th Street belonged to a merchant named Edgar Irving. This, and the fact that Irving Place *had* been named for the Knickerbocker writer, may have been responsible for the error memorialized in a misplaced plaque today. When Washington Irving visited the city from Sunnyside in Tarrytown, he stayed with his nephew John Treat Irving at East 21st Street. When the poet Orrick Johns came to live at 53 Irving Place in 1911, he in turn mistakenly believed O. Henry had lived in his house.

Fourth Avenue, now Park Avenue South above 14th Street, was one of Porter's favorite streets and he describes it in "A Bird of Bagdad":

Fourth Avenue — born and bred in the Bowery — staggers northward full of good resolutions.

Where it crosses Fourteenth Street it struts for a brief moment proudly in the glare of the museums and cheap theatres. It may yet become a fit mate for its high-born sister boulevard to the west, or its roaring, polyglot, broad-waisted cousin to the east. It passes Union Square; and here the hoofs of the dray horses seem to thunder in unison, recalling the tread of marching hosts — Hooray! But now come the silent and terrible mountains — buildings square as forts, high as the clouds, shutting out the sky where thousands of slaves bend over desks all day. On the ground floors are only little fruit shops and laundries and book shops . . . And next — poor Fourth Avenue! — the street glides into mediaeval solitude. On each side are the shops devoted to "Antiques."

With a shriek and a crash Fourth Avenue dives headlong into the tunnel at Thirty-fourth and is never seen again.

When Porter died, a funeral service was held at a neighborhood landmark, the Little Church Around the Corner at Fifth Avenue and West 29th Street.

In the late teens and twenties, the *Dial* had several outposts in the area around Gramercy Park. Sibley Watson, who financed the magazine, lived in Rochester but his wife had a house at 140 East 19th Street, one of the area's loveliest blocks. There was a bronze nude by Gaston Lachaise in the two-story living room and expressionist canvases by E. E. Cummings lined the staircases. Down the block at 77 Irving Place lived Paul Rosenfeld, who was the *Dial*'s music critic for seven years. (He had previously lived in an apartment at 20 Gramercy Park, where his friends Waldo Frank, Van Wyck Brooks and Randolph Bourne visited; Bourne died there after being cared for by Rosenfeld in his last illness.)

The *Dial* was a magazine primarily run by mail. What socializing did take place among members of the staff and contributors was likely to occur in Rosenfeld's apartment. Alyse Gregory, the managing editor, described it as "an interior that might have been lifted out of some European capital — Vienna, Paris, Florence — and without disarranging a single picture, or overturning a single vase, set down on the chill, dusty sidewalk of Irving Place, New York. It was an interior both intimate and spacious, an interior for pleasures that were grave and thought that was gay, for conversation witty and civilized." Edmund Wilson remembered it as a place where "poets read their poetry and composers played their music" and recalled conversation "beneath his little collection of Hartleys and O'Keeffes and Marins, surrounded by his shelves full of Nietzsche and Wagner, Strindberg, Shaw and Ibsen . . ." Among the guests who gathered here were Darius Milhaud, Aaron Copland, Edgar Varèse, E. E. Cummings, Hart Crane, Marianne Moore, Alfred Stieglitz, the Stettheimer sisters and Allen Tate.

In 1926 the Irving Place apartment became the unofficial offices of the *American Caravan,* an annual magazine that published new American writers. Rosenfeld and Alfred Kreymborg had conceived the idea and asked Van Wyck Brooks and Lewis Mumford to join with them in selecting manuscripts. Each Saturday afternoon the editors, with the exception of Brooks, who was having a nervous breakdown, gathered at Irving Place to read the manuscripts that had been submitted during the week. Often they would take writers to lunch at Lüchow's on 14th Street, the area's most prominent restaurant, which was also a favorite of Dreiser and Mencken and George Jean Nathan when they were in town.

Robert Penn Warren, then a graduate student at Yale, met Rosenfeld in 1927. He would visit New York on weekends and Rosenfeld took him to exhibits and taught him about art. "The really important thing for me, however," Warren said, "was not the mere fact that Rosenfeld introduced me to modern painting. The important thing was that he managed to set it for me in relation to the impulse behind modern literature." Rosenfeld encouraged Warren, who had been writing poetry, to try fiction. He did, and wrote "Prime Leaf," a novelette about rural Kentucky life, which was published in *American Caravan IV*. When the depression came, Rosenfeld's private income was diminished and he moved to a small apartment on West 11th Street.

During the twenties, writers must have bumped into one another coming and going on 19th Street. Carl Van Vechten and Ernest Boyd, whose homes were also gathering places, were living on the same block as the Sibley Watsons. In 1923 Van Vechten was at 151 East 19th Street in an apartment on the top floor. Although the place was tiny — there was a two-burner stove on top of the icebox — the Van Vechtens made it distinctive by covering the living room walls with red, gold-dotted Chinese tea paper. Ernest Boyd, a critic and litterateur who had come from Ireland, lived at 131 East 19th Street, where he entertained frequently. At one dinner party Scott and Zelda Fitzgerald arrived an hour late, after the others had finished eating, and fell asleep at the table over their soup. "Someone gathered Zelda up, with her bright cropped hair and diaphanous gown, and dropped her on a bed in a room nearby . . ." Van Wÿck Brooks wrote. "Scott slumbered in the living room, waking up suddenly again to telephone an order for two cases of champagne, together with a fleet of taxis to take us to a night-club."

Several blocks away, in contrast to the high intellectual and social life of 19th Street, a struggling young writer was making an unexceptional hotel a gathering place of quite a different sort. In 1927, through the aid of a rich uncle, Nathanael West got a job as night manager of the Kenmore Hall Hotel at 145 East 23rd Street. West's biographer, Jay Martin, describes the hotel: "Badly designed, with small rooms, no restaurant, and neither conference rooms nor a mezzanine, it was saved by its faults; in some ways, it had been planned as a kind of glorified rooming house, its small rooms renting at low rates, its lobby and drugstore, where all the guests naturally congregated, becoming popular as unostentatious meeting places for young men and women."

With little to do after midnight, West read for long hours and entertained his fellow writers — Quentin Reynolds, Dashiell Hammett, Maxwell Bodenheim, Michael Gold and S. J. Perelman — in the early morning hours. Often West, who was called Pep by his friends, would let them stay at the hotel without paying. One night Reynolds discovered that Hammett was halfway through a serial for a pulp detective story magazine called *Black Mask* and was about to be thrown out of his room at another hotel. Reynolds called up West to tell him about it and make a suggestion.

"'Register him under a phony name,' I said. 'When he finishes his serial he can run like a deer and you can say that he was some skip artist who just blew the joint.' There was silence at the other end of the line. 'What is it, Pep?' I asked anxiously. 'I was just trying to think of a good name to register him under,' Pep said mildly. 'How do you like "T. Victrola Blueberry"?' "

Reynolds took Hammett to the hotel and the three drank a bottle of gin together. The serial was *The Maltese Falcon.* As Reynolds recalled, he and West read *Black Mask* avidly because Hammett was the first writer either of them knew who had actually sold his stories.

West worked on *The Dream Life of Balso Snell,* a fantasy about the adventures of a man who enters the Trojan Horse through its "Anus Mirabilis," in the hotel office from 1927 to 1929. In 1930 one of the owners of the Kenmore bought stock in the Sutton Club Hotel on East 56th Street and West moved uptown to become manager there.

Since the twenties, the Gramercy Park area has played little part in the lives of writers or their work. However, two landmarks with literary associations have remained through the years. The Players Club, an actors' club founded in 1888 by Edwin Booth, occupies an old brownstone house, remodeled by Stanford White, at 16 Gramercy Square. Booth thought actors should mix with those in other professions and a number of writers, including Mark Twain, Booth Tarkington, Edgar Lee Masters and Vachel Lindsay, were made members. Next door at 15 Gramercy Square is the National Arts Club. Founded in 1898 to provide exhibition facilities for the visual arts, it has also numbered literary people among its members, including Richard Watson Gilder, editor of the *Century,* S. S. McClure, Padraic Colum and W. H. Auden. Currently, however, neither club serves any important function for writers. Like the neighborhood, both institutions are only reminders of a literary past.

Gramercy Park

Gramercy Park Tour

1. 110–112 East 14th Street. Lüchow's Restaurant. With its immense high-ceilinged, dark-paneled rooms, it resembled a German banquet hall. Theodore Dreiser, H. L. Mencken, and George Jean Nathan often dined here, and it was a favorite luncheon spot for the editors of the *American Caravan*—Paul Rosenfeld, Alfred Kreymborg and Lewis Mumford. Now only the façade exists. The restaurant has been closed and gutted. The entrance was at number 112 (p. 157).

The area one block east and west of Irving Place is O. Henry country.

(1a) The Hotel America stood seventy-five yards east of Fourth Avenue (now Park Avenue South) on the south side of 15th Street. It found its way into O. Henry's stories as the Hotel Español (p. 154).

2. 122 East 17th Street, on the southwest corner of Irving Place. O. Henry, like many others, believed that this house had once been Washington Irving's. Although a plaque to that effect marks the house, Irving never lived there (pp. 154–55, 381).

3. 17th Street at 201 Park Avenue South. The Guardian Life Insurance Building, where Theodore Dreiser rented an office in 1925 while he was finishing *An American Tragedy.* He also used the office to rendezvous with women. Originally called the Germania, it was built in 1911 by architects D'Oench and Yost.

4. 55 Irving Place. O. Henry lived here from 1903 to 1907.

5. 53 Irving Place. The poet Orrick Johns lived here in 1911. The three houses at 51 to 55 Irving Place have been remodeled with a new brick façade to form one apartment building. A restaurant, Sal Anthony's, occupies the same spot as the front parlor-room floor where O. Henry used to sit, watching the passing scene. There is a plaque (p. 153).

6. 66 Irving Place. Pete's Tavern, diagonally across from O. Henry's home. In his time it was Healy's Café, or the Club. Dating from 1864, it is not the oldest saloon in New York as claimed; McSorley's Old Ale House preceded it in 1854. Today O. Henry memorabilia hang on its walls (p. 154).

7. At 190 Third Avenue between 18th and 17th streets, is Scheffel Hall, which O. Henry described in "The Halberdier of the Little Rheinschloss." Although the beer hall now has a modern overlay in its reincarnation as Tuesday's, much of the atmosphere of the old restaurant remains. Built in 1894 by architects Weber and Drosser, it was for many years called Joe King's Rathskeller (p. 154).

8. 241 East 17th Street. William Dean Howells lived in this house in 1891. Set back from the street behind an iron grillwork fence, the four-story house is ornamented by a second-floor balcony. The exterior has been "modernized" above the ground floor. The house faces Stuyvesant Park, an island of serenity on busy Second Avenue (p. 150).

(8a) 330 East 17th Street. Howells had lived earlier at this address. Beth Israel Hospital now occupies the entire block (pp. 150–51).

East 19th Street between Third Avenue and Irving Place is known as "the Block Beautiful." During the 1920s its mid-nineteenth-century houses and former stables were remodeled, and it has been maintained as an attractive architectural unit to this day. During the twenties the homes of four residents served as gathering places for the artistic elite:

9. 151 East 19th Street. Carl Van Vechten lived on the top floor of this small six-story apartment house (p. 157).

10. 140 East 19th Street. James Sibley Watson, who provided the main financial support for the *Dial*, lived in this building (p. 156).

11. 131 East 19th Street. Ernest Boyd resided in this five-story brick building with bay windows (pp. 157–58).

12. 77 Irving Place, on the southwest corner of 19th Street. Paul Rosenfeld lived in this five-story red brick building (pp. 156–57).

Gramercy Park was planned as a fashionable residential development in the 1830s. This is the only surviving private park in the city, and only tenants occupying the original surrounding plots have keys to the locked park gates.

13. 22 Gramercy Park South. Paul Rosenfeld had lived here before moving to Irving Place (p. 156).

14. 16 Gramercy Park South. Edwin Booth, the actor, bought this 1845 Gothic Revival house in 1888 and had it remodeled by Stanford White to serve as a club for those associated with the theatre. To this day the brownstone house with its two-story balcony supported by columns is the Players Club, whose literary members have included Mark Twain, Booth Tarkington, Maxwell Anderson, Robert Benchley, Heywood Hale Broun, John O'Hara, Carl Van Doren, and Ernest Hemingway (p. 159).

15. 15 Gramercy Park South. The National Arts Club. Originally two connecting houses built in 1845, the building was remodeled in 1874 in Victorian Gothic style by Calvert Vaux as a residence for Samuel J. Tilden. In 1906 it was bought by the National Arts Club, which had been founded in 1898 (p. 159). For many years its top floor was home to the Poetry Society of America.

West of Park Avenue South are three addresses from the 1850s when the neighborhood was at its height.

16. 35 East 19th Street was Horace Greeley's house in the early 1850s. Soon after the accompanying picture was taken, the building was extended five or six feet to the sidewalk line with a very cheap façade, which still survives on the second and third floors.

17. 28 East 20th Street, a few doors east of Broadway. Theodore Roosevelt was born here in 1858 in a house built in 1848. The original building was demolished and replicated from the foundations up in 1923.

Horace Greeley's house at 35 East 19th Street as it
looked in 1905, when the lower floor was a café.

Architect, Theodate Pope Riddle; it is open to the public (p. 147).

18. 46 East 21st Street. John Treat Irving lived here, and his uncle
Washington Irving often visited. All three buildings here were probably
similar to the two top floors of number 42, with a double-door entrance as
in number 44, and wrought-iron stairs and a railing like that of number 42
(pp. 147, 155, 381).

19. 145 East 23rd Street. Nathanael West worked as night manager at the twenty-two story, red-brick Kenmore Hall Hotel, which was probably built in the mid-1920s (pp. 158–59).

(19a) 143 East 23rd Street. In 1893 Stephen Crane was living with three friends in a studio, in a building located here that had housed the Art Students League (pp. 152–53).

20. 68 Lexington Avenue. The Armory (originally home to the 69th Regiment of the New York National Guard) occupies most of the block from Lexington toward Park Avenue South between 25th and 26th streets. It was constructed in 1904 by architects Hunt and Hunt. Here was held the Armory Show in 1913 which masked the bombshell entry of postimpressionist painting to America (p. 148). When it was built several literary landmarks were lost:

(20a) 111 East 25th Street. Henry James stayed here for six months in 1875.

(20b) 115 East 25th Street. When James visited America in 1881, he stayed with Edwin Godkin, his former editor at the *Nation*. These two houses, located about midblock, were in a row of thirteen houses (pp. 149–50).

(20c) 104 East 26th Street. Herman Melville lived from 1863 until his death in 1891 in a house which was just about where the loading dock at the west end of the Armory now stands (pp. 148–49).

21. 1 East 29th Street. "The Little Church Around the Corner" was the site of O. Henry's funeral in 1910. The church was built 1849–61 by architect Frederic Clarke Withers; the lych-gate was added in 1896 (p. 155).

V. Chelsea

As a neighborhood with a literary past, Chelsea is dominated by one overshadowing landmark, the Hotel Chelsea. Standing impressively at the midpoint of the area's main thoroughfare, between Seventh and Eighth avenues on 23rd Street, this Victorian Gothic anomaly, with its slate roof, gables and ironwork balconies, has housed artists and writers since it opened in 1884. Boasting a roster of residents that includes William Dean Howells, O. Henry, Edgar Lee Masters, Thomas Wolfe and Arthur Miller, it has, perhaps, been home to more writers than any other single New York building.

Yet long before the hotel's clientele drew attention to it, the neighborhood was rich in literary associations. Edith Wharton was born two blocks east at 14 West 23rd Street in 1862, when the area around Madison Square was at its most fashionable. The rich lived in houses made of the brownstone quarried primarily in Portland, Connecticut. A rich man was known as a "brownstone" and what today is the silk-stocking vote was then the brownstone vote, but Wharton found the architectural fashion oppressive. "One of the most depressing impressions of my childhood," she wrote, "is my recollection of the intolerable ugliness of New York, of its untended streets and the narrow houses so lacking in external dignity, so crammed with smug and suffocating upholstery . . . this little low-studded rectangular New York cursed with its universal chocolate-coloured coating of the most hideous stone ever quarried, this cramped horizontal gridiron of a town without towers, porticoes, fountains or perspectives, hide-bound in its deadly uniformity of mean ugliness . . ."

It was this New York and the passing of the older society that Wharton chose to chronicle in *The Age of Innocence.* Her hero, Newland Archer, lived on West 28th Street and the world he found so stifling, where society "cultivated ferns in Wardian cases, made macramé lace and wool embroidery on linen, collected American revolutionary glazed ware, subscribed to *Good Words,* and read Ouida's novels for the sake of the Italian atmosphere," was the same one that oppressed her. Born Edith Jones and as a child called Pussy, she spent most of her time reading and writing in the library of her home, where the collected works of an old family friend, Washington Irving, adorned the shelves "in comely type and handsome binding." In 1882, after her father died, she moved with her mother to 28 West 25th Street. She was married from the church that still stands across the street; it was then called Trinity Chapel.

Even in Wharton's time, the neighborhood a short block to the west created a striking contrast to the upper-class respectability of Madison Square. All along Sixth Avenue from 14th Street to 42nd was the Tenderloin, an area of shops and department stores by day, and bars, dance halls, brothels and gambling houses by night. The district was said to have earned its name because it was so rich in graft; in 1876 when Alexander "Clubber" Williams became precinct captain he told a reporter that from then on tenderloin was all he meant to eat. The area was as prime a territory for two writers — Stephen Crane and O. Henry — as it was for the police. Crane lived in the area, in the peripatetic way characteristic of him, for a month at a time from 1893 to 1895. Then, after *The Red*

Badge of Courage had made him famous, he moved to 165 West 23rd Street to research a series of sketches for the *New York Journal*. A reporter visiting the apartment in 1896 described it as decorated with impressionistic landscapes and war trophies Crane had collected on a trip to the Fredericksburg battlefield. It was while living here that Crane had one of his most notorious experiences. He was with three women one evening, and while he escorted one of them to a streetcar another was arrested for streetwalking. Crane came to her defense and said he had spent the evening interviewing her and her two companions for his articles and had not observed her soliciting. During the trial, in an attempt to discredit Crane as a witness, the prosecution implied that he was a libertine, drug addict and pimp. Two weeks later he jumped at an offer from William Randolph Hearst to cover the insurrection in Cuba.

Several sketches describing Tenderloin life survive to record Crane's stay. In "When Every One Is Panic Stricken" Crane describes a fire in "one of those ancient dwellings which the churning process of the city had changed into a hive of little industries," a variety of building surviving in the district that is now part of the garment center. "The Duel That Was Not Fought" takes place in a Sixth Avenue bar, and "A Detail" describes the daytime Sixth Avenue shopping district, "where from the streams of people and vehicles went up a roar like that from headlong mountain torrents."

Close upon Crane's heels came William Sydney Porter, who arrived in New York in 1902 after having served three years in prison on an embezzlement conviction in Columbus, Ohio. Katharine Anne Porter told the story this way: "He was my father's second cousin — I don't know what that makes him to me. And he was more known in the family for being a bank robber. He worked in a bank, you know, and he just didn't seem to find a talent for making money; no Porter ever did. But he had a wife who was dying of TB and he couldn't keep up with the doctor's bills. So he took a pitiful little sum — oh, about three hundred and fifty dollars — and ran away when he was accused. But he came back, because his wife was dying, and went to prison."

In the city Porter found his ideal subject and described the lives of its inhabitants lovingly. "Silent, grim, colossal," he once wrote, "the big city has ever stood against its revilers. They call it hard as iron; they say that no pulse of pity beats in its bosom; they compare its streets with lonely forests and deserts of lava. But beneath the hard crust of the lobster is found a delectable and luscious food." His first address here was the far from glamorous Marty Hotel at 47 West 24th Street. He had a small room on an air shaft with a bed and chair and used his trunk as a writing table. Although he moved the following year to the East Side when a contract with the *Sunday World* gave him a steady income, he continued to patronize his West Side haunts. His favorite among these was Mouquin's, at 38th Street and Sixth Avenue, a popular gathering place for artists and writers, who called it Mook's. In "Cosmopolite in a Café" Porter describes the atmosphere generally attributed to the restaurant although he does not refer to it by name. (He usually altered a few details of the settings he used in order to prevent positive identification.) "Invoke your consideration of the scene — the marble-topped tables, the range of leather-upholstered wall seats, the gay company, the ladies dressed in demi-state toilets, speaking in an exquisite visible chorus of taste, economy, opulence or art; the sedulous and largess-loving *garçons,* the music wisely catering to all with its raids upon the composers, the mélange of talk and laughter — and, if you will, the Wurzburger in the tall glass cones that bend to your lips as a ripe cherry sways on its branch to the

beak of a robber jay." In search of material, Porter also frequented the Haymarket, a dance hall at Sixth Avenue and 30th
Street, where he sometimes paid the prostitutes their usual
rates to sit and talk with him at his table.

From 1906 until his death in 1910, Porter's office and sometime home was a room at the Caledonia Hotel, a tan brick building that stands at 28 West 26th Street. To avoid people he
didn't want to see, he gave his friends a secret number, which
he frequently changed, to be repeated to the hotel operator
or clerk. He lived at the Chelsea Hotel briefly in 1907 and
again in 1910, when he had a six-room apartment furnished
only with a work table, a chair and a bed. Finally, after a lifetime of heavy drinking, he died at the Caledonia of cirrhosis
of the liver. Nine empty whiskey bottles were found under the
bed.

At the time of Porter's death, the area of the Tenderloin from
23rd to 33rd streets between Sixth and Seventh avenues was a
Negro bohemia. It was to this neighborhood that the protagonist of James Weldon Johnson's *Autobiography of an
Ex-Coloured Man* first came when he left his native South.
"New York City," wrote Johnson, "is the most fatally fascinating thing in America. She sits like a great witch at the gate
of the country, showing her alluring white face and hiding her
crooked hands and feet under the folds of her wide garments
— constantly enticing thousands from far within, and tempting
those who come from across the seas to go no farther. And all
these become the victims of her caprice." "The Club," a meeting place for Negro writers, entertainers, musicians and composers, which was in fact located on West 53rd Street, is set in
the novel in a three-story house on 27th Street near Sixth
Avenue.

•

Although the Hotel Chelsea had existed before the time of Crane and O. Henry, its literary reputation came later. It was originally an apartment house and among its first occupants was William Dean Howells, who took a four-room suite when he arrived in the city in 1888 after leaving Boston. The same year Mark Twain stayed there while on a lecture tour. The Chelsea became a hotel in 1905. "This is not a bourgeois hotel that has gone artistic," said contemporary resident Virgil

Edgar Lee Masters on the roof of the Chelsea Hotel in the 1940s.

Thomson, the composer. "It started as an expensive artistic hotel." John Sloan had a studio there and O. Henry had been in residence in 1907 and 1910. But it was not until the thirties, when Edgar Lee Masters moved into the hotel, became interested in its past and gave it a social focus, that it came into its heyday. Masters even glorified the hotel in a poem:

> . . . Then who will know
> About its ancient grandeur, marble stairs,
> Its paintings, onyx mantels, courts, the heirs
> Of a time now long ago?
>
> Who will remember that Mark Twain used to stroll
> In the gorgeous dining room, that Princesses,
> Poets and celebrated actresses
> Lived here and made its soul . . .

Late in 1937 Thomas Wolfe stopped by the Chelsea to look at the rooms and met Masters, who urged him to stay and vouched for him at the desk. Wolfe took a corner suite on the eighth floor with a foyer, bedroom, living room, office and bath. He had just left his publisher, Scribner's, and spent the next few months trying to decide on a new one. He frequently sat in the hotel bar, now a Spanish restaurant named El Quijote, and often ate at Cavanaugh's, a famous restaurant, now defunct, down the block at 256. He had a special table in the rear, from which he watched the other patrons.

Wolfe eventually settled on Harper's and on December 31, 1937, his editor, Edward Aswell, brought the contract to him at the Chelsea. Aswell described Wolfe's apartment: "The rooms were dark and dingy, but they had the advantage of ceilings high enough so that he ran no risk of bumping his head. The most impressive feature of the suite was the bathroom, which was quite large, with a toilet set on a raised platform: Tom called it 'The Throne Room.'"

In May 1938, Wolfe put together the manuscripts that were to become *The Web and the Rock* and *You Can't Go Home Again* from the four thousand pages he kept in packing cases in the middle of the living room floor. He left for a trip to the West where he became ill and died four months later in Baltimore.

In the fifties, the Chelsea's famous literary residents included James T. Farrell, Mary McCarthy and Dylan Thomas. Farrell lived here from June 1951 to December 1953, while he was writing the last volume of *Yet Other Waters*, a semiauto-biographical novel in his Bernard Carr trilogy, which describes a writer's involvement with the Communist party. In *Judith*, published in 1969, he chronicled the affair he had with a cele-brated pianist when he lived at the Chelsea. Mary McCarthy was in residence during the winter and spring of 1952–53 and the spring of 1954. Dylan Thomas made a practice of staying at the Chelsea when he came to America, and in November 1953 was taken from the hotel to St. Vincent's Hospital, where he died. Another writer in the hard-drinking tradition, Bren-dan Behan, went to the Chelsea in 1961 after being asked to leave the Algonquin, where, it is said, he chased the maids through the halls. In *Brendan Behan's New York*, he wrote: "I would hope that Mr. Bard, the proprietor, and his son Stanley . . . would leave space on their plaque for myself. I am not humble enough to say that I do not deserve one, but I hope it does not come too soon, because of all the names on the plaque, as far as I know, James T. Farrell is the only one that's alive and kicking very much." Behan had his wish and a plaque bearing his name was affixed after his death in 1964. Arthur Miller maintained an apartment in the hotel for seven years in the early sixties. "It is the only hotel I know which has no class lines," he said.

Throughout the years there have been other notable literary visitors — Nelson Algren, William Burroughs, Vladimir Nabokov, Gregory Corso and Julius Lester. Most recently, Edgar Lee Masters's old rooms were occupied by Clifford Irving, who achieved notoriety by writing a bogus biography of multimillionaire Howard Hughes. Today the grandeur Masters described is largely gone, but here and there vestiges remain. The hotel office, once the ladies' sitting room, still boasts an ornate fireplace and ceiling decorated with cherubs hand-painted on canvas. And Virgil Thomson's apartment recaptures the elegant past. The oak floor is polished and covered with Persian rugs. The fireplace, one of many in the Chelsea rooms, is in its original condition, with carved rosewood mantel, deep green glazed tile facing and brass trim and fender. Rosewood Victorian gingerbread decorates each window and the archway between rooms. At one end of the long living room there are built-in rosewood bookcases and cupboards with beveled mirrors. Here the old Chelsea lives.

.

To the west beyond the Tenderloin lies yet another Chelsea, the true Chelsea, which gave the rest of the area its name. In the eighteenth century Chelsea was the estate, named after the Chelsea district in London, of Captain Thomas Clarke. It reached from 14th to 27th streets and from Seventh Avenue to the Hudson River. In the early nineteenth century the property descended to Clarke's grandson, Clement Clarke Moore, a scholar of the Bible and of Hebrew and Greek literature, who is best remembered for his poem, "A Visit from St. Nicholas." As the implementation of the New York City grid plan progressed, Moore took steps to plan Chelsea as an elegant residential neighborhood. He divided his property into lots but controlled its development by covenants written into the deeds. Chelsea never became as fashionable as Fifth Avenue but its streets of middle-class homes, many of which remain and are now protected by designation within the Chelsea Historic District, were of high architectural quality and imparted a harmony found in few other sections of the city.

Several writers found this area a pleasant way station in the early decades of the present century. Edwin Arlington Robinson was a habitué of the Café Francis on West 23rd Street, a haunt, like Mouquin's, of artists and writers. When the proprietor learned that Robinson was penniless and couldn't pay his rent, he offered him a room on the top floor of his house, a four-story brownstone that can be seen at 450 West 43rd Street. Robinson stayed there throughout most of the period between 1901 and 1906. From 1909 until he moved to Hartford in 1916, Wallace Stevens lived at 441 West 21st Street, a red brick house that stands today. After a short-lived job as a reporter for the *Tribune,* Stevens entered New York University Law School. He remarked in later life that "he had been no more serious about poetry during his early days in New York than he had been at Harvard." His first important publication did not come until 1914.

Sherwood Anderson lived in the area in the fall of 1918. "I got a cheap room," he wrote in his *Memoirs,* "somewhere over on the West Side in the twenties between Ninth and Tenth avenues, and there I worked . . . It was a good room. There was the hoarse cry of steamers in the river at night. I was in the back of the house, upstairs, and looked across little city back yards into many other people's rooms. At night I could turn off my lights and sit by my window. There were people making love, dining, quarreling." The room was in a house at 427 West 22nd Street, a brownstone painted gray that even now has the air of a rooming house. Anderson was much older than most of his literary acquaintances in New York — Van Wyck Brooks, Waldo Frank and Paul Rosenfeld

— and wondered whether he had a place in their world. "And so there I was," he wrote, "an American rapidly approaching middle life, sitting in my room over in west Twenty-Second street at night after a day spent listening to the talk of the new men and trying with all my might to be one of the new men myself." With the publication of *Winesburg, Ohio* in 1919, Anderson's standing in the world of letters was established. He had a place in the New York world but he did not choose to live there.

Among Anderson's "new men" was Van Wyck Brooks, soon to become one of the dominant figures in criticism of the twentieth century. As a young man, he had lived one block north of Anderson in the row of houses called London Terrace from 1909 to 1911. The houses, since replaced by a mammoth apartment complex bearing the same name, were noteworthy for their design when they were built in 1845. They were set back about thirty-five feet from the street with gardens in front and were uniformly pilastered to give the effect of a colonnade. Brooks wrote of his house:

> There were three big trees in the front yard, with a cast-iron fountain and a bench, and, within, the kind of furnished rooms that O. Henry so often described with half-broken chairs and the odour of mildewed woodwork. It was kept by a brawny Scotswoman with a drunken husband, and there was an ancient libidinous chambermaid, always dressed in rusty black, who might have stepped out of an eighteenth-century novel. It was a discouraging household, especially in winter, when the trains of "Death Avenue" [Ninth] at the corner ploughed through the snow and one had to resort to the free-lunch counter at the saloon across the street that was one of Edwin Arlington Robinson's haunts. For Robinson had lived eight years before in a brownstone house a hundred yards away . . ."

During this period Brooks often went to a small French

John Sloan's *Yeats at Petitpas*, 1910. Sloan's identifications were, from left to right around the table: Van Wyck Brooks, John Butler Yeats, Alan Seeger, Dolly Sloan, Robert W. Sneddon, Anne Squires, Fred King, John Sloan, Mrs. Charles Johnston and, serving, Mlle. Celestine Petitpas.

hotel at 317 West 29th Street run by three sisters from Brittany named Petitpas. William Butler Yeats's brother, the painter Jack Yeats, was in residence there from 1908, when he first visited New York and decided to stay, until his death thirteen years later. W. B. Yeats visited his father at the hotel in 1911 and again in 1914. Conrad Aiken, who lived in London Terrace one summer while an undergraduate at Harvard, remembered encountering Jack Yeats, "who invariably, when asked if he was the father of the great Yeats, replied, '*I* am the great Yeats!' "

There was a restaurant in the backyard at Petitpas' where Yeats would sit at the end of one of the long tables surrounded by the men who were to become the most important American painters of the period — Robert Henri, John Sloan, George Bellows, William Glackens and the Prendergast brothers — and a number of young writers, including Brooks, Alan Seeger, and Padraic and Mary Colum. Yeats's talk "abounded in recollections not only of 'Willie' but of Æ and Synge, Lady Gregory, the Abbey Theatre, George Moore, Dunsany," wrote Brooks. "We had special reasons for our interest in this, for we felt we were on the verge of a not dissimilar movement of our own, the first phase of another revival that expressed an American coming-of-age, an escape from our old colonial dependence on England. Yeats himself said, 'The fiddles are tuning all over America' . . ."

In 1914 the *New Republic* started publication in three old houses at 419 to 423 West 21st Street. Unfortunately, this is one of the few buildings that has been replaced on an otherwise architecturally intact, tree-lined block. The magazine began to achieve literary distinction in 1928 with Edmund Wilson as literary editor. Malcolm Cowley became his assistant in 1929 and when Wilson left to travel around the country reporting on the depression, Cowley replaced him. Cowley lived nearby at 360 West 22nd Street in a sixty-five-dollars-a-month studio from 1930 to 1934. It was under his direction that the magazine reached its height as a literary force. As Alfred Kazin, who began his career as a reviewer for the magazine, remembered, "The lead review in the *New Republic,* a single page usually written by Cowley himself, brought the week to focus for people to whom this page, breathing intellectual fight in its sharp black title and solid double-columned lines of argument, represented the most dramatically satisfying confrontation of a new book by a

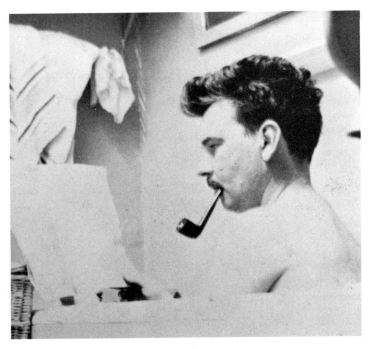

Malcolm Cowley reading a *New Republic* manuscript in
the bathtub at 360 West 22nd Street in the early 1930s.

gifted, uncompromising, critical intelligence." Lunch for staff
members and distinguished guests was served in a dining room
on one of the lower floors, and in the thirties, after work, the
staff drank gin and lime and played quoits and deck tennis
in the garden.

In the fifties Chelsea gained yet another literary dimension
when Jack Kerouac wrote the first complete version of *On the
Road* in a loft at 149 West 21st Street in 1951. His friend
Lucien Carr brought home a 120-foot roll of teletype paper from
United Press, which enabled Kerouac to type nonstop. He
claimed he had originated "spontaneous prose," which involved
writing without pausing to calculate or revise. But, in fact, he
had begun *On the Road* in 1948 and was to rework it consider-

ably before it was published in 1957. Later in the decade another writer who, like Kerouac, would come to be associated with the East Village, lived in Chelsea. In the fall of 1958 LeRoi Jones moved to 402 West 20th Street and stayed there for about a year.

All in all, Chelsea has been a neighborhood of immense diversity. During the last decades of the nineteenth century an area only five blocks wide included the fashionable residential district of Madison Square, the gambling halls and brothels of the Tenderloin and the middle-class respectability of Chelsea Square. Its literary history has been similarly diverse, encompassing Edith Wharton's commentary on New York society, descriptions of the city's underside by Stephen Crane and O. Henry, the influential criticism of the *New Republic* and Jack Kerouac's Beat prose. Today the old houses in the Chelsea Historic District have been restored and form one of the most attractive enclaves on Manhattan. But the larger area is now New York's garment center and is primarily given over to

LeRoi Jones at 402 West 20th Street, around 1959.
(Allen Ginsberg on bongos.)

commercial uses. In terms of the neighborhood's literary associations only the Hotel Chelsea, which still houses an occasional writer, remains.

Chelsea

Chelsea Tour

Madison Square, once a fashionable residential area, borders Chelsea on the east.

(a1) 14 West 23rd Street, where Edith Jones, later Wharton, was born in 1862, is a house several times altered; the cast-iron façade was added in 1892 (p. 165).

(b1) 28 West 25th Street. Wharton's family home was located here at

A glimpse of Edith Wharton's birthplace, the house shown in part on the right. This is the only existing photograph of 14 West 23rd Street.

the time of her marriage (p. 166).

1. 15 West 25th Street. Trinity Chapel, where Wharton was married, was just across the street from her home. It served the uptown parishioners of Trinity Church. In the English Gothic style, it was built between 1851 and 1856 by the architect Richard Upjohn, and is now the Serbian Orthodox Cathedral of St. Sava. To the right are the parish house and school constructed in 1860 by architect J. Wrey Mould, which are a treasury of Victorian architectural details (p. 166).

2. West 28th Street. Along either side of the street a few brownstones and brick houses remain from the era Wharton described in *The Age of Innocence*. Wharton's brother lived here, as well as her fictional characters, the Archers (p. 166).

Going west to Sixth Avenue one enters the area once known as the Tenderloin. Many of the grand department stores, where the shopgirls O. Henry wrote about worked, are still standing but have been converted to other uses. At night the action shifted to the street's dance halls and gambling houses, though there is nothing to see of them now. At Sixth Avenue and 30th Street, on the southeast corner was the Haymarket, the famous dance hall painted by John Sloan and visited by O. Henry and Eugene O'Neill (p. 169).

3. 28 West 26th Street. The Caledonia Hotel, where O. Henry had a room he used for writing from 1906 on, and where he died in 1910 (p. 169). The building is now apartments, but the façade is largely unaltered.

(3a) 47 West 24th Street. The location of the Marty Hotel, O. Henry's first address in New York (p. 168).

4. 165 West 23rd Street. Stephen Crane lived here for nearly a year in 1896 while researching city life for a series of articles for the *New York Journal* (p. 167).

5. 148 West 21st Street. An old five-story house, where Jack Kerouac wrote most of *On the Road* in a loft (p. 178).

6. 222 West 23rd Street. The Chelsea Hotel is one of the few remaining Victorian Gothic apartment houses once common in New York; it became a hotel in 1905. French doors open onto balconies decorated with ironwork leaves and flowers. The building has been designated both a historical and an architectural landmark. In the lobby only a vestige of its former elegance can be seen in the ornately carved fireplace mantel. Paintings and sculpture by former and present Chelsea residents, such as Larry Rivers, are now displayed there. Plaques at the entrance honor writers who have lived here—from Mark Twain to Yevgeni Yevtushenko. The building was constructed in 1884 by architects Hubert, Pirsson, and Co. (pp. 165, 170–73).

7. 226 West 23rd Street. El Quixote, a Spanish restaurant now occupies the space which was originally the Chelsea Hotel bar (p. 171).

8. 215 West 23rd Street, across the street from the Chelsea. The YMCA, where William Saroyan stayed at the age of nineteen when he first came to New York. He had lost his luggage, including a hundred dollars, all the money he had, and paid one dollar in change as an advance on his room. Among the various Chelsea residents who have used the YMCA pool are Brendan Behan and Edgar Lee Masters.

(8a) 256 West 23rd Street. The location of Cavanaugh's restaurant. Famous for more than a hundred years, the restaurant opened in 1876 (p. 171).

(8b) 360 West 22nd Street. Malcolm Cowley lived in a sixty-five-dollar-a-month studio in a row house here from 1930 to 1934 (p.177).

The original London Terrace in Chelsea.

The Chelsea Historic District, with its lovely tree-lined blocks of nineteenth-century houses, runs mainly between 20th and 22nd streets and Ninth and Tenth avenues.

(a9) 419 to 423 West 21st Street is the site of three houses that served the *New Republic* as offices (pp. 177–78). In 1938 they were replaced by a brick apartment building.

9. 441 West 21st Street. Wallace Stevens lived in this pleasant brick house with a high stoop from 1909 to 1916 (p. 174).

10. 427 West 22nd Street. This was a rooming house when Sherwood Anderson lived here in 1918 (p. 174).

11. 450 West 23rd Street. Edwin Arlington Robinson lived in one of a row of brownstone houses here from 1901 to 1905 (p. 174).

(11a) Across the street was a row of four-story houses collectively named London Terrace which once housed, at various times, Van Wyck Brooks and Conrad Aiken (p. 175). A vast apartment complex built in 1930 and bearing the same name now occupies the site.

12. 317 West 29th Street. In what was once a French neighborhood stands the house that was the famous Petitpas, a small hotel where J.B. Yeats lived and where John Sloan, Van Wyck Brooks, Alan Seeger and others visited (pp. 176–77). The building has now been totally modernized, and has a new façade.

VI. Midtown

WALT WHITMAN once noted that "while New York was a bad place for literary farming, it was a good market for the harvest." Although he would eventually be proven wrong on the first part of his proposition as more and more good writing came out of New York, he was prescient on the second. Around 1900 the center of publishing moved from Boston to New York. The old nineteenth-century firms were joined in the twentieth by new companies that would change the cast of publishing and shift the balance of influence. Where the New England Brahmins had taken a conservative moral, political and literary tone, the new firms launched the publication of works by Continental European authors, writings about radical politics, literature that was experimental in style, and books whose breakthroughs in subject matter would often plunge the publishers into battle with the censors.

At the same time New York, in its role as capital of style and sophistication in America, was producing a series of publications that kept the fashionable abreast of the latest in art, theater and writing and provided a steady diet of highly literate entertainment. The prototype of such magazines, the *Smart Set,* was followed by *Vanity Fair,* the *American Mercury* and, still thriving today, the *New Yorker.* By the twenties, Midtown — the business district of the city extending from 34th Street to West 59th Street — was bustling with literary activity, mostly of the harvest but sometimes of the farming variety. Like the Park Row area in the mid-nineteenth century, Midtown was the center of both the theater and commercial publishing. Authors came to do business with their publishers and stayed in the great hotels. Journalists, playwrights, critics and celebrities socialized in Midtown restaurants, speakeasies and living rooms. And some writers even came to write.

One of the area's earliest residents symbolized the rise in the city's literary significance. When William Dean Howells moved from Boston to New York, his action was viewed as a sign that the country's literary center had shifted. As editor, critic and novelist, Howells was considered so much the representative sensibility of his time that the last third of the nineteenth century has often been called "the Age of Howells." A native of Ohio, Howells had worked for the *Atlantic* in Boston, eventually becoming editor and enjoying a wide influence on American writing. In 1886, however, he contracted with *Harper's Magazine* in New York to write "The Editor's Study," a column he called "a symposium of one," in which he used reviews of current books as a springboard for discussing his critical ideas. For a while he commuted between Boston and New York, finally moving here in the early nineties. Although he wrote about the Stuyvesant Square area in *The Coast of Bohemia* and *A Hazard of New Fortunes* (see Chapter IV, Gramercy Park), he spent his years as America's pre-eminent literary figure in a series of addresses on or near West 59th Street. Here, where tall hotels and apartment buildings have replaced a row of smaller hotels and brownstones, he wrote *The Coast of Bohemia, A Traveler from Altruria* and *Literary Passions*. The mansions of the rich lined nearby Fifth Avenue. Around the corner between 57th and 58th streets stood "Marble Row." This series of houses with shimmering white façades had been built by Edith Wharton's great-aunt, Mary Mason Jones, in 1870. Mrs. Jones appears in

The Age of Innocence as Mrs. Manson Mingott, an eccentric aristocrat who had "put the crowning touch to her audacities by building a large house of pale cream-coloured stone (when brown sandstone seemed as much the only wear as a frock-coat in the afternoon) in an inaccessible wilderness near the Central Park." The old Plaza Hotel was on its present site at the corner of 59th Street, and the columned Hotel Savoy and the Romanesque Netherland Hotel, the predecessor of the present Sherry-Netherland, were across the way. Howells would have been fairly well at home, at least economically, in this district of fabulous mansions and elegant hotels. One biographer, Kenneth S. Lynn, estimates that the 1970 equivalent of his income during the 1890s would have been around $120,000 a year, which he earned through his great productivity and his acumen in negotiating royalties up to 25 per cent. At the same time, he reflected on the disparity between the rich dashing by in their carriages and the poor seated on the benches of Central Park, whom he could see from his window.

In 1908 Howells moved to 130 West 57th Street, his address until his death in 1920. Van Wyck Brooks, then twenty-three-years old, interviewed him there in 1909 for a publication called *The World's Work*. Howells was seventy-two. "He goes into his little study after breakfast, and sits down at a very clean, plain writing-table, and writes. It is a habit of half a century . . ." Frank Norris, another author who had met Howells in the late nineties, represented him as Trevor in "The Lost Story." "He was a short, rotund man," wrote Norris, "rubicund as to face, bourgeois as to clothes and surroundings, joyful in manner, indulging even in slang. One might easily set him down as a retired groceryman — wholesale, perhaps, but nonetheless a groceryman."

A few other literary people lived nearby. Lincoln Steffens had a seven-room apartment at 341 West 56th Street in 1897.

William Dean Howells at 130 West 57th Street in 1909.

The décor of the apartment was eclectic; a samovar from the Lower East Side and a silver tea service presented to his wife's father during the Civil War shared the dining room sideboard. James Weldon Johnson lived several blocks south in the Marshall Club at 260 West 53rd Street. In the early 1900s, the area around West 53rd was a center for black writers, musicians and performers. The Marshall was the most popular meeting place and Johnson portrayed it as "The Club" in his *Autobiography of an Ex-Coloured Man.* There was a restaurant and ragtime music but no bar. The main floor had lace-curtained windows and pictures of every Negro who had attained distinction — athletes, performers, political leaders. Some whites went "slumming" at the club, but many of those who came were theatrical performers of Negro roles; they based their characterizations on what they saw there. Johnson, who was a successful songwriter at the time, lived on the second floor of the Marshall for a while, using the back rooms as a studio.

The area around the Art Students League, which had moved from East 23rd to its present site on West 57th Street, was a center for artists, who lived in small rooms near the school. Vachel Lindsay came to New York to study there with Robert Henri in 1905. He had rooms with a friend on the top floor of a building on 57th Street. There was a trap door in the ceiling leading to the attic, where he lived when he had no rent money. Around 1908 Lindsay began to turn his energies to poetry. He had very little money and, to test the idea that ordinary people could appreciate his poetry, he decided to sell it on the street. "About eleven o'clock in the evening in accordance with a plan matured for some weeks," he wrote ". . . I put twelve copies of the 'We Who Are Playing' in my overcoat pocket, and made a plunge for Tenth Avenue . . . Well, I tried a sleepy big shock-headed baker first. I tried to give the poem to him. He considered the thing for some time as I explained it, but finally handed it back saying he had no use for it . . . So the next place I said to the proprietor, 'I will sell you this for two cents.' At once I saw the thing take . . ." After selling several poems on Tenth Avenue, Lindsay went over to Ninth, where he sold only to druggists — "the confectioners and delicatessens refused." He concluded that "there is more poetry in the distribution of verse than in the writing of it."

·

In 1902 Howells wrote: "New York society has not taken to our literature. New York publishes it, criticizes it, and cir-

culates it, but I doubt if New York society much reads it or
cares for it, and New York is therefore by no means the literary
centre that Boston once was, though a large number of our
literary men live in or about New York . . . New York is a
vast mart, and literature is one of the things marketed here . . ."

New York's importance as a literary market was reflected in
the fact that the *Smart Set* had become the proving ground for
literary careers. The magazine came into its most important
period in November of 1914, when H. L. Mencken and George
Jean Nathan took over as its editors. Nathan's function was
administrative: he ran the office and supervised the daily
routine; Mencken dealt with authors and selected manuscripts for publication. Each also wrote a column, Nathan
on theater and Mencken on books. Through his column and
his editorial power on the magazine, Mencken was the most influential voice in American letters for fifteen years. Before the
tenure of Mencken and Nathan, the *Smart Set* had helped
found the careers of O. Henry and James Branch Cabell. Now
it was to introduce its readers to a whole new era in literature. It "discovered" Eugene O'Neill by publishing three of
his plays; it gave James Joyce his first exposure in the United
States with two of his Dubliners stories; and it bought the work
of F. Scott Fitzgerald regularly enough to enable him to quit
his advertising job and complete his first novel, *This Side of
Paradise*. In addition, Mencken popularized a new standard
in literature. He praised Mark Twain, Conrad and Melville
and was the first prominent critic to champion Walt Whitman. He introduced Americans to Flaubert, Stendhal and
Goethe.

Mencken himself was never a New Yorker and it is a measure of the primacy of the city that, despite his hatred of it, he
came here regularly from Baltimore to do his work on the
Smart Set. "I thoroughly detest New York, though I have to go

there very often," he said. "Have you ever noticed that no
American writer of any consequence lives in Manhattan.
Dreiser tried it . . . but finally fled to California." Mencken
was discounting the new bohemians in Greenwich Village. He
told a young writer, "Don't ever, if you can possibly help it,
go below Fourteenth Street. The Village literati are scum."
He and Nathan would venture that far downtown only to
visit Dreiser and take in dinner at Lüchow's.

Mencken's visits to New York gradually settled into a
routine. He would arrive at the Algonquin Hotel at 59 West
44th Street late Sunday afternoon, check in, call Nathan across
the street at the Hotel Royalton and join him for an evening
out at a bar or a party. (Nathan maintained an apartment on
the top floor of the Royalton from 1908 until his death in
1958.) Monday morning Mencken would go to the *Smart Set*
office, which occupied various addresses on Fourth, Fifth and
Eighth avenues before finally settling down at 25 West 45th
Street. The reception room was decorated with original art
work for covers and had a golden oak church pew as a visitors'
bench. There was a yellow tea cosy woven from hundreds of
cigar bands, cigars being Mencken's trademark, and a tapestry
depicting a Newfoundland dog rescuing a baby — thrown over
a claw-foot gilt chair. The tapestry also served as a cover for
a table made from saw horses and an alabaster slab that
Mencken had filched from a Maryland graveyard. During the
long work sessions when he was in town, immense lunches
sent in from a nearby German café were served here with a
sign saying POETS' FREE LUNCH tacked above the slab.

In between the serious writing, the *Smart Set* sprinkled its
pages with fillers, epigrams, quotes and inane news stories
reprinted without comment, divertissements later to be taken
up by the *New Yorker*. Eventually, however, the lightness
infected the whole periodical and came to undermine it. By

1923 Mencken and Nathan concluded that the *Smart Set* had become too frivolous, and decided to leave it and form a more serious magazine, the *American Mercury,* published by Alfred Knopf. Unfortunately, they could never agree on what to be serious about. Nathan stepped down as coeditor in 1925 and became a contributing editor, withdrawing entirely in 1930. Mencken once characterized their difficulty in a letter to Nathan: "*The Smart Set* went to pot because it was too trivial — because it interested intelligent readers only intermittently, and then only when they were in trifling moods — when they were, so to speak, a bit stewed intellectually." Dreiser had voiced the same criticism years earlier when Mencken had asked him for a promotional blurb. "Under you and Nathan the thing seems to have tamed down to a light, non-disturbing period of persiflage and badinage . . . Everything, apparently, is to be done with a light, aloof touch, which to me is good but like a diet of soufflé."

The *American Mercury* took offices first at the Heckscher Building at 730 Fifth Avenue (57th Street), where Knopf had his publishing company. The office was so drab that Mencken called it "the undertaking parlor." To save the space of files, no carbons were made and there was a house rule that only in cases of emergency did anyone speak to anyone else before 11:00 A.M.

While the *Smart Set* found itself becoming too smart, another magazine was making a virtue of taste and fashion. *Vanity Fair* had some of the same contributors — Edna St. Vincent Millay, Theodore Dreiser, D. H. Lawrence, Elinor Wylie — but set them in a different context. On its heavy satin pages it published the newest writers alongside reproductions, often in color, of avant-garde paintings and photographs of personalities, actors and celebrities that today recall a gentler, more civilized and optimistic era. Here is the young Gary Cooper photo-

Neysa McMein's
portrait of
Dorothy Parker.

graphed in all his lanky elegance by Cecil Beaton next to
Matisse's *White Plumes*. Here is the luminous Garbo side by
side with the latest from the pen of Gertrude Stein. Interspersed are the wittiest efforts of Dorothy Parker and Robert
Benchley. Before it was through, *Vanity Fair* had published
the work of virtually every important new writer and painter of
the 1920s and 1930s. At its offices at 19 West 44th Street, three

who were to become midtown literary celebrities were employed. Robert Benchley was managing editor, Robert Sherwood was drama editor and Dorothy Parker filled in as drama critic for P. G. Wodehouse. Benchley, who had written a paper on undertaking when he was in school, subscribed to two undertaking magazines. Parker cut out a picture illustrating how and where to inject embalming fluid and hung it over her desk until editor Frank Crowninshield asked her to take it down. When the office manager sent around a memo forbidding the discussion of salaries, Parker, Benchley and Sherwood wrote theirs on signs, which they wore around their necks. Finally, when Parker was fired in January 1920 for panning three plays in a row, Sherwood and Benchley resigned in protest. Sherwood got a job reviewing films for the humor magazine *Life,* and Parker and Benchley went off to free-lance from an office they shared together. They took a room on the third floor of the Metropolitan Opera House studios for thirty dollars a month and discussed using "Parkbench" as a cable address. Benchley said the room was so small that "one cubic foot less of space, and it would have constituted adultery." It was widely rumored, though apparently not true, that Parker had a sign saying MEN lettered on the door. Three months later Benchley left and went to *Life* as drama editor. Parker left soon afterward.

Dorothy Parker and Robert Benchley were among the few writers to make homes of sorts in Midtown. Parker had been born in the West Seventies and had lived in a boarding house at 103rd Street and Broadway when she took her first job at *Vogue* at ten dollars a week. In 1917 she went to *Vanity Fair.* She was briefly married to Edwin Pond Parker II but separated from him in 1920 and took a small apartment at 57 West 57th Street, where her friend Neysa McMein, a magazine illustrator and artist, had a studio. According to her biographer,

John Keats, Dorothy Parker had "a cheaply furnished room, utterly without taste, as anonymous as a room in a traveling salesmen's hotel . . . She was so seldom home that her private life was, in a sense, nonexistent."

Benchley had left his family in Scarsdale and went to live first at the Algonquin and then at the Royalton, where he had a two-room suite. With its mahogany trim and cross-latticed windows, the place looked Victorian. "Oh, so they think they're Victorian," he said. "I'll show them something Victorian, if that's the way they want to play." He furnished the room with a dark red rug, red draperies, a red velvet tasseled cover on an oak table, brass student lamps with green shades and three pictures of Queen Victoria. He collected books for their titles alone — such works as *Forty Thousand Sublime and Beautiful Thoughts, Success with Small Fruits, Talks on Manure* — and acquired so many oddities — a cello and music stand, a model of the Erie steamboat, a collection of beer mugs and Brueghel prints — that his motto became "Dig It Up, Dust It Off, and Give It to Benchley."

In his long career as a drama critic, first for *Life* and later for the *New Yorker,* Benchley spent most of his time out on the town. A typical day consisted of breakfast at eleven-thirty, fooling around at the typewriter for a while, late lunch at the Algonquin, answering mail, telephoning his wife or visiting friends in the afternoon. At six or seven he would go for drinks to Jack and Charlie's Puncheon Club, the forerunner of the "21" Club at 42 West 49th Street, or Tony's, a speakeasy where Heywood Broun and Franklin P. Adams also gathered, then to the theater, then back to Jack and Charlie's for dinner and, after it closed, on to Harlem to Dickie Wells', the Nest or the Savoy Ballroom. He even went out to write and sometimes rented a room at Polly Adler's, the "house" run by the well-known madam. When he died, a wake, presided over by Marc Connelly, was held at "21," and a plaque reading "Robert Benchley, His Corner, 1889–1945" was placed over the table where he customarily sat.

Benchley and Parker were two of the regulars in a group called the Round Table, which began to gather at the Algonquin Hotel in 1919. The group is said to have originated when press agent John Peter Toohey took *New York Times* drama critic Alexander Woollcott to the Algonquin to sample the angel cake. Woollcott, Franklin P. Adams, who under the byline F. P. A. wrote a famous column for the *New York World* called "The Conning Tower," and Heywood Broun, then a sportswriter for the *Tribune,* formed a weekly luncheon habit. Others joined them. The story goes that the midgets from the Hippodrome across the street teased Robert Sherwood, who was extremely tall, whenever he left the office of *Vanity Fair.* "As a result," records Nathaniel Benchley, "Sherwood wouldn't go out to lunch alone, and he took to asking Robert [Benchley] and Mrs. Parker if they would mind walking on either side of him, at least until they got past the midgets. This led to the three of them having lunch together every day." So Sherwood, Parker and Benchley joined Toohey, Woollcott, Broun and Adams and soon they were all meeting daily first in the Pergola Room (now the Oak Room), then in the Rose Room at a long table and finally at the round table from which the group drew its name. Eventually the group also included Edna Ferber, George S. Kaufman, Marc Connelly, Harold Ross, his wife, Jane Grant, and others, and became known to the public through F. P. A., who would report the group's witticisms in his column.

Woollcott's biographer, Samuel Hopkins Adams, explained that "leadership in the group went, by tacit consent, to F. P. A., due to his reputation, already national, his wit, and in some degree to his financial status as by far the highest paid newspaperman of the lot. He was . . . a lean, sinewy man, faintly demonic of expression, with a passion for Horatian odes and base-line tennis; fast as a boxer on his mental feet, and endowed with an intolerant manner masking a tolerant mind."

Edna Ferber wrote of the group: "Their standards were high, their vocabulary fluent, fresh, astringent and very, very tough. Theirs was a tonic influence, one on the other, and all on the world of American letters. The people they could not and would not stand were the bores, hypocrites, sentimentalists and the socially pretentious. They were ruthless toward charlatans, toward the pompous and the mentally and artistically dishonest. Casual, incisive, they had a terrible integrity about their work and a boundless ambition." Still, this collection of witty critics, playwrights and journalists should not be confused with writers in a more serious literary tradition. "People romanticize [the Round Table]," said Dorothy Parker. "These were no giants. Think of who was writing in those days — Lardner, Fitzgerald, Faulkner, and Hemingway. Those were the real giants. The Round Table was just a lot of people telling jokes and telling each other how good they were."

Today the round table stands in the Oak Room, where it is occasionally reserved by Marc Connelly, one of the few surviving members of the group. The Rose Room, restored some years ago by theatrical designer Oliver Smith, is much as it was in the twenties. *New Yorker* people still lunch there regularly — editor William Shawn usually sits at table number one — as do editors from the nearby publishing houses. The lobby, with its dark wood paneling, Chinese lamps, grandfather clock, velvet-covered sofas and wing chairs, has never been changed, except for new upholstery, and is a favorite cocktail place for literary people.

On Saturday nights in the early twenties, the Round Table extended itself into a poker game called the Thanatopsis Pleasure and Literary Club, a name taken from Sinclair Lewis's *Main Street,* later modified to the Thanatopsis Poker and In-

side Straight Club. The poker game, which included Harold
Ross, Raoul Fleischmann, an heir of the baking family, and
Herbert Bayard Swope, editor of the *New York World,* as well
as Kaufman, Toohey, Connelly, F. P. A., Broun and Woollcott,
had its origins in a wartime game in Paris. Ross, who was to
found the *New Yorker,* promoted the resurrection of the game
at his 11th Street apartment. Later the players moved to an
upstairs room at the Algonquin and later still to Ross's 47th
Street house, "21," and the Colony restaurant.

The founding of the *New Yorker* magazine in 1925 can be
seen as a product of Harold Ross's association with the people
of the Round Table and the Thanatopsis Club. From 1917
to 1919 Ross had worked in Paris with Woollcott and F. P. A.
as editor of *Stars and Stripes,* the armed services magazine.
When he came back to New York he started *Home Sector,* an
unsuccessful stateside version of the magazine. In 1920 he
married Jane Grant, a reporter for the *New York Times,* and
on the day of the wedding signed a contract to edit the *American Legion Weekly.* The two lived on her salary and saved
his for a publishing venture.

After the *American Legion Weekly,* Ross briefly edited a
humor magazine called *Judge.* Then in 1924 he met Raoul
Fleischmann over the Thanatopsis poker table. He sold Fleischmann on his idea for a weekly magazine of humor and satire that
would incorporate the Algonquin's sophisticated, debunking
attitude toward life. With $25,000 from Fleischmann and $20,-
000 from Ross and Grant, the *New Yorker* (the name was contributed by John Peter Toohey) began publication at 25 West
45th Street, the building that had housed the *Smart Set.*

If the *Smart Set* had started out as a serious literary forum
and ended as a "soufflé," the *New Yorker* took the reverse direction. The first issue, one critic remarked, looked as if "it had
been made up by the office cat's knocking over the wastebasket."
It was filled with sophomoric humor and half-baked Broadway

gossip. Gradually, however, Ross assembled the staff that would give the magazine its distinctive quality. E. B. White arrived in 1926 and took over the lead "Notes and Comment" column. James Thurber came in 1927 and set the tone for "The Talk of the Town," editing and rewriting the offerings of amateurs and several reporters. The editorial influence of the two extended far beyond their departments. Both contributed pieces regularly and so much set the tone of the magazine as to be considered its soul. And both also fulfilled Ross's dream of publishing humor of such high caliber that it could be called literature. A third staff member helped to establish the *New Yorker*'s literary importance. Katharine Sergeant, who later married E. B. White, came to the *New Yorker* as a reader in 1925. She eventually became managing editor and took responsibility for the literary aspects of the magazine. Of the Algonquin group, Robert Benchley wrote "The Wayward Press" and later covered the theater, and Alexander Woollcott contributed a weekly column, "Shouts and Murmurs."

In the mid-thirties, some members of the editorial staff complained that Ross, who had invested in some outside ventures, had lost interest in the magazine and should be replaced. The story goes that Fleischmann invited Thurber to the Algonquin and asked whom he would suggest. This so incensed the humorist that he picked up the baked potatoes from an adjoining table and began to hurl them across the room. When they were gone, he turned to hard rolls. In *Here at the New Yorker,* Brendan Gill questions the accuracy of the story and suggests that Thurber made it up. "No restaurant keeps baked potatoes in baskets on tables . . ." he says, "and at that time the Algonquin served not hard rolls but popovers . . . It is just possible that a drunken Thurber . . . tossed a single warm popover in Fleischmann's direction . . ."

It was Thurber who best described the *New Yorker* in its

early days. "The new magazine reflected the reckless detachment of the period," he wrote.

> It wore no armor and it sought no grail; it did not carry a sword cane or even an umbrella. Since neither trumpet nor banner had called it into existence, it was not going anywhere to do anything about anything. It was just walking along, like any other visitor from out of town, looking into the expensive store windows, gazing up at the tall buildings, widening its eyes and dropping its jaw at impressive statistics or unusual facts. The amiable periodical tiptoed away from disputes and disturbances, since it had nothing particularly in mind to prove or disprove, to attack or defend. Now and then it jostled the celebrated, or thumbed its nose at the powerful, but all in a spirit of gay mockery. The *New Yorker* was not really angry. It just didn't give a good goddam.

As Dwight Macdonald, who was later to become a member of the *New Yorker* staff, observed in 1937 in a highly critical essay called "Lie Down and Laugh," this position already represented a radical change from the magazine's purposes at its founding. "The *New Yorker*," he remarked, "was established to exploit commercially two groups of sophisticated readers: those who followed Mencken and Nathan and those who looked to the Manhattan wits centering around the Algonquin Hotel . . . The brash Menckenians and the aggressively sophisticated Algonquins have been superseded by the timorous and bewildered Thurber." In recent years, however, the *New Yorker* has changed again, most noticeably perhaps in the editorial "Notes and Comment," which has become decidedly angry and has taken as strong stands on such issues as the Vietnam War and the impeachment of President Nixon as any periodical with a popular following. As Macdonald later reported in 1966, the magazine had begun to be weightier and more thoughtful when William Shawn became managing editor. "Do we have to run that in our funny little magazine?" Ross would ask when presented with something he considered too serious. When Shawn succeeded to the editorship after Ross's death in 1951, the change became more pronounced, with a shift to what Macdonald called "elaborately researched reportage and 'intellectual stuff' . . . The different temperaments of the two editors were responsible," he wrote. "Also the difference between the pre-war and the post-war periods. By 1940, Ross, Benchley, Thurber, White, Dorothy Parker and the other original 'New Yorker wits' found themselves in a less clement atmosphere."

Today the New Yorker has come to represent the highest standards in literature and journalism. It survives as the major mass market for serious fiction and poetry and each year publishes important nonfiction books in advance of publication. It now occupies offices on the eighteenth, nineteenth and twentieth floors of 25 West 43rd Street, where writers, editors and artists work out of a series of warrens identified only by numbers handpainted in the same curving style as the typeface used on the magazine's cover. The atmosphere has been described as "donnish," an impression reinforced by the old wooden desks and threadbare carpets that furnish the rooms. With the exception of a Fabian Bachrach photographic portrait of Ross, the halls are decorated only with maps — subways maps, a Hammond International World Map, a postal zone map, "Sorties de Paris" — each so commonplace that finally, taken as a whole, they transcend their ordinariness, like a work of conceptual art.

·

The crowd that gathered at the Algonquin had two additional Midtown meeting places. One was Neysa McMein's studio on 57th Street. Edna Ferber, who modeled her character Dallas O'Mara in So Big on McMein, described the apartment: "At her untidy hospitable studio you might encounter, any day between three and six, anyone from Irving Berlin to the reigning Van-

derbilt; from Father Duffy to H. G. Wells. And in the midst
of the talk, and the music made by someone at the piano,
and the roar of the L train on Sixth there was Neysa working calmly away at her canvas in the middle of the room,
her hair wrung into a careless knot at her neck, her smock
smeared with paint, her face smudged but wreathed in lovely
smiles." Although the Round Table group was present en
masse at every McMein party, her circle was a wider one.
Alexander Woollcott noted:

> The population is . . . wildly variegated. Over at the piano
> Jascha Heifetz and Arthur Samuels may be trying to find what
> four hands can do in the syncopation of a composition never
> thus desecrated before. Irving Berlin is encouraging them.
> Squatted uncomfortably around an ottoman, Franklin
> P. Adams, Marc Connelly and Dorothy Parker will be play-
> ing cold hands to see who will buy dinner that evening. At
> the bookshelf Robert C. Benchley and Edna Ferber are amusing
> themselves vastly by thoughtfully autographing her set of Mark
> Twain for her. In the corner, some jet-bedecked dowager from
> a statelier milieu is taking it all in, immensely diverted. Chap-
> lin or Chaliapin, Alice Duer Miller or Wild Bill Donovan,
> Father Duffy or Mary Pickford — any or all of them may be
> there.

The second address where the Algonquin crowd gathered was
a kind of commune far west on 47th Street. Hawley Truax, a
lawyer who had been Woollcott's classmate at Hamilton College
and helped to finance the *New Yorker,* bought twin brick
houses at 412 and 414 West 47th Street and, in partnership with
Harold Ross and Jane Grant, set about modernizing them to
be used as a joint residence. Woollcott invited himself into the
cooperative. The houses had no electricity but were heated by
potbellied stoves and fireplaces in every room. The two original
kitchens were combined and made into a communal dining
room, which opened into a backyard in which they installed a

large fountain. There was a Chinese cook and anyone could bring guests for dinner as long as advance warning was given. The dining room, furnished with a black lacquered sideboard and walnut tables, was the headquarters for the weekly Thanatopsis poker games.

The Rosses had an apartment with a sitting room on the first floor, Truax and Woollcott were on the second (Woollcott characterized his apartment as "a small and disordered flat in the Gas House district") and Kate Ogleby and William Powell, friends of Woollcott's from Cleveland, had apartments on the third floor. A housewarming was held in 1923; playwright Charles MacArthur had invitations printed and passed them out on the street. Along with Dorothy Parker and Harpo Marx, he rented a merry-go-round and gave the neighborhood children rides. Also present were F. Scott Fitzgerald, Edna St. Vincent Millay, who read her poems, and George Gershwin, who played a new composition called "Rhapsody in Blue." The house acquired various names — Chinaman's Chance and the Speakeasy, because of a mysterious-looking peephole in the door, Wit's End, coined by Dorothy Parker, and the Gash House, Woollcott's favorite. Life consisted of periods of guerrilla warfare between truces — Woollcott disrupted the household by invading the Ross apartment at any hour of the night, crashing noncommunal parties and raiding gatherings to carry guests off to his own apartment. He left in the spring of 1926 and the following year both Ross and Grant moved when their marriage broke up.

Two other Midtown living rooms served as literary and intellectual centers in the twenties and thirties. Carl Van Vechten, who arrived in New York in 1906 to be assistant music critic for the *New York Times,* made his home, no matter how modest, a gathering place from the very beginning. His first address was "a large room at 39 West 39th Street where Sinclair

Lewis occupied an adjoining chamber." The two would nod to one another in passing. In 1907 Van Vechten was at 528 Seventh Avenue near 40th Street. Although he had only a single room without bath or kitchen, he entertained regularly, usually serving grapefruit, which was then "as exotic as pomegranates." It was not until the early twenties, when Van Vechten and his wife, the actress Fania Marinoff, moved to 150 West 55th Street, that their celebrated parties began. Van Vechten had by this time begun his association with and sponsorship of the writers and other figures of the Harlem Renaissance. So many prominent Negroes attended his parties that they were reported as a matter of course in black society columns and Walter White called his apartment the Midtown branch of the NAACP. In addition, many white writers — Somerset Maugham, Hugh Walpole, Witter Bynner, Arthur Davison Ficke, Louis Untermeyer — visited at various times. The double apartment had a black and orange cubist study, a sea green, purple and raspberry drawing room, and was "full of silver fishes and colored glass balls and ceiling-high shelves of gaily-bound books." Here after all-night parties or jaunts to Harlem, Van Vechten worked as long as twelve hours a day on his most controversial book, *Nigger Heaven* (see Chapter IX, Harlem).

Emily Clark, who wrote *Innocence Abroad,* a literary memoir, described one party "with George Gershwin at the piano playing and singing bits from his current musical show to a crowd of people, among whom Theodore Dreiser sat, heavy and brooding, the direct antithesis, almost a contradiction, of all that Gershwin means. And Elinor Wylie sat, aloof and lovely, a contradiction and denial of all that both Dreiser and Gershwin mean. Later some woman danced, and later still Paul Robeson sang. Last of all, James Weldon Johnson recited his 'Go Down, Death' and Carl hovered about in doorways, his face, as always on such evenings, benevolent and shining."

Carl Van Vechten, Alfred A. Knopf, Jr., and James Weldon
Johnson at a joint birthday party in the 1930s.

For several years Van Vechten gave an annual party for himself, James Weldon Johnson and Alfred A. Knopf, Jr., because
their birthdays all fell on June 17. In 1936 the Van Vechtens
moved to Central Park West, where Van Vechten continued
his unique role in the artistic life of New York. As Edward
Lueders wrote in the *New Republic:* "In the fifty years since
he took up residence in New York, Van Vechten has been

friend, host, adviser, champion, and appreciative audience to three generations of celebrities in society, literature, and the arts. In the process, he has become perhaps the most successful dilettante in the land, a sophisticated ringleader among the intelligentsia and a genial patron of the arts."

Near Van Vechten's 55th Street address, in the Alwyn Court, an apartment building with an extraordinary, ornate façade cast in terra cotta, lived the three Stettheimer sisters, Ettie, Carrie and Florine. Ettie wrote two novels, Florine was a painter and Carrie worked for twenty years on a ten-room doll house, decorated with miniature but authentic works of art by William Zorach, Archipenko, Gaston Lachaise and others, now in the Museum of the City of New York. At their home, recalled Virgil Thomson, who was one of the visitors, gathered "a selection of New York's rather fine intellectual life." The apartment was done in "the marble and gold and red velvet German-royalty style with a fluffy overlay of modern Baroque," wrote Thomson. "There were crystal pendants everywhere and gold fringes and lace and silk curtains so much longer than the windows that they stood out in planned puffs and lay no less than two feet on the waxed floors." In the evenings Ettie usually wore red taffeta with puffy skirts tightly closed around each ankle, Carrie wore gold and white and Florine wore black velvet.

.

The Algonquin's reputation as a literary hotel had predated the Round Table group, going back to Mencken's visits there in 1914, and was to continue after the famous wits stopped meeting. When Heywood Broun ran for Congress on the Socialist ticket in 1930, he had his campaign offices at the hotel. When Gertrude Stein visited America in 1934 after an absence of twenty-five years, she and Alice B. Toklas took a three-room suite at the Algonquin. On her first evening in the city Stein took a walk to Times Square and saw the lights of the Times Building repetitiously announcing her arrival in New York. The same year, James Thurber went to live at the Algonquin after the breakup of his marriage. One evening he met F. Scott Fitzgerald, who was also staying there. They spent the night drinking at Tony's and drove up to the hotel in a cab at daylight. When they discovered they had something in common — they were nearly the same age and both had daughters — they got back in the cab. They drove around the park, discussing Ring Lardner. Thurber was also a habitué of Costello's Bar and Grill at 44th Street and Third Avenue and there, in ninety minutes one night, he drew a mural depicting the battle of the sexes. When the drawings were painted over, Thurber did another set. Since then Costello's has moved twice, murals and all, and is now at 225 East 44th Street.

From the thirties to the fifties, William Faulkner frequently stayed at the Algonquin when he came to New York to see his publishers. One year his wife and friends were unable to reach him and finally found him unconscious on the floor of his Algonquin room. He had been drinking and had burned his back leaning against a steam pipe. When he won the Nobel Prize in 1949, he wrote his acceptance speech on Algonquin stationery. Parts of "Barn Burning," *Requiem for a Nun, A Fable, The Mansion* and *The Reivers* were written at the hotel.

There is a myth that anything written at the Algonquin must be a success. Perhaps in hope, if not belief, many writers — including Tennessee Williams, John Updike, Bruce Catton, Peter De Vries, Gore Vidal, Graham Greene, Günter Grass, Art Buchwald, Thornton Wilder and John Osborne — still stay at the hotel.

Other Midtown hotels have, to a lesser degree, acquired

something of a literary history. Amy Lowell stayed at the St. Regis at Fifth Avenue and 55th Street in the early years of the century and at the Belmont in the twenties. She always reserved a suite of five rooms — a bedroom with vacant rooms on either side, a sitting room and a room for her companion, Ada Russell. She ordered all the clocks to be stopped and any objects that reflected light covered with dark cloths. She worked at night, slept from 6:00 A.M. to 2:30 P.M. and saw visitors only after 5:00. She was astute at the "harvesting" end of publishing, which she conducted in New York. She would call all the major newspapers and magazines to find out who was reviewing her latest book. Then she invited each reviewer to tea, explained her intentions in the book and insisted he write as he pleased. This usually assured the success of the review.

William Saroyan had a special affection for the Great Northern Hotel at 118 West 57th Street, where he stayed in 1935 after his first book was published. "I loved being at The Great Northern Hotel," he wrote, "and I went back to the hotel again and again when I was in New York — until at last it just wouldn't do any more: the hotel had changed, I had grown more worldly, I had become wealthy, and the world itself had changed, so I moved on and up, as the saying is." Most recently he has stayed at the Royalton.

Ernest Hemingway rewrote the galley proofs of *For Whom the Bell Tolls* in the Hotel Barclay at 111 East 48th Street in ninety-six consecutive hours, never leaving his room. In later years he always stayed at the Sherry-Netherland because he liked the "good protection" — no name on the register, phone calls screened, newsmen and photographers thrown off the scent. But in 1959 he gave up the hotel for a three-room pied-à-terre at 1 East 62nd Street, a once luxurious town house that had been divided into apartments.

F. Scott Fitzgerald conducted most of his New York life in

hotels and portrayed the city as the visitor's glamorous mecca of public places rather than the homes and offices where people lived and worked. "To this day," Alfred Kazin has written, "Fitzgerald remains the only poet of New York's upper-class landmarks . . . New York was a dreamland to Fitzgerald. It represented his imagination of what is forever charming, touched by the glamour of money, romantically tender and gay." His characteristic view is expressed in the first pages of *This Side of Paradise,* in which he describes the city as seen by Amory Blaine:

> New York burst upon him on Washington's birthday with the brilliance of a long-anticipated event. His glimpse of it as a vivid whiteness against a deep blue sky had left a picture of splendor that rivalled the dream cities in the Arabian Nights; but this time he saw it by electric light, and romance gleamed from the chariot-race sign on Broadway and from the women's eyes at the Astor, where he and young Paskert from St. Regis' had dinner. When they walked down the aisle of the theatre, greeted by the nervous twanging and discord of untuned violins and the sensuous, heavy fragrance of paint and powder, he moved in a sphere of epicurean delight.

Amory Blaine's New York is compounded of afternoons at the Plaza, the theater, dinner at the Ritz or the Princeton Club and cocktails at the Biltmore bar, as was Fitzgerald's. Scott and Zelda were married in the rectory of St. Patrick's Cathedral in April 1920 and spent their honeymoon in Room 2109 of the Biltmore. When they were asked to leave because of their disruptiveness — Fitzgerald did handstands in the lobby, for instance — they moved to the Commodore. Late in 1920 they took an apartment at 38 West 59th Street and had their meals delivered from the Plaza Hotel. They held parties attended by H. L. Mencken, George Jean Nathan, Edna Ferber, Dorothy Parker, John Peale Bishop and Edmund Wilson. It was during this period that Zelda took her famous dips into the Pulitzer Fountain opposite the hotel. Then they were off to Europe and St. Paul, Minnesota. In September 1922 they stayed at the Plaza while looking for a place to settle in New York, finally choosing a house in Great Neck. *The Great Gatsby*, set against the Great Neck background, also used the Plaza for the critical scene in which Gatsby and Daisy confront Tom Buchanan with their love for one another.

.

Among the publishers the writers came to visit, the most colorful was Horace Liveright, whose offices in a four-story brownstone at 61 West 48th Street became another of the gathering places of the era. Liveright had started in publishing with Albert Boni, who had run the Washington Square Book Shop in Greenwich Village (see Chapter II, Greenwich Village). In 1917 Boni and Liveright was founded with headquarters at 105 West 40th Street. Gradually the established nineteenth-century publishing firms — D. Appleton and Company; Dodd, Mead; Doubleday, Page; E. P. Dutton; Harper and Brothers; Henry Holt; G. P. Putnam's and Charles Scribner's — were being joined by a new breed. These publishers, who were generally Jewish (Jews had been excluded from advancement in the established companies), launched into fresh areas. B. W. Huebsch, who entered publishing in 1902 and was to merge with Harold K. Guinzburg in 1925 to form the Viking Press, found his authors abroad and published H. G. Wells, D. H. Lawrence and James Joyce as well as translations of Gorky, Chekhov and Strindberg. Alfred and Blanche Knopf, who started in 1915, also published Europeans, like Tolstoy, Gogol, Dostoevsky, Nietzsche and Mann, but added the Americans Mencken, Nathan and Cather to their lists. But Boni and Liveright were the first to publish such Village writers as Mary Heaton Vorse, Hutchins Hapgood, Harry Kemp, Max Eastman, Maxwell Bodenheim, John Reed and Eugene O'Neill. In 1928 the two publishers tossed a coin to determine who would control the firm. Liveright won, and with the Modern Library, which Boni had founded, as the backstop of the company broadened out and soon became spectacularly successful. "When I went to work for Horace Liveright in 1924," Bennett Cerf wrote in an article on Liveright's death, "his list included Dreiser, O'Neill, Anderson, George Moore, Atherton, Lewisohn, Jeffers, Van Loon, Rose Macaulay, Sigmund Freud . . . and for good measure he had the Modern Library, which although almost completely neglected, was already selling over three hundred thousand copies a year. What a list for a one-man publishing house!"

Horace Liveright also had an unusually talented staff. In addition to editor-in-chief T. R. Smith, whom he hired away from the *Century Magazine* of which he was editor, there was Cerf, who later cofounded Random House; Richard Simon, who left to form Simon and Schuster; and Donald Friede, who left to start the now defunct Covici-Friede. The readers at various times included Beatrice Kaufman, the wife of George S. Kaufman, who provided a link to the Algonquin group, and Lillian Hellman. Yet in spite of all these assets and a steady stream of best sellers (the firm had six in 1928 alone), Liveright seemed determined to fail. He risked large sums producing plays on Broadway and speculating in the stock market, and, by selling the Modern Library to Bennett Cerf in 1925, committed a suicidal error. Without the steadily selling backlist the Modern Library had provided, the firm was forced to produce best sellers on demand in order to survive. By 1930 Liveright was bankrupt and in 1933 he was dead at the age of forty-six.

While in its heyday, however, the firm occupied a special place in publishing. As Lillian Hellman put it:

A job with any publishing house was a plum, but a job with Horace Liveright was a bag of plums . . . Liveright, Julian Messner, T. R. Smith, Manuel Komroff, and a few even younger men had made a new and brilliant world for books . . . They discovered or persuaded over Faulkner, Freud, Hemingway, O'Neill, Hart Crane, Sherwood Anderson, E. E. Cummings . . . all of them attracted by the vivid, impetuous, high-living men who were the editors. It didn't hurt that Horace was handsome and daring, Julian serious and kind, Tom Smith almost erudite with his famous collection of erotica and odd pieces of knowledge . . . that the advances they gave were large and the parties even larger, full of lush girls and good liquor; that the sympathy and attention given to writers, young or old, was more generous than had been known before, possibly more real than has been known since.

Liveright and his firm occupied the entire brownstone. The stock room and shipping department were in the basement and the business offices on the first floor. At the back of the second floor, reached by a nineteenth-century staircase, was a reception room with an enormous fireplace, three Italian double doors and a bust of Theodore Dreiser. Beyond the doors on the extension roof was an awning-covered roof garden with furniture upholstered in shades of coral, mauve and jade. Here and in the reception room were held the famous parties. In addition to any Liveright authors who were in town, guests might include Otto Kahn, New York Mayor Jimmy Walker, Herbert Bayard Swope, Paul Robeson, John Barrymore, Thomas Wolfe, the Millay sisters, Carl Van Vechten, Elinor Wylie and Sinclair Lewis. The parties sometimes spilled over into Liveright's office in the front half of the second floor, which also served the publisher as a studio apartment. There was a narrow carved Italian desk, a huge Chinese jar for wastepaper, a fireplace, lounging chairs, grand piano and bar and an adjoining zinc-lined shower.

Other publishing offices would fulfill more than the usual
function. The former Random House offices in the architecturally historic Villard Houses, designed by Stanford White,
on Madison Avenue between 50th and 51st streets, for instance,
became one of William Faulkner's favorite writing places when
he found he could no longer work well in Oxford, Mississippi.
He liked the ornate rooms with their high ceilings, paneled
walls and heavy draperies, and would often arrive early in the
morning when the doors were still locked and sometimes sleep
over in the fifth-floor employees lounge. But no other publishing house would ever approach Liveright's in boldness or in
style.

·

One other Midtown institution served as a focal point for
literary life from the twenties onward. On the first day of
January 1920, Frances Steloff opened a bookstore at 128 West
45th Street. It was called the Gotham Book and Art, and a sign
designed by John Held, Jr. — depicting three men in a boat
and bearing the store's motto, "Wise Men Fish Here" — was
hung outside. In 1923 the store moved to 51 West 47th Street
and called itself the Gotham Book Mart. Here Steloff began to
stock an impressive number of little magazines and a wide
selection of the newest poetry and prose. It became known as
"the place where you can buy *transition*," and because young
writers were grateful to Steloff for stocking their work, they
often came to the store. The poet, novelist and essayist Christopher Morley, who lived across the street at 46 West 47th,
helped to make the place a literary hangout when he established
the Three Hours for Lunch Club, which was joined by Buckminster Fuller, William Rose Benét, book exporter Bill Hall
and others. The members came in the early afternoon, had
food passed to them from Chez Maurice next door and ate in

The garden of the Gotham Book Mart, with Paris-inspired book stalls,
at 51 West 47th Street, where it was located until 1946. The umbrella
at left sheltered the "Three Hours for Lunch Club."

the garden. Mencken visited the store regularly when he was in the city. One day he and Dreiser came in and found some of their own books among the first editions. They embellished them with long inscriptions and then began to dedicate other books, including more than one Bible, which they signed "With the compliments of the authors."

In the thirties the Gotham was used for a series of lectures initiated by Samuel Putnam, editor of the *New Review,* a short-lived international quarterly. He called them the Dog Star evenings, in reference to Pope's *Dunciad.* Another time about a hundred writers, nearly all of whom had lived abroad, met to establish an expatriates' group called the Left Bank Club of America. The store also frequently held publication parties and celebrations for foreign writers. Among the many honored were Edith and Osbert Sitwell, Dylan Thomas, Paul Goodman, Anaïs Nin, Jean Cocteau, Katherine Anne Porter and William Carlos Williams. In 1939 a "wake" was held to celebrate the publication of Joyce's *Finnegans Wake;* clay pipes and tobacco were imported from Belfast and Old Bushmills from Dublin. The Gotham is also the home of the James Joyce Society. When it was organized in 1947, T. S. Eliot bought the first membership.

Frances Steloff went out of her way to help writers and other artists. Edmund Wilson once phoned from Cape Cod to tell her

The invitation to "Finnegans Wake," a 1939 celebration for the publication of James Joyce's book.

The Dead Come to Life at "Finnegans Wake"

Who, confidentially, will be the life of the party

on May 4th at the

Gotham Book Mart

51 West 47th Street

Obsequies will be held in the garden, beginning at 5 p.m.

You are invited to be a mourner   R.S.V.P.

At the "wake," from left: Christopher Morley, Frances Steloff, Arthur Davison Ficke, book collector Wilbur Macy Stone, Joyce's biographer Herbert Gorman, Mrs. Steloff's assistant Kay Steele, Mrs. William Carlos Williams (with hat), William Carlos Williams (with hat), actor Albert Hecht.

that John Dos Passos needed $200 to pay his insurance premium. She wired the money and was sent the holograph manuscript of *Manhattan Transfer* as collateral. Wilson himself would sometimes borrow money out of the cash register and leave an IOU. Martha Graham borrowed $1000 to stage her first dance concert. Henry Miller sent regular SOS's for food, clothing, a car, money to go to Mexico, and they were posted on the store's bulletin board. In 1941, this philanthropy was institutionalized in a group called the Writers' Emergency Fund, which loaned money to young writers with no strings attached.

In 1946, when Steloff had to move and couldn't find another shop, Christopher Morley and Mark Van Doren discovered that Columbia University owned the brownstone at 41 West 47th

At a Gotham Book Mart party: front row, from left, Malcolm
Cowley, Marianne Moore, Frances Steloff and Kenneth Burke.
Standing, Allen Tate (left) and Stephen Spender.

Street. They went to see the trustees, who eventually sold her the building. Today the Gotham remains much the same as it always was, cramped and cluttered with half a million books and hundreds of photographs of writers, the great and near great, peering down from the moldings. At eighty-six, Miss Steloff still works in the shop daily, commanding an alcove of works on metaphysics and theosophy. In 1967 she sold the store to Andreas Brown, a bibliographer and appraiser of rare books, who has attempted to preserve the ambiance while making the operation more efficient. Now, once again, the store is planning to move.

•

Midtown remains the center of American publishing and the harvesting continues as it did in Whitman's day. Several of the publishers have new, modern buildings of their own — Random House at 201 East 50th Street, Harper & Row at 10 East 53rd and Harcourt Brace Jovanovich at 757 Third Avenue. The two-hour lunch is the literary institution of the seventies, and the haunts of writers and editors today are likely to be the restaurants that serve an elegant midday meal rather than the night-spots that distinguished the twenties. The names change as the restaurants open and close and as the publishing community tires of the old and goes on to the new. Midtown still has two prime literary landmarks in the Algonquin Hotel and the Gotham Book Mart. It still has the Broadway theater and perhaps the last traces of the urban glamour Fitzgerald cherished. William Dean Howells's observation about the city and literature holds true: New York still publishes it, criticizes it and circulates it — with the important difference that today New York, by far the largest market for serious books, reads it too.

•

Midtown Tour

With the exception of a few interesting houses, Midtown literary landmarks consist primarily of hotels and office buildings. You can sit in the restaurant of the Park Lane Hotel and imagine yourself in the apartment of Zelda and Scott Fitzgerald, or have a drink at the Café de la Paix at the St. Moritz and enjoy the same view William Dean Howells did at the turn of the century. Or you can patronize the surviving restaurants and bars with literary associations.

1. Fifth Avenue and Central Park South. The Plaza Hotel, immortalized in *The Great Gatsby* by F. Scott Fitzgerald, is one of the city's architectural landmarks. Designed by Henry J. Hardenbergh (1907), it is richly detailed with dormers, balconies and balustrades (p. 208).

2. 781 Fifth Avenue, on the northeast corner of 59th Street. The Sherry Netherland Hotel was designed by Schultze & Weaver, architects in 1927. Hemingway stayed here for its "good protection" (p. 207).

3. 1 East 62nd Street. Beginning in 1959, Hemingway had a three-room pied-à-terre in this once-luxurious town house (p. 207).

(3a) 38 West 59th Street. The Park Lane Hotel now occupies this address, but the Fitzgeralds lived in an apartment house here in the early 1920s (p. 208).

(3b) 40 West 59th Street. William Dean Howells lived here at the turn of the century. Now on this site is a restaurant called "Mickey Mantle's." There is a plaque: "New York Yankees 1951-69."

(3c) 48 West 59th Street. Now the St. Moritz Hotel. There is a plaque memorializing Howells's residence at this location.

4. 911 Seventh Avenue, also known as 180 West 58th Street, on the southeast corner of Seventh Avenue. The Stettheimer sisters lived and entertained in this unique building, the Alwyn Court Apartments. The profuse terra-cotta decoration consists of French Renaissance detail, featuring the crowned salamander, symbol of Francis I, king of France. The building was designed in 1909 by architects Harde & Short (p. 205).

5. 215 West 57th Street. The Art Students League, which was designed in 1892 by Henry J. Hardenbergh, architect (p. 188).

6. 130 West 57th Street. William Dean Howells lived here from 1908 to 1920. The exterior seems to be largely in its original condition, except for one storefront (p. 186).

(6a) 118 West 57th Street. The Great Northern Hotel. William Saroyan first stayed here in 1935 (p. 207).

(6b) 57 West 57th Street. Dorothy Parker had a small apartment, and Neysa McMein a studio in a building at this location, once frequented by the Algonquin crowd (pp. 193-94).

7. 730 Fifth Avenue, on the southwest corner of 57th Street. The *American Mercury* rented offices in 1924 here in the Heckscher (now Crown) Building which was designed in 1921 by Warren & Wetmore, architects (p. 191).

8. 150 West 55th Street. Carl Van Vechten and his wife Fania Marinoff had a double apartment in this red-brick apartment building from 1924 to 1936 (p. 203).

9. 55th Street and Fifth Avenue. The St. Regis Hotel, where Amy Lowell stayed early in the century was designed in 1904 by Trowbridge & Livingston, architects (p. 207).

10. 21 West 52nd Street. The "21" Club, a with plaque over Robert Benchley's table. This Duggin and Crossman building dates from 1872. "21" is the direct descendant of Jack & Charlie's Puncheon Club which was at 42 West 49th Street until about 1930, where the Algonquin wits and others often met (p. 195).

11. 50th–51st streets at Madison Avenue. The Villard Houses designed in 1884 by architects McKim, Mead, & White. These four different houses intended to look like one, were modeled on the Palazzo della Cancelláría in

Rome. Random House owned the mansion on the 51st Street corner from 1946 to 1969. The famous photograph of Ayn Rand on the book jacket of *Atlas Shrugged* shows her seated in a second floor window at the corner of the court (p. 212).

12. 51st Street and Madison Avenue. On the southwest corner is the rectory of St. Patrick's Cathedral, where Scott and Zelda Fitzgerald were married in 1920. The building was designed in 1880 by architect James Renwick (p. 208).

13. 111 East 48th Street, on the northwest corner of Lexington Avenue. Once the Barclay Hotel and now the Hotel Inter-Continental, where Hemingway rewrote the galleys of *For Whom the Bell Tolls* in ninety-six hours, never leaving his room. (p. 207)

(13a) 46th–47th streets, on the west side of Madison Avenue. This was the location of "the Ritz" (p. 208).

(13b) 43rd–44th streets, on the east side of Madison Avenue. The site of the Hotel Biltmore. In the early 1980s it was stripped down to its steel frame and rebuilt as an office building (p. 208).

14. 225 East 44th Street. Costello's Bar and Grill. The Thurber drawings are still here, although the business has moved from its original location at 44th Street and Third Avenue. This is an old building, probably much like the original (p. 206).

(14a) 125 East 42nd Street, on the northwest corner of Lexington Avenue. This was once the Commodore Hotel. In 1980 it was rebuilt as the Grand Hyatt Hotel (p. 208).

(14b) 41st–42nd Streets and the west side of Park Avenue. The location of the Belmont Hotel, where Amy Lowell stayed in the 1920s (p. 207).

(14c) 39th Street and Park Avenue, on the northwest corner. In Fitzgerald's day this was the Princeton Club (p. 208).

15. 20 West 43rd Street and through the block to 28 West 44th Street. The *New Yorker* moved here in 1935 (p. 200) and remained until it moved across the street to 25 West 43rd Street early in 1991.

16. 19 West 44th Street and through the block to 45th Street. *Vanity Fair* had its offices here in the 1920s in the Berkeley Building, which was designed in 1917 by Starrett & Van Vleck, architects (p. 192).

17. 25 West 45th Street. The Central Building. The *Smart Set* offices were here in 1923 (p. 190) and the *New Yorker* was located on the 13th floor, from its beginning in 1924 until 1935 (pp. 190, 197).

18. 59 West 44th Street. The Algonquin Hotel, which was designed in 1902 by architects Goldwin & Starrett (pp. 195-97, 205-06).

19. 44 West 44th Street. The Royalton Hotel, where George Jean Nathan and Robert Benchley, at various times, maintained permanent suites. In the mid-1980s, it was converted to an international jet-set hostelry (pp. 190, 194).

(19a) 44th–45th streets and the west side of Broadway. The Astor Hotel was located here. It's now site of a fifty-story office tower, the Astor Plaza (p. 208).

(19b) 43rd Street and Broadway, on the northeast corner. This was the site of Eugene O'Neill's birthplace, the Barrett House, a family-style hotel. It is now a skyscraper, just completed in 1990. A plaque, here for many years, is now on the other corner of the block, at 44th and Broadway.

(19c) 41st Street and the west side of Eighth Avenue. During the depression the WPA Federal Writers' Project occupied a huge loft here in the Port Authority Building. Among the writers on the project were John Cheever, Richard Wright, Muriel Rukeyser, Alfred Kazin, Claude McKay, Ralph Ellison and Philip Rahv. Legmen received $21.67 a week, and the editors, $23.86. As a rule those on the project were not allowed to work on their own writing. Their major achievement was the still-excellent guide to New York City. When Philip Rahv was asked to do an essay for the book dealing with New York's literary history, he refused the assignment, claiming the city had none. After being told about Poe, Melville and the rest, he did the job. Several books eventually came out of the Negro unit of the project, including Claude McKay's *Harlem: Negro Metropolis* and *The Negro in New York*, edited by Roi Ottley and William J. Weatherby. The present Port Authority Building was built in 1950, expanded upward in 1963 and northward in 1980.

20. 412 West 47th Street. This was originally two houses, each twelve-and-a-half feet wide, with separate high stoops and entrances, numbered 412 and 414. They were occupied by Harold Ross, Jane Grant, Alexander Woollcott, and others (pp. 201-02).

21. 46 West 47th Street. Christopher Morley's pied-à-terre; his home was in Roslyn, Long Island (p. 212).

22. 41 West 47th Street. The Gotham Book Mart, perhaps Midtown's most interesting literary landmark, occupies an old brownstone here. The long-time owner, Frances Steloff died in 1989 at the age of 101 (pp. 212-17).

VII. The East Side

IN 1844, shortly after moving to New York, Edgar Allan Poe began a series of letters about the city for the *Columbia Spy,* a newspaper in Pottsville, Pennsylvania. Documenting his wanderings, Poe voiced what would become a perennial protest. He lamented the destruction of the old New York as it made way for urban development. But Poe had more to mourn than the loss of buildings, for what was taking place in his time was the implacable leveling of the island terrain for the implementation of the city's grid plan. He was particularly disturbed by the destruction of the area facing what was then called the Sound on the East Side. For his third letter to the *Spy,* he explored the area around Turtle Bay, a cove that today is the site of the United Nations Park. "A day or two since I procured a light skiff, and with the aid of a pair of sculls . . . made my way around Blackwell's Island, on a voyage of discovery and exploration," he wrote. "The chief interest lay in the scenery of the Manhattan shore, which is here particularly picturesque. The houses are, without exception, frame, and antique . . . I could not look on the magnificent cliffs, and stately trees, which at every moment met my view, without a sigh for the inevitable doom — inevitable and swift."

The leveling Poe anticipated soon took place. The remnants of the magnificent cliffs are barely discernible under the apartment buildings perched on Beekman Place and Sutton Place.

The stately trees have been replaced by frail, constrained city sycamores and oaks surrounded by wickets and ivy. But the East Side today has regained the social ascendancy it had in Poe's time. The region where John Jacob Astor built "Astoria," at 88th Street and First Avenue, and Edith Wharton's first families kept their country homes has been primarily a place for writers to live when their financial standing was assured. And the literature that has used the East Side as its setting has been mainly concerned with society and success.

When Poe was visiting Turtle Bay, Horace Greeley, publisher of the country's most influential paper, the *New York Tribune,* was living there with his family in a spacious old country mansion (see Chapter I, Lower Manhattan). The house, as Greeley wrote, "was located on eight acres of ground, including a wooded ravine, or dell, on the East River, at Turtle Bay, nearly opposite the southernmost point of Blackwell's Island." Accustomed to "the rumble and roar of carriages," Greeley at first found the stillness at night "so sepulchral, unearthly," that he had difficulty in sleeping.

The same year, 1844, Margaret Fuller had published *Summer on the Lakes,* an account of her travels in the "West," which at that time meant Illinois and Wisconsin. Impressed by the book, Greeley invited her to come to New York to write for his newspaper and board at his home. Fuller, who had received, under her father's guidance, the thorough classical education accorded only boys at that time, was a major figure in the New England transcendentalist movement. Famous for her Conversations, discussion groups on high-minded subjects attended first by the best-educated women of Boston and later the men as well, Fuller had edited the *Dial* and moved as an equal in the society of such thinkers as Emerson, Thoreau and Hawthorne. She was reported to have said, "I now know all the people worth knowing in America, and I find no intellect comparable to my own."

Fuller accepted Greeley's offer and arrived at Turtle Bay in December. She described the house:

> Stopping on the Harlem road, you enter a lane nearly a quarter of a mile long, and going by a small brook and pond that locks in the place, and ascending a slightly rising ground, get sight of the house, which, old-fashioned and of mellow tint, fronts on a flower garden filled with shrubs, large vines, and trim box borders . . . Passing through a wide hall, you come out on a piazza stretching the whole length of the house, where one can walk in all weathers; and thence, by a step or two, on a lawn with picturesque masses of rocks, shrubs, and trees overlooking the East River . . . And owing to the currents and the set of the tide, the sails glide sidelong, seeming to greet the house as they pass by.

In New York Fuller became one of the two most important literary critics of her time. She reviewed Carlyle, Browning, Shelley, Tennyson, Longfellow, Hawthorne, Poe, Emerson and Lowell, making judgments that are, for the most part, valid to this day. She also did a series of exposés on New York hospitals and prisons, including the one on Blackwell's Island, and during her stay Greeley published her *Woman in the Nineteenth Century*. This was the first considered feminist statement since Mary Wollstonecraft's *Vindication of the Rights of Women* and the intellectual impetus for the American feminist movement, which would flower in the 1850s. When she left for Europe in August of 1846, she wrote in her farewell column: "New York is the focus, the point where American and European interests converge . . . Twenty months have presented me with a richer and more varied exercise for thought and life, than twenty years could in any other part of these United States."

The other great critic of the era, Edgar Allan Poe, had once written that humanity may be divided into three classes, "men, women, and Margaret Fuller." In the spring and summer of

1846 Poe was also at Turtle Bay, living at a farm belonging to Mr. and Mrs. John L. Miller. The house, at 47th Street and Second Avenue, had an attic with three rooms, where the Poes stayed. They were almost penniless and left a bed behind as payment for their board when they moved to Fordham.

The mansions and farmhouses that Poe, Fuller and Greeley knew were replaced in the 1860s by rows of the brownstones characteristic of New York. After the building of the Second and Third Avenue Els in 1880 and the development of water-front industry, the neighborhood began to deteriorate. By the early twentieth century, it had become the slum, inhabited by a variety of ethnic groups, depicted in Sholem Asch's *East River*. In 1914 the Irish literary critics Padraic and Mary Colum took advantage of the depressed real estate values to find lodgings they liked in the neighborhood. "We rented a furnished apartment in Beekman Place, then an unfashionable and dingy part of the city, though amazingly characterful," Mary Colum wrote.

> For the five-room furnished apartment in a walk-up brown house we paid the sum of 35 dollars a month. All the section east of Third Avenue, around the 50s and below was very foreign and like the moldy and rundown part of a European city — like the Bastille section of Paris, for instance — into which drifted men and women of all European nationalities; in the 50s, Polish and Russian Jews were in the majority. Beekman Place at the time was certainly dingy, but with the bright New York sun shining on the water, the boats and the barges, all the life of the river which we could view from our windows, we felt we had struck the pleasantest living quarters in the City.

The Colums held at-homes with tea and cake on Sundays. J. B. Yeats came often, walking all the way from Petitpas', and John Quinn, the New York lawyer and patron of Irish literature, also visited frequently. One day he was there when Amy Lowell came. "We heard Amy's voice screaming for someone to bring her a chair, as she wanted to rest on the landing before mounting the next flight," Mary Colum recalled. "Quinn bolted down the stairs, and as I followed and introduced them he looked at the bulk of Amy with fairly open astonishment. 'So you are the great John Quinn?' said Amy, rising to the occasion. He should have answered 'So you are the great Amy Lowell?' But he did not."

In the twenties the area began to undergo renewal. One of the most successful efforts was Turtle Bay Gardens, a group of twenty houses back to back on 48th and 49th streets renovated by Mrs. Walton Martin. She painted or stuccoed their brownstone fronts and filled in the swampy backyards to create a communal garden. Still in existence today, the gardens have a central flagstone path, a fountain copied from one at the Villa Medici in Rome and low masonry walls adorned with iron or stone turtles, cobras and snails. Two old willow trees and plantings of holly, laurel, ivy and rhododendron fill the garden. The houses were sold to their owners, among them a number of literary figures, subject to restrictive covenants that have preserved the character of the enclave. The distinguished editor Maxwell Perkins lived at 246 East 49th Street during the thirties.

Perkins, who discovered and launched F. Scott Fitzgerald, Ernest Hemingway, John P. Marquand, Erskine Caldwell, James Jones and others, had a special relationship with Thomas Wolfe. Working almost as a collaborator, he helped Wolfe cut and revise the voluminous drafts of his early books sentence by sentence and line by line. Following conferences at Chatham Walk, an outdoor café at the Hotel Chatham at Vanderbilt Avenue and 48th Street, where the two went after working late, Wolfe would walk Perkins home. They continued talking until

Perkins went out for the early edition of the morning paper. Wolfe's *Of Time and the River* was one of approximately sixty-five books dedicated to Perkins by grateful authors. In 1935 Wolfe moved to a three-room apartment at 865 First Avenue near Perkins's house and spent many evenings at his editor's. There was a break between the two when Wolfe transferred to Harper, presumably to prove he could write his books without Perkins's help. The editor is portrayed as Foxhall Edwards in Wolfe's *The Web and the Rock* and *You Can't Go Home Again*.

Perkins's office at Scribner's, at 597 Fifth Avenue, a few blocks from his home, was the scene of a famous literary confrontation. In 1933 Max Eastman had written an article about Ernest Hemingway, called "Bull in the Afternoon," for the *New Republic*. Four years later Hemingway walked into Perkins's office unexpectedly one afternoon to find Eastman there. Hemingway ripped open his shirt to display his hairy chest, then reached over and opened Eastman's, revealing an expanse of skin that, in Perkins's words, was "bare as a bald man's head." A fight ensued and the two fell to the floor, grappling. Each gave a different version of the story to the newspapers.

Some years later, when writing his memorable appreciation, *Here Is New York*, E. B. White recalled the incident. "I am sitting at the moment in a stifling hotel room in 90-degree heat, halfway down an air shaft, in midtown. No air moves in or out of the room, yet I am curiously affected by emanations from the immediate surroundings. I am twenty-two blocks from where Rudolph Valentino lay in state, eight blocks from where Nathan Hale was executed, five blocks from the publisher's office where Ernest Hemingway hit Max Eastman on the nose, four miles from where Walt Whitman sat sweating out editorials for the Brooklyn Eagle, thirty-four blocks from the street Willa Cather lived in when she came to New York to write books about

Nebraska . . ." and so on. White did not usually live in a hotel room. In fact, of the eight New York apartments he occupied at various times, three were in Turtle Bay: 245 East 48th Street from 1936 to 1938, 239 East 48th during a winter sometime later and 229 East 48th from 1945 to 1957. Here he had what the poet Louise Bogan described as "a dream-duplex." The apartment had "a circle of lemon-colored couches; one fine painting over the fireplace; a broad black cocktail table; and, best of all, four windows (one of them behind a concert grand) onto the communal garden." He chose a tree in the garden as the definitive symbol of New York. "In Turtle Bay," he wrote, "there is an old willow tree that presides over an interior garden. It is a battered tree, long suffering and much climbed, held together by strands of wire but beloved of those who know it. In a way it symbolizes the city: life under difficulties, growth against odds, sap-rise in the midst of concrete, and the steady reaching for the sun. Whenever I look at it nowadays, and feel the cold shadow of the planes, I think: 'This must be saved, this particular thing, this very tree.' If it were to go, all would go — this city, this mischievous and marvelous monument which not to look upon would be like death."

Dorothy Thompson was another resident of Turtle Bay Gardens. In 1941, after her divorce from Sinclair Lewis, she bought the house at 237 East 48th Street. The apartment, decorated primarily in Bauhaus-style, had a vestibule with eight sketches painted on glass of Thompson as she went through the activities of a typical day, a library with some three thousand books, a living room dominated by a black leather couch about eight feet long and a feminine bedroom in pale green satin and ivory. Her studio had "the air of a command post," according to her biographer, Marion K. Sanders. "Walls papered with maps, an illuminated globe, and a short-wave radio enabled her to follow the progress of the war on land, sea, and air." Like White,

Dorothy Thompson on her eight-foot couch with movable
arm rests, in her Turtle Bay house, 1942.

Dorothy Thompson sold her house in 1957. Today, Robert
Gottlieb, editor-in-chief of Knopf, is in Dorothy Thompson's
house; and literary agent Julian Bach lives at 241 East 48th.
Forty-ninth Street is the theatrical side of the Gardens; here
there are houses owned by Ruth Gordon and Garson Kanin,
Stephen Sondheim, and Katharine Hepburn.

With renewal, Beekman Place became even more elegant
than Turtle Bay. In 1937, after winning the Pulitzer Prize for
The Late George Apley, John P. Marquand took a duplex

apartment overlooking the river at 1 Beekman Place. Marquand, whose mother was Margaret Fuller's niece, wrote most often about New England, but two books were set in New York. In *So Little Time,* a writer for the theater married to an independently wealthy society woman (like Marquand's second wife, Adelaide Hooker) lives in an East Side duplex, and *Point of No Return* tells the story of a suburban banker who works in New York. Of its hero, Charles Gray, Marquand wrote: "It did not matter that he had not been born and raised there, because New York belonged almost exclusively to people who had come from other places. New York in the end was only a strange, indefinable combination of triumph, discouragement and memories. It did not matter what the weather was there, or the season of the year, or whether there was war or peace . . ."

Mary McCarthy, then a young free-lance writer, lived across the street in the apartment house at 2 Beekman Place from 1933 to 1936, when she was married to Harold Johnsrud. Kay, the heroine of her novel *The Group,* lived, like her creator, in the east Fifties. In the summer of 1937, after an interlude in the Village, McCarthy was again living on Beekman Place, in a borrowed apartment with Philip Rahv. Two Beekman Place had another literary resident when Antoine de Saint-Exupéry took a six-room suite there in 1941. A visitor described the apartment, which had been decorated for the previous tenant, Greta Garbo, and still held her furnishings: "Tawny wall-to-wall carpeting, large faded mirrors, an old dark green library, a sort of Venetian patina where the ships glide by in front of the windows as though on a level with the carpets." During this period, Saint-Exupéry began writing *Le Petit Prince,* which had come to him when he was entertaining friends with drawings on napkins at the Café Arnold on Central Park South.

The final step in the renewal of the Turtle Bay area was the construction in 1966 of the United Nations Plaza, twin apartment towers rising from what had once been an area of tenements and slaughterhouses. Truman Capote lives there today in a five-room cooperative apartment with a living room described by Gloria Steinem as "a dusty-plush 'best' parlor in the South seen through the eyes of Vuillard, and suspended twenty stories above Manhattan."

.

The rest of the East Side, particularly the area near Fifth, Madison and Park avenues, was not subject to the alternation in social standing that afflicted Turtle Bay. Edith Wharton, a social barometer as always, was living in "a little house in Madison Avenue" after her marriage when her work was first accepted for publication. Three poems were taken simultaneously by *Scribner's, Harper's* and the *Century* magazines. "As long as I live," she wrote, "I shall never forget my sensations when I opened the first of the three letters, and learned that I was to appear in print. I can still see the narrow hall, the letter-box out of which I fished the letters, and the flight of stairs up and down which I ran, senselessly and incessantly, in the attempt to give my excitement some muscular outlet!" Later the Whartons moved to a town house at 884 Park Avenue, which Edith furnished in accordance with the views she had expressed in her first book, *The Decoration of Houses.* Henry James, who stayed there on a visit to New York in 1905, called it "a bonbonnière of the last daintiness naturally." James described the visit to a friend: ". . . She was charming, kind and ingenious, and taste and tone and the finest discriminations, ironies, and draperies mantelled us about."

At the close of the twenties a good quotient of the Algonquin wits, prosperous by now, went to live on the East Side. Edna Ferber was at 791 Park Avenue, George S. Kaufman was at 14 East 94th and Alexander Woollcott had a penthouse with a

river view at 450 East 52nd Street, then one of New York's
most luxurious apartment houses. Woollcott had a valet and a
chauffeur, and the St. Regis barber came to shave him every
morning. In 1936 he sold the apartment to Noel Coward.

In 1930 Nathanael West again provided a center of poverty
in the midst of prosperity, as he had earlier in Gramercy Park.
Formerly the night manager of the Kenmore Hall Hotel on 23rd
Street, he took the same job at the Sutton Club Hotel at 330
East 56th. Here again he let friends — Erskine Caldwell, S. J.
Perelman and his wife (West's sister Laura), Edmund Wilson,
and Robert Coates — stay for little or no money. James T.
Farrell and his wife were welcomed after they had been evicted
from their hotel, and Lillian Hellman and Dashiell Hammett
came and occupied the Diplomat's Suite. Hammett had skipped
from the Hotel Pierre, wearing, layer upon layer, all the clothing he owned. He was writing *The Thin Man* and put Laura
Perelman's dog, Asta, in the novel. Quentin Reynolds often
stayed over rather than travel home to Flatbush late at night.
"I would go to the Sutton . . . and be given a room and
no nonsense about signing the register or paying. Besides this
attractive feature, the Sutton had a swimming pool, and many
a midnight when the hotel was quiet, Nat would turn over his
duties to the head bellboy and we'd go swimming. After that,
sitting around with something to drink, we would talk, usually
about writing . . ."

West was fascinated by the sordid lives and suffering of the
people in the hotel. He referred to the sundeck as "suicide
leap," because so many people jumped from it during the depression. He and Lillian Hellman steamed open the guests' letters to see the difference between the reality and the façade of
their lives. He was preoccupied with loneliness, fear and desperation, the disease of the spirit W. H. Auden would call
"West's Disease," in an essay on his work. Both of West's major

works, *Miss Lonelyhearts* and *The Day of the Locust*, draw heavily on the atmosphere of the hotels where he worked.

The same year, 1931, Dorothy Thompson and Sinclair Lewis were living prosperously at 21 East 90th Street. They had two sitting rooms so that each could entertain guests separately. And in 1932 Willa Cather moved to 570 Park Avenue, where all her windows faced the blank wall of the Colony Club.

In the thirties two East Side homes were gathering places of very different kinds. Kirk Askew, a 57th Street art dealer, and his wife, Constance, had at-homes at 166 East 61st Street, known to habitués as the Askew Salon. The salon was held on Sunday afternoons during "r" months from 5:00 P.M. on. There was a large drawing room with tall windows overlooking a garden and a small cork-lined library for more serious discussions. The at-homes were not parties but "a continuing, well-organized operation with a clear and consistent objective" — the advancement of the careers of a group of art dealers and curators to which Askew belonged. In addition to painters and composers, many writers were guests: Carl Van Vechten, Emily Hahn, Glenway Wescott, Elizabeth Bowen, E. E. Cummings, Gilbert Seldes and Archibald MacLeish. Elizabeth Bowen once stayed in the guest bedroom and Virgil Thomson lived there on and off from 1932 to 1935.

Several blocks away, at 220 East 69th Street, Stephen Vincent Benét's home became a haven for young poets seeking help and advice. Like Howells in his day, Benét was one of the few writers who commanded the respect of the young and at the same time made himself available to them. He had won the Pulitzer Prize in 1929 for *John Brown's Body* and wrote his famous story, "The Devil and Daniel Webster," in 1936. Benét said the house on 69th Street "looks like something you build out of those pink stone building blocks when you are a child and has more wasted hall-space than the Grand Canyon."

He and his family lived there until 1939, when they moved to 215 East 68th Street. He took long walks, often through Central Park, every morning before working.

During the late thirties and early forties the war brought a number of expatriates to New York and some of them settled on the East Side. Saint-Exupéry was living on Beekman Place, Thomas Mann was at the Hotel Bedford at 118 East 40th Street and André Maurois was at the Ritz Tower, on the northeast corner of Park Avenue and 57th Street. Maurois had no money but the management allowed him to pay when he could and told his wife to furnish their three-room apartment with French antiques and send them the bills. When he left to spend several months in Kansas City, Maurois wrote:

> I shall miss this tiny New York apartment where there is nothing ugly. On our lamp shades, in transparency, the two pink houses of the Place Royale and the poplars of the Dordogne. On our wall, the Angel of Chartres bending above the Beauce plain. In the morning, at sunrise, the soaring towers of New York, amber or rose, take on the smooth luminous softness of walls by Vermeer or Guardi. I have loved this part of town . . . the Greek grocer who gave me chocolate for my French friends, because I had written a life of Byron; the young salesman, cool and cultured, of the Chaucer Head Bookshop, who preferred fine texts to best sellers; the Canari d'Or restaurant where Monsieur Robert, the French proprietor, always has a corner for us; the florist who, everytime we pass her shop, makes Simone a little gift: a rose or a violet; Klebanoff, the newspaper seller, who also sells books, theatre tickets, cigarettes, cough drops, and is a notary public besides . . .

Maurois and his wife saw other expatriates: Saint-Exupéry, Mann, Jules Romains, Pierre Claudel, Fernand Léger and André Gide.

The forties also brought John Steinbeck, who had come to New York from San Francisco in 1925. Then he had first worked as a laborer pushing wheelbarrows of concrete for the construction of Madison Square Garden. After a stint on a newspaper and a period in which, jobless and weak with hunger, he tried to write stories, he shipped back to San Francisco. "The city had beaten the pants off me," he wrote. "Whatever it required to get ahead, I didn't have. I didn't leave the city in disgust — I left it with the respect plain unadulterated fear gives." With success behind him, he returned in 1943 and took an apartment at 330 East 51st Street. "My new home consisted of the first and second floors of a three-story house and the living room looked out on a small sootfield called a garden. I was going to live in New York but I was going to avoid it. I planted a lawn in the garden, bought huge pots and planted tomatoes, pollinating the blossoms with a water-color brush." In 1951 Steinbeck moved to 206 East 72nd Street, where he lived until his death in 1968. He summed up his feelings about the city in an article called "The Making of a New Yorker": "New York is an ugly city, a dirty city," he stated. "Its climate is a scandal, its politics are used to frighten children, its traffic is madness, its competition is murderous. But there is one thing about it — once you have lived in New York and it has become your home, no place else is good enough. All of everything is concentrated here, population, theater, art, writing, publishing, importing, business, murder, mugging, luxury, poverty. It is all of everything. It goes all night. It is tireless and its air is charged with energy. I can work longer and harder without weariness in New York than any place else."

Eugene O'Neill, who disliked city life, took a six-room penthouse with his third wife, Carlotta Monterey, at 35 East 84th Street in 1946. (The O'Neills had an apartment at 1085 Park Avenue for several months in 1931.) The apartment had a terrace on three sides with panoramic views of the city, and

Eugene O'Neill on the terrace of his penthouse at
35 East 84th Street, around 1946.

the walls of the rooms were painted in strong colors — deep purple, royal blue, Chinese red. In O'Neill's combination bedroom-study there were pictures of clipper ships and an oil painting of Broadway during the theater rush hour. "There's the whole story of the decline of America," O'Neill told a *New Yorker* interviewer, pointing to the pictures, "from the most beautiful thing America has ever made, the clipper ship, to the most tawdry street in the world."

In 1944 Mary McCarthy and Edmund Wilson lived at 14 Henderson Place, a cul-de-sac off 86th Street between York and East End avenues, until the end of their marriage. After their separation Wilson brought Anaïs Nin to visit. She described the experience: "A street lined with old-fashioned English brick houses. Pointed slate roofs, ivy and trees, but all of them so narrow and bleak; the windows long and narrow. He had forgotten his key, so we entered through the basement. The place had an air of devastation. 'Mary took away all the furniture.' We entered the parlor, a deep and narrow room. In the middle of the empty room stood two rocking chairs. On the walls, a series of Hogarth prints."

In 1953 Sylvia Plath spent a brief but traumatic month in New York as a guest editor of *Mademoiselle* magazine. She stayed at the Barbizon, a hotel for young women at Lexington Avenue and 63rd Street, which she called the Amazon in her autobiographical novel, *The Bell Jar*. ". . . It reminded me of my dormitory at college," she wrote. "It wasn't a proper hotel — I mean a hotel where there are both men and women mixed about here and there on the same floor. This hotel — the Amazon — was for women only, and they were mostly girls my age with wealthy parents who wanted to be sure their daughters would be living where men couldn't get at them and deceive them; and they were all going to posh secretarial schools like Katy Gibbs." The visit to New York triggered a depression that culminated in a suicide attempt when Plath returned to Massachusetts. Friends and critics speculated that she found the world of fashion journalism artificial and banal, that she was brought up short before the inadequacy of her preparation for life in New York as an editor and writer and that, despite the protection of the Barbizon, she had some unfortunate sexual experiences, including an attempted rape by a South American playboy.

The same year, Dorothy Parker, who had been in California for most of the preceding two decades, returned to New York to live in a "stark, bare, colorless, and impersonal room" in the Volney, a residential hotel at 23 East 74th Street. After another trip to California, she returned to the Volney in 1963 and lived there until her death in 1967. In her last years she was extremely poor. Her good friend Lillian Hellman took two paintings, presents from Dorothy in more prosperous times, sold them and gave her the money. Hellman was living at this time in a house at 63 East 82nd Street, which she had bought in 1944. In 1969 she sold the house and a year later moved to Park Avenue in the Sixties, where she still lives. Her apartment is furnished with fine furniture: an early American highboy, an Empire love seat, Sheraton chairs, pieces from her plays and paintings by Toulouse-Lautrec, Rouault, Picasso and Ben Shahn. Her parties there are considered among New York's most exclusive literary events.

Other writers currently living on the East Side are Edward Albee, who has a painting-filled apartment on Fifth Avenue; Dwight Macdonald, who, though often associated with the West Side intellectuals, lives on East 87th Street; and Kurt Vonnegut, who lives across from Turtle Bay Gardens on 48th Street. George Plimpton, who, as an expatriate, began the *Paris Review* in 1953, returned to New York in the late fifties to live in a house overlooking the East River on 72nd

A party around 1965 at George Plimpton's for the formation of Film-wrights, a cooperative of playwrights and novelists. Plimpton is at left front. In right foreground with his back to the camera is Arthur Kopit with Frank and Eleanor Perry behind him. Standing to their right are Jack Richardson and, holding a drink, Mario Puzo. Truman Capote is on the couch, his dog at his feet. William Styron is talking to Capote, and Harold L. Humes, a founder of the *Paris Review,* is the man with the pipe listening in. The group at left rear includes (left to right) Jonathan Miller, Gore Vidal and filmmaker Richard Leacock. At far rear, right, Ralph Ellison is talking to Peter Matthiessen.

Street. Norman Podhoretz speculates that Plimpton performed a unique literary function. "He brought writers and intellectuals into contact with the rich, the powerful, and the fashionable for the first time in any of their lives, and thereby did much to increase the standing and power of the former, if not the comfort and happiness of the latter."

In recent years only a few authors of stature have chosen

to write about the East Side. Marquand wrote several novels set there, but unlike his close dissections of New England they deal with the city in an abstract way. Truman Capote's *Breakfast at Tiffany's,* which he wrote when he lived in Brooklyn Heights, opens in an East Seventies brownstone said to be based on his first New York apartment. "It was one room crowded with attic furniture, a sofa and fat chairs upholstered in that itchy, particular red velvet that one associates with hot days on a train . . . The single window looked out on a fire escape. Even so, my spirits heightened whenever I felt in my pocket the key to this apartment; with all its gloom, it still was a place of my own, the first, and my books were there, and jars of pencils to sharpen, everything I needed, so I felt, to become the writer I wanted to be." In the novel Holly Golightly had occupied the apartment below. John O'Hara came to New York from Pennsylvania in 1927 and immediately began to live a dissolute life, to the detriment of his work. "God, to think that I recognize the faces of scores of cops and doormen between 42nd Street and 59th!" he said. "Waiters in speakeasies and the Algonquin and Sardi's and B-G sandwich shops know me by name . . . and in essence I don't like it." In 1934 he wrote about this life in *Butterfield 8,* a book named for a telephone exchange then serving the fashionable East Side. He had lived at the Pickwick Arms Hotel at 230 East 51st Street while writing the football column for the *New Yorker* and starting *Appointment in Samarra;* and he wrote *Butterfield 8* in a brownstone on East 55th Street. In 1940, after several stints in Hollywood, he could at last afford Butterfield 8 himself. He rented a ground-floor apartment in a remodeled town house at 27 East 79th Street, and later, from 1945 to 1949, he lived at 55 East 86th Street.

Finally, Louis Auchincloss has been the only writer born and bred on the East Side to chronicle life among old New

York society as Edith Wharton did in the early part of the century. He lived at 66 East 79th Street from 1935–1945. *Portrait in Brownstone,* set on 53rd Street, is based on his grandmother's family, which occupied what was called "Dixon Alley" in the 1890s. There were six Dixons on 49th Street between Fifth and Sixth avenues and one on 48th. After attending Groton, Yale and the University of Virginia Law School, Auchincloss went to work at the law firm of Sullivan and Cromwell. When he resigned in 1952 to devote himself to full-time writing, he was living at 24 East 84th Street. He has long since gone back to another law firm and lives today on upper Park Avenue.

Auchincloss is alone in writing from his own experience about the world of law and business. "No writer today has anything to do with Wall Street," he says. "No major people have anything to do with business at all. Even Marquand didn't come by it naturally; he boned up. Writers don't have to go into business anymore. The universities support them . . . or the magazines." Auchincloss remains the only major writer to use the characteristic upper-class life of the upper East Side as his subject.

East Side Tour

1. 118 East 40th Street, between Park and Lexington. The Hotel Bedford, where Thomas Mann lived for a time about 1940 (p. 234).

2. 5 Tudor City Place. James T. Farrell lived in this block-long, 22-story building in the 1960s, and Louise Bogan lived here from 1930 to 1932.

3. 48th and 49th streets, between Third and Second avenues. Turtle Bay Gardens. There are two rows of ten houses each, remodeled in 1920. The brownstone houses, most of which have been painted or stuccoed, share a private garden. A number of prominent literary figures have lived

E. 96th St.

E. 94th St.

E. 90th St.

E. 86th St.

E. 84th St.

E. 82nd St.

E. 79th St.

E. 72nd St.

E. 68th St.

E. 57th St.

E. 56th St.

E. 52nd St.

E. 51st St.

E. 48th St.

E. 42nd St.

←Henderson Pl.

CENTRAL PARK

EAST RIVER

Fifth Ave.

Madison Ave.

Park Ave.

Lexington Ave.

Third Ave.

Second Ave.

First Ave.

York Ave.

East End Ave.

F.D. Roosevelt Drive

Sutton Pl.

Beekman Pl.

←United Nations Plaza

←Tudor City Place

Grand
Central →
Station

The East Side

in this complex throughout the years (pp. 226–28). On 48th Street: Dorothy Thompson was at 237 from 1941 to 1957; number 239 was home to E. B. White, though he also lived at 245 (1936–38), and 229 (1945–57); Julian Bach lived at number 241. Max Perkins lived at 246 East 49th Street during the 1930s.

4. 865 First Avenue, between 48th and 49th streets. Thomas Wolfe lived here in 1935 (p. 227).

In the 1840s Edgar Allan Poe, Margaret Fuller, and Horace Greeley lived in the Turtle Bay area. Poe stayed at the Miller farmhouse, located at what is now 47th Street and Second Avenue, and Margaret Fuller boarded with the Greeleys in their house at about 50th Street. Turtle Bay itself is now filled in and is United Nations Park.

5. 870 United Nations Plaza, at 49th Street. Truman Capote lived here for a number of years until his death in 1984. The building was constructed in 1966 by architects Harrison, Abramovitz and Harris (p. 231).

The area overlooking the river around Beekman Place has become one of the most desirable in the city, but in 1914, when Padraic and Mary Colum lived here, it was "unfashionable and dingy" (p. 225).

6. 1 Beekman Place at Mitchell Place, 49th Street. John P. Marquand lived in a duplex in this immense apartment building in 1937 (pp. 229–30).

7. 2 Beekman Place. Mary McCarthy lived here from 1933 to 1936 during her first marriage. In the summer of 1937, she was again at Beekman Place with Philip Rahv. In 1941, Antoine de Saint-Exupéry took a six-room apartment here which had previously belonged to Greta Garbo (pp. 230, 234).

8. 450 East 52nd Street. The Campanile, where Alexander Woollcott lived during the early 1930s. Then and now it is one of New York's most luxurious apartment houses (pp. 231–32).

9. 330 East 51st Street. John Steinbeck lived here in 1943, and had a little garden which he called a "soot-field" (pp. 234–35).

10. 230 East 51st Street. The Pickwick Arms Hotel, where John O'Hara began writing *Appointment in Samarra* (p. 240).

11. 60 East 54th Street. The Hotel Elysee, where Tennessee Williams often stayed and where he died in 1983. He called it the "Hotel Easy Lay" because of its proximity to Rounds, a hustler bar he frequented.

12. 111 East 56th Street. The Hotel Lombardy. Hemingway stayed here in 1941; Sinclair Lewis lived here in 1940; and Edna Ferber was in residence from 1930 to 1935.

13. 330 East 56th Street. The Sutton Club Hotel; it is now vacant, presumably to be renovated. Nathanael West was night manager here during the depression. So many people jumped from the sundeck that he called it "suicide leap" (pp. 232–33).

14. 57th Street and Park Avenue, on the northeast corner. The Ritz Tower, built in 1925 by architects Emery Roth and Thomas Hastings. André Maurois lived here during the war and Marlene Dietrich kept an apartment in the building for many years (p. 234).

(14a) 38 East 57th Street. The Chaucer Head Bookshop was here until the early 1960s (p. 234).

15. 134 East 61st Street. Originally Au Canari d'Or Restaurant, it is now Le Pistou, with a new red granite façade (p. 234).

16. 570 Park Avenue, on the southwest corner of 63rd Street. Willa Cather lived here from 1932 until her death in 1947 (p. 233).

17. 63rd Street and Lexington Avenue, on the southeast corner. The Barbizon Hotel, constructed in 1927 by architects Murgatroyd and Ogden; the interior public spaces were remodeled in 1986. Sylvia Plath stayed here in 1953 (pp. 237–38).

18. 630 Park Avenue at 66th Street. Lillian Hellman lived here from 1970 until her death in 1984 (p. 238).

19. 730 Park Avenue at 71st Street. Edna Ferber lived here from 1950 to 1968.

(19a) The homes of Stephen Vincent Benét, first at 220 East 69th Street and later at 215 East 68th were gathering places for young poets. Both houses were replaced by the same gigantic apartment house.

(19b) 206 East 72nd Street, east of Third Avenue. John Steinbeck lived in a house located here from 1951 until his death in 1968. The house is gone, but number 208 next door is probably very similar (p. 235).

20. 23 East 74th Street, near Madison Avenue. The Volney Hotel. Dorothy Parker resided here from 1953 until her death in 1967 (p. 238).

21. 791 Park Avenue, on the southeast corner of 74th Street. Edna Ferber went to live here at the end of the 1920s (p. 231).

(21a) 884 Park Avenue, four doors north of 78th Street. The Whartons' town house was located here in the early 1900s (p. 231).

22. 66 East 79th Street. Louis Auchincloss, a great admirer of Wharton, lived here from 1935 to 1945 (pp. 240–41).

23. 27 East 79th Street. John O'Hara lived here in a ground-floor apartment in 1940. The building is now the headquarters of a high-style design firm, Hanae Mori (p. 240).

24. 63 East 82nd Street. Lillian Hellman owned this house from 1944 to 1969 (p. 238).

25. 24 East 84th Street. Louis Auchincloss lived here in 1952 when he decided to write full-time for a while (p. 240).

26. 35 East 84th Street, on the northeast corner of Madison Avenue. Eugene O'Neill had a penthouse apartment here in the 1940s (pp. 235–37).

27. 55 East 86th Street. John O'Hara lived here from 1945 to 1949 (p. 240).

28. 1085 Park Avenue, on the northeast corner of 88th Street. O'Neill lived here briefly in 1931 (p. 235).

29. 21 East 90th Street, on the northwest corner of Madison Avenue. Dorothy Thompson and Sinclair Lewis lived here in 1931 (p. 233).

30. 1111 Park Avenue, at 90th Street. This is the present residence of Louis Auchincloss.

31. 1133 Park Avenue, at 91st Street. J. D. Salinger lived here with his parents.

32. 14 East 94th Street. George S. Kaufman lived here in the late 1920s in a town house which is now painted white (p. 231).

33. 1395 Lexington Avenue, on the southeast corner of 92nd Street. Young Men's-Young Women's Hebrew Association. Since the late forties readings by distinguished American and visiting European poets have been held here.

(33a) 88th Street and 2nd Avenue. This is the region where John Jacob Astor built his country estate, Astoria, in the early decades of the 1800s (p. 223). Wide lawns swept down to the East River. Washington Irving stayed here now and then in 1834 and 1835.

34. 14 Henderson Place, (a cul-de-sac off 86th Street between York and East End avenues). Mary McCarthy and Edmund Wilson lived here in 1944, when they were married. The group of brick Queen Anne houses along Henderson Place, East End Avenue, and 87th Street was built in 1881 for "persons of moderate means" by John H. Henderson. They now comprise the Henderson Place Historic District (p. 237).

VIII. The West Side

NEW YORK today has no thriving literary center like the Greenwich Village of the 1910s and 1920s. There is not one area where writers live in great concentration and share a sense of community, collaboration and mutual stimulation, although various institutions scattered around the city serve as focal points. But if New York has anything approaching a literary center today, it is the upper West Side.

Lionel Trilling wrote that in 1929 he "signalized [his] solidarity with the intellectual life by taking an apartment in Greenwich Village." But most recently, until his death in 1975, Trilling, like many other literary people, lived on the West Side. In part the shift uptown of the literary community is a matter of practicality; the large apartments on West End Avenue and Riverside Drive have provided reasonably priced housing for the writers whose families expanded during the fifties. But additionally, the West Side is the geographic area most closely associated with certain contemporary literary currents. In a time when the New York literary scene is dominated by critics and essayists writing about social and political problems, West Siders encounter these problems with stunning immediacy on their own teeming, anarchic streets. And in a time when a Jewish sensibility dominates New York fiction and criticism, the West Side, once "the golden ghetto" of prosperous immigrants, is an appropriate ground for its flowering.

Yet the West Side is a literary neighborhood with a difference. Unlike the majority of writers of the past who abhorred bourgeois lifestyles, those on the West Side embrace them in massive, impersonal middle-class buildings. And unlike most neighborhoods with large concentrations of literary people, the West Side has no public place — no bar, restaurant or cafeteria — where writers and intellectuals gather. They are most likely to meet in Zabar's, a gourmet delicatessen, where each arrives and departs separately. Although the West Side literati are presumably connected by ephemeral intellectual filaments, they claim hardly ever to see one another.

The West Side, like all of New York, was originally lovely countryside. Washington Irving described it in *A History of New York* as "a sweet rural valley, beautiful with many a bright flower, refreshed by many a pure streamlet, and enlivened here and there by a delectable little Dutch cottage, sheltered under some sloping hill; and almost buried in embowering trees." Several decades later, in the days when John James Audubon recorded catching a 200-pound sturgeon in the Hudson below his house at 156th Street, Edgar Allan Poe was living in a farmhouse on a rocky knoll at what is now 84th Street between Broadway and Amsterdam Avenue. Poe spent the summer of 1844 there while finishing "The Raven." He and his wife lived in a garret under the eaves, but Poe worked in a spacious study on the floor below. The fireplace mantel, where he carved his name, is now in Philosophy Hall at Columbia University.

Residential development on the West Side began in the 1880s. Numerous blocks of row houses were succeeded by luxury apartment houses as the preferred style of building. The first, and forever the most distinguished, was the Dakota, built in 1884 on Central Park West at 72nd Street. Next came the Ansonia, completed in 1904, at 73rd and Broadway. Although the building was constructed in the style of the resort hotels of the French Riviera, the architect and builder, W. E. D. Stokes, kept goats, ducks, chickens and a small pet bear in the roof garden and sold eggs to the tenants at half price. The West Side streets, however, were never to become truly fashionable, with the exception of Central Park West. From the early 1900s the grand buildings overlooking the Park drew a number of literary residents who had achieved financial success. Although the apartment houses sometimes were numbered according to their cross streets, they were all on Central Park West.

First among the literary gathering places was 1 West 87th Street, the home of John Quinn, the New York lawyer who was a patron of Irish literature, a collector of postimpressionist art and defender of the *Little Review* in the obscenity suit

The farmhouse at 84th Street and Broadway where Edgar Allan Poe lived in the summer of 1844.

resulting from its publication of *Ulysses*. William Butler Yeats stayed with Quinn in November of 1903 while on an American lecture tour. He had his own key and treated the apartment as his home in New York; his poem "Never Give All the Heart" grew out of a conversation he had there with Quinn. In later years, when Quinn was living at 58 Central Park West, Yeats, Lady Gregory and Standish O'Grady all stayed with him at various times. The lawyer had an unexpected literary connection through his Paris collector, Henri Pierre Roché, who wrote the apparently autobiographical *Jules et Jim* at the age of seventy-five.

Ellen Glasgow lived at 1 West 85th Street from 1911 to 1916 in an apartment overlooking the Park. She was writing *Life and Gabriella,* a book set on East 57th Street and in London Terrace, where her friend Van Wyck Brooks lived (see Chapter V, Chelsea). In 1917 Sara Teasdale and her husband moved to the Beresford at 211 Central Park West. Teasdale, who considered herself extremely delicate, was almost a recluse and seldom went out. John Hall Wheelock recalls that she was so sensitive she was incapable of saying good-by, and simply went into another room and closed the door when it was time for a guest to leave.

In 1923 Edna Ferber sublet an apartment at 50 Central Park West in an ornate building with cast-iron bay windows. The following year she took a five-year lease on another apartment in the same building, with eight windows facing the Park. Another of the Algonquin wits, Marc Connelly, has been living since 1929 at 25 Central Park West, the Century, a prime example of the art deco apartment houses built in the twenties and thirties.

In 1943 Sinclair Lewis telephoned a rental agency and announced that he wanted an apartment with a view of all the New York bridges and a living room sixty feet long and twenty feet high. The agent rented him a duplex at the Eldorado Towers, an orange stone art deco building at 300 Central Park West. Lewis wrote to a friend: "I have taken a gaudy flat, a cross between Elizabeth Arden's Beauty Salon and the horse-stables at Ringling Circus Winter Headquarters: 29 floors up in the air and commanding a fair view of the Orkney Isles on the West, of Girard Avenue South on the North and West." Lewis called the apartment "Big Intolerable" or "Intolerable Towers." On the upper floor were a living room, dining room and sitting room with a fireplace. Below, there were bedrooms and Lewis's study, which was dominated by an enormous map of Minnesota. The apartment was decorated with pale gray walls, terra-cotta tile floors, dull green, beige and yellow upholstery and bleached woodwork. The same building would serve to symbolize the ultimate in nouveau-riche upward mobility as the home of Herman Wouk's Marjorie Morningstar.

Among the most distinctive West Side blocks is 67th Street from Central Park West to Columbus Avenue. Four of the buildings on the block were constructed by the same developer, Walter Russell, who wanted them to be the best possible artists' housing. Most of the apartments have two-story studio living rooms. The Hotel Des Artistes at 1 West 67th Street, most magnificent of the buildings, originally had its own communal kitchen, squash courts, swimming pool, theater and ballroom. It now has a restaurant on the first floor, the Café Des Artistes, decorated by Howard Chandler Christy with murals of nude women against fields of flowers. Fannie Hurst, the highly successful writer of popular fiction, lived here from 1932 until her death in 1968. She had a triplex with a study brought in its entirety, including wall panels and stained-glass windows, from a sixteenth-century Italian palazzo. She described the apartment: "Baronial living room, thirty-foot-high ceiling. Woodburning fireplaces. Balconies. A roof terrace halfway across the building. My workroom, overlooking this terrace, oak paneled, with stained-glass windows, seemed to have a hush built into it." Other tenants of the Des Artistes have been Isadora Duncan, Alexander Woollcott and Noel Coward. In 1929 the building was the scene of a famous literary murder/suicide; Harry Crosby, publisher of the Black Sun Press in Paris, killed a woman companion and then himself. His wife, Caresse Crosby, was at the theater with Hart Crane when the news came. E. E. Cummings wrote a poem about it:

> 2 boston
> Dolls; found
> with
> Holes in each other
>
> 's lullaby.

The neighborhood behind the elegant façade of Central Park West has always been primarily middle-class. Theodore Dreiser used its characteristic ambiance in *Sister Carrie,* which he began when he was living at 6 West 102nd Street in 1899. It is evidence of the sparse settlement of the area that Carrie can see the Hudson to the west and the tops of the trees in Central Park to the east from her third-floor apartment on 78th Street near Amsterdam Avenue. Dissatisfaction with the middle-class housewifely life and a yearning for the glamour of the big city downtown lead Carrie to seek a career in the theater.

In the winter of 1902, after a trip to Europe with her brother, Gertrude Stein stayed with three friends in a wooden apartment building overlooking the Hudson on West 100th Street. Here she started her first novel, *Q.E.D.,* in which the main character, Adele, returns to New York from London, as Stein had, and says, "I simply rejoiced in the New York streets, in the long spindling legs of the elevated, in the straight high undecorated houses, in the empty upper air and in the white surface of the snow. It was such a joy to realize that the whole thing was without mystery and without complexity, that it was clean and straight and meagre and hard and white and high." The novel, which discusses a Lesbian affair, was published under the title *Things As They Are* after Stein's death.

In 1916 Louis Untermeyer was living on the West Side, leading what he described as "two separate lives." In frequent visits to the Village, where he was working on the *Masses*, he mingled with the bohemian set. Back home at 310 West 100th Street, he lived the life of "the upper-class bourgeoisie" and entertained Vachel Lindsay, Robert Frost and Amy Lowell — and one exception from downtown, Edna St. Vincent Millay. Often the poets would read their work. Untermeyer recalled that "Frost read with just a slight New England tang, sort of down country." Amy Lowell read "wonderfully, colorfully. When she died her poems died with her because they needed her flamboyant personality; they needed all her feminine-masculine vigor . . . Edna Millay read very well because of her particular quality, her combination of elfin and gamin." Sometimes the Village crowd would come uptown for a cheese and beer party. Untermeyer remembered serving "tea, coffee, fine sandwiches and very good Viennese pastries for the other crowd."

F. Scott Fitzgerald, just discharged from the army, was living in a cheap room at 200 Claremont Avenue in 1919. He was working for an advertising agency and trying to make his way as a writer. At one time he had "one hundred and twenty-two rejection slips pinned in a frieze" around his bedroom. When Zelda broke their engagement because Fitzgerald had no money and could offer her little security, he went home to St. Paul to rewrite *This Side of Paradise*. (They were married as soon as Scribner's accepted the book.) Fitzgerald's own West Side neighborhood may well have provided the setting in *The Great Gatsby* for the apartment Tom Buchanan keeps for assignations with his mistress, in "one slice in a long white cake of apartment-houses" on West 158th Street.

.

The vast middle-class precincts of the West Side were the rearing ground for a number of children who would later distinguish themselves as writers. Young Dorothy Rothschild, later Dorothy Parker, spent her early years in a comfortable house at 57 West 68th Street and attended the Blessed Sacrament Convent on 70th Street. Later, when she began working for *Vogue*, she roomed in a boarding house at 103rd Street and Broadway. She earned ten dollars a week and paid eight dollars for her room and two meals a day. Lillian Hellman came to New York from New Orleans when she was six and lived on the West Side, frequently visiting her mother's family nearby. "The Newhouse apartment," she wrote in *An Unfinished Woman*, "held the upper-middle-class trappings, in touch of things and in spirit of people, that never manage to be truly stylish. Heavy weather hung over the lovely oval rooms." Nathanael West's father, who was a contractor involved in the building boom, wanted his son to go to the progressive Public School 81 on 119th Street between Seventh and St. Nicholas avenues and accordingly built an apartment house a block from the school and moved his family into it. Despite, or perhaps because of, his father's efforts, West was absent as many as thirty times a semester and never got a grade higher than a B. In 1917 his family moved to Tenth Avenue and 59th Street and he attended DeWitt Clinton High School, where his schoolmates included Countee Cullen and Lionel Trilling. Here his grades were spectacularly bad. He left school without graduating and got into college by altering his

high school transcript. Anaïs Nin, who had spent her earliest
years in Europe, lived with her mother and brother on the
first floor of a rooming house at 158 West 75th Street from
1914 to 1919. Here she began the diary, intended as a record
for her father, who had abandoned the family, that would be
her major literary work. A few years later, J. D. Salinger was
growing up on the West Side; he lived at 390 Riverside Drive
on the corner of 111th Street. The childhood he attributes to
the Glass children in *Seymour, Raise High the Roof Beam,
Carpenters* and other works must have been very similar to his
own. Before moving to the East Side, as Salinger's family also
did, the Glasses live in the Hotel Alamac on Broadway and 71st
Street and then in an apartment building at 110th Street and
Riverside Drive with a canopy lit by "bulby bright lights."
They play curb marbles and stoopball. "As we played it,"
Salinger wrote, "a rubber ball was thrown against some architectural granite fancy-work — a popular Manhattan mixture of
Greek Ionic and Roman Corinthian molding — along the
façade of our apartment house, about waist-high." They went
for haircuts in a barbershop "at 108th and Broadway, nested
verdantly . . . between a Chinese restaurant and a kosher
delicatessen" and bought Louis Sherry ice cream from a drugstore at 113th and Broadway.

In 1932 Herman Wouk's family moved from the Bronx to a
"luxurious Manhattan apartment building on the northwest
corner of 101st Street and West End Avenue." His years there,
Wouk said, "furnished the milieu, the story and the characters"
for *Marjorie Morningstar,* although he set his heroine on Central Park West.

·

It was only in the fifties that the West Side began to be viewed
as a place for writers and intellectuals to live. Some observers

speculate that this came about as a result of a child-bearing trend. "The Village was more radical in the thirties; people were childless," said Elizabeth Hardwick. "In the nineteen fifties people were searching for the large house. It was a phenomenon of the Eisenhower era — babies, the stress on family, have a big apartment, gather your books." Then, too, many of the fifties writers and intellectuals were Jewish and found the West Side comfortably familiar. Meyer Levin, Chicago-born author of *Compulsion,* took a humorous view of the phenomenon. "I was rehabilitating this brownstone — when was it? Six years ago? Suddenly it came to me. I'm an obsessive-compulsive! Back in the late twenties I worked in Palestine. And now I'm doing it all over again on the West Side — reclaiming ancient Jewish land."

Frederic Morton, in an article on the West Side written for the *New York Times,* speculated that "the mass migration of intellectuals to the West Side often implies a frank coming to terms with the probity of their origins . . . It's *really* all right to be Jewish." Alfred Kazin put it another way: "If you're interested in Jewish history, there's no shame to living on the West Side."

In any case, the West Side has come to be associated with "New York intellectuals," a group defined primarily by Irving Howe in his 1968 *Commentary* essay, "The New York Intellectuals, A Chronicle and A Critique," and by Norman Podhoretz, editor of *Commentary,* in his autobiography, *Making It.* Howe, who lives on Riverside Drive, wrote: "They are, or until recently have been, anti-Communist; they are, or until some time ago were, radicals; they have a fondness for ideological speculation; they write literary criticism with a strong social emphasis; they revel in polemic; they strive self-consciously to be 'brilliant'; and by birth or osmosis, they are Jews." Norman Podhoretz added that what he calls "the

Alfred Kazin in his book-lined living room on West End Avenue.

family" has produced its share of books, "but its characteristic form has been the short piece."

In addition to Howe and Podhoretz themselves, members of the West Side intelligentsia include Susan Sontag (Riverside Drive), James Baldwin (470 West End Avenue on occasional visits home from Paris), Barbara and Jason Epstein (West 67th Street), Alfred Kazin (West End Avenue), Murray Kempton (West End Avenue) and Elizabeth Hardwick (West 67th Street). Reports have it that Kempton once quipped, "Only Norman Podhoretz would think that 'making it' and living on West End Avenue and One hundred and fifth Street were the same thing."

The intellectuals, who originally gathered around the *Partisan Review,* now have a variety of forums — Podhoretz's *Commentary,* Howe's *Dissent,* and the *New York Review of Books.* The *New York Review* was conceived one night during the 1963 newspaper strike when Robert Lowell and Elizabeth Hardwick, then married to one another, were having dinner at the Epsteins'. The first issue was dummied up on the dining room table of the Lowell-Hardwick apartment, one of the West 67th Street studio duplexes described by Lowell as "the last gasp of true Nineteenth-Century Capitalistic Gothic." The apartment is still filled with furnishings from Lowell's parents' house in Boston — a red velvet sofa, oriental rugs and American primitive paintings. Lowell described its "oak panels, mantel" and "book ladders on brass rods" in his poem "The Golden Middle."

The *New York Review's* second issue came from the identically laid-out Epstein apartment several buildings west. As Merle Miller noted in an article called "Why Norman and Jason Aren't Talking," Jason Epstein used to cook on his restaurant stove for the Podhoretzes as well as other West Siders who are no longer on speaking terms since feuding began between *Com-*

mentary and the *New York Review.* Although there was a time when West Side intellectuals got together, it seems there is now no gathering place, to say nothing of a salon. "The reason there are no successful salons is simple," journalist and critic Victor Navasky wrote in 1966. "To have a salon, enemies must at least be friends. But as Columbia English professor Albert Goldman has pointed out, 'We don't have enough social quality. We don't like each other enough . . .' And Irving Kristol theorized, 'A lot of New York intellectuals have roots in Eastern Europe where, unlike England and France, there was no tradition of civility.' "

Alfred Kazin has observed that "until recently, the writers most sensitive to the city were indeed strangers to it." Kazin was thinking back to William Dean Howells, but his observation holds true of the present-day West Side. Although New York area writers Philip Roth, in *Letting Go;* Salinger, in his Glass family stories; and Herman Wouk, in *Marjorie Morningstar,* have made some use of the West Side, the writer who has best absorbed, described and raised it to a level of symbolic significance is Saul Bellow. Bellow, who was born outside Montreal and grew up in Chicago, did not come to New York until the forties. His novel *The Victim* uses New York only as a barely noticeable backdrop although it begins with a vivid description of the city: "On some nights New York is as hot as Bangkok. The whole continent seems to have moved from its place and slid nearer the equator, the bitter gray Atlantic to have become green and tropical, and the people, thronging the streets, barbaric fellahin . . ." From 1950 to 1952 Bellow was a visiting lecturer at New York University, living at least part of the time in the Village at 17 Minetta Lane. Later he moved to 333 Riverside Drive, a beautiful white brick limestone-trimmed house from which he had a view of the river from one room, his bathroom. *Seize the Day,* published in 1956, makes full use of the West Side locale. It is set in the fictional Hotel Gloriana, near the Ansonia, which Bellow described as looking "like a baroque palace from Prague or Munich enlarged a hundred times, with towers, domes, huge swells and bubbles of metal gone green from exposure, iron fretwork and festoons." Bellow is fascinated by the old men and women who live along Broadway in the Seventies, Eighties and Nineties. "Unless the weather is too cold or too wet they fill the benches about the tiny railed parks and along the subway gratings from Verdi Square to Columbia University, they crowd the shops and cafeterias, the dime stores, the tea-rooms, the bakeries, the beauty parlors, the reading rooms and club rooms." In *Herzog,* the protagonist has a small apartment on West 17th Street, but all his women live on the upper West Side. Finally, in *Mr. Sammler's Planet,* the neighborhood itself takes center stage. Bellow's descriptions become more graphic and intense as he raises the city to the level of symbol. Sammler parts his curtain and looks out: "Brownstones, balustrades, bay windows, wrought-iron. Like stamps in an album — the dun rose of buildings canceled by the heavy black of grilles, of corrugated rainspouts . . . Such was Sammler's eastward view, a soft asphalt belly rising, in which lay steaming sewer navels. Spalled sidewalks with clusters of ash cans. Brownstones. The yellow brick of elevator buildings like his own. Little copses of television antennas . . . Westward the Hudson came between Sammler and the great Spry industries of New Jersey. These flashed their electric message through intervening night. SPRY." Bellow writes of upper Broadway: "It was aware of being a scene of perversity, it knew its own despair. And fear. The terror of it. Here you might see the soul of America at grips with historical problems, struggling with certain impossibilities, experiencing violently states inherently static." As one character in *Mr. Sammler's Planet* says, "New York makes one think about the collapse of civilization, about Sodom and Gomorrah, the end of the world." And of all New York, Broadway and 96th Street most forcefully conveys this idea. "By a convergence of all minds and all movements the conviction transmitted by this crowd seemed to be that reality was a terrible thing, and that the final truth about mankind was overwhelming and crushing . . . Sammler could not swear this was really accurate, but Broadway at Ninety-sixth Street gave him such a sense of things."

Though none find it as compelling a subject as the visitor Bellow, a host of other important contemporary writers live on the West Side. Joseph Heller, author of *Catch 22* and *Something Happened,* maintains an apartment on West 80th Street although he spends much of his time in Amagansett, near the tip of Long Island. Jack Gelber, whose play *The Connection* was a turning point in American theater when it was produced in 1959, lives on West End Avenue in the Nineties. (The Living Theatre, which produced the play, had its origins in a large apartment at 789 West End Avenue inherited by Julian Beck from his father. Here he and Judith Malina first put on plays. Later they used a loft at 110th Street and Broadway as a theater.) According to Gelber there is little West Side socialization based on literary affinities. "Most of the interaction I get is on the street, in the supermarket, walking the dog," he has said. "I'll meet someone and he'll say, 'What are you doing, Jack?' Writers don't talk about writing anyway. As far as I can gather, their main topic of conversation is money — what kind of an advance did you get, how many performances did you have."

Isaac Bashevis Singer has lived on the West Side for over thirty years — "as long as I lived in Poland," one of his characters says. "I know each block, each house . . . I have the illusion of having put down roots here. I have spoken in most

Isaac Bashevis Singer at his desk in his apartment
on West 86th Street.

of the synagogues. They know me in some of the stores and in
the vegetarian restaurants. Women with whom I have had
affairs live on the side streets. Even the pigeons know me; the
moment I come out with a bag of feed, they begin to fly toward
me from blocks away." Singer currently lives on 86th Street
between Broadway and Amsterdam Avenue.

.

Merging with the West Side group but having its own distinct identity is the literary circle associated with Columbia University. Young critics, poets and fiction writers who studied there or are on the faculty tend to live in the buildings above 110th Street. And a number of Columbia alumni who left the area have become writers. Harlem Renaissance writer Zora Neale Hurston did graduate study with Columbia anthropologist Franz Boas after graduating from Barnard, and Langston Hughes attended Columbia College, living in Hartley Hall, in 1921. When he came to New York in 1929, Federico García Lorca stayed in John Jay Hall with a friend who was a Columbia professor. Herbert Gold went to Columbia, living for a time in Hartley Hall. Bernard Malamud got an M.A. at Columbia, and J. D. Salinger took Whit Burnett's course in the short story. Historically, a number of Columbia professors have had a literary influence, most notably the Van Doren brothers, Carl and Mark. Although they both lived in the Village, their influence was strongly felt on campus. Carl taught at Columbia from 1911 to 1930, during which time he was also, in succession, literary editor of the *Nation* and of the *Century Magazine*. He played an important part in the rediscovery of Herman Melville, assembling the first bibliography of Melville's work and encouraging Raymond Weaver to write the first Melville biography. Alfred Kazin said that "Carl Van Doren got me to write *On Native Grounds.*" Mark Van Doren taught at Columbia from 1920 until 1959 and succeeded his brother as literary editor of the *Nation.* Among his students were John Berryman, Thomas Merton, Herbert Gold, Allen Ginsberg and Jack Kerouac. Van Doren was particularly influential with the poets; he himself won the Pulitzer Prize for poetry in 1940. On Mark Van Doren's death, Allen Ginsberg remembered that the professor "taught Kerouac Shakespeare and gave him an 'A.' Kerouac quit the Columbia football team to spend more

Allen Ginsberg on the roof of his apartment building
at 114th Street, around 1947.

time studying Shakespeare with Van Doren. Most of the other
professors were interested in careers in literature and he was
interested in illuminated wisdom."

The Beat movement was born in the forties out of the interaction between Ginsberg and Kerouac and William Burroughs,
who met in the area around Columbia. Two young women
named Edie Parker and Joan Adams were living in an apartment on 118th Street between Amsterdam Avenue and Morningside Drive. In 1943 Kerouac went to live there with Edie, to
whom he was later married for a short time. Burroughs moved
in with Joan, whom he married in 1944, and Ginsberg stayed
with them all for a while in 1945. "This," said Ginsberg, "was
the seminal situation" in terms of the Beat sensibility. "Something happened in Joan Adams's apartment to all of us. Listening to her and Burroughs talk, make fun of the public consciousness. We'd sit around talking very ironically, cynically,
about public persons. I guess everyone else was hypnotized by
the officialese mentality." In 1945 Ginsberg was suspended
from Columbia for letting Kerouac stay in his room in Hartley
Hall and for writing an obscenity in the dust on his window-
pane. "The dean called me in and said, 'Mr. Ginsberg, I hope
you realize the enormity of what you've done.' I took that
phrase back to Burroughs and Joan. It represented the official
world in which the entire bedrock of economics and foreign
policy and law was based. They burst into screams of laughter. I realized the dean of Columbia was crazy, literally
crazy; a madman was running the entire college." Here, too,
Burroughs did his first writing when Kerouac persuaded him
to undertake alternate chapters of a detective novel in the
style of Dashiell Hammett. The three spent a great deal of
time in a Columbia hangout, the West End Café on Broadway, making it the only West Side saloon with literary connections.

Mark Van Doren in his office at Columbia about 1945.

Since the Van Dorens, the major literary influence at Columbia has been Lionel Trilling. Trilling, who himself had been a student and was later a colleague of Mark Van Doren, held a special significance for the young Jewish intellectuals as the first Jew to be given a permanent appointment in the Columbia English department. He was regarded as the pre-eminent "New York intellectual." In Trilling the two main West Side literary traditions — Columbia and the New York intellectuals — met. And if Greenwich Village in the late twenties had a special literary valuation because Edmund Wilson lived there — "He seemed in his own person . . . to propose and to realize the idea of the literary life," Trilling wrote — Trilling, in turn, conferred that significance on the West Side.

The West Side

The
West
Side

*West Side
Tour*

Claremont Ave.→
Columbia Univ.
Barnard Col.→
Riverside Dr.→
Morningside Dr.
W. 110th St.

Broadway

HUDSON RIVER

PKWY

Hudson

Henry

West End Ave.
Broadway
Amsterdam Ave.
Columbus Ave.

CENTRAL PARK

W. 127th St.
W. 125th St.
W. 116th St.

W. 100th St.

W. 85th St.
W. 84th St.
W. 81st St.
W. 80th St.
Amer. Museum of
Natural History

Central Park W.

W. 75th St.
W. 73rd St.
W. 68th St.
W. 67th St.

Lincoln Center →
W. 61st St.

1. 25 Central Park West, between 62nd and 63rd streets. The Century

Apartments is one of New York's most attractive art deco buildings. Marc Connelly moved here in 1931, the year it was built (p. 249).

2. 50 Central Park West, on the southwest corner of 65th Street. Edna Ferber lived here from 1924 to 1929 in an eighth-floor apartment (p. 249).

3. Numbers 1, 15, 27, and 33 West 67th Street were constructed by the same developer, Walter Russell, as housing for artists. Number 1, the Hotel Des Artistes was built in 1916, and the Café was redecorated in 1979 (pp. 250–51). Number 15 was designed in 1906. Robert Lowell and Elizabeth Hardwick lived here in the 1960s (p. 257).

4. 57 West 68th Street. Dorothy Parker lived here as a child, in one of a row of five-story stone houses with bay windows which are now painted white (p. 253). Anaïs Nin spent her young teenage years in a similar house several blocks away at 158 West 75th Street.

5. 1 West 72nd Street on Central Park West. The Dakota, one of New York's most famous luxury apartment houses, was built in 1884 by Henry J. Hardenbergh. It has been home to such well-known tenants as Boris Karloff, Zachary Scott, Leonard Bernstein, and Lauren Bacall. It was also the home of John Lennon and Yoko Ono, and was, sadly, the site of Lennon's murder.

6. 160 West 71st Street, on the southeast corner of Broadway. The Hotel Alamac. J.D. Salinger's fictional Glass family lived here; it's now an apartment building, "160" (p. 254).

7. 146 Central Park West at 74th Street. Carl Van Vechten lived here from 1936 until his death in 1964 (p. 204).

8. 73rd Street and Broadway, on the northwest corner. The Ansonia Hotel. Many famous people have lived here, including Theodore Dreiser (pp. 247–48).

9. 2245 Broadway, on the northwest corner of 80th Street. Zabar's, a gourmet delicatessen frequented by West Side intellectuals (p. 247).

10. West 84th Street, "Edgar Allan Poe Street." A plaque at 255 West 84th Street, about twenty feet west of Broadway, marks the site where Poe put the finishing touches on "The Raven," though the exact location is 206 West 84th, east of Broadway, a crumbling tenement without any markings (p. 247).

11. 300 Central Park West, between 90th and 91st streets. The Eldorado Towers. Sinclair Lewis lived here 1943–45 (pp. 250–51.) Herman Wouk also used it as the fictional home of his heroine Marjorie Morningstar.

12. 6 West 102nd Street. The first of three existing row houses, now gentrified as part of an apartment complex. Theodore Dreiser was living here in 1902 when he began *Sister Carrie.*

13. 310 West 100th Street. In 1916, Louis Untermeyer was living in this interesting structure with ironwork balconies and decorative grills in front of its long casement windows. He entertained many poets here (p. 252).

14. 845 West End Avenue, on the northwest corner of 101st Street. Herman Wouk lived here with his family during his college years (p. 254).

15. 333 Riverside Drive, between 105th and 106th streets. Saul Bellow lived here during the 1950s in a lovely white-brick, limestone-trimmed home within the Riverside-West 105th Street Historic District. The houses within the district, which covers Riverside Drive from 105th to 106th and most of 105th Street from Riverside Drive to West End Avenue, were all built from 1899 to 1902 in the French beaux arts style (p. 258).

16. 404 Riverside Drive, at the southeast corner of 113th Street, is the only building in this stretch of the drive which has a canopy lit by "bulby bright lights." Just in front is the Kossuth statue, where the Glass boys played football or soccer on a patch of grass. The only stretch of wall in this whole area lending itself to "stoopball" is at 420 Riverside Drive, at the northwest corner of 114th Street; it has two rows of simple moldings, waisthigh (p. 254).

17. 2911 Broadway, between 113th and 114th streets, on the west side. The West End Café, commonly called the West End bar, was a hangout for the Beat writers during the forties (p. 264).

18. Several writers lived on the Columbia University campus. Federico García Lorca stayed at John Jay Hall with his friend and teacher Ferdinando de los Rios when he came to New York in 1929 (p. 262). Langston Hughes, Herbert Gold, and Allen Ginsberg all lived in Hartley Hall at various times. Hughes didn't like Columbia because he felt it was too big and "the buildings looked like factories." Ginsberg was suspended for letting Jack Kerouac stay in his room and for writing obscenities in the dirt on his window (p. 264).

19. 421 West 118th Street. This sixth-floor walkup apartment of Edie Parker and Joan Adams, where Allen Ginsberg, Jack Kerouac, and William Burroughs often met, "was the seminal situation" in terms of Beat sensibility (p. 264).

20. 200 Claremont Avenue, on the southeast corner of 127th Street (Tieman Street). In 1919, Scott Fitzgerald had a cheap room in this building, "a high horrible apartment house in the middle of nowhere," while trying to become a writer (p. 252).

IX. Harlem

FOR MOST OUTSIDERS, Harlem is simply the quintessential ghetto — a precinct riddled with poverty, drugs, crime and violence. Some may temper this image with memories of the speakeasy and cabaret life of the twenties or nostalgia for the jazz era, when Dizzy Gillespie, Charlie Parker and Charlie Christian hammered out their art in Harlem clubs. But for black people, particularly black writers, Harlem is immeasurably more.

In the twenties, while downtown New York used Harlem as its playground, black intellectuals and writers assigned it a far more serious function. To them it was mecca, the big, beautiful capital of the black world. They came from all over the country to write, think and socialize together in the vital community that was developing·in Harlem. Few among them are well-remembered — Countee Cullen and Langston Hughes perhaps are the only widely familiar names — but when the twenties were over and the depression came, they left behind them the beginnings of black American literature.

In the forties, black writers began to document the effects of the depression on the people of Harlem. The neighborhood was never to recover from its heavy toll or to regain the innocence and optimism of the twenties. By the fifties, however, two towering literary figures, Ralph Ellison and James Baldwin, were to come to grips with Harlem, transmuting it in their writing. Today, again in a period of heightened consciousness, black writers are rediscovering their literary past and attempting to build cultural institutions in Harlem that will survive where those of the twenties did not. Although they may not choose to live physically in Harlem, it is in some way their mental residence — a focal point for their artistic consciousness.

Harlem was first settled in 1637 when two brothers named Isaac and Hendrick de Forest bought strips of land in the area, then a wilderness inhabited by wolves, rattlesnakes and hostile Indians. Soon a community developed and by 1658 it was sufficiently large to be established as the village of Nieuw Haarlem. By the early nineteenth century, the farms had been replaced by elaborate estates owned by the most prominent New York families — the De Lanceys, Beekmans, Bleeckers, Rikers and Coldens. One reminder of this era, Hamilton Grange at 141st Street and Convent Avenue, still survives. A gracious country house designed by John McComb, one of the foremost architects of the time, it was built by Alexander Hamilton in 1802. Here, in a finely furnished library and greenhouses filled with tropical and subtropical plants, he spent the last few years of his life.

In the 1840s and '50s Harlem had declined as a farming area; the soil was worn out and many of the estates were sold off. But the press of population northward from downtown was soon to transform the area. With each subsequent improvement in transportation — in 1881 the elevated reached 129th Street, in 1884 it was extended to 145th Street, and in 1901 the IRT Lenox Avenue subway line was constructed — the population grew. One of the builders who participated in the construction boom at the turn of the century was Nathanael West's father, Max Weinstein, known for his large luxury apartment houses adorned with ornamental work in limestone. In 1908 West lived with his family in one of them, the De Peyster, which stands on Seventh Avenue between 119th and 120th streets. During this period more and more Jews began moving to the area between 110th and 125th streets. Among them were Arthur Miller's parents, and in 1915 Miller was born on 111th Street. While he was still an infant his family moved to apartment 6B in the yellow brick building facing the Park at 45 West 110th Street.

The boom of the early 1900s caused overbuilding; many apartment houses were empty, the landlords desperate for tenants, and as a result the rather extraordinary events occurred that made the Harlem Renaissance possible. An enterprising Negro realtor named Philip A. Payton approached several landlords with the proposal that he fill their apartments with black tenants. The landlords accepted and in 1903 several houses on 134th Street were rented. Payton and a partner, J. C. Thomas, later bought two five-story apartment buildings, dispossessed the whites and put in Negro tenants. Other realtors did the same. And after selling its property in the Pennsylvania Station area, St. Philip's Episcopal Church, a Negro congregation, turned around and invested the proceeds in thirteen apartment houses on 135th Street between Lenox and Seventh avenues. By dint of initiative and cooperative effort, Negroes, who had previously lived in the Tenderloin and San Juan Hill areas, were able to do the unprecedented: secure for themselves new housing in one of New York's prime residential areas.

Obviously, Harlem then was not a ghetto in the usual sense of the term. James Weldon Johnson described it as "one of the most beautiful and healthful sites in the whole city." Writing in 1930 he said, "It is not a slum, nor is it a 'quarter' consisting of dilapidated tenements. It is a section of new-law apartment houses and handsome dwellings, with streets as well paved, as well lighted, and as well kept as in any other part of the city."

The desirable community soon attracted the black elite.

W. E. B. Du Bois in the office of the *Crisis* magazine.

W. E. B. Du Bois came to New York from Atlanta in 1910 to edit the *Crisis,* a publication of the NAACP. James Weldon Johnson moved to Harlem in 1914 after seven years as a diplomat. And in 1917 Marcus Garvey, later to lead the Back-to-Africa movement, founded the Universal Negro Improvement Association. Harlem represented a spirit of protest, militancy and self-assertion — a new kind of identity for the Negro. The new consciousness drew the talented young men and women who were to create the movement known as the Negro Renaissance. In literary terms the Renaissance was in fact only an awakening — the first emergence of black writers in force. Little more than half a century after the end of slavery, America had produced only a few Negro writers, among them Paul Laurence Dunbar, Charles W. Chestnutt, James Weldon Johnson and W. E. B. Du Bois. But in a larger sense, the term "Renaissance" characterized a rebirth of the race, as in the phrase "the New Negro." And as a social phenomenon it involved not only writers, but musicians, actors, dancers and a hitherto unprecedented exchange with white people that was expressed both on a personal level and in a wholesale influx of sight-seers, curiosity-seekers

"The New Negro Has No Fear" reads the sign carried in a Harlem parade in the twenties.

and speakeasy habitués to Harlem. Langston Hughes captured the uniqueness and extravagance of the Renaissance when he wrote:

> It was a period when, at almost every Harlem upper-crust dance or party, one would be introduced to various distinguished white celebrities as guests. It was a period when almost any Harlem Negro of any social importance at all would be likely to say casually: "As I was remarking the other day to Heywood —," meaning Heywood Broun. Or: "As I said to George —," referring to George Gershwin. It was a period when local and visiting royalty were not at all uncommon in Harlem. And when the parties of A'Lelia Walker, the Negro heiress, were filled with guests whose names would turn any Nordic social climber green with envy . . . It was a period when every season there was at least one hit play on Broadway acted by a Negro cast. And when books by Negro authors were being published with much greater frequency and much more publicity than ever before or since in history.

The beginnings of the literary strands of the Renaissance, as most beginnings, are vague and subject to dispute. Most seem to recognize West Indian poet and novelist Claude McKay as forerunner of the movement, whether they mark its start with his poem "Harlem Dancer," which appeared in *Seven Arts* under the pen name Eli Edwards in 1917, or his sonnet "If We Must Die," two years later. In any case, the movement was well under way when the anthology *The New Negro,* edited by Rhodes Scholar and Howard University professor Alain Locke, was published in 1925.

The movement had an old guard and a new: elder statesmen and gurus as well as fresh, young talent. "Jessie Fauset at the *Crisis,* Charles Johnson at *Opportunity,* and Alain Locke in Washington, were the three people who midwifed the so-called New Negro literature into being," wrote Langston Hughes in a capsule description. "Kind and critical — but not too critical for the young — they nursed us along until our books were born. Countee Cullen, Zora Neale Hurston, Arna Bontemps, Rudolph Fisher, Wallace Thurman, Jean Toomer, Nella Larsen, all of us came along about the same time."

The Renaissance writers did not constitute a school in the sense of possessing a common style, political attitude or subject matter, though many critics generalized about "primitivism and exoticism." If anything, it was marked by extraordinary diversity. What could be more disparate than Cullen's Keatsian sonnets, Jean Toomer's experimental prose, Langston Hughes's jazz rhythms and Zora Neale Hurston's rediscovered folk tales? What the writers of the Renaissance had in common was that they were the first to focus on the question of Negro identity. Venturing into areas of Negro life previously ignored or denied, they were attempting the self-description that is the first step toward the independence and autonomy of mind necessary to create art.

Alain Locke, who taught philosophy at Howard, is often credited with being the "father" of the Negro Renaissance. Zora Neale Hurston, who was a member of the Stylus, the literary club he advised, suggested that more of the credit should have been shared with Charles Johnson, editor of *Opportunity*, the magazine of the Urban League, and later first Negro president of Fisk University. Johnson, who arrived in Harlem in 1921 and founded *Opportunity* in 1923, saw a story she had written for the Stylus and asked her to send something to him. She sent "Drenched in Light" and he published it. "He wrote me a kind letter and said something about New York. So, beginning to feel the urge to write, I wanted to be in New York. This move on the part of Dr. Johnson was the root of the so-called Negro Renaissance. It was his work, and only his hush-mouth nature has caused it to be attributed to many others." Langston Hughes concurred: "Mr. Johnson, I believe, did more to encourage and develop Negro writers during the 20s than anyone else in America. He wrote them sympathetic letters, pointing out the merits of their work. He brought them together to meet and know each other. He made the *Opportunity* contests sources of discovery and help."

Jessie Fauset was helpful and hospitable to the young writers although she often disapproved of their subject matter and attitudes. She, with W. E. B. Du Bois, was dedicated to proving that there were no differences between black and white. They took the position that it was preferable to portray the lives of those well-traveled Negroes who discussed Shakespeare over tea than to dwell upon the problems of the poor, the mulatto or the very dark-skinned black. Fauset's home at 1947 Seventh Avenue, an attractive building with Ionic columns just north of the elegant Graham Court Apartments at 116th, was a center for what Langston Hughes called "cultural soirées." At her parties, he wrote, "there was always quite a different atmosphere from that at most other Harlem good-time gatherings. At Miss Fauset's, a good time was shared by talking literature and reading poetry aloud and perhaps enjoying some conversation in French . . . At her house one would usually meet editors and students, writers and social workers, and serious people who liked books and the British Museum, and had perhaps been to Florence. (Italy, not Alabama.)" Jessie Fauset and her husband, Herbert Harris, later moved to a cooperative in the Paul Laurence Dunbar Apartments.

Among the principal elder statesmen of the Renaissance was James Weldon Johnson, who lived in 1927 at 180 West 135th Street. Johnson, at various times in his life, was principal of a public school, member of the Florida bar, U.S. Consul to Venezuela and Nicaragua, professor at New York University and successful musical comedy writer. His 1912 novel, *Autobiography of an Ex-Coloured Man*, with its descriptions of

Negro life in New York, is considered by many to anticipate the Harlem Rennaissance school by more than a decade. It was in 1927, however, with *God's Own Trombones,* that he had his greatest literary success.

During the Renaissance years Johnson served as executive secretary of the NAACP and was in an ideal position to act as liaison between the Negro community and influential whites. His parties, at which he often introduced young writers to the publishing establishment, tended to be sedate. Blanche Ferguson wrote in *Countee Cullen and the Negro Renaissance* that "Mr. Johnson's appearance and background did not inspire levity. He was tall, lean and immaculate . . . But as a host he was modest and self-effacing, always focusing attention on others. And in the well-appointed home that exuded culture and comfort the Johnson's guests could generally count on meeting interesting personalities such as Van Vechten or Clarence Darrow." Johnson himself recalled a farewell party he gave for Claude McKay in a letter to him in 1930: "We often speak of that party back in '22 . . . Do you know that was the first getting together of the black and white literati on a purely social plane. Such parties are now common in New York, but I doubt if any has been more representative. You will remember there were present Heywood Broun, Ruth Hale, F. P. Adams, John Farrar, Carl Van Doren, Freda Kirchwey, Peggy Tucker, Roy Nash — on our side you, Du Bois, Walter White, Jessie Fauset, [Arthur] Schomburg, J. Rosamond Johnson — I think that party started something."

The phenomenon of the Negro Renaissance was very much a collaboration with the white world, and master collaborator of them all was Carl Van Vechten, author, photographer and master of ceremonies of the twenties. As a white writer, Van Vechten was able to introduce black writers to publishers and producers; also, he demonstrated with his novel *Nigger Heaven* that people might buy a book that went beyond stereotypes and described black people as they were. The success of *Nigger Heaven* in 1926 helped the other novelists of the Renaissance to find publishers.

Van Vechten's choice of a title was unfortunate, however, and earned him the undeserved scorn of some members of the black community. There were many who never understood that it was meant to be ironic: "Nigger Heaven!" moans the novel's protagonist, a tormented aspiring writer. "That's what Harlem is. We sit in our places in the gallery of this New York theater and watch the white world sitting down below in the good seats in the orchestra. Occasionally, they turn their faces up towards us, their hard, cruel faces, to laugh or sneer, but they never beckon . . . Harlem! The Mecca of the New Negro! My God!" Van Vechten, better than many of the black writers, understood that Harlem might be Mecca for the black elite but that there were many, like his protagonist, so mutilated by past oppression that they couldn't seize the opportunities opened up by the Renaissance.

Older than most of the writers associated with the Renaissance (Hurston, Bontemps, Hughes, Thurman and Cullen were all born in 1902 or 1903), Claude McKay was a precursor of the movement and a strong influence on those who came after him. Born in Jamaica in 1890, he came to the United States in 1912 and spent two years at Tuskegee Institute in Alabama and the University of Kansas before settling in Harlem in 1914 to become a writer. Until 1921, when he became associate editor of the *Liberator* under Max Eastman, he worked as porter, houseman, longshoreman, barman and dining car porter.

McKay's first novel, *Home to Harlem,* published in 1928 while he was abroad, was the first fictional work by a Negro to make the best-seller list. In rhapsodic prose, punctuated profusely with exclamation points, *Home to Harlem* romanticized the simple, instinctive life of an AWOL soldier turned dining car waiter named Jake. McKay's great facility with language— the novel is written primarily in a lyrical Harlem dialect — makes this one of the most beautiful of the Renaissance novels. Some years later McKay was to write, "Like a flock of luxuriant, large-lipped orchids spreading over the side of a towering rock, the color of African life has boldly splashed itself upon the north end of Manhattan." This was the way he saw Harlem and his first novel described its every exoticism — from the cabarets and speakeasies to "the Block Beautiful," an all-white enclave in the midst of black Manhattan on 130th Street between Lenox and Fifth avenues.

McKay was abroad from 1922 to 1934 and therefore absent during the honeyed days when black writers were pampered and courted. When he returned, he lived in an apartment, decorated with tapestries he had brought back from Africa, in a tenement building that stands at 147 West 142nd Street. Gradually, however, he became more and more isolated and impoverished.

Nella Larsen, too, belonged to a slightly older generation. Born in Chicago in 1893 of a West Indian father and Danish mother, she came to New York after attending Fisk University and the University of Copenhagen. She was at various times a nurse and a librarian and lived at 236 West 135th Street during her marriage to Dr. Elmer S. Imes. Her first novel, *Quicksand,* is generally conceded to be one of the best literary achievements of the Renaissance. Psychologically it is the most real, perhaps because unlike the other writers Larsen was describing a situation she knew intimately — the dilemma of the mulatto alienated from both the dominant culture and the black world because of her mixed blood. In 1930 she became the first black woman to win a Guggenheim Fellowship.

Of all the Renaissance writers, Countee Cullen was the only native New Yorker. Born Countee Porter in 1903, he was adopted by the Reverend Frederick Cullen when he was eleven years old and went to live with Cullen and his wife first at 234 West 131st Street and later in the parsonage that adjoined the Salem Methodist Episcopal Church at 2190 Seventh Avenue. Countee showed achievement from an early age. He won the Federation of Women's Clubs Prize for his poetry at DeWitt Clinton High School, the poetry prize established by poet, dramatist, translator and silk-manufacturing heir Witter Bynner at New York University, and received a master's degree from Harvard. His first volume of poetry, *Color,* appeared in 1925, and the following year he became assistant editor of *Opportunity* and started writing a column that he called "The Dark Tower." The most important social event of the twenties was undoubtedly Cullen's marriage in 1927 to W. E. B. Du Bois's daughter, Yolande. The ceremony took place before thirteen hundred people in Cullen's father's church. Du Bois directed the rehearsal himself, organizing the sixteen bridesmaids and the ushers, who included the poets Langston Hughes and Arna Bontemps. At the ceremony, canaries in gilded cages provided musical accompaniment. Shortly after the wedding Cullen went off to Paris on a Guggenheim Fellowship, leaving his bride behind. The marriage, less spectacular than the wedding, was dissolved in 1929.

Cullen returned to New York in the fall of 1930. His only novel, *One Way to Heaven,* published in 1932, presents a panorama of Harlem life, including a rather cynical view of the church. He juxtaposes the life of a Harlem maid with that of her Negro socialite mistress, whose chaotic parties bring together black intellectuals and celebrities and white curiosity-seekers.

Langston Hughes arrived in Harlem in 1921 and stayed at

From left, Langston Hughes, Charles S. Johnson, E. Franklin Frazier, Rudolph Fisher, Hubert Delaney on the roof of 580 St. Nicholas Avenue.

the 135th Street Y while making preparations to enter Columbia University. He had just graduated from high school in Cleveland, where he had lived with his mother. His father — lawyer, rancher, money-lender and manager of an electric company in Toluca, Mexico — provided the money for him to go to college. Hughes's grandmother was the widow of one of the five Negroes who attacked Harper's Ferry with John Brown, and the poet was also related to John Mercer Langston, a Reconstruction Congressman from Virginia and one-time dean of law at Howard University. After a year at Columbia, Hughes transferred to Lincoln University in Philadelphia, making frequent trips to New York to keep in touch with other young Harlem writers. He also corresponded with Claude McKay, then in Europe, who influenced him considerably.

While Hughes was a student at Columbia, Arna Bontemps came to New York from Los Angeles, where he had studied at Pacific Union College. Bontemps's first poetry appeared in the *Crisis* in 1924. From 1924 to 1931 he taught at the Harlem Academy, living during these years at various addresses; 305 Edgecombe Avenue and 75 St. Nicholas Avenue were two. Most of his work was published in the thirties, beginning with a novel, *God Sends Sunday,* in 1931. He and Cullen collaborated on a dramatization of it; it was renamed *St. Louis Woman* and was produced in 1946 with music and lyrics by Harold Arlen and Johnny Mercer. The production, introducing Pearl Bailey, ran 113 performances on Broadway.

Rudolph Fisher was one of the Renaissance's most versatile and intelligent figures. A brilliant student at Brown University, where he received his B.A. and M.A., he was Paul Robeson's accompanist and arranger on concert tours at the same time as he was earning his M.D. at Howard. He came to New York in 1924 to study bacteriology and pathology at Columbia's College of Physicians and Surgeons and went into the practice of radiology in 1927. From 1929 to 1932 he was superintendent of a hospital while living at 2816 Eighth Avenue at the Dunbar Apartments. He had begun writing when he was in medical school and published the first mystery to use all Negro characters, *The Conjure Man Dies,* in 1932. His later novel, *The Walls of Jericho,* describes the integration of white sections of Harlem.

In 1925 Zora Neale Hurston arrived in New York to attend Barnard. A desperately poor young woman from Eatonville, Florida, daughter of a tenant farmer, she made her way in the world on charm and determination as well as talent. At the age of fourteen, she left home employed as a maid with a traveling Gilbert and Sullivan company. Eighteen months later she quit the company in Baltimore, got a job as a waitress and started night school. She was soon convinced that literature was to be her world. Although she had no money, she immediately enrolled in the high school department of Morgan College. During the two years she spent there, she worked in the home of one of the trustees for room and board and two dollars a week. She then went to Howard but dropped out after a year and a half for lack of money. It was at this time that the letter from Charles Johnson inspired her to go to New York and try her luck there. She arrived the first week of January 1925 with "$1.50, no job, no friends, and a lot of hope." After she won a prize for a short story at an *Opportunity* dinner in May, Fannie Hurst offered her a job as secretary and one of Barnard's founders got her a scholarship there. She entered in the fall and graduated in 1928.

During her years at Barnard, she was very much present on the Harlem scene although she lived downtown at Fannie Hurst's 67th Street duplex (see Chapter VIII, The West Side). Langston Hughes remembered that "she went about Harlem with an anthropologist's ruler, measuring heads for Franz Boas." After graduation she was in New York intermittently, between trips to the South and the Caribbean to collect Negro folklore. In 1932 she was living at Graham Court, a white granite building at 116th Street and Seventh Avenue, then the most luxurious apartment house in Harlem.

Wallace Thurman also arrived in 1925 and set up housekeeping at what was probably the main gathering place of the younger writers of the Renaissance, a brick and brownstone building still standing at 267 West 137th Street. Langston Hughes had a room here one summer, and Zora Neale Hurston, Gwendolyn Bennett and the painter Aaron Douglas were frequent visitors.

Thurman, who had a biting sense of humor, called the Harlem literati the "niggerati" and immortalized his rooming house as Niggerati Manor in *Infants of the Spring,* a satirical roman à clef on the Renaissance. He took a pessimistic view of the future of Negro literature and alone seems to have understood the dimensions of the psychological obstacles Negroes faced. ". . . 99 and 99/100 per cent of the Negro race is patently possessed and motivated by an inferiority complex," says Raymond, the autobiographical protagonist of *Infants of the Spring.* "Being a slave race actuated by slave morality, what else could you expect?"

Thurman was managing editor of the *Messenger,* a radical weekly founded by A. Philip Randolph and Chandler Owen, and later worked as a reader at Macaulay's ("the only Negro reader, so far as I know, to be employed by any of the larger publishing firms," Langston Hughes wrote) and coauthored *Harlem,* the first successful play written by a Negro to appear on Broadway. And in 1926 Thurman edited the one and only issue of *Fire,* intended to be a Negro literary quarterly. Zora Neale Hurston, Aaron Douglas, Gwendolyn Bennett and Langston Hughes were on the staff. "The idea," said Hughes, was "that it would burn up a lot of the old, dead conventional Negro-white ideas of the past, *épater le bourgeois* into a realization of the existence of the younger Negro writers and artists, and provide us with an outlet for publication not available in the limited pages of the small Negro magazines then existing . . ." Although everyone else contributed fifty dollars, Thurman, the only steadily employed participant, bore most of the expenses. In the end, the first number cost almost a thousand dollars, and since nobody could afford to pay the bills there was no second issue.

The year 1926 stands out as the high point of the Negro Renaissance. It was the year of *Fire* and of Hughes's *The Weary Blues* and Van Vechten's *Nigger Heaven.* All the young writers were in New York, working on the books that would be published in the late twenties and early thirties. Even Jean Toomer, acknowledged by his contemporaries as well as most critics as the finest writer of the Renaissance, was in Harlem that year.

Toomer's *Cane,* the first novel of the Negro Renaissance, had been published in 1923. It sold only 500 copies, but was clearly a succès d'estime and had an importance to black writers far out of proportion to its sales figures. While most writers of the Renaissance, with the possible exception of Hughes, were stylistically way behind their times, Toomer was treated as an equal in the avant-garde magazines. *Cane,* portions of which originally appeared in *Broom,* the *Little Review* and the *Liberator,* was a formally experimental composite of portraits and stories, interspersed with poems, dealing with life in the South.

Although seldom present in Harlem, Toomer exercised a strong influence on the imaginations and aspirations of the younger Renaissance writers. "I know of only one Negro who has the elements of greatness, and that's Jean Toomer," says Wallace Thurman's Raymond in *Infants of the Spring.* "The rest of us are merely journeymen, planting seed for someone else to harvest." Unfortunately, Toomer's work appeared infrequently after the late twenties, and that fact has given rise to the notion that he stopped writing. In fact, unpublished novels and plays are among his papers at Fisk.

Soon after the publication of *Cane,* Toomer developed an interest in the mysticism of Gurdjieff, which culminated in a visit to the Gurdjieff Institute in Fontainebleau, France, during the summer of 1926. He returned to Harlem to spread his beliefs. Among those who became adherents were Wallace Thurman, Dorothy Peterson, Aaron Douglas and Nella Larsen. However, as Langston Hughes has observed, everyone in Harlem had to make a living and could not afford the amount of time required in study and meditation. Toomer's efforts were not very successful and he "shortly left his Harlem group and went downtown to drop the seeds of Gurdjieff in less dark and poverty-stricken fields."

In later years Toomer was to become a rather enigmatic figure. In 1922, in response to a request from the *Liberator* for some biographical information, he had written: "My family is from the South. My mother's father, P. B. S. Pinchback, born in Macon, Georgia, left home as a boy and worked on the Mississippi River steamers . . . Later, in the days of Reconstruction, he utilized the Negro's vote and won offices for himself, the highest being that of lieutenant, and then acting governor of Louisiana . . . Racially, I seem to have (who knows for sure) seven blood mixtures: French, Dutch, Welsh, Negro, German, Jewish, and Indian. Because of these, my position in America has been a curious one. I have lived equally amid the two race groups. Now white, now colored . . . I have strived for a Spiritual fusion analagous [sic] to the fact of racial intermingling . . . Within the last two or three years, however, my growing need for artistic expression has pulled me deeper and deeper into the Negro group. And as my powers of receptivity increased, I found myself loving it in a way that I could never love the other."

Later, Toomer married two women from socially distinguished white families. The first, whom he married in 1932, was Marjory Latimer, a descendant of Anne Bradstreet's. She died giving birth to their child the following year. The second was Marjorie Content, daughter of a member of the New York Stock Exchange and former wife of Harold Loeb, founder of *Broom*. (Her home at 3 East 9th Street was *Broom* headquarters; see Chapter II, Greenwich Village.) When asked at the time of his second marriage whether he was Negro or white, Toomer replied, ". . . I have not lived as [a Negro], nor do I really know whether there is any colored blood in me or not. My maternal grandfather, Pickney Benton Stewart Pinchback, was the 'carpet-bag' governor of Louisiana. In order to gain colored votes, he referred to himself as having colored blood. His two brothers never did so however; so the fact is, I do not know whether colored blood flows through my veins."

.

Negro Harlem in the twenties extended approximately from 130th to 145th streets, bounded on the east by Madison Avenue and on the west by Seventh, with its hub at 135th Street between Fifth and Seventh avenues. Seventh Avenue, "Harlem's Broadway during the week and its Fifth Avenue on Sunday," as Rudolph Fisher described it in *The Walls of Jericho,*

> remains for six days a walk for deliberate shoppers, a lane for tumultuous traffic, the avenue of a thousand enterprises and the scene of a thousand hairbreadth escapes; remains for six nights a carnival, bright with the lights of theaters and night clubs, alive with darting cabs, with couples moving from house party to cabaret, with loiterers idling and ogling on the curb, with music wafted from mysterious sources, with gay talk and loud Afric [sic] laughter. Then comes Sunday, and for a few hours Seventh Avenue becomes the highway to heaven; reflects that air of quiet, satisfied self-righteousness peculiar to chronic churchgoers. Indeed, even Fifth Avenue on Easter never quite attains to this; practice makes perfect, and Harlem's Seventh Avenue boasts fifty-two Easters a year."

Harlem, with its broad avenues, was as given to the promenade as any European city, and much of the action of the twenties' novels revolves around strolls and chance encounters on Seventh Avenue. Helga, the protagonist of Nella Larsen's *Quicksand,* remarks, "They say . . . that if one stands on the corner of 135th Street and 7th Avenue long enough, one will eventually see all the people one has ever known or met."

The fashionable district of the time is described in Wallace Thurman's *The Blacker the Berry* as the area between Seventh and Edgecombe avenues on 136th through 139th streets and the apartment buildings on Edgecombe, Bradhurst and St. Nicholas avenues. Most of the homes inhabited and visited by the Renaissance writers fall within these elegant precincts. The most popular social center of the twenties was the $90,000 mansion at 108 West 136th Street, built in 1913 of Indiana limestone by Madame C. J. Walker, a St. Louis laundress who had made a fortune with the discovery of a hair-straightening process. Mme. Walker's daughter, A'Lelia Walker Robinson, was Harlem's foremost hostess. Hughes says that the "big-hearted, night-dark, hair-straightening heiress, made no pretense at being intellectual or exclusive. At her 'at homes' Negro poets and Negro number bankers mingled with downtown poets and seat-on-the-stock-exchange racketeers. Countee Cullen would be there and Witter Bynner, Muriel Draper and Nora Holt . . . And a good time was had by all." She also helped writers with money; Pulitzer Prize-winning journalist Ted Poston has called her "a one-woman foundation." In 1928 A'Lelia Walker attempted to establish one floor of her house as a café for writers and artists. "She saw a real need for a place, a sufficiently sympathetic place in which they could meet and discuss their plans and arts, to which they could bring their friends, and at which they could eat for a price within their very limited means," wrote Roi Ottley and William J. Weatherby in *The Negro in New York*. "But the plans never jelled, because A'Lelia was always too busy with parties to find time to give approval, or the artists could not be found because of similarly important distractions." Finally, the café, its walls covered with lettered verses by Cullen and Hughes, opened. Named the Dark Tower after Cullen's column in

Opportunity, it served for a short time as a place where "the Negro Intelligentsia met influential white people, particularly publishers, critics, and potential 'sponsors.'" Less than two years after its opening, A'Lelia closed it and moved her social activities to her apartment at 80 Edgecombe Avenue.

Behind the site of the Walker mansion (now occupied by the Countee Cullen branch of the New York Public Library), stands a Harlem literary landmark of a different sort. The attractive, white, neoclassic building was the 135th Street branch of the New York Public Library during the twenties, when it served as a meeting place for all the people of the Renaissance. Today it houses the material on black history collected by Arthur A. Schomburg, a Puerto Rican Negro who dealt in rare books, and continues to function as one of the community's most influential literary centers. In addition to lending books, the library was the scene of innumerable meetings, debates and plays. In 1938, Langston Hughes's *Don't You Want to be Free?* played 135 performances here after its run at the Harlem Suitcase Theater. In later years, James Baldwin and Ralph Ellison have visited often, and today most black writers use the library at one time or another for researches into the Negro past.

Several blocks away is Striver's Row, made up of what were, during the twenties, Harlem's most fashionable homes. Actually four blocks of attached houses, the "Row" is mentioned in virtually every work of the Renaissance. At a time when working-class families paid between ten dollars and eighteen dollars a month for rent, these homes, which rented for about eighty dollars, symbolized affluence. Negroes, especially doctors and entertainers, first began to live in the houses in 1919. In 1933, Abram Hill, founder of the American Negro Theater, wrote a play, *On Striver's Row,* whose main characters were the Van Strivens.

Aaron Douglas, a painter closely associated with the Renais-

Aaron Douglas, whose book jackets were a hallmark of the Harlem
Renaissance.

sance, and his wife, Alta, lived on Striver's Row at 227 West 139th Street in 1927 but later moved up the Harlem Heights to 409 Edgecombe Avenue, in the exclusive area called Sugar Hill. The Douglases, who are portrayed in Thurman's *The Blacker the Berry* and *Infants of the Spring*, were frequent hosts to their friends. "Everybody dropped in; this was really a meeting place for all the artists and intellectuals in Harlem," remembered Arna Bontemps. "We talked about all of the literary subjects, historical subjects, about everything related to the black experience . . . Every night was memorable. The apartment was decorated with Douglas's own paintings. It almost became a hallmark of the Harlem period in literature to have a book jacket by him."

Upstairs in the same building lived Walter White, assistant and later successor to James Weldon Johnson at the NAACP. He was often present at the Douglases' and also had his own share of parties. Among the guests at what was sometimes called "the White House of Negro America" were such celebrities as Sinclair Lewis, Willa Cather, Heywood Broun and George Gershwin.

In addition to gathering at the homes of friends, Renaissance writers visited and wrote about Harlem's theaters, casinos and cabarets. One of the most famous of these institutions was the Lafayette Theater, at Seventh Avenue and 131st Street, which was originally a complete entertainment center with ballrooms, restaurant and tavern. In the early years of the century the Lafayette housed a repertory company that repeated downtown successes. By the twenties the program had changed to Negro sketches and musical shows. As a scene of entertainment for the common man, the Lafayette made its appearance in *The Blacker the Berry, Nigger Heaven* and other Harlem novels.

The casinos where Harlem went to dance the exuberant steps of the Charleston, the Lindy Hop and the Black Bottom included the Harlem Casino, at Seventh Avenue and 124th Street (now the Refuge Temple), and the Renaissance, at Seventh Avenue and 138th Street (now the New Lafayette Theatre). Harlem cabarets, each with its own clientele and personality, existed in great profusion. Some were known for catering to whites and many were owned by whites. Other clubs refused to admit whites at all. On one occasion Claude McKay took Max Eastman to Ned's Place, a cabaret mentioned in *Home to Harlem*. Despite McKay's intimacy with the owner, Ned told them, "Ride back! Ride back, or I'll sick mah bouncers on you-all!"

In the twenties Ed Smalls' Sugar Cane Club, a dimly lit cellar on 135th Street and Fifth Avenue, was Harlem's principal "jump joint." The minuscule dance floor, surrounded by a few dozen tables, necessitated the phenomenon known as "dancing on a dime." Arna Bontemps recalls the emcee admonishing, "Get off that dime!" Later the club moved to its present location at 136th Street and Seventh Avenue, and, as Smalls' Paradise, continued to figure importantly in black social life. W. E. B. Du Bois celebrated his eighty-third birthday there in 1950; Malcolm X worked there as a waiter when he first came to New York at the age of sixteen; and James Baldwin was honored at Smalls', his favorite restaurant, in 1960 with a publication party for *Another Country*. Today, owned by basketball star Wilt Chamberlain, Smalls' still thrives.

Best known among whites in the twenties was the Cotton Club, "the Aristocrat of Harlem," on Lenox Avenue and 143rd Street. It was here that Duke Ellington and Cab Calloway held court with a "high yaller" chorus line so famous that white girls tried to "pass" to join it. Lena Horne, a member of the chorus for a time, recalls that "the most galling thing was that

the club was owned by whites . . . who based their business
on giving their white brethren a thrilling peek at the 'exotic'
world of the Negro, but refused to allow Negroes into their
club as paying customers. There were bouncers at the door
to keep out Negroes."

.

The depression brought an abrupt end to the concept of a
"New Negro" and the image of Harlem as an exotic utopia,
and exposed the poverty and struggle that had underlaid it all
along. The literary output continued through the early
thirties — Bontemps and Hurston began to publish only after
the twenties had ended — but for most, the good days were
over. Rudolph Fisher and Wallace Thurman died the same
week in December of 1934; Thurman, after long bouts of
alcoholism, of tuberculosis in a charity ward at Bellevue. Cullen spent his last years as a teacher of French and English at
Frederick Douglass Junior High School at 301 West 149th
Street, and died of ulcers in 1946. McKay grew progressively
more cynical and isolated until his death in 1948. The same
year, Zora Neale Hurston was indicted on a charge of being a
party in sexual relationships with two mentally ill boys and an
older man. The charge, brought by the mother of the boys,
was totally unsubstantiated; Hurston was out of the country
when the incident was supposed to have occurred. Yet the
scandal dealt her a deathly psychological blow. In a letter to
Carl Van Vechten she wrote: "I care for nothing anymore.
My country has failed me utterly. My race has seen fit to destroy
me without reason, and with the vilest tools conceived of by
man so far . . . All that I have tried to do has proved useless.
All that I have believed in has failed me. I have resolved to
die." In the fifties she stopped writing and went to work as a
maid in Florida. Her employers were unaware of her former

career until they came upon a story of hers in the *Saturday Evening Post*. She died penniless in 1960. Nella Larsen never completed the novel she had planned to write on her Guggenheim Fellowship. She disappeared from public life, went back to nursing as a supervisor at Bethel Hospital in Brooklyn and died in obscurity in 1963. Clearly, most of the writers lacked the psychic strength to survive the terrible pressure of their positions and aspirations. The high optimism and promise of Alain Locke's New Negro was not fulfilled, but the work of the Renaissance laid the foundations for what was to come afterward. Thurman was right after all: the Renaissance writers planted the seed that was to be harvested by Richard Wright, James Baldwin, Ralph Ellison and a profusion of black writers in the sixties.

Langston Hughes was one of the few Renaissance writers to survive the era. He alone made some vital connection with the real life of Harlem, which enabled him to continue when the fad for black writers had passed. And he alone, drawing the rhythms of his poetry from blues, created a literature stylistically based on black culture. Hughes earned his familiarity and friendship with the common man of Harlem through long hours spent in the ginmills and barrooms between 125th and 128th streets on Lenox Avenue. In later years his favorite hangout was the Palm Café on 125th between Seventh and Eighth. Here, during the early years of World War II, he met a man who worked in a war plant making cranks but hadn't any idea what the cranks were for. "You know white folks don't tell colored folks what cranks crank," he told Hughes. It was this man who provided the model for Jess B. Semple (Just Be Simple), Hughes's prototype of the common man of Harlem.

"More than Paris, or the Shakespeare country, or Berlin, or the Alps, I wanted to see Harlem," Hughes had written of the time before he came to New York. It was a feeling he was

Langston Hughes.

never to lose. "Had I been a rich young man," he wrote of his
early years, "I would have bought a house in Harlem and
built musical steps up to the front door, and installed chimes
that at the press of a button played Ellington tunes." But
Hughes was not rich and instead lived in a series of rooming
houses between his frequent travels until he was able to afford
a studio apartment on 141st Street in 1942. He took his meals
with an adopted uncle and aunt, Mr. and Mrs. Emerson Harper,
who lived a short stroll down the hill at 634 St. Nicholas
Avenue.

When the opportunity came for the Harpers to move into larger quarters, they asked Hughes what he thought of a place on 153rd Street and Riverside Drive. "It's a nice place, Aunt Toy, and I'll help you buy it. But I won't live in it with you. It is not Harlem; it never was Harlem, and it never will be Harlem — and I'll never leave Harlem for anywhere else." Instead, the Harpers moved to a three-story brownstone at 20 East 127th Street. Hughes had a workroom at the top of the house. Two long walls were covered with books, and a T-shaped desk stood between the windows. During the forties and fifties Hughes's many friends — musicians and actors as well as writers — visited the house on 127th Street; there were Canada Lee, Burl Ives, Robert Earl Jones, Ann Petry and Margaret Walker. In 1938 Hughes established the Harlem Suitcase Theater, in a loft on 125th Street, to present plays by black writers with black actors, directors and scene designers. His most enduring work, however, was his poetry. In the twenties he wrote about the blues and jazz scene in *The Weary Blues;* in *Shakespeare in Harlem,* published in 1942, he treated the effects of the depression on the community; and in *Montage of a Dream Deferred* he caught the underlying unrest and frustration that eventually surfaced in the protest of the sixties. Lorraine Hansberry's play *A Raisin in the Sun* takes its title from some lines in one of the poems, "Harlem":

> What happens to a dream deferred?
>
> > Does it dry up
> > like a raisin in the sun?
> > Or fester like a sore —
> > And then run?

During the thirties black literary output dwindled. Zora Neale Hurston published *Jonah's Gourd Vine* in 1934 and *Their Eyes Were Watching God* in 1937. Arna Bontemps, a late bloomer, started the decade with *God Sends Sunday* and published his best novel, *Black Thunder,* in 1936. Many black writers found work with the WPA Federal Writers' Project. A group that included Henry Lee Moon, Ellen Tarry, Richard Wright, Claude McKay, Ralph Ellison, Roi Ottley and Ted Poston worked on a project that was to be published years later as *The Negro in New York: An Informal Social History.*

The publication of Richard Wright's *Uncle Tom's Children* in 1936 foreshadowed the social realism of black writing in the forties. Although he lived in Harlem only briefly, Richard Wright dominated the decade. Most prominent among what has been called the Wright School was Ann Petry, a graduate of the University of Connecticut College of Pharmacy, who came to Harlem in 1938. Petry lived at 2 East 129th Street and worked for local newspapers, the *Amsterdam News* and the *People's Voice.* She sold her first short story to the *Crisis* and two years later won the 1945 Houghton Mifflin Fellowship Award for her first novel, *The Street.* The Harlem portrayed in *The Street* — 116th between Seventh and Eighth avenues — is radically different from the Harlem described just fifteen years earlier by James Weldon Johnson. The houses are no longer new; in fact, the dirt has become so deeply ingrained as to be ineradicable. "Layers and layers of paint won't fix that apartment," thinks Lutie Johnson, the book's heroine. "It would always smell; finger marks and old stains would come through the paint; the very smell of the wood itself would eventually win out over the paint. Scrubbing wouldn't help any." Petry later wrote two more novels, *Country Place* (1947) and *The Narrows* (1953), and a novella, "In Dark Confusion" (1947), set against the background of the Harlem riots of 1943.

The Harlem of the late thirties and early forties is the setting of the two great fifties' novels, Ellison's *Invisible Man* and Baldwin's *Go Tell It on the Mountain.* Both bring to it a new

perspective: Ellison is concerned with Harlem not in a natural-
istic or realistic sense, but as symbol. Baldwin is the first writer
born and bred in Harlem.

Ellison first came to New York in the summer of 1936, after
his junior year at Tuskegee, intending to earn money to return
to school that fall and study music and sculpture. He stayed
at the 135th Street YMCA and on his second day in the city
met Langston Hughes and Alain Locke on the steps of the
library across the street. He introduced himself and asked about
meeting Richard Wright. Hughes lent him Malraux's *Man's
Fate* and *Days of Wrath,* which were to affect him profoundly.
A short time later Hughes arranged the meeting with Wright.
"[He] had just come to New York and was editing a little
magazine," Ellison remembered. "I had read a poem of his
which I liked, and when we were introduced . . . he suggested
that I try to review a novel for his magazine. My review was
accepted and published and so I was hooked." Ellison later
wrote a short story for Wright's magazine, *New Challenge,*
but it was not published.

Like the narrator of *Invisible Man,* Ellison never got the
job that he anticipated would pay his school expenses and
therefore never went back to Tuskegee. He had very little
money and his living arrangements were improvised. Sometimes he slept on benches in St. Nicholas Park and for several
weeks he slept on the sofa at the home of Hughes's "aunt and
uncle," the Harpers. Wright continued to play a catalytic role
in Ellison's development as a writer. He gave him *Native Son*
to read as it came out of the typewriter and continued to advise
him. Ellison remembered his saying, " 'You must learn how
Conrad, Joyce, Dostoievsky get their effects . . .' He guided
me to Henry James and to Conrad's prefaces, that type of thing."

Between 1939 and 1945, Ellison lived at a series of addresses
on the western borders of Harlem. From 1945 to 1953, the

period covering the writing of *Invisible Man,* he lived at 749 St. Nicholas Avenue. Currently, he lives on upper Riverside Drive, in an apartment furnished with a Mies van der Rohe chair, which Ellison calls his equivalent of a Cadillac, and a collection of Hopi and Zuñi kachina dolls.

Ellison's attitude toward Harlem is a complex one. He seems always to have been somewhat aloof: "I did *not* come to New York to live in Harlem," he once explained. Instead, he sought "a wider world of opportunity. And, most of all, the excitement and impersonality of a great city. I wanted room in which to discover who I was." Although Ellison's experience in the most general sense is reflected in *Invisible Man* — its narrator leaves a college in the South, comes to stay in the "Men's House" and ends up living not in Harlem but "in a border area" — the novel is not a realistic one and Ellison has specifically denied that it is autobiographical. In it as well as in his essays, Ellison portrays Harlem in a symbolic way. At the same time, he has participated in its institutions and gloried in its pleasures, visiting the 135th Street library, Lewis Michaux's bookstore, then located at the corner of 125th Street and Seventh Avenue and, most of all, Minton's — the famous forties' jazz club in the Hotel Cecil on 118th Street, which Dizzy Gillespie, Charlie Christian, Charlie Parker, Thelonius Monk and many other musicians used as a jazz workshop. Ellison was one, as he wrote in an *Esquire* article, "who shared, night after night, the mysterious spell created by the talk, the laughter, grease paint, powder, perfume, sweat, alcohol and food — all blended and simmering, like a stew on the restaurant range, and brought to a sustained moment of elusive meaning by the timbres and accents of musical instruments locked in passionate recitative."

On the one hand, Ellison sees Harlem as a place where nightmares mingle with reality. "Harlem is a ruin — many of its ordinary aspects (its crimes, its casual violence, its crumbling buildings with littered areaways, ill-smelling halls and vermin-invaded rooms) are indistinguishable from the distorted images that appear in dreams, and which, like muggers haunting a lonely hall, quiver in the waking mind with hidden and threatening significance." On the other hand, Harlem is a symbol of liberation and light. "In my novel," he has said, "the narrator's development is one through blackness to light; that is, from ignorance to enlightenment: invisibility to visibility. He leaves the South and goes North; this, as you will notice in reading Negro folktales, is always the road to freedom — the movement upward." In the trip from the South to Harlem, the century from slavery to postindustrial society is radically telescoped. "Here," he writes,

> it is possible for talented youths to leap through the development of decades in a brief twenty years, while beside them white-haired adults crawl in the feudal darkness of their childhood. Here a former cotton picker develops the sensitive hands of a surgeon, and men whose grandparents still believe in magic prepare optimistically to become atomic scientists. Here the grandchildren of those who possessed no written literature examine their lives through the eyes of Freud and Marx, Kierkegaard and Kafka, Malraux and Sartre . . . The real and the unreal merge, and the marvelous beckons from behind the same sordid reality that denies its existence.

James Baldwin was born in 1924 in Harlem Hospital. His early years were spent in a house on upper Park Avenue, where the New York Central trains rattled by. It was the typical Harlem apartment: a railroad flat on the top floor, so thoroughly impregnated with dirt that it resisted all cleaning. Later Baldwin moved to an apartment at 2171 Fifth Avenue, since replaced by a housing project, where he spent his adolescence. His neighborhood, today called "Junkie's Hollow," was bounded by Lenox Avenue, the Harlem River, where "he and other children had waded into the water from the garbage-heavy bank or dived from occasional rotting promontories," 130th and 135th streets. In his short story "Sonny's Blues," a schoolteacher who has escaped Harlem revisits it with feelings that must have been Baldwin's own:

> These streets hadn't changed, though housing projects jutted up out of them now like rocks in the middle of a boiling sea. Most of the houses in which we had grown up had vanished . . . But houses exactly like the houses of the past yet dominated the landscape, boys exactly like the boys we once had been found themselves smothering in these houses, came down into the streets for light and air and found themselves encircled by disaster. Some escaped the trap, most didn't. Those who got out always left something of themselves behind, as some animals amputate a leg and leave it in the trap.

Baldwin went to Frederick Douglass Junior High School, where Countee Cullen was one of his teachers. A hill in the middle of Central Park near the reservoir was his refuge. From it, "cloudy, and far away, he saw the skyline of New York." Later, he went on to DeWitt Clinton High School, where he was editor-in-chief of the literary magazine, the *Magpie,* whose former editors included Paddy Chayefsky, Paul Gallico, Countee Cullen and the photographer Richard Avedon, who became Baldwin's close friend.

Baldwin's religious life, which he describes in *Go Tell It on the Mountain,* dominated his adolescence. He experienced a religious conversion at Mount Calvary of the Pentecostal Faith Church, known as Mother Horn's Church. (Mother Horn was the model for Sister Margaret in his play *The Amen Corner.*) There he came under the influence of Arthur Moore, a devoted communicant, who was also a fellow student at Frederick Douglass. The two boys often browsed on 125th

Street and picked up used books — one for a nickel and six
for a quarter. Later, Baldwin followed Moore to the Fireside
Pentecostal Assembly at 136th Street and Fifth Avenue. He
went to church several nights a week from eight to midnight,
and preached once a week on Young Ministers' Night.

In 1942, when he was eighteen, Baldwin left Harlem for
Greenwich Village. Soon afterward he met Richard Wright,
who seems to have functioned in his life as a spiritual father.
(John Grimes's father in *Go Tell It on the Mountain* is named
Richard.)   By the time he was twenty-four, he told his biographer, Fern Marja Eckman, "since I was not stupid, I realized
that there was no point in my staying in the country at all.
If I'd been born in Mississippi, I might have come to New York.
But, being born in New York, there's no place that you can
go. You have to go *out*. *Out* of the country." Despite Baldwin's recognition and abhorrence of the destructive nature of
Harlem, it still retains the meaning and emotional force of
home for him. He has described it as "the only *human* part
of New York" and in an interview in 1970 said that the only
place outside Europe he felt at home in the world was Harlem,
"where people know what I know, and we can talk and laugh,
and it would never occur to anybody to say what we all know."

·

In 1945, the Harlem Writers' Workshop was founded at the
YMCA by writer and historian John Henrik Clarke and others.
James Baldwin dropped in and out at the Sunday evening meetings and Langston Hughes read his poetry at workshop meetings
and acted as a critic for the group. In 1949 twelve members
pooled their resources and founded a quarterly of their own
because they were having trouble getting their work published.
Parties, attended by such celebrities as Sidney Poitier, Harry
Belafonte, Leon Bibb and Judy Holliday, were held to raise
funds. The group often met at Clarke's apartment at 311 West

136th Street. Today his present home, an elegant brownstone on 137th Street, is still a meeting place for young writers and intellectuals.

In 1950 and 1951, writers Rosa Guy and John Oliver Killens got together to form the Harlem Writers' Guild, an institution completely unrelated to the Workshop of the late forties. The purpose was to train young black people in writing, for which a group also called the Harlem Writers' Workshop was set up, and to promote the writers' work by means of parties and publicity. Killens served as chairman of the Guild until 1960, and the Workshop met most often at his apartment in Brooklyn because he had the biggest place. Today it meets at the Countee Cullen branch of the New York Public Library.

Through the Harlem Writers' Workshop have passed a large percentage of the black writers who came to prominence during the fifties and sixties. It was there that Killens first read *Youngblood,* Guy read *A Bird at My Window* and Maya Angelou read *I Know Why the Caged Bird Sings.* Paule Marshall, Louis Meriwether, Lonne Elder III, Douglas Turner Ward and Julian Mayfield were also members of the Workshop. Its meetings featured open and intense criticism of structure, character building, style — every aspect of writing. A number of the novels by writers who came out of the Workshop were set in Harlem. Rosa Guy's *A Bird at My Window* is a story of ghetto life in the area around Lenox Avenue between 110th and 125th streets. Louise Meriwether's *Daddy Was a Number Runner* portrays the futility of Harlem life during the depression. Julian Mayfield also describes the numbers game in *The Hit,* and uses Harlem for the setting of *The Long Night.*

Two best sellers of the sixties were set in Harlem and portrayed its life vividly. *The Autobiography of Malcolm X* told the story of Malcolm Little from his childhood in Michigan and youth in Boston to his arrival in Harlem in 1941 as a sixteen-year-old sandwich hawker on the Yankee Clipper between Boston and New York. His first tour of Harlem included a stop at Smalls' Paradise, a show at the Apollo Theater on 125th Street and a few drinks at the Braddock Hotel on 126th Street. Malcolm, like so many of the literary figures who preceded him, first stayed at the 135th Street Y. In 1942 he took a job at Smalls' and roomed in the 800 block of St. Nicholas Avenue. With the loss of his job the following year, his descent into drug addiction and crime began, culminating in his imprisonment in Boston in 1946. He emerged in 1952 as Malcolm X. In 1954, he returned to Harlem to establish Temple 7 on the top floor of a four-story building at 116th Street and Lenox Avenue. Ten years later, he broke with the Muslims and established the Organization of Afro-American Unity at the Hotel Teresa. He was shot at a rally at the Audubon Ballroom on 166th Street between Broadway and St. Nicholas Avenue on February 21, 1965.

Claude Brown's *Manchild in the Promised Land* focuses on the block where he grew up — 145th Street between Seventh and Eighth avenues, particularly the concrete alley behind the tenements on his block, where much of its action takes place. After the publication of his book, he revisited it with journalist Tom Wolfe. "The strip is practically a block long but only 2-feet wide," wrote Wolfe. "It is like a six-story tar vat, with all that bright sky up above and this weird twilight at the bottom. The place is a garbage heap, all this junk piled up, beer cans, scraggly old gray cabbage heads, every damned thing, with nice great fluffy fumes of human urine rising up."

In the mid-sixties, LeRoi Jones changed his name to Amiri Baraka and moved up to Harlem for about seven months to found the Black Arts Repertory Theater School at 146 West 130th Street. The theater announced itself with a parade down Lenox Avenue led by jazz conductor Sun Rah. During 1965, the Black Arts Repertory Theater produced outdoor plays, poetry readings and concerts — "perhaps the first street theater of recent years," said poet Larry Neal. While in Harlem, Jones spent some time in Jock's Place, a bar at 2350 Seventh Avenue, which provides the setting for his story "Unfinished." Neal described Jock's, across the street from the New Lafayette Theatre, as the hangout of a "hip, bourgeois crowd, hip in a suave way, that included fast women, good-looking women."

Since the late sixties, a rebuilding of Harlem's cultural life has been taking place. Some of the old institutions — the Schomburg Collection, Lewis Michaux's National Memorial African Bookshop at its new location at 101 West 125th Street, the Harlem Writers' Guild — are still vital centers for black literary development, and now they are being joined by new ones, such as the New Lafayette Theatre and the Studio Museum at 2033 Fifth Avenue. "Folks are trying to settle down and build some institutions rather than use the place as a playground," said Neal. Like the members of the Harlem Writers' Workshop, who called their group by that name though few of them lived in Harlem and they seldom met there, many contemporary black writers, who also live elsewhere, use Harlem as a symbolic reference point. Neal called them "uptown folks" who are "in and around Harlem, and whose thinking is about Harlem." A few live there: Neal is on Jumel Terrace, which he regards as within the community's boundaries ("Harlem is where *we* are," he has said), and Albert Murray, Evan Walker and Frank Hercules are in a complex of buildings around 132nd Street and Fifth Avenue. Others — David Henderson, Rosa Guy and Maya Angelou — are among those who come to Harlem to see everything produced at the New Lafayette and attend every concert, poetry reading or exhibition at the Studio Museum. Although vastly different today from what it was during the twenties, when it was called Mecca, Harlem remains the center of the black literary world.

Harlem

W. 154th St. ㉓

㉔ W. 149th St.

㉒ Convent Ave.

㉕

W. 142nd St. ㉑ Edgecombe Ave.

HARLEM RIVER

Harlem River Drive

City Col. ㉖

of ㉗

N. Y. ⑳ W. 139th St.

⑱ ⑲ ⑮ W. 138th St.

⑰ ⑭ W. 136th St.

⑯ W. 135th St.

⑪ ⑬

⑫

⑩ W. 132nd St.

⑨ ㉘ W. 130th St.

⑧

Broadway

W. 125th St. W. 127th St. EAST HARLEM

㉙

㉚ E. 125th St.

Riverside Dr.

Barnard Col.

Columbia Univ.

Amsterdam Ave.

Morningside Dr.

St. Nicholas Ave.

Eighth Ave.

⑦ W. 124th St.

Mount Morris Park

Madison Ave.

Park Ave.

Lexington Ave.

Third Ave.

⑥ W. 119th St.

⑤ Ave. ④

② ③ W. 116th St.

Lenox Ave.

Fifth Ave.

Seventh

Henry Hudson Pkwy.

①

W. 110th St.

CENTRAL PARK

HUDSON RIVER

Harlem Tour

In Harlem, Eighth Avenue is now called Frederick Douglass Boulevard, and Seventh Avenue is Adam Clayton Powell, Jr. Boulevard.

1. 45 West 110th Street. Arthur Miller lived as a child in apartment 6B, facing the park (p. 271).

2. 116th Street between Seventh and Eighth avenues is the block which Ann Petry chose as the setting for her novel *The Street* (p. 297).

3. 116th–117th streets, on the east side of Seventh Avenue. The Graham Court Apartments, designed in 1901 by architects Clinton and Russell are the most luxurious in Harlem. Zora Neale Hurston lived here in 1932 (p. 283).

4. 1947 Seventh Avenue, between 117th and 118th streets. Jessie Fauset lived in this attractive building with Ionic columns (p. 276).

5. 118th Street, on the southeast corner of St. Nicholas Avenue. The Hotel Cecil was the location of Minton's, the famous forties jazz club (p. 299).

6. 119th Street, on the northwest corner of Seventh Avenue. Nathanael West's father, Max Weinstein, built the DePeyster apartments, and he lived here with his family in 1908 (pp. 270–71).

7. 2081 Seventh Avenue, on the northeast corner of 124th Street. The Harlem Casino provided space for dancing in Harlem's heyday. Since 1966, when the interior was renovated, this building has been the Refuge Temple. It has a stylish façade done with ceramic tile (p. 292).

(7a) 125th Street, on the northeast corner of Seventh Avenue. This is the original location of Lewis Michaux's National Bookshop which was later moved to the other end of the block on Lenox Avenue, and called the National Memorial African Bookshop. Both are now gone (p. 299).

(7b) 209 West 125th Street, between Seventh and Eighth avenues. The Palm Café, Langston Hughes's favorite hangout in later years (p. 294), was here. The building is now a branch of Chemical Bank.

8. 2180–88 Seventh Avenue, on the northwest corner of 129th Street. The Salem Methodist Episcopal Church, built in 1887 and enlarged in 1890 has a notable bell tower and arched doors. Countée Cullen's foster father was the minister, and the family lived in the parsonage at number 2190 (p. 280).

9. 146 West 130th Street. LeRoi Jones founded the Black Arts Repertory Theatre School in the mid-sixties in this row house (p. 304).

10. 2225 Seventh Avenue, between 131st and 132nd streets. Since 1951 this building has been the Williams Christian Methodist Episcopal Church, but it was formerly the Lafayette Theatre, built about 1910. The opening of the Darktown Follies here in 1913 started the vogue of whites visiting in Harlem (p. 291).

11. 2294 Seventh Avenue, near the southwest corner of 135th Street. Smalls' Paradise, in its day, was Harlem's most famous restaurant. Founded in 1925 in a cellar at Fifth Avenue and 135th Street, it soon moved to this spot. In later years it was owned by Wilt Chamberlain, and called Big Wilt's Smalls' Paradise (pp. 292, 304). It is now closed, and the sign, dating probably from the early eighties, reads: "The New Small's (sic) Paradise." The building is in the beginning stages of renovation.

12. 180 West 135th Street, on the south side, between Lenox and Seventh avenues. The YMCA was built as an annex to the small, original "Y" across the street in 1932. James Weldon Johnson once had a house on this site. The "Y" has been an important Harlem cultural center. In 1945 the Harlem Writers' Workshop was founded there. Ralph Ellison stayed at the "Y" in 1936 (pp. 298, 302, 304).

13. 179–181 West 135th Street. The original YMCA, built in 1919. At this writing it is called the Jackie Robinson YMCA Youth Center, now closed for renovation. Langston Hughes stayed here in 1921 (pp. 280–81).

14. 103 West 135th Street. The New York Public Library, 135th Street branch, designed in 1905 by architects McKim, Mead and White. In 1991, it was being renovated. This was the unofficial headquarters of the Black Literary Renaissance in the twenties. In 1927 the Schomburg Collection of Black History, Literature and Art was installed, now it is in a huge building on Lenox Avenue.

15. 104–110 West 136th Street, west of Lenox Avenue. The Countée Cullen Branch of the New York Public Library was restored in 1988. This art moderne library was built in 1942 as an extension through the block of the library at 103 West 135th Street. Previously, the Harlem residence of Madame C. J. Walker, inventor of a hair-straightening process which made her rich, was at 108 West 136th Street. An adjoining building (number 110) housed the Walker College of Hair Culture, with beauty parlors and splendidly furnished apartments (p. 288).

16. 236 West 135th Street. Nella Larsen lived in this five-story building, and worked as a librarian at the 135th Street branch of the public library (p. 279).

17. 311 West 136th Street. John Henrik Clarke's apartment was a meeting

Striver's Row on the north side of 139th Street, Harlem's
most fashionable houses during the 1920s.

place for the Harlem Writers' Workshop during the forties (p. 302).

(17a) One block east at 267 West 136th Street was a rooming house in which Wallace Thurman lived during the twenties. It was an important meeting place for Renaissance figures, including Langston Hughes, Zora Neale Hurston, Gwendolyn Bennett and Aaron Douglas. Thurman portrayed it satirically as Niggerati Manor in his novel *Infants of the Spring* (p. 283).

18. 2350 Seventh Avenue, three doors south of 138th Street. Jock's Place, a bar with a "hip, bourgeois crowd," where LeRoi Jones spent some time (p. 305). It is now closed.

19. 2351 Seventh Avenue, on the southeast corner of 138th Street. This was the Casino Renaissance Theatre and ballroom complex in the twenties. In the seventies and eighties it was the New Lafayette Theatre, where contemporary black plays (pp. 292, 305) were performed. It is now closed, and dilapidated. The original Casino corner sign and marquee remain, like relics of ancient Egypt.

20. 138th and 139th Streets, between Seventh and Eighth avenues. Striver's Row (1891) is actually four rows of attached houses. A designated landmark, the development represents a highly successful experiment in urban planning. David H. King, builder of the Times Building and the original Madison Square Garden, commissioned three of New York's most prominent architectural firms to build houses here. The red brick brownstone-trimmed houses on the south side of 138th Street as far as number 250, and the three houses around the corner on Seventh Avenue, were designed in the Georgian tradition by James Brown Lord. The entire block bounded by 138th and 139th streets, including the ends on Seventh and Eighth avenues, was done by Bruce Price and Clarence Luce; inside the block were gardens with flower beds and fountains. The north side of 139th Street, and around the corners, was done by McKim, Mead and White in the Italian Renaissance style, in brown mottled brick (p. 289).

21. 287 Convent Avenue, between 141st and 142nd streets. Alexander Hamilton spent the last years of his life here, at Harlem's most important architectural landmark. Designed by John McComb, Jr. in 1802, Hamilton Grange, as the house was called, originally stood about one hundred yards from its present site. It was moved to this location in 1889. The parlor rooms which are open to the public, have some furnishings of the period. The house has charming octagonal rooms and room-high three-sash windows (p. 270). The building is open on Wednesdays, Thursdays, and Fridays.

22. 749 St. Nicholas Avenue, between 147th and 148th streets. Ralph Ellison lived here from 1945 to 1953, while he was writing Invisible Man (p. 299).

Return to 145th Street and walk up to:

23. 409 Edgecombe Avenue, south of 155th Street. This is one of Harlem's most fashionable addresses, in the exclusive area called Sugar Hill. Aaron Douglas, the painter whose work adorned many book jackets during the Renaissance, lived here, as did Walter White, whose parties were attended by many celebrities (p. 291).

Cross on the 155th Street viaduct and begin working your way south again to:

24. 149th to 150th streets, from Seventh to Eighth avenues. This entire block is occupied by the Paul Laurence Dunbar Apartments, built in 1928 by architect Andrew J. Thomas. Named after the early black writer (he was from Dayton, Ohio), the brick buildings feature decorative friezes and portrait medallions of Dunbar. Financed by John D. Rockefeller, Jr., the apartments were originally cooperatives. Residents have included Jessie Fauset, W.E.B. DuBois and Rudolf Fisher (p. 282).

25. West 145th Street, between Seventh and Eighth avenues. Claude Brown's *Manchild in the Promised Land* focuses on this block where he grew up (p. 304).

26. 147 West 142nd Street. Claude McKay moved into this tenement in 1934 when he returned from a decade abroad (p. 279). The building is now an empty shell, but the façade is in very good condition.

(26a) 142nd Street and Lenox Avenue, on the northeast corner. The location of the Cotton Club, in the twenties "the Aristocrat of Harlem" (p. 292–93).

27. 120 West 140th Street, between Lenox and Seventh avenues. PS 139, Frederick Douglass Junior High School, where Countee Cullen spent his last years (he died in 1946) as a teacher. One of his students was James Baldwin (pp. 293, 301). The school is now a senior citizens' apartment complex called "PS 193 Apartments."

28. 130th Street, on the south side, from Fifth to Lenox avenues. This was "the Block Beautiful," then an all-white enclave, which Claude McKay described in his first novel, *Home to Harlem* (1928). The three-story brick houses are in sad disrepair, and most of the porches, long ago painted green and white, are either gone or falling down (p. 278–79).

29. 20 East 127th Street. Langston Hughes lived here with his good friends, the Emerson Harpers. During the forties and fifties, many writers, musicians and actors visited him (p. 296). The block is now named Langston Hughes Place.

30. 2033 Fifth Avenue, between 125th and 126th streets. As part of the new cultural life of Harlem, the Studio Museum was founded here; it is now at 144 West 125th Street, between Lenox and Seventh avenues, a center for local and national black art. Now active at the museum's original location is the National Black Theatre (p. 305).

X. The Bronx, Queens and Staten Island

The Bronx

THE BRONX has literary associations dating back to the Knickerbocker period. Joseph Rodman Drake, best known for his poem "The American Flag," lived here in the area around Hunts Point. His closest friend was Fitz-Greene Halleck and the two writers are commemorated in the names of adjacent Hunts Point streets. Drake died at the early age of twenty-five and is buried in a park named for him at Hunts Point and Oak Point avenues. Another Knickerbocker writer, James Fenimore Cooper, set his novel *Satanstoe* in the Bronx. "Satanstoe" was a name given to what is now Throgs Neck. Legend had it that when Satan was driven away by the Indians he used the rocky islets between Throgs Neck and City Island as stepping stones. Before jumping off, he left his toe print and that point of land became known as Satanstoe.

The Bronx's best-known literary resident was Edgar Allan Poe, who took a cottage in Fordham from 1846 to 1848 in the hope that it would improve the health of his wife, Virginia. He himself was none too well at the time. "I am living out of town about 13 miles, at a village called Fordham, on the railroad leading north," he wrote in a letter. "We are in a snug little cottage, keeping house, and would be very comfortable, but that I have been for a long time dreadfully ill." The house

Edgar Allan Poe's cottage in its original location on Kingsbridge Road near Fordham Road, where it stood until 1913.

was unheated and Virginia lay on a straw mattress with Poe's West Point greatcoat wrapped around her and the cat hugged close to her body for warmth. In 1847 Virginia died and was buried in a nearby churchyard. (Her body was later moved to Baltimore to be buried near Poe's.) Poe was found many times at her tomb that winter in the middle of the night, having wandered there from his bed.

The Fordham cottage, moved a few hundred feet north of its original location, now stands at 2460 Grand Concourse in Poe Park. It is a simple, frame farmhouse, built around 1813. During his time here, Poe wrote "Ulalume" and "The Bells" and probably started "Annabel Lee."

The Bronx's next prominent literary resident lived in the greatest possible contrast to the impoverished Poe. In 1901 Mark Twain, at the height of his success, moved to one of the borough's most magnificent houses, Wave Hill. The fieldstone mansion stands overlooking the Hudson at 252nd Street and Sycamore Avenue. "We drifted from room to room on our tour of inspection," Clemens wrote, "always with a growing doubt as to whether we wanted that house or not; but at last, when we arrived in a dining room that was 60 feet long, 30 feet wide, and had two great fireplaces in it, that settled it." In 1902, Clemens's wife, like Poe's, became ill. He was permitted to see her two minutes a day by the clock. His bedroom was separated from hers by a bathroom and he left notes there for her every night; she answered as best she could on scraps of paper. This continued until her death two years later. The house, which had also been the home of Theodore Roosevelt, among others, has been given to the Parks Department and is now the Wave Hill Environmental Center.

Sholom Aleichem, known as the Jewish Mark Twain, also lived in the Bronx. Among the first to visit him was Clemens, who said, "Please tell him that I am the American Sholom Aleichem." Another Yiddish writer, Sholem Asch, guaranteed a loan to Leon Trotsky so that the revolutionary could buy furniture when he lived in the Bronx in 1917. Trotsky wrote, "We rented an apartment in a workers' district, and furnished it on the instalment plan." Trotsky stayed only two and a half months, working on the editorial board of *Novy Mir* on the Lower East Side, and returned to Russia when the revolution occurred. Asch had to complete the payments on the furniture.

The neighborhood in which Aleichem and Trotsky lived was a flourishing Jewish community in the period between the two World Wars. Herman Wouk was born in 1915 in a tenement here on 167th Street, just west of Southern Boulevard. He lived at several addresses in the neighborhood and attended Public School 48, the Joseph Rodman Drake School, in Hunts Point. The milieu of his novel *The City Boy: The Adventures of*

Herbie Bookbinder is the area around 1091 Longfellow Avenue, where he lived during his adolescence. In the novel he described his apartment building as "a brick cliff very much like the other brick cliffs that stood wall to wall for many blocks along the less rocky side of the street. It was gray, square, five stories high, punctured with windows, and saved from bleakness only by the entrance, which tried on a little matter of plaster gargoyles overhead and dead shrubs in cracked plaster urns on either side of the iron-grilled glass doors."

The playwright Clifford Odets spent his childhood in roughly the same neighborhood. *Awake and Sing* is set in an apartment on Longwood Avenue near Beck Street. Frank Gilroy wrote about another generation in another Bronx neighborhood in his play *The Subject Was Roses*. Gilroy grew up at 116 West 176th Street near University Avenue.

In 1931 Ogden Nash wrote:

> The Bronx? No thonx.

By 1964 he had revised his opinion:

> I wrote those lines, "The Bronx? No thonx."
> I shudder to confess them.
> Now I'm an older, wiser man I cry,
> "The Bronx? God bless them!"

Queens

Queens has had only the most fragmentary literary history. It is known as the home of Jupiter Hammon, said to be the first Negro poet. Hammon was a slave living in Queens Village and his first literary effort was a broadside called "An Evening Thought: Salvation by Christ, with Penitential Cries." His next known work was "A Poetical Address to Phyllis Wheatley,"

written in 1778. In the 1830s James Fenimore Cooper spent
the summers in the area of Queens known as Astoria, sailing
over to Manhattan daily on a sloop. Walt Whitman was working for the *Long Island Democrat* in 1839 and lived at the home
of the editor, James J. Brenton, in Jamaica. Jack Kerouac
lived with his mother in an apartment over a drugstore on
Cross Bay Boulevard in the late forties while writing *The
Town and the City*. In 1952 they took a two-story frame house
at 94–21 134th Street in Richmond Hill. He was writing *Dr.
Sax* and the following year would write *The Subterraneans*
there. Malcolm X lived in Queens in the late fifties.

The only major work in which Queens figures importantly
is F. Scott Fitzgerald's *The Great Gatsby*. In 1922 Fitzgerald
was living in Great Neck, outside the city limits. However, his
frequent trips into the city, either on the Long Island Railroad
or driving on Northern Boulevard and over the Queensboro
Bridge, gave him an opportunity to become familiar with
Queens. The climactic scene in *Gatsby,* the killing of Myrtle
Wilson in front of her husband's gas station, takes place near
Northern Boulevard in the area then known as the Corona
Dumps. "This is a valley of ashes," Fitzgerald wrote, " — a
fantastic farm where ashes grow like wheat into ridges and hills
and grotesque gardens; where ashes take the forms of houses
and chimneys and rising smoke and, finally, with a transcendent
effort, of men who move dimly and already crumbling through
the powdery air."

The most inspiring thing about Queens for Fitzgerald, however, was the view it gave of Manhattan from the Queensboro
Bridge. "Over the great bridge," he wrote, "with the sunlight
through the girders making a constant flicker upon the moving
cars, with the city rising up across the river in white heaps and
sugar lumps all built with a wish out of non-olfactory money.
The city seen from the Queensboro Bridge is always the city

seen for the first time, in its first wild promise of all the mystery and the beauty in the world."

Staten Island

In the nineteenth century Staten Island was a lovely rural paradise. As such it drew a number of distinguished visitors who have given it something of a literary history. In the 1840s, Dr. Samuel MacKenzie Elliott, who practiced in Manhattan and lived on Staten Island, had a reputation as an eye specialist among the literati. When writers outside the city came to consult him, they would often live at his house or nearby while undergoing treatment. James Russell Lowell stayed with him in 1843, and the historian Francis Parkman consulted him in 1846. Elliott had his patients lie on the floor and operated on their eyes with a knife, holding their heads between his knees. Although Parkman stayed under Elliott's care for two years, he later wrote that the doctor had "nearly blinded me, and for this and other reasons hated me to the extent of his capacity." Other writers who came to visit Elliott included Henry Wadsworth Longfellow and Richard Henry Dana. Elliott lived in thirty houses during the twenty-eight years he spent on Staten Island. One of them, a vine-covered stone house with aquamarine trim, still stands at 69 Delafield Place.

During the same period, the home of Ralph Waldo Emerson's brother William, on what is now known as Emerson Hill, had its share of visitors. Waldo, as the writer was known to his family and friends, spent several summers here and early in 1843 suggested that Henry David Thoreau come and serve as his nephew's tutor. He returned to Concord and from there wrote his brother: "I have to say that Henry Thoreau listens very willingly to your proposition he [sic] thinks it exactly fit

The "Snuggery," the Emerson house on Staten Island where Henry
David Thoreau served as tutor.

for him & he rarely.finds offers that do fit him. He says that
it is such a relation as he wishes to sustain, to be the friend &
educator of a boy, & one not yet subdued by schoolmasters
. . . I have told him that you will give him board, lodging
(washing?) a room by himself to study in, when not engaged
with Willie, with fire when the season requires, and a hundred
dollars a year."

The arrangements were agreed to and Ralph Waldo Emerson
advanced Thoreau twenty dollars, which he used for clothes
and traveling expenses. On Staten Island he lived with the
Emersons (William was the county judge) in their house, a
low brown-shingled building with grapevines on the piazza,
called the Snuggery. This house burned down in 1855 but the
stone gate to the property remains on Douglas Road near
Richmond Road. Thoreau's schedule was to breakfast at six-

thirty, take his charge for long walks in the early morning, and tutor him from nine until two. Less than three weeks after his arrival, he was writing to Sophia Emerson in Concord:

> The cedar seems to be one of the most common trees here, and the fields are very fragrant with it. There are also gum and tulip trees . . . The woods are now full of a large honeysuckle in full bloom, which differs from ours in being red instead of white, so that at first I did not know its genus. The painted cup is very common in the meadows here. Peaches, and especially cherries, seem to grow by all the fences. Things are very forward here compared with Concord. The apricots growing out-of-doors are already as large as plums. The apple, pear, peach, cherry, and plum trees have shed their blossoms. The whole island is like a garden, and affords very fine scenery . . . Garlic, the original of the common onion, grows here all over the fields, and during its season spoils the cream and butter for the market, as the cows like it very much.

Thoreau was not impressed with Manhattan but was attracted by the sea. "I want a whole continent to breathe in," he wrote to his family in Concord, "and a good deal of solitude and silence, such as all Wall Street cannot buy — nor Broadway with its wooden pavement. I must live along the beach, on the Southern Shore, which looks directly out to sea, and see what that great parade of water means, that dashes and roars, and has not yet wet me, as long as I have lived."

William Emerson introduced Thoreau to several literary people. The writer reported to Waldo after a three-hour talk with Henry James, Sr., that "he has naturalized and humanized New York for me." But ultimately Thoreau found his situation uncongenial. His tuberculosis flared up; he suffered from chronic sleepiness; and he was homesick for Concord. Unlike Waldo, William Emerson was very conventional, and he and Thoreau agreed on nothing. Shortly before Thanksgiving, Thoreau returned to Concord.

The Pavilion, the Staten Island hotel where Henry James's family vacationed.

The Jameses spent summer vacations on Staten Island and the younger Henry recalled, "I seem more or less to have begun life with impressions of New Brighton." His family stayed at the Pavilion, a hotel on the north shore that had many famous visitors. James remembered that "to childish retrospect," its form "was that of a great Greek temple shining over blue waters in the splendour of a white colonnade and a great yellow pediment."

Another visitor was Herman Melville, who came frequently to see his brother Tom during the years between 1867 and 1884, when he was governor of Sailors' Snug Harbor. A home for old seamen, Sailors' Snug Harbor was established by a trust left by Captain Robert Richard Randall. The governor's mansion where Tom Melville lived has been torn down, but the remaining Greek Revival buildings are now the headquarters of the Staten Island Institute of Arts and Sciences and the Staten Island Council on the Arts.

Among the literary figures who actually lived on Staten Island was George William Curtis, editor of *Harper's Weekly*. Curtis said, "God might have made a more beautiful spot than Staten Island, but he never did." In 1856 Curtis was living in a gabled house at 234 Bard Avenue, which still stands today. During the draft riots of July 1863 Horace Greeley sought refuge here from mobs seeking to kill him for his abolitionist activities.

Later in the century, in the 1890s, the poet Alan Seeger was living with his family on top of Tompkins Hill in a gabled Victorian house surrounded by four acres of land. Seeger attended the Staten Island Academy before going to war.

In 1901 Edwin Markham came to Staten Island from Brooklyn. He lived first in a house at the corner of Waters and Livermore, then on the border of meadows extending toward Willowbrook Road. From 1909 until his death in 1940 he lived at 92 Waters Street, a brown-shingled house with yellow porches and a carved wood door. In addition to writing poetry (in 1910 he founded the Poetry Society of America), Markham frequently reviewed books. Virgil Markham, the poet's son, described their house: "It was evident to anyone setting foot inside the door that books were here the cornerstone and indeed the whole foundation of life. There were books on walls and floor and in every nook and cranny. There were books on every horizontal surface except the top of the piano, which had to be opened sometimes, and the seats of some often-sat-upon chairs." Since there were books and manuscripts on the dining room table where the Markhams did their literary work, eating was generally done in the kitchen. "When we had guests for meals, the debris was pushed to one end of the dining table and the vacant area set for places," Virgil recalled. "Unless, that is, there were several outsiders, when the cloth might be laid over a carefully leveled plateau of books."

The Bronx

Other than Markham, twentieth-century literary figures have spent little time on Staten Island. Theodore Dreiser, who moved frequently and lived virtually everywhere in New York, stayed for a time at 109 St. Mark's Place. Maxim Gorky once spent a night in a house on Grymes Hill. In 1922, after Langston Hughes quit Columbia, he found a job on a Staten Island truck farm owned by a Greek family. He got bed and board — he slept in the hayloft — and fifty dollars a month. Jane and Paul Bowles once spent a summer on the island, an experience reflected in Jane's *Two Serious Ladies*. But throughout the nineteenth and twentieth centuries, Staten Island has been too remote from Manhattan and the literary mainstream for its associations with writing to be anything but incidental.

Bronx Tour

A literary tour of the Bronx encompasses the most radical extremes of New York City life. The area of the South Bronx that was a Jewish community between the wars and home to several writers is now a region of such desperate poverty and chaos that all who can have fled it. In contrast the Riverdale where Mark Twain lived is still an area of mansions and lovely gardens.

From Midtown take the Lexington Avenue subway, number 6 train, to Hunt's Point Avenue.

1. Joseph Rodman Drake Park, at Hunt's Point and Oak Point avenues, has as its center the nineteenth-century graveyard where the poet is buried. Note that streets and avenues in the area—Bryant, Longfellow, Whittier, Drake and Halleck—are named for nineteenth-century writers (p. 314).

Walk back to Spofford Avenue, southwest to Longwood Avenue, and west about six blocks to:

2. Beck Street and Longwood Avenue, the area where Clifford Odets grew up. His play *Awake and Sing* is set in an apartment on Longwood (p. 315).

Walk one block up to Intervale, one block west to Kelly, and continue up to:

3. 968 Kelly Street, between East 163rd Street and Westchester Avenue. Sholom Aleichem was living here at the time of his death in 1916. His building was one in an attached row of four-story red brick houses (p. 314).

4. 974 Aldus Street, between Hoe Avenue and Faile Street. Herman Wouk moved here as a child, and soon after lived next door at 978 Aldus Street. These two buildings, typical five-story apartment houses, were two and three doors east of Hoe Avenue; they have now been replaced by a block-long apartment building (pp. 314–15).

5. 1091 Longfellow Avenue, opposite Lowell Street. Wouk spent his adolescence here. This was the setting for his novel *The City Boy: The Adventures of Herbie Bookbinder.* The building seems to have been remodeled, with a new façade in red brick (p. 315).

6. East 167th Street, just west of Southern Boulevard. Herman Wouk was born here in May 1915 in a tenement no longer standing.

7. 1522 Vyse Avenue, on the northeast corner of East 172nd Street. Leon Trotsky lived here for a few months in 1917, in a five-story brick apartment building called the Mildred, now vacant and blocked up with its upper windows empty (p. 314).

8. Detour (unless you are driving, there is little reason to make the trip here): 116 West 176th Street, at Andrews Avenue South. Frank Gilroy lived in this area called Tremont in a 1920s six-story brick apartment. He wrote about this neighborhood in his play called *The Subject Was Roses* (p. 315).

Walk west to Southern Boulevard and take the number 19 bus to Fordham Road; then walk, or transfer to the number 9 or number 22 bus, to Grand Concourse.

9. 2640 Grand Concourse, at Kingsbridge Road. Now at the north end of Poe Park is the cottage, dating from about 1812, in which Edgar Allan Poe lived from 1846 to 1848. It originally stood a few hundred feet south, at about 261 Kingsbridge Road. Moved to its present location in 1913, it was opened as a museum in 1917 (pp. 312–13).

Take the number 9 bus (westbound) on Kingsbridge Road at Grand Concourse or Fordham Road. At Broadway and 231st Street transfer to the number 7 and go to West 252nd Street. Walk west about five blocks to Sycamore Avenue. Or, if coming here directly from Midtown, take the Metro North from Grand Central Station to Riverdale Station.

10. 675 West 252nd Street, on the southwest corner of Sycamore Avenue. Wave Hill mansion. Mark Twain moved here in 1901 and stayed about four years (pp. 313–14). This was also the home, at various times, of Theodore Roosevelt and Arturo Toscanini.

Queens Tour

Take the A Train to Rockaway Boulevard–Liberty Avenue. Walk four or five blocks south to:

1. 133-01 Cross Bay Boulevard, on the corner of 133rd Avenue. Jack Kerouac lived here on the second floor with his parents (his father died in 1946) from 1943 to 1950. Here he wrote *The Town and the City*. Across the street the bar where he often went with his father (now called McNulty's) still stands, although it has been much refurbished (p. 316).

Get back on the A Train and go three stops east to Lefferts Boulevard–Liberty Avenue. Walk east on Liberty Avenue about fourteen blocks to 134th Street, then a few blocks north to:

Queens

2. 94-21 134th Street. Kerouac lived here with his mother from 1952 to 1955 in this two-story frame house in a small yard. Here he wrote *Maggie Cassidy and The Subterraneans* (p. 316).

Return the same way, or walk a block or two north to Archer Avenue, about seven blocks east to Sutphin Boulevard and north to the Sutphin Boulevard–Archer Avenue Station. Take the E Train back to Manhattan.

Staten Island Tour

From the ferry terminal to Snug Harbor is a brisk walk of about thirty minutes.

1. Sailors' Snug Harbor (now Snug Harbor Cultural Center), on Richmond Terrace between Tysen Street and Kissel Avenue. Herman Melville's brother Tom Melville lived in the Governor's House between 1867 and 1884; now torn down, it was near the northwest corner of the property. Five of the Greek Revival buildings remain (p. 320).

2. 69 Delafield Place, between Davis and Bard avenues. This is one of the thirty houses Dr. Samuel MacKenzie Elliot lived in during the twenty-eight years he spent on Staten Island. Constructed of fieldstone with Gothic details, it was designed by the doctor himself about 1850 (p. 317).

3. 234 Bard Avenue, on the northwest corner of Henderson Avenue. George W. Curtis was living here in 1856 and later. The house has a hipped roof with four gables; it would appear that the decorative wood trim at the eaves and porch has been stripped (p. 321).

Walk west on Henderson Avenue to Broadway; catch a number 54 bus to Goodwin Avenue (a little south of the Armory). Walk west, crossing Jewett Avenue, into Waters Avenue.

4. 92 Waters Avenue, on the southeast corner of Willard Avenue. Edwin Markham lived from 1910 to 1940 in this wooden Victorian house with a two-story front porch. The stair windows on the east side with the wooden tracery design are probably original (p. 321).

To return to Manhattan, walk south a few blocks to Watchogue Road; catch a number 57 (not 67) bus to Victory Boulevard; transfer to a number 61 bus to St. George, the ferry terminal. If you want to visit what is left of the Emerson estate, ask the locals for directions.

5. Douglas Road near Richmond Road, a short distance from the Staten Island Expressway. The stone gate that once led to the property of Judge William Emerson, Ralph Waldo Emerson's brother, still exists. The house, called the Snuggery, burned down in 1855. Henry David Thoreau lived here while serving as a tutor for the judge's son (pp. 317–19).

XI. Brooklyn and Brooklyn Heights

Brooklyn

LIKE MANHATTAN, Brooklyn began as a series of villages, the first of which was settled near Red Hook in 1636. Some of the borough's many neighborhoods — Flatbush, New Utrecht, Gravesend and Bushwick — retain the names of these original towns. The village of Brooklyn itself originally centered on what are now Fulton and Smith streets, where downtown Brooklyn is today. Eventually all the villages joined to form the City of Brooklyn, which was incorporated into New York in 1898.

The borough's first and most significant writer, Walt Whitman, spent most of his life in the region north of downtown Brooklyn. In 1823, when Whitman was four years old, his family moved from Long Island to a house on Front Street, an area of taverns and grog shops near the waterfront. Whitman's father was a carpenter who built one house after another for his family, intending to sell them at a profit. In *Specimen Days* Whitman reminisced about these early years: "From 1824–'28 our family lived in Brooklyn in Front, Cranberry and Johnson streets. In the latter my father built a nice house for a home, and afterwards another in Tillary Street. We occupied them one after the other, but they were mortgaged, and we lost them." All of Whitman's houses are gone today, and housing projects and roadways to Manhattan have replaced most of the old neighborhood.

Whitman's father was never very successful at his house-building occupation, and in 1834 moved his family back to Long Island to earn his living at farming. Walt, only fifteen years old, stayed behind and found work in printing houses. In 1836, he rejoined his family and spent the next three years teaching and working on small Long Island papers. In the early 1840s he found work as a printer and newspaperman in Manhattan and then returned to Brooklyn in 1845. For the next five years he worked consecutively as a writer for the *Long Island Star,* editor of the *Brooklyn Daily Eagle* and editor of the *Brooklyn Freeman.* William Cullen Bryant came to visit him several times during this period. "We were both walkers," Whitman recalled at Bryant's death, "and when I work'd in Brooklyn he several times came over, middle of afternoons, and we took rambles, miles long, till dark, out towards Bedford or Flatbush, in company. On these occasions he gave me clear accounts of scenes in Europe — the cities, looks, architecture, art, especially Italy — where he had travel'd a good deal." During the next decade Whitman was variously occupied; for a while he was a real estate speculator, and from 1857 to 1859 he edited the *Brooklyn Times.* He was writing poetry throughout these years and in 1855 published the first edition of *Leaves of Grass* at the print shop of friends, setting some ten pages of type himself (see Brooklyn Heights in this chapter). In 1862 he went south to Fredericksburg, Virginia, to look for his brother George, who had been injured in battle, and began to visit the wounded in hospitals in Washington, D.C. He never came back to live in Brooklyn although he made several long visits.

Whitman, like most New Yorkers of the time, was enormously attached to the waterfront, and he especially enjoyed

Walt Whitman's house at 106 Myrtle Avenue, where he
lived when he was editor of the *Brooklyn Freeman*.

the ferry trips he made to Manhattan to attend the opera and
other entertainments or simply to walk the streets. "Living in
Brooklyn or New York City from this time forward," he wrote
of the period around 1840,

> my life . . . was curiously identified with Fulton ferry already
> becoming the greatest of its sort in the world for general im-
> portance, volume, variety, rapidity, and picturesqueness.
> Almost daily, later, . . . I cross'd on the boats, often up in
> the pilot houses where I could get a full sweep, absorbing
> shows, accompaniments, surroundings . . . The river and bay
> scenery . . . the hurrying, splashing sea-tides — the changing

panorama of steamers, all sizes, often a string of big ones out-
ward bound to distant ports — the myriads of white-sail'd
schooners, sloops, skiffs, and the marvelously beautiful yachts
— the majestic sound boats as they rounded the Battery and
came along toward five, afternoon, eastward bound — the
prospect off toward Staten island, or down the Narrows, or the
other way up the Hudson — what refreshment of spirit such
sights and experiences gave me . . ."

Brooklyn's next major writer was not to arrive until the end
of the century. In 1892 Henry Miller, then an infant, moved
with his family from Yorkville in Manhattan to the Williamsburg section of Brooklyn. "In my dreams I come back to the
Fourteenth Ward as a paranoiac returns to his obsessions,"
Miller wrote. "Where others remember of their youth a beautiful garden, a fond mother, a sojourn at the seashore, I remember, with a vividness as if it were etched in acid, the grim,
soot-covered walls and chimneys of the tin factory . . . and
the bright, circular pieces of tin that were strewn in the street,
some bright and gleaming, others rusted, dull, copperish, leaving a stain on the fingers . . ."

Opposite Miller's home, a three-story brick house still
standing at 662 Driggs Avenue, was the veterinary and on the
corner was a place where raw hides were stacked up in the
street. Like the tin factory, the place where the hides were
trimmed stank frightfully. But across from the factory was a
bakery, from which emanated the "sweet, irresistible odor of
bread and cake."

Miller's old neighborhood has undergone relatively little
renewal. In his time, the ground floor of his house was a barber shop and it remains a storefront today. Diagonally across
from the house was Miller's favorite street, Fillmore Place.
With the opening of the Williamsburg Bridge came the destruction of some of its houses. "Soon" he wrote, "the street

looked like a dirty mouth with all the prominent teeth missing, with ugly charred stumps gaping here and there, the lips rotting, the palate gone." By today's standards, the street, with its nineteenth-century houses renewed and repainted, is relatively intact.

When he was ten years old Miller moved to what he called "the street of early sorrows" — Decatur Street at number 1063. His new home was in Bushwick, a German-American neighborhood. Why he disliked it was unclear even to Miller, since his memories are not unhappy ones. "I recall some wonderful days in the autumn in empty lots in the neighborhood," he wrote. "We would dig caves in them. Some days we would shoot sparrows and roast them over a fire."

Growing up in Williamsburg, which gave Miller so much of his artistic material, was also the subject of Betty Smith's 1943 best seller, *A Tree Grows in Brooklyn*. The tree, *ailanthus glandulosa,* a variety of sumac imported from China, found great popularity in swampy areas like Williamsburg for its supposed power to dispel disease-producing vapors. Behind the house on Grand Street where Smith's heroine, Francie Nolan, lives, stood the tree. "It had pointed leaves which grew along green switches which radiated from the bough and made a tree which looked like a lot of opened green umbrellas," she wrote. ". . . No matter where its seed fell, it made a tree which struggled to reach the sky. It grew in boarded-up lots and out of neglected rubbish heaps and it was the only tree that grew out of cement."

With the opening of the Williamsburg Bridge in 1903, Jews from the Lower East Side began to cross over to Brooklyn. Around 1940 they were joined by Hassidic Jews fleeing persecution in Eastern Europe. The Hassidic community, which has only recently moved out of Williamsburg to Crown Heights, became the background of several books by Chaim Potok — *The Chosen, The Promise* and *My Name Is Asher Lev* — which deal with the conflict between Hassidic tradition and the development of the individual.

Although many Jews settled in Williamsburg and other parts of Brooklyn, the borough's pre-eminent Jewish community for many years was Brownsville. Jews, most of them in the needle trades, began to arrive in 1892. At first the community preserved the customs of an Eastern European *shtetl*, speaking Yiddish and reading Yiddish-language newspapers. But later generations, which included a number of writers — Matthew Josephson, Henry Roth, Alfred Kazin, Norman Podhoretz, Irving Shulman, Gerald Green and Murray Schisgal — broke away. Kazin, who grew up in the twenties at 256A Sutter Avenue, describes the neighborhood in *A Walker in the City:* "Every time I go back to Brownsville it is as if I had never been away. From the moment I step off the train at Rockaway Avenue and smell the leak out of the men's room, then the pickles from the stand just below the subway steps, an instant rage comes over me, mixed with dread and some unexpected tenderness . . . The early hopelessness burns at my face like fog . . . I can smell it in the air as soon as I walk down Rockaway Avenue." Growing up on Sutter Avenue, Kazin had a typical urban boyhood. "On the block itself everything rose up only to test me. We worked every inch of it, from the cellars and the backyards to the sickening space between the roofs. Any wall, any stoop, any curving metal edge on a billboard sign made a place against which to knock a ball; any bottom rung of a fire escape ladder a goal in basketball; any sewer cover a base; any crack in the pavement a 'net' for the tense sharp tennis that we played by beating a softball back and forth with our hands between the squares."

In *Making It,* Norman Podhoretz, who came a generation after Kazin, documents the social aspects of growing up in the forties in Brownsville at 2027 Pacific Street. "One of the longest journeys in the world," his book begins, "is the journey

Marianne Moore and her mother, Mary Warner Moore, at 260 Cumberland Street in the 1930s.

from Brooklyn to Manhattan — or at least from certain neighborhoods in Brooklyn to certain parts of Manhattan." *Making It* documents the journey in speech, clothes, manners from lower-class Brownsville, where Podhoretz was a member of the red-satin-jacketed Cherokees, to the unaccented parlors of the American literary elite.

·

Another old Brooklyn neighborhood, Fort Greene, was home to two prominent writers, Marianne Moore and Richard Wright. In 1931 Moore moved to an apartment building up the street from the magnificent old mansions, now mostly rooming houses, facing Fort Greene Park. She told George Plimpton, who came to interview her at 260 Cumberland Street in 1964, "am on right, middle of the block, with what look like mothballs on iron stands flanking the entrance." She lived on the fifth floor. "Piles of books were everywhere," Plimpton wrote. "Tea-colored oils on the walls, and a fine clutter of memorabilia, of which she pointed out a marlinspike from Greely's expedition to the Arctic." When Moore died (she had moved to Greenwich Village), funeral services were held at the Lafayette Presbyterian Church half a block away, where she had regularly attended Sunday morning and Wednesday evening services during her years in Fort Greene.

Richard Wright lived several blocks from Marianne Moore in 1938 when he moved in with his friends Jane and Herbert Newton at 175 Carlton Avenue. Here he began *Native Son.* As soon as the sun had taken the chill off the morning air, around five-thirty during the summer, he went to write at the top of the hill in Fort Greene Park. At 10:00 A.M. he would return to the house for breakfast and type up what he had written. When the Newtons moved, he went with them because he felt the atmosphere of their home helped him to write. They were briefly at 522 Gates Avenue and then moved to 87 Lefferts Place, a brownstone in an area near Bedford-Stuyvesant. When *Native Son* was finished, Wright and his friends read the whole book aloud here, accompanied sometimes by a Shostakovich prelude played at full volume. Wright later returned to this neighborhood after his marriage. From 1943 to 1945 he and his wife lived at 89 Lefferts Place, a brick apartment building. Here Wright organized a tenants' strike and had the rent lowered to the OPA level. He was writing *Black Boy* at the time.

Bedford-Stuyvesant itself was the home and subject of another black writer, Paule Marshall, who wrote about the area's West Indian community in *Brown Girl, Brownstones*. Black novelist John O. Killens now lives on Union Street near Kingston Avenue. When he first moved there fifteen years ago it was considered Crown Heights, but is now often referred to as part of Bedford-Stuyvesant. In the early years Killens's house was a meeting place for the Harlem Writers' Guild (see Chapter IX, Harlem). Among those who gathered to read and discuss their work were John Henrik Clarke, Rosa Guy, Paule Marshall, Louise Meriwether, Maya Angelou and Ossie Davis. The neighborhood was then mixed. Today, Killens writes, "my turf is mostly black. The houses, like most of the folk who live here, have a quiet grace and dignity. In the summer the front lawns are sparkling green and manicured. The proud majestic oak trees form a long green tunnel, as their leafy limbs reach over the streets and grasp each other in a fine display of brotherhood."

·

The newer area of Brooklyn south of Prospect Park was home to Arthur Miller when he was growing up. In 1929 he and his family moved from 110th Street in Manhattan to a two-story brick house at 1277 Ocean Avenue. Two or three years later they moved to a small house at 1350 East 3rd, "the version ten years later," Miller says, "of the kind of two-family house Willy Loman lived in. These were post-World War One, a little more jerry-built. They were square-front buildings, made of wood, with flat roofs. They were often built in sets of three and might be surrounded by tomato fields, beautiful elm trees, hickories, woods. The little guys used to go out there and hunt rabbits and snakes." To get there from New York, one rode an hour and a half on the Culver Line. Each car had a coal stove which the passengers fed and sat around for heat.

Miller recalls life in Brooklyn as being like that in a small town:

> My mother didn't go to Manhattan more than once or twice a year. The neighborhood was psychologically divorced from New York. There was a terrific autonomy in these neighborhoods. It was as if they were demarcated by an iron fence. One knew when he was passing into foreign territory. My neighborhood was bounded by Gravesend Avenue and Ocean Parkway, a matter of six blocks, and from Avenue M over to Avenue J. Once you got out of there you might as well have been taking a voyage to Kansas. You didn't know anyone. There were some blocks that you liked better than others. My block was a dead-end street with a great college track star and a Colgate University football star. It was great to live on because you never knew when they would be out playing touch football.

Growing up in a neighborhood like his, Miller said, "gives a sense of hierarchy — one belongs somewhere, a well-oriented, well-grounded sense of touch, a sense of history, people growing older, people getting married, careers. It was a stable, ongoing, articulated community in a sense that the suburb today is not . . . In my neighborhood there were always Swedes, Italians, black people, Jews, Irish. There was quite a mélange. I'm glad I grew up that way. You get a sense of the *moyenne* man — God help us — the man who is the back-bone of the country. It never leaves you; you get a good sense of how he views the world."

Today many young writers live in Brooklyn. Paula Fox lives in Cobble Hill, Sol Yurick in Park Slope, L. J. Davis in Boerum Hill. Davis explained Brooklyn's appeal in an article for the *New York Times:*

> Once one gets off the main commercial streets, one finds that the 19th century city is surprisingly intact and, in parts, it is unusually handsome, with its low skyline and big old trees and rows of sculptured houses in brick and brownstone . . . Compared to Manhattan, housing is relatively inexpensive and considerably more spacious; it is possible to achieve a measure of stability by purchasing one's own home . . . and it is easier to be alone. There is much to be said for the back parlor of the old house on Dean Street where I am writing this essay, with its generous proportions and shelves of books and high ornamental ceiling. The windows look out over trees and flower gardens. It is a good room to write in. Brooklyn is full of such rooms.

Brooklyn Heights

Brooklyn Heights has always had a greater affinity with Manhattan than with its own borough. While the rest of Brooklyn was still farmland and small villages, the Heights became what architectural historian Clay Lancaster called "America's first suburb." In the early 1880s it was a bedroom community for the merchants and businessmen who worked in Lower Manhattan. Since then, Brooklyn Heights has maintained its connection with Manhattan, and its literary history is more closely allied with that of the sophisticated island across the river than with that of the neighboring flatlands.

In a quiet, gentle way Brooklyn Heights has nurtured an impressive collection of major American writers, among them Hart Crane, Thomas Wolfe, W. H. Auden, Carson McCullers, Truman Capote, Arthur Miller and Norman Mailer. None was formed by the Heights — Wolfe, McCullers and Capote came from the South, Crane from small-town Ohio, Auden from England, and Mailer and Miller from yeastier areas of Brooklyn. But all found the Heights a good place to live when it came time to write.

First among the Heights' attractions was its physical beauty. In 1816, residents found it a great bluff, whose face and brow were covered with "a beautiful growth of cedar and locust." From its summit, the land stretched away in orchards, gardens and pasture. Today, a smaller population of locust trees still scents the air and geranium-filled window boxes are symbols of the larger gardens of the past. Unlike many of New York's neighborhoods, however, what the Heights has lost in natural beauty it has gained in the manmade achievements of the industrial age. Its view of the Manhattan skyline is unequaled, and the Brooklyn Bridge, a magnificent marriage of esthetics and engineering, is its link with the mainland. Great ships, looming up beside the promenade, compensate somewhat for the loss of the river's fishing and swimming.

The Heights is also one of the most architecturally distinguished areas of the city; over 700 of its houses predate the Civil War. A homogeneous, isolated enclave — only four of its streets connect with greater Brooklyn — it possesses a sense of history and community. Yet, paradoxically, its residents have always felt more of a connection with Manhattan than the rest of Brooklyn.

As early as 1870, the remark that "Brooklyn is only a large bedroom for the businessmen of New York" was a cliché. In fact, even a century earlier, when it was still farmland, it had boasted three residents with businesses in the city. By 1819 land was specifically advertised for its suburban virtues: "Families who may desire to associate in forming *a select neighborhood and circle of society, for a summer's residence or a whole year's,* cannot anywhere obtain more desirable situations," read an advertisement extolling the health of the location and, especially, its proximity to the business center. The suburban development of the Heights had been made possible by the granting of a franchise to steamboat-inventor Robert Fulton and his partner, William Cutting. In 1814 they began the operation of a steam ferry — it connected the present Fulton Street in Manhattan with Fulton Street in Brooklyn (both, of course, named after the owner of the ferry) — for a charge of four cents a passenger. Later, in 1854, the Wall Street Ferry was established at the foot of Montague Street and further spurred the suburban development of the Heights. It made access to the financial and shipping district easy for bankers, brokers, lawyers and export and import merchants. "Shipping men especially felt drawn to the Heights as from it they could view their own gallant ships arriving and departing," wrote James Callender in his history of the neighborhood. "The cargoes from 'India and Cathay' were unloaded almost at their very doors."

The Heights' earliest literary resident was Thomas Paine, who spent some time in his last years "in a quiet and somewhat dreary existence" in the home of John Harmer at the corner of Sands and Fulton streets. Next, almost half a century later, came Henry Ward Beecher, Walt Whitman and John Greenleaf Whittier. Brooklyn is known as "the city of churches" and Beecher's Plymouth Congregation, still located on Orange Street between Henry and Hicks, was the most renowned church of its time, estimated to have the largest congregation in the country. As the church was also the largest auditorium in the city, it was here that all the famous readers and lecturers of the day spoke, among them Dickens, Thackeray and Emerson. Beecher, who was paid the then staggering salary of $20,000 a year, lived at 22 Willow Street in 1848 and at 176 Columbia Heights from 1851 to 1855.

During the same era, although with much less notice, the young Walt Whitman was supervising the typesetting of *Leaves of Grass* in a print shop on the southwest corner of Cranberry and what was then Fulton, now Cadman Plaza West. Unfortunately, this building, in recent years a little brick luncheonette, was torn down in 1964. Whitman was a long-time Brooklynite, but always lived on "the other side of Fulton," the boundary that separated the elite Heights from more common neighboring districts, except for a short time in 1824, when his family lived on Cranberry Street.

In 1867 a charter was granted for the construction of the Brooklyn Bridge, setting in motion a process that was to have great literary significance for the Heights. John A. Roebling, a native of Germany who had been a favorite pupil of Hegel's, conceived and designed the bridge. His foot was crushed by a ferry in 1869 when he was surveying to determine the exact location of the bridge's Brooklyn tower; he contracted tetanus and died within two weeks. His son Washington took charge, determined to fulfill his father's vision. Three years later Washington too met misfortune. He suffered an attack of caisson bends but, despite his illness, continued to press himself to the limit. Overwork, the residual effect of the bends and frustration at being unable to do more physical work resulted in what at the time was called "nervous prostration." From then on he directed construction of the bridge from a second-floor window at 110 Columbia Heights, using binoculars or a telescope to watch the work in progress.

Among those at work on the bridge down below was a sixteen-year-old Irish boy named Frank Harris, author in later years of *My Life and Loves*. Harris wrote of the disease that afflicted all who worked in the caissons:

> In a bare shed where we got ready, the men told me no one could do the work for long without getting the "bends" . . . When we went into the "air-lock" and they turned on one air-cock after another of compressed air, the men put their hands to their ears and I soon imitated them, for the pain was acute . . .
>
> When the air was fully compressed, the door of the air-lock opened at a touch and we all went down to work with pick and shovel on the gravelly bottom . . . The six of us were working naked to the waist in a small iron chamber with a temperature of about 80 degrees Fahrenheit: in five minutes the sweat was pouring from us, and all the while we were standing in icy water that was only kept from rising by the terrific pressure. No wonder the headaches were blinding. The men didn't work for more than ten minutes at a time, but I plugged on steadily, resolved to prove myself and get constant employment . . .

Had Harris been able to last, he would have earned enough in a month to live on for a year. But after the fifth or sixth day he was told he might be going deaf. A few days later, after seeing one of the men fall and writhe on the ground with blood spurting from his nose and mouth, he quit.

The bridge was completed at great human cost, but has perhaps repaid its debt better than other similar structures. In *The Brown Decades*, Lewis Mumford wrote: "A stunning act was necessary to demonstrate the aesthetic possibilities of the new materials . . . That act was the building of the Brooklyn Bridge — not merely one of the best pieces of engineering the 19th century can show anywhere but perhaps the most completely satisfactory structure of any kind that had appeared in America." In addition to being an immense architectural achievement, the bridge became an inspiration and a potent symbol to many.

One of the first to use its meaning in a work of art was Hart

Hart Crane on the roof of 110 Columbia Heights
with the Brooklyn Bridge in the background.

Crane, who in 1924 went to live in the very same house Washington Roebling had occupied. Crane previously had moved from one furnished room to another in the Village and was in constant search of more permanent inexpensive living quarters. A meeting with a young ship's steward named Emil Opffer seemed to offer a solution. Opffer's family had several rooms in a building that had been formed by connecting 110 Columbia Heights with the two adjoining houses at 106 and 108. An art school occupied the lower floors, and apartments and rooms were rented out upstairs. Opffer, who was to become Crane's intimate friend, suggested that the poet move to his building. Crane's room was on the fourth floor but he mistakenly fantasized that it was the very same one from which Roebling had directed the construction of the bridge. The view fascinated him. "Everytime one looks at the harbor and the New York skyline across the river it is quite different," he wrote, "and the range of atmospheric effects is almost endless. But at twilight on a foggy evening . . . it is beyond description. Gradually the lights in the enormously tall buildings begin to flicker through the mist . . . And up at the right Brooklyn Bridge, the most superb piece of construction in the modern world, I'm sure, with strings of light crossing it like glowing worms as the Ls and surface cars pass each other going and coming."

The bridge, finally, was the catalyst that caused the elements of the long poem he had been working on, eventually called *The Bridge,* to fall in place. The same perceptions found their way into the poem:

> O harp and altar, of the fury fused,
> (How could mere toil align thy choiring strings!)
> Terrific threshold of the prophet's pledge,
> Prayer of pariah, and the lover's cry, —
>
> Again the traffic lights that skim thy swift
> Unfractioned idiom, immaculate sigh of stars,

Beading thy path — condense eternity:
And we have seen night lifted in thine arms.

Emil, the bridge, Roebling's house together created for Crane a rare period of contentment and relative tranquility. Nevertheless, there were still drunken binges. John Dos Passos, who also had a room in 106–110 Columbia Heights, sometimes met Crane walking home across the bridge late at night after a round of Village parties. Appalled by the poet's generally disheveled, drunken state, Dos Passos would implore him to go home to bed. To avoid arguing, Crane would pretend to comply and then sneak back down the stairs to prowl among the bars along Sands Street near the navy yard.

Crane's stay in this room, interrupted by occasional travels, continued until 1929. He then took a trip to Europe, where Harry and Caresse Crosby encouraged him to complete *The Bridge* for publication by their Black Sun Press in France. When he returned, he moved to 130 Columbia Heights. On December 7, 1929, he gave a party attended by William Carlos Williams, Malcolm and Peggy Cowley, E. E. Cummings and the Crosbys to celebrate the near completion of the poem. On the day after Christmas he finished it.

Since Crane, the bridge has impressed its symbolism on many others. Marianne Moore, who lived near the Heights in Clinton Hill for many years, habitually took the Manhattan Bridge when crossing the East River to get a better view of the Roeblings' masterpiece. "Brooklyn Bridge," she wrote, recalling their sacrifices, "is synonymous with endurance . . . It was opened May 24, 1883 — a stern triumph, this feat — memorialized by the cables, towers, and centrally fixed arcs of filament united by stress, refined till diaphanous when seen from the Manhattan Bridge, silhouetted by the sun or the moon."

Arthur Miller, who used to walk home over the bridge from

Midtown when he lived in the Heights, has said that it was impossible not to respond to its symbolism. "It was so esthetically pleasing, such a wonderful model of how a utilitarian device could be done so beautifully. It seemed to hold a certain promise that we could build a society that would work and that would be inspiring at the same time. It is the most beautiful structure I know."

.

If Brooklyn Heights belonged to Hart Crane in the twenties, it was Thomas Wolfe's in the thirties. Where Crane had sought love, Wolfe fled it; he moved to the Heights to avoid Aline Bernstein, who for many years had encouraged and nurtured his writing. His first home was a few blocks away from the Heights at 40 Verandah Place. He described his apartment, which consisted of a high-ceilinged bedroom and, beneath it, a study opening onto a little garden, in *You Can't Go Home Again:* "The place may seem to you more like a dungeon than a room that a man would voluntarily elect to live in. It is long and narrow, running parallel to the hall from front to rear, and the only natural light that enters it comes through two small windows rather high up in the wall, facing each other at the opposite ends, and these are heavily guarded with iron bars . . ."

Wolfe left Verandah Place for the less miserable precincts of the Heights in October 1931. His first address was 111 Columbia Heights, one of a pair of Greek Revival row houses that have survived. He reported to his mother that he had "an entire floor — two big sunny rooms, a big fine kitchen, a good bath room." By August of 1932, he had moved again, this time a few doors away to 101 Columbia Heights. He wrote his mother that he had two "very nice rooms, a bath, and a kitchen, and although the place is not as big as the place I had

Thomas Wolfe with the manuscript of *Of Time and the River* in his Montague Terrace apartment.

before, it is cleaner and more modern and more private. The owners put in an electric icebox for me and the rent is $15 a month lower than it was at the other place. In addition, the place is cool and I have a very nice view of New York harbor and of the skyscrapers . . ."

Wolfe remained at 101 Columbia Heights until October of 1933, when he moved to 5 Montague Terrace, one of a row of seven brownstone houses. Here he did the final work on *Of Time and the River*. He lived on the fourth floor and had a large living room and moderate-sized bedroom. A visitor described the apartment:

> The chief piece of furniture was an old table, work worn and ancient but still sturdy. It was marked by many cigarette burns and its surface was dented like a shield after a hard battle . . . At the right, as one entered, and opposite the windows, was one alcove containing a gas range and another with an electric refrigerator which bumped and hummed as refrigerators did then. Tom claimed that this sound stimulated him by its rhythm. On the old table and on this refrigerator he did most of his writing . . . The adjoining bedroom contained a cot, an old battered bureau, and a straight chair.

In 1934, after an interview that mentioned his address, Wolfe was forced to give up this apartment. The day the article appeared fans began swarming to the building and Wolfe moved out of Brooklyn into a hotel.

•

Early in the 1940s, one address in Brooklyn Heights — 7 Middagh Street — became the gathering place for an extraordinary collection of people. George Davis, literary editor of *Harper's Bazaar,* claimed the house had appeared to him in a dream one night when he still lived in Manhattan. The next day he went to Brooklyn Heights and found it, exact in every detail.

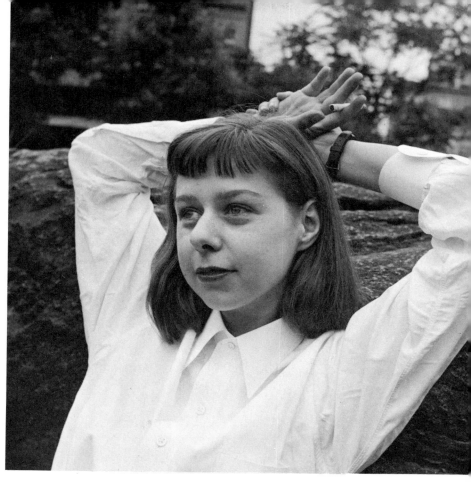

Carson McCullers in Central Park, 1941.

By fortunate coincidence, it was for rent. He called his friend
Carson McCullers, who had just decided to leave her husband,
and asked if she wanted to take the house with him. She agreed,
and they soon found a third in W. H. Auden. In the beginning, the housekeeping chores fell to McCullers as the only
regular female occupant. Sometimes, with the assistance of
Auden (she always pronounced Wystan "Winston"), she cooked
dishes she had learned to make as a child in Columbus, Georgia.
Later their friend Gypsy Rose Lee found them a cook — a

former Cotton Club chorine. Auden collected the rents "as George Davis was rather shy about money matters." He recalled that he "paid $25 a month for a floor, and I imagine the others paid about the same." According to Auden, the permanent residents included George Davis, Carson McCullers, theatrical designer Oliver Smith, Golo Mann (Thomas Mann's son), Jane and Paul Bowles and himself. "Then there were those who came fairly often for a few days, Benjamin Britten, Peter Pears, Louis MacNeice. And then there were those who may have spent a night or two, like Christopher Isherwood. Gypsy Rose Lee, who at that time was engaged to George Davis, was a frequent visitor (as was Tchelitchev) but never, so far as I can recall, stayed there. The 'permanents' had floors and there was usually a room or two for transients." Others — Anaïs Nin, Lincoln Kirstein, Leonard Bernstein, Salvador Dali, Marc Blitzstein and Aaron Copland — came for an evening or two.

Richard Wright, his wife and child, lived on the parlor floor and in the basement for a time in 1940, but didn't stay long enough to be considered permanent residents. The house didn't suit them; as Anaïs Nin reported: "When he [George Davis] invited them to live in his house, there were difficulties with the neighbors. His superintendent, a faithful Negro who had tended the furnace, resigned because he would not tend a furnace for another Negro." In addition, the Wrights were unhappy in what they considered an atmosphere of "general overstimulation and excitement." Eventually Wright told his wife, "This is not a proper environment in which to raise a child," and they moved.

In her *Diary*, Anaïs Nin has recorded something of the physical character of 7 Middagh: "An amazing house, like some of the houses in Belgium, the north of France, or Austria. He [George Davis] filled it with old American furniture, oil lamps, brass beds, little coffee tables, old drapes, copper lamps, old cupboards, heavy dining tables of oak, lace doilies, grandfather clocks. It is like a museum of Americana . . ." Though the name never took, Nin called it February House because she, Auden, George Davis and Carson McCullers were all born in February.

The best descriptions of 7 Middagh and its environs remain those of Carson McCullers: "The street where I now live has a quietness and sense of permanence that seem to belong to the nineteenth century. The street is very short. At one end, there are comfortable old houses, with gracious façades and pleasant back-yards in the rear." Like Hart Crane, McCullers was a habitué of Sands Street, where she frequently went at night with George Davis:

> At three o'clock in the morning, when the rest of the city is silent and dark, you can come suddenly on a little area as vivacious as a country fair. It is Sands [sic] Street, the place where sailors spend their evenings when they come here to port. At any hour of the night some excitement is going on in Sands street. The sunburned sailors swagger up and down the side-walks with their girls. The bars are crowded, and there are dancing, music, and straight liquor at cheap prices . . .
>
> In one bar, there is a little hunchback who struts in proudly every evening, and is petted by every one, given free drinks, and treated as a sort of mascot by the proprietor. There is a saying among sailors that when they die they want to go to Sands Street.

Unfortunately, were the sailors' souls to seek out Sands Street today, they would find no traces of it. The gaudy bars have been replaced by undifferentiated apartment-house projects. The hunchback, however, lives on in Carson McCullers's portrayal of Cousin Lyman in *The Ballad of the Sad Café*.

No one has immortalized 7 Middagh in prose or verse. Like

Brooklyn Heights, it provided the conditions rather than the material for creation. Paul Bowles has written: "It was just a nice old house with a comfortable atmosphere and rather uncomfortable furnishings. Each one did his work and minded his business; residents saw one another generally only at meal-times. Auden sat at the head of the table and conducted the conversations." Jane and Paul Bowles lived on the second floor of the house during the winter of 1940–41. He recalled being in a room with a life-size cut-out photograph of Gypsy Rose Lee, "something from the lobby of a burlesque theatre, standing nearly six feet high."

With its heady assortment of creative people, it is a wonder that 7 Middagh functioned at all. There were arguments, of course, and Bowles's memory of one of them captures some of the spicier tones of the house's atmosphere:

I remember having measles at Seven Middagh. It was mid-winter, and I got grippe immediately after my recovery. I always kept a room to escape to, around the corner, on Columbia Heights, and it was to this room, I suppose, that Auden imagined I would go when he casually remarked to me one evening: "I shall be requiring your room over the weekend." However, I intended to stay in bed over the weekend, and not to stir out of Seven Middagh. I told him this, but he seemed not to want to understand. "I have a friend coming from Michigan, and he will go into your room." When I stated clearly that I was not giving up my room to anybody for any reason, Auden turned very white and went downstairs and out into the street, slamming the front door violently. I decided Auden disliked me because I was a Stalinist. (There was great feeling at the time between pro-Moscow Marxists and anti-Moscow Marxists.) From then on I would not let anything be said at the table without giving the Party's viewpoint on the subject; I knew this would annoy my antagonist rather more than anything else. It certainly made for unpleasant meals.

Bowles seems to have regarded himself as the stepchild of 7 Middagh. He recalled also that "Benjamin Britten used the big piano in the salon on the first floor, and I installed an upright in the coal room behind the furnace in the cellar, where it was both freezing and airless."

The household at 7 Middagh lasted for about five years. Following the death of her father, Carson McCullers took a house with her mother and sister in Nyack. Finally, in 1945, the entire block where the house stood was condemned for the construction of a wider access to the Brooklyn-Queens Expressway and the last residents moved out.

•

During the same period, unaware of the unusual ménage at Middagh Street, the young Arthur Miller had come to live in the Heights. His first home was an ornate apartment house crazily adorned with round rooms, towers and cupolas at 62 Montague Street. It was 1940 and Miller had just returned from the University of Michigan and gotten married to Mary Grace Slattery. He and his wife shared her seven-room apartment with her roommates. "We lived there because it was the cheapest place in New York," he recalled. "It was about eighty dollars a month for the whole apartment." The poet Willard Maas and his wife, filmmaker Marie Menken, were residents of a duplex in the same building; their home was the scene of frequent literary parties until their deaths in the early 1970s.

From Montague, the Millers moved to 18 Schermerhorn Street, one of the first Heights houses to be remodeled and converted into apartments. There the rent was thirty dollars a month, and Norman Rosten, a friend of Miller's from the University of Michigan, also lived in the building. Miller's window looked out on the backyard of a mosque. "I used to sit and watch the Moslems holding services," Miller wrote. "They had a real Moorish garden symmetrically planted with curving lines of white stones laid out in the earth, and they would sit in white robes — twenty or thirty of them, eating at a long table, and served by their women who wore the flowing purple and rose togas of the East."

In 1944 Miller moved to a duplex at 102 Pierrepont Street, which harbored another then unknown author. As Miller remembered it, "The rooms were very dark — wood-paneled. It had been a very elaborate home. We never could see anything. Norman Mailer lived upstairs, but much of the time he was away at war." Here, after the war, Mailer, who lived with his parents, wrote *The Naked and the Dead* and Miller wrote *All My Sons*.

In 1947 Miller bought 31 Grace Court and there wrote *Death of a Salesman*. In 1951 he bought one of the Heights' architectural prizes, a charming Federal brick row house at 155 Willow Street, and sold the Grace Court house to W. E. B. Du Bois. "We couldn't have rented here," Du Bois remarked at the time. "We had to buy. When we first came, the FBI swarmed around the neighborhood asking questions." Du Bois, who had joined the Communist party publicly, lived there until 1961.

During his time in Brooklyn Heights, Miller "never gravitated toward a society of writers." He was far more likely to explore the livelier neighborhoods just beyond the Heights. "I loved walking along the waterfront," he recalled. "When I got interested in the longshoremen, I spent a lot of time in Red Hook around Columbia Street. There was a movement at the time to rid the union of racketeers . . . I knew a newly graduated lawyer involved in that struggle. There were lots of murders, bodies dropping into the river in concrete slabs. He called me. He thought I could get some publicity in the

papers. Then I became a supernumerary of that movement."
Miller's experience in Red Hook gave him the background for
A View from the Bridge and the young lawyer furnished part
of the characterization of Alfieri.

In spite of his solitary habits, Miller did visit his old friend
Norman Rosten, who had moved to 84 Remsen Street, where he
still lives. Miller met Carl Sandburg at the Rostens' and went
with Rosten to visit Louis Untermeyer, who had moved from
Manhattan to the top floor of 88 Remsen Street next door.
Robert Frost was there that evening and Rosten described the
occasion: "Everybody tried to hold forth and Frost wouldn't
let anybody have the floor. Frost was a very opinionated guy
who knew that he was immortal. He was the only man I knew
who could take the floor away from Untermeyer." Remsen
Street had had another writer as resident when Henry Miller
lived at 91 in 1924. He had quit his job and was writing full-
time. In a letter to Anaïs Nin he reminisced about the apartment "where I refused to clutter the place with furniture,
where I moved the bed or divan into the middle of the big
open room and thought I was in Japan all the time, everything
so clean, so polished, so decorative, so bare."

.

After Columbia Heights, Willow Street has probably housed
more literary people than any other Brooklyn Heights thoroughfare. Down the block from Miller's former home is 128 Willow,
one of the Heights' few apartment buildings, where Norman
Mailer lived before moving to 142 Columbia Heights. Hart
Crane stayed at 77 Willow for a short time in 1928, and 22
Willow was once the home of Henry Ward Beecher.

Marianne Moore, a frequent visitor to the Heights, wrote
fondly of the street. "At No. 27 there is still one remaining
willow, all curves and angles as though by Harunobu. Willow

became official, it is *said*, when a Miss Middagh, undetected, substituted for the name 'Jones,' shingles on which she had painstakingly inscribed 'Willow' . . . On Willow Street the doors are black or green, their brass knobs complementing the old-style italic numeral in gold leaf on glass above the door. The numeral is usually repeated, one above the left and one above the right double door, with a gold dot between." One of the most impressive houses on Willow Street is number 70, the home of theatrical designer Oliver Smith and, for a time, his basement tenant, Truman Capote. Unlike the attached row houses that predominate on the Heights, this grand residence was originally surrounded by open space on all sides. Capote described how the house looked to him one night in 1957 when Smith invited him to visit:

> I was most impressed; exceedingly envious. There were twenty-eight rooms, high-ceilinged, well proportioned, and twenty-eight workable, marble-manteled fireplaces. There was a beautiful staircase floating upward in white, swan-simple curves to a skylight of sunny amber-gold glass. The floors were fine, the real thing, hard lustrous timber; and the walls! In 1820, when the house was built, men knew how to make walls — thick as a buffalo, immune to the mightiest cold, the meanest heat.
>
> French doors led to a spacious rear porch reminiscent of Louisiana. A porch canopied, completely submerged, as though under a lake of leaves, by an ancient but admirably vigorous vine weighty with grapelike bunches of wisteria. Beyond, a garden! a tulip tree, a blossoming pear, a perched black-and-red bird bending a feathery branch of forsythia.

Capote convinced Smith to let him live in part of the house and he set up housekeeping in the five-room basement apartment where he was to write *Breakfast at Tiffany's* and *In Cold Blood*. There was a bedroom that opened onto the garden, a kitchen with its floor painted lemon yellow and a Victorian parlor containing all Capote's personal treasures. Hanging over the sofa was a pair of gold mirrors in the shape of butterflies; on polished tables and bamboo bookcases were a golden Easter egg brought back from Russia, an iron dog, a Fabergé pillbox, blue ceramic fruit, a coquille bouquet, Battersea boxes, marbles, paperweights, old photographs — one of Capote with Jane and Paul Bowles in Africa — and, propped up in a corner, a Spanish saint.

Capote regularly took a walk that led past "a ghost hotel" down to the waterfront. "In aggravated moments," he wrote of the hotel, "I imagine retiring there, for it is as secluded as Mt. Athos, remoter than the Krak Chevalier in the mountains of wildest Syria. Daytimes the location, a dead-end Chiricoesque piazza facing the river, is little disturbed; at night, not at all; not a sound, except foghorns and a distant traffic whisper from the bridge which bulks above. Peace, and the shivering glow of gliding-by tugs and ferries." The hotel still stands at 1 Water Street. From here, Capote would walk along the waterfront past "silent miles of warehouses with shuttered wooden windows, docks resting on the water like sea spiders," past ships and the men who work on them. "Every kind of sailor is common enough here," he noted. "Even saronged East Indians, even the giant Senegalese, their onyx arms afire with blue, with yellow tattooed flowers, with saucy torsos and garish graffiti . . . Runty Russians, too — one sees them flapping in their pajama-like costumes."

Like Capote, many of the Heights residents of the fifties and sixties have departed. Alfred Kazin, who lived at 91 Pineapple Street in 1952, moved to the city; Louis Untermeyer to the country. But some have stayed, and there are always new, young writers to replace those who have left. Among the most loyal have been Norman Mailer and Norman Rosten. During

Norman Mailer standing beneath the gabled work area in his Brooklyn Heights house.

the forties Rosten had a furnished room he used for writing in a house at 20 Remsen Street. Mailer took over the studio for a while when he came back from the war and then used a room in the Ovington Building at 246 Fulton Street. At that time he had already written *Barbary Shore,* which concerned a writer who became involved with a group of spies living in his rooming house. Later Mailer commented:

> . . . Writing about F.B.I. agents and Old Bolsheviks in *Barbary Shore,* the greatest single difficulty with the book was that my common sense thought it was impossible to have all these agents and impossible heroes congregating in a rooming house in Brooklyn Heights. Yet a couple of years later I was working in a studio on Fulton Street . . . On the floor below me, worked one Colonel Rudolph Abel, who was the most important spy for the Russians in this country for a period of about eight or ten years, and I am sure we used to be in the elevator together many times. I think he literally had the room beneath me.

Mailer now lives in the upper two floors of a brownstone at 142 Columbia Heights, where he has designed a unique work place: "Lofty, tenting, glass-and-wood gable that he pushed right through his roof like a small pyramid. Inside this structure, it is like a ship's forecastle. There are many different ways to reach many upper levels, but none of them is easy: climbing ropes, boarding nets, trapezes, deck ladders, catwalks and, for those who wish to rest halfway, a rope hammock slung between two beams over the dried-out skeletons of dead sea skates that roll like mobiles in the cross-ventilation below." Mailer's carrel "is tucked way up under the peak of the gable, its only ingress being a 6-inch-wide plank across the long drop down to the patrolling sea skates below. A lot of important people have bothered to inch their way across that plank for a visit, but what Norman really appreciates is any

N. 7th St.
N. 3rd St.
N. 1st St.
Bedford Ave.
Driggs Ave.
Roebling St.
Expwy.
①
②
Fillmore Pl.
Metropolitan Ave.
Brooklyn - Queens
Grand St.
Broadway

Carlton Ave.
Cumberland St.
Myrtle Ave.
④
③
Fort
Greene
Park
De Kalb
Ave.
⑤
Lafayette Ave.
⑥
Washington Ave.
Fulton St.
⑦ ⑧
Lefferts Pl.
Grand Ave.
Classon Ave.

Williamsburg Bridge →
Manhattan Bridge →
Brooklyn Bridge →

*BROOKLYN
HEIGHTS*

Fort Hamilton Pkwy.
Flatbush Ave.
E. 3rd
Ocean Parkway
⑭ ⑬ Ave. M
St.
Kings
Highway
Shore
Parkway

*Verrazzano -
Narrows
Bridge*

Shore Parkway

Brooklyn

Evergreen Ave.
Decatur St.
Bushwick Ave.
Broadway
Fulton St.
Atlantic Ave.
⑨ Pacific St.
Ralph Ave.
Howard Ave.
Eastern
Parkway
New York Ave.
Rockaway Parkway
⑪ Pitkin Ave.
Chester St.
Belmont Ave.
⑩ Sutter Ave.

Brooklyn Ave.
Kingston Ave.
⑫
Eastern Parkway
Union St.

cat sure-footed enough to cool it without using the handholds along the gable roof."

Today, in addition to Rosten and Mailer, writers James Purdy and Frank Conroy also live in the Heights. Undoubtedly, they will not be the last, for as Carson McCullers noted, "Comparing the Brooklyn that I know with Manhattan is like comparing a comfortable and complacent duenna to her more brilliant and neurotic sister." The Heights offers qualities writers have always valued — beauty, quiet, privacy, tradition and a sense of community.

Brooklyn Tour

Take the L Train (14th Street Crosstown) to Bedford Avenue in Williamsburg.

1. 662 Driggs Avenue, between North 1st Street and Metropolitan Avenue. Henry Miller spent his childhood, beginning in 1892, in this three-story brick house, once part of a row (p. 331).

2. Fillmore Place, diagonally across the way; Miller's favorite street. Most of the three-and-a-half story brick row houses from Miller's time remain today, although one can see the gaps he compared to missing teeth. This little street is a time warp. (pp. 331–32).

Walk to the Metropolitan Avenue—Grand Street Station, and take the G Train to Fulton—Lafayette Avenue (seven stops). Fort Greene has several literary landmarks.

3. 175 Carlton Avenue. Richard Wright moved here in 1938, where he began writing *Native Son*. The old three-and-a-half story brick house, one of a pair in a row, is still in good condition (p. 355).

4. Fort Greene Park. Every morning Wright went to the top of the hill in the park to write. The park was originally designed by Olmsted and Vaux, in 1876; in 1908, from designs by McKim, Mead and White, the high column, plaza, comfort station, and new flight of steps to Willoughby Street were added. A row of once-magnificent brownstone mansions on Washington Street faces the park; most of them are now broken up into apartments.

5. 260 Cumberland Street. Marianne Moore lived from 1931 to 1965 in this six-story 1920s building which has bay windows and inlaid tile mosaics.

The iron stands with the "mothballs" Moore described to George Plimpton are gone (p. 335).

6. The Lafayette Avenue Presbyterian Church, which Moore attended regularly twice a week, is on the southeast corner of Lafayette Avenue and South Oxford Street. It was built in 1862 and has numerous Tiffany windows (p. 335).

7. 87 Lefferts Place, between Grand and Classon avenues. Richard Wright, after living in Fort Greene, moved to this high, three-and-a-half-story Victorian brownstone with bay windows and an attractive iron fence (pp.335–36).

8. 89 Lefferts Place. After his marriage, Wright moved back to this neighborhood and lived in this long four-story brick apartment house from 1943 to 1945 (p. 336).

At Franklin—Fulton Street take the C Train (weekdays only) to Ralph Avenue (four stations).

9. 2027 Pacific Street, in Crown Heights, between Howard Avenue and Ralph Avenue. Norman Podhoretz lived here in the forties in this four-story brick apartment house, now called Pacific Court (p. 334).

10. 256A Sutter Avenue, on the southeast corner of Chester Street and Sutter Avenue. Alfred Kazin grew up here in the twenties in a building now gone. He says that the street numbering was changed in the thirties, no one knew why, and he remembers his house as originally numbered 234; but a 1929 street atlas shows it as 236, and the twin building next door as 238 (p. 333).

11. The Belmont market, on Belmont Avenue between Thatford Street and Stone Avenue (now Mother Gaston Boulevard), was once reminiscent of the Orchard Street market on the Lower East Side. It is a street of sidewalk stands and small one-story clothing and food shops, many still Jewish owned.

12. 1390 Union Street, between Kingston and Brooklyn avenues. John Oliver Killens lived here in Bedford-Stuyvesant for many years, beginning in 1961. This is a block of double three-story brick houses, many with Dutch gables facing the street. Killens wrote of it, "Softly silent is our tree-lined block, save for the squealing laughter of children, the chirping of birds, the chattering of crazy crickets and the gentle rustling of wind in the trees that made the world around our house sound like continuous summer showers" (p. 336).

Take the number 2 Train at Nostrand Avenue (two blocks west of Brooklyn Avenue) and President Street (one block south of Union Street) to Borough Hall—Court Street and on in to Manhattan. If you want to transfer to the F Train, you must continue into Manhattan to 14th Street, or leave the subway and reenter a block or two away at Jay Street—Borough Hall.

Take the F Train and go toward Coney Island to Avenue M. Exit from the north end of the platform and walk east on Avenue M toward:

13. 1277 Ocean Parkway, north of Avenue M. Arthur Miller's first Brooklyn address was this two-story, two-family house where he lived with his parents (p. 336). He grew up in the area bordered by Avenue J and Avenue M, Ocean Parkway and Gravesend Avenue (today McDonald Avenue).

14. 1350 East 3rd Street, north of Avenue M. Miller's second address, a small house on which Willy Loman's house in *Death Of A Salesman* was modeled, is near the end of a dead-end street (p. 337).

Brooklyn Heights Tour

1. 2 Water Street. This was originally Franklin House, a hotel to which Truman Capote imagined retiring. It was built in 1835 and remodeled in the 1850s. Now on the ground floor is the colorful Harbor View Restaurant.

2. Sands Street (now the end of Middagh Street) and Fulton Street (now Cadman Plaza West). In his later years, Thomas Paine, Brooklyn's earliest literary resident, stayed at the home of John Harmer which was once at this corner (p. 340).

3. Cranberry and Fulton streets, on the southwest corner. The little building housing a printshop where *Leaves of Grass* was typeset survived here until 1964. The town houses now on this site are called Whitman Close (p. 341).

4. 91 Pineapple Street, now open space in Cadman Plaza. Alfred Kazin lived here in 1952 (p. 357).

5. Orange Street, east of Hicks Street. Plymouth Church, designed in 1849 by architect Joseph C. Wells, where Henry Ward Beecher preached from 1847 to 1887. The Tuscan porch was added after his death (pp. 340–41).

6. 7 Middagh Street, four doors east of Columbia Heights. A "nice old house" here was a gathering place for an extraordinary collection of people—W. H. Auden, Carson McCullers, Jane and Paul Bowles, etc.—

Brooklyn Heights

EAST RIVER

UPPER BAY

Brooklyn Bridge

Water St.

Manhattan Bridge

Queens Expressway

Sands St.

Brooklyn

Poplar St.

Middagh St.

Cranberry St.

Orange St.

Pineapple St.

Clark St.

College Pl.

Heights

Willow St.

Columbia

Promenade

Love Lane

Pierrepont St.

Montague St.

Montague Ter.

Grace Court

Grace Ct. Alley

Remsen St.

Hunts Lane

Joralemon St.

Cadman Plaza W.

(Fulton St.)

Monroe Pl.

Clinton St.

Adams St.

Court St.

Aitken Pl.

Livingston St.

Schermerhorn St.

State St.

Columbia Pl.

Willow Pl.

Hicks St.

Garden Pl.

Henry St.

Sidney Pl.

Atlantic Ave.

Pacific St.

Amity St.

Congress St.

Verandah Pl.

Warren St.

from about 1941 until 1945, when it was demolished for wider access to the Brooklyn-Queens Expressway (pp. 348–53).

7. 22 Willow Street, in a row of Greek Revival houses built in 1846. Henry Ward Beecher lived here in 1848; the house is now painted gray (pp. 341, 355).

8. 27 Willow Street. In the courtyard stands the ten-foot-high stump of a willow tree, with some willow branches remaining, which was Marianne Moore's favorite (pp. 355–56).

9. 70 Willow Street. The wide Greek Revival house, dating to 1839, is the home of theatrical designer Oliver Smith. Truman Capote wrote *Breakfast at Tiffany's* and *In Cold Blood* in the basement apartment here (pp. 356–57).

10. 77 Willow Street. Hart Crane lived here for a short time in 1928 (p. 355).

11. 111 Columbia Heights, one of a pair of Greek Revival houses. This was Thomas Wolfe's second Brooklyn address, from October 1931 to August 1932 (p. 346).

12. 101 Columbia Heights. Wolfe lived at this location from August 1932 to October 1933. The building has been replaced by high rises (pp. 346–48).

13. 97 Columbia Heights, on the northeast corner of Orange Street. The site of the Hotel Margaret, demolished in 1980 after a disastrous fire. At various times its guests included H. G. Wells and Sigrid Undset. The new building is called the Margaret Apartments.

14. 110 Columbia Heights; this was exactly opposite the Hotel Margaret. The invalid Washington Roebling directed construction of the Brooklyn Bridge by telescope from a room here. The same building was the residence of Hart Crane in 1924, when he began writing *The Bridge*, and of John Dos Passos in 1929 (pp. 341, 344–45).

15. 130 Columbia Heights, where Crane finished *The Bridge* in 1930. The original building has been replaced by high rises.

16. 142 Columbia Heights. Norman Mailer has lived for many years on the top two floors (pp. 358–59).

17. 176 Columbia Heights. Henry Ward Beecher lived here from 1851 to 1855 (p. 341).

18. 128 Willow Street. Mailer lived here in one of the Heights' few apartment buildings before moving to 142 Columbia Heights (p. 355).

19. 155 Willow Street. Arthur Miller owned this landmark house from 1951 to 1956. A plaque designates the house and its attached neighbors at 157 and 159. The carriage house at 151 was once connected to number

159 by an underground passage, and the glass panes of the passage's skylight can be seen near the gate to 157 (p. 354).

20. 62 Montague Street. Arthur Miller's first home in the Heights was this strange, ornate apartment house built about 1880 (p. 353).

21. The east side of Montague Terrace is a "terrace" in the English sense, meaning a row of houses. Numbers 1 to 15 were built about 1886. W. H. Auden lived at number 1. Thomas Wolfe finished *Of Time and the River* while at number 5 in the fall of 1933 and on into 1934 (p. 348). Number 11 was home to Jules Feiffer.

22. 10 Montague Terrace, directly across the street. Maxwell Bodenheim worked on the white balcony off his living room. The balcony can be seen from the street.

23. 20 Remsen Street. During the forties Norman Rosten and Norman Mailer consecutively used the same studio here.

24. 31 Grace Court was owned by Arthur Miller from 1947 to 1951, and was where he wrote *Death of a Salesman*. It was then owned by W.E.B. DuBois from 1951 to 1961 (p. 354). Until it was covered with stucco and remodeled, the house was probably a mate to the Renaissance Revival building next door at number 29.

25. 84 Remsen Street, where Norman Rosten lived for many years (p. 355).

26. 187 Hicks Street, on the northeast corner of Pierrepont Street. Rosten now lives in this turn-of-the-century apartment building.

27. 102 Pierrepont Street. Arthur Miller moved to this brownstone in 1944 and stayed until 1947. Here he wrote *All My Sons*. Norman Mailer lived upstairs with his parents, and after the war wrote *The Naked and the Dead* here (p. 354). The building has been modernized and painted white since then.

28. 91 Remsen Street was the home of Henry Miller in 1924 (p. 355).

29. 88 Remsen Street. Louis Untermeyer lived on the top floor in the early fifties (p. 355).

30. 18 Schermerhorn Street. Arthur Miller, in the early forties, lived here in one of the first houses in the Heights to be remodeled and converted into apartments. His friend Norman Rosten also lived in the building (pp. 353–54).

31. 40 Verandah Place. Thomas Wolfe's first Brooklyn address, where he stayed until October 1931. It is an old three-story brick house in an alley running between Clinton and Henry streets about four blocks south of Atlantic Avenue. In Wolfe's time there was a church across the street (p. 346).

Notes to the Introduction

page

i. "Do Not Disturb!" Hank O' Neal, *Life is painful, nasty and short...in my case it has only been painful and nasty* (New York: Paragon House, 1991), p. 5.

ii. "I've had eighteen . . ." John Malcolm Brinnin, *Dylan Thomas in America* (Boston: Atlantic Monthly Press, 1955), p. 272.

ii. "In a biography of the poet . . ." Jean Gould, *The Poet and Her Book* (New York: Dodd, Mead & Co., 1969), pp. 77–84.

vi. "In the office in which I work . . ." Joseph Heller, *Something Happened* (New York: Random House, 1984).

ix. ". . . at the fifty-ninth hour . . ." Marianne Moore, *Tell Me, Tell Me* (New York: Viking Press, 1966), p. 40.

xi. "when we finally . . ." and "I found myself . . ." *Newsweek,* June 25, 1984.

xi. "Today it houses . . ." *Fund Raising Management,* Feb. 1990, p. 53.

xii. " . . . if there are more than ten . . ." John Rockwell, "A Conversation with Virgil Thomson," *A Virgil Thomson Reader* by Virgil Thomson (New York: E. P. Dutton, 1984), pp. 525–54.

xiv. "All those writers . . . " Blair Fuller, Pati Hill, Archibald Macleish, George Plimpton, Irwin Shaw, Tony Southers, William Styron and others, "The Paris Review Sketchbook," *The Paris Review,* 79, 1981, p. 397.

xv. "'Paul Desmond Room' because the late saxophonist . . ." Conversation with George Plimpton, January 12, 1991; see also Plimpton's amusing piece, "Elaine's Restaurant," in *The Best of Plimpton* (New York: Atlantic Monthly Press, 1990), pp. 251–254.

xv. "One writer who was not . . ." Gerald Clarke, *Capote: A Biography* (New York: Simon & Schuster, 1988), p. 374.

xv. "A second party . . ." Tom Wolfe, *The Purple Decade* (New York: Farrar, Straus & Giroux, 1982), pp. 181-200; and Joan Peyser *Bernstein: A Biography* (New York: Beech Tree Books, 1987), p. 409.

xvi. "What many people remembered . . ." George Plimpton, "The Paris Review Sketchbook," *The Paris Review,* 79, 1981, p. 400.

xvii. "The book was, Capote claimed . . ." George Plimpton, "The Story Behind a Nonfiction Novel," *New York Times Book Review,* January 16, 1966, p. 2.

page

xvii. "A beginning, a middle, and an end." Robert McDowell, "The New Narrative Poetry," *Crosscurrents*, VIII, 2, 1989, p. 34.

xviii. "linguistic exercises" . . . Robert McDowell, "The New Narrative Poetry," *Crosscurrents*, VIII, 2, 1989, p. 34.

xxi. "Everything . . . I said once . . ." and "on the grounds that . . ." Carol G. Herman, *Mary McCarthy.* (New York City: St. Martin's Press, 1988), p. 332.

xxi. "I think she has always disliked me . . ." Herbert Mitgang, "Miss Hellman Suing a Critic for 2.2 Million," *New York Times*, February 16, 1980, p. 12.

xxi. "I didn't want her . . " Samuel G. Freedman, "McCarthy Is Recipient of MacDowell Medal," *New York Times*, Aug. 27, 1984, c14.

xxi. "just picked Gore up . . ." "Truman Capote Talks About His Crowd," *Playgirl,* Sept. 1975, p. 54.

xxi. "great mental anxiety and suffering . . ." Gerald Clarke, *Capote: A Biography* (New York: Simon & Schuster, 1988), p. 480.

xxii. "Q: What occurred on that occasion? . . ." Gerald Clarke, *Capote: A Biography* (New York: Simon & Schuster, 1988), p. 480.

xxii. "Dear Gore . . ." Gerald Clarke, *Capote: A Biography* (New York: Simon & Schuster, 1988), p. 520.

xxii. "on the grounds that even if Ms. Malcolm . . ." Linda Greenhouse, "A Debate on What Is Truth," *New York Times*, Jan. 15, 1991, A16.

xxiii. "The Poetry Center was started . . ." Karl Kirchwey, "About the Poetry Center" (program notes for a photographic exhibition marking the anniversary of the Poetry Center), Spring 1989, p. 1.

xxvi. "cherished eccentricity" Deirdre Carmody, "There at *The New Yorker,* with Thurber," *New York Times*, Feb. 19, 1991, p. B1, B8.

xxvii. Petition of protest and following quote, "supports governments that silence . . ." "The PEN International Congress—a Retrospect," *PEN American Center Newsletter*, #58, Spring 1986, p. 1, p. 16.

xxvii. "I did not bring . . ." "The PEN International Congress—a Retrospect," *PEN American Center Newsletter*, #58, Spring 1986, p. 17.

xxvii. "more in common than you think . . ." As reported in *The Village Voice,* the remark did not appear in the *New York Times.*

xxvii. "there are not many women who are . . ." Glenn Collins, "Festival of Arts Lowers its Sights," *New York Times*, Feb. 27, 1991, C11, C12.

Notes

I. Lower Manhattan (pages 1–34)

page

1 "After a hundred . . ." Lawrence C. Wroth, *The Voyages of Giovanni da Verrazzano: 1524–1528* (New Haven: Yale University Press, 1970) , pp. 85–86.

2 "Safe from the fury . . ." Rodman Gilder, *The Battery* (Boston: Houghton Mifflin Co., 1936) , p. 3.

3 "See, two streams . . ." Meyer Berger, *Meyer Berger's New York* (New York: Random House, 1960) , pp. 37–38.

6 "What a contrast . . ." William Smith, quoted in Moses Coit Tyler, *A History of American Literature, 1607–1783*, abridged and edited by Archie H. Jones (Chicago: University of Chicago Press) , p. 116.

"I offered my services . . ." Benjamin Franklin, *The Autobiography of Benjamin Franklin and Selections from His Other Writings* (New York: Random House, Modern Library, 1950) , p. 26.

"a monkey of the . . ." Edward Ellis, *The Epic of New York City* (New York: Coward McCann, 1966) , p. 120.

8 "all you have to do . . ." reprinted in *The American Literary Revolution: 1783–1837*, edited by Robert E. Spiller (New York: Doubleday & Co., 1967) , p. 6.

9 "a free newspaper . . ." Lewis Leary, *That Rascal Freneau* (New Brunswick: Rutgers University Press, 1941) , p. 14.

"He was regarded . . ." Vernon Louis Parrington, *Main Currents in American Thought* (New York: Harcourt, Brace & Co., 1958) , p. 328.

11 "Both were staunch . . ." Alfred Owen Aldridge, *Man of Reason: The Life of Thomas Paine* (Philadelphia: Lippincott Co., 1959) , p. 295.

12 "It was exceedingly pleasant . . ." Spiller, *American Literary Revolution*, p. 225.

page

13 "DISTRESSING" and all subsequent quotations from the hoax, Washington Irving, *Diedrich Knickerbocker's History of New York* (New York: The Heritage Press, 1940), pp. xv–xvi.

17 "one of two recently . . ." Susan Cooper, "Small Family Memories" (1883), in *Correspondence of James Fenimore Cooper,* edited by his grandson James Fenimore Cooper (New Haven: Yale University Press, 1922), p. 48.

"The number of rats . . ." Cooper, *Correspondence,* p. 53.

"the bark of the cinnamon . . ." William Cullen Bryant, "Discourse on the Life, Genius, and Writings of J. Fenimore Cooper," in James Fenimore Cooper's *Precaution and Ways of the Hour* (Boston: C. T. Brainard Publishing Co., n.d.), pp. 32–33.

19 "the disagreeable, disgusting drudgery . . ." John Bigelow, *William Cullen Bryant* (New York: Arno and the *New York Times,* 1970), p. 62.

20 "is the strong temptation . . ." Allan Nevins, *The Evening Post: A Century of Journalism* (New York: Russell & Russell, 1968), p. 350.

21 "he believed that . . ." John Bigelow, quoted in Charles Brown, *William Cullen Bryant* (New York: Charles Scribner's Sons, 1971), note p. 250.

"I do not know . . ." Bigelow in Brown, *Bryant,* p. 292.

"Cooper, burly, brusque . . ." Nevins, *The Evening Post,* p. 191.

"As Audubon . . ." Van Wyck Brooks and Otto L. Bettmann, *Our Literary Heritage: A Pictorial History of the Writer in America* (New York: E. P. Dutton & Co., 1965), p. 40.

22 "The face of the island . . ." Asa Greene, *A Glance at New York* (New York: A. Greene, 1837), pp. 1–2.

"As certain kings . . ." Greene, *A Glance at New York,* p. 152.

23 "To the Readers . . ." Nevins, *The Evening Post,* p. 159.

24 "Coming up Broadway . . ." Joseph Jay Rubin and Charles H. Brown, *Walt Whitman of the New York Aurora* (State College, Pa.: Bald Eagle Press, 1950), p. 18.

25 "a strange, natural . . ." Walt Whitman, *Specimen Days* (New York: E. P. Dutton & Co., n.d.), p. 19.

"Mannahatta," Walt Whitman, *Leaves of Grass and Selected Prose,* edited by Sculley Bradley (New York: Rinehart & Co., 1949), p. 413.

"Leading traits . . ." Gay Wilson Allen, *The Solitary Singer: A Critical Biography of Walt Whitman* (New York: Macmillan, 1955), p. 103.

page

26 "very kindly and human . . ." Perry Miller, *The Raven and the Whale* (New York: Harcourt, Brace & Co., 1956), p. 148.

27 "I have been roaming . . ." Edgar Allan Poe, *Doings of Gotham,* collected by Jacob E. Spannuth, with preface, introduction and comments by Thomas O. Mabbott (Pottsville, Pa.: J. E. Spannuth, 1929), Letter I, p. 25.

28 "In a week . . ." Jay Leyda, *The Melville Log, A Documentary Life of Herman Melville, 1819–1891,* Vol. 1 (New York: Harcourt, Brace & Co., 1951), p. 414.

29 Murray speculates . . . Herman Melville, *Pierre; or, the Ambiguities,* edited by Henry A. Murray (New York: Hendricks House, 1962), p. 484.

Another scholar . . . Correspondence with Hans Bergmann.

30 "the multitudinous . . ." Henry James, *The American Scene* (New York: Charles Scribner's Sons, 1946), p. 76.

"the new landmarks . . ." James, *The American Scene,* p. 81.

"the special skyscraper . . ." James, *The American Scene,* p. 83.

"'Jimmy the Priest's' . . ." Louis Sheaffer, *O'Neill, Son and Playwright* (Boston: Little, Brown & Co., 1968), p. 190.

32 "a receptacle of all the . . ." Gilder, *The Battery,* p. 75.

"a small country jail . . ." Poe, *Doings of Gotham,* p. 26.

II. Greenwich Village (pages 35–110)

The Nineteenth-Century Village: Washington Square

35 "It has a kind . . ." Henry James, *Washington Square* (New York: Random House, Modern Library, 1950), p. 22.

37 "too magnificent . . ." James Fenimore Cooper, *The Letters and Journals of James Fenimore Cooper,* edited by James Franklin Beard (Cambridge: Harvard University Press, 1964), p. 4.

39 "I suppose the Knights . . ." Letter of Melville to Duyckinck, November 7, 1851, Duyckinck Collection, New York Public Library.

40 "The grey and . . ." Henry James, *The American Scene* (New York: Charles Scribner's Sons, 1946), p. 91.

"a stout red-faced . . ." Henry James, *A Small Boy and Others* (New York: Charles Scribner's Sons, 1913), p. 17.

41 "in 'grounds' peopled . . ." James, *A Small Boy and Others,* p. 24.

"the ideal of quiet . . ." James, *Washington Square,* p. 21.

page

42 "was as if the wine . . ." James, *The American Scene*, p. 88.

43 "I was a failure . . ." Edith Wharton, *A Backward Glance: The Autobiography of Edith Wharton* (New York: Charles Scribner's Sons, 1962), p. 119.

"The Jameses were . . ." Louis Auchincloss, *Edith Wharton, A Woman In Her Time* (New York: Viking Press, 1971), p. 12.

"then just within . . ." Wharton, *A Backward Glance*, p. 18.

45 "'purest 1830,' with . . ." Edith Wharton, *The Age of Innocence* (New York: Random House, Modern Library, [c.] 1920), p. 24.

47 "One could never begin . . ." Clara Clemens, *My Father, Mark Twain* (New York: Harper & Brothers, 1931), p. 217.

"his efflorescence . . ." and "Until he imagined . . ." William Dean Howells, *My Mark Twain* (New York: Harper & Brothers, 1910), p. 96.

48 "But all I remember . . ." John Dos Passos, *The Best Times: An Informal Memoir* (New York: New American Library, 1966), p. 14.

"with his white hair . . ." Van Wyck Brooks, *An Autobiography* (New York: E. P. Dutton & Co., 1965), p. 158.

"a self-conscious entity . . ." Max Eastman, *Enjoyment of Living* (New York: Harper & Brothers, 1948), p. 416.

The Birth of Bohemia

49 "do not know how . . ." Roi Ottley and William J. Weatherby, editors, *The Negro in New York* (New York: The New York Public Library, 1967), p. 73.

"Of all the ambitions . . ." Van Wyck Brooks, *The Confident Years: 1885–1915* (New York: E. P. Dutton & Co., 1955), p. 265.

50 "In 1906 . . ." Edith Lewis, *Willa Cather Living* (New York: Alfred A. Knopf, 1953), p. xv.

51 "Forty-Two Washington Square," in Allen Churchill, *The Improper Bohemians* (New York: E. P. Dutton & Co., 1959), p. 37.

"I used to go . . ." Steffens, *Autobiography*, p. 654.

52 "Why don't you . . ." Richard O'Connor and Dale L. Walker, *The Lost Revolutionary: A Biography of John Reed* (New York: Harcourt, Brace & World, 1967), p. 75.

53 "she sat quietly . . ." Steffens, *Autobiography*, p. 655.

56 "You are elected . . ." Churchill, *The Improper Bohemians*, p. 93.

"Voting! . . . Poetry is something . . ." Churchill, *The Improper Bohemians*, p. 108.

page

57 "We had a custom . . ." Eastman, *Enjoyment*, p. 439.

58 "Before O'Neill . . ." Louis Sheaffer, *O'Neill, Son and Playwright* (Boston: Little, Brown & Co., 1968), p. 481.

"that there is always . . ." Interview with Karl Schriftgiesser for the *New York Times* quoted in Crosswell Bowen, *The Curse of the Misbegotten, A Tale of the House of O'Neill* (New York: McGraw-Hill, 1959), p. 310.

61 "It was wonderful . . ." John Dos Passos, *The Fourteenth Chronicle: Letters and Diaries of John Dos Passos,* edited and with a biographical narrative by Townsend Ludington (Boston: Gambit, 1973), p. 75.

62 "We bought gold . . ." Margaret Anderson, *My Thirty Years' War* (New York: Horizon Press, 1969), p. 152.

63 "At auction rooms . . ." Lewis, *Willa Cather,* p. 89.

"so popular, in fact . . ." Lewis, *Willa Cather,* p. 134.

64 "the sounds the leopards . . ." Lewis, *Willa Cather,* p. 139.

66 "The thing that interested me . . ." Theodore Dreiser, *Color of a Great City* (New York: Boni and Liveright, 1923), pp. 1–2.

"the ponderous battering ram . . ." Allen Churchill, *The Literary Decade* (Englewood Cliffs: Prentice-Hall, 1971), p. 18.

67 "with a large eraser . . ." Floyd Dell, *Homecoming, An Autobiography* (New York: Farrar & Rinehart, 1933), p. 269.

68 "I decided I would go . . ." *Sherwood Anderson's Memoirs,* edited by Ray Lewis White (Chapel Hill: University of North Carolina Press, 1942), p. 452.

The Lost Generation

69 "After college and the war . . ." Malcolm Cowley, *Exile's Return: A Literary Saga of the 1920's* (New York: Viking Press, 1951), p. 48.

70 "Marianne had two cords . . ." quoted in Donald Hall, *Marianne Moore, The Cage and the Animal* (New York: Pegasus, 1970), p. 25.

"an astonishing person . . ." Hall, *Marianne Moore,* p. 24.

71 "Lola Ridge had a party . . ." Hall, *Marianne Moore,* p. 57.

"She lived in that . . ." Floyd Dell, *Love in Greenwich Village* (New York: George H. Doran Co., 1926), p. 33.

72 "One cannot really . . ." Edmund Wilson, *The Shores of Light* (New York: Farrar, Straus & Young, Inc., 1952), p. 751.

73 "never a great fan . . ." John Unterecker, *Voyager: A Life of Hart Crane* (New York: Farrar, Straus & Giroux, 1969), p. 89.

page

73 "inquisitive landlady . . ." Hart Crane, *The Letters of Hart Crane, 1916–1932*, edited by Brom Weber (New York: Hermitage House, 1952), pp. 134–35.

74 "Italian speakeasy of the moment . . ." Dos Passos, *The Best Times*, p. 83.

"'4' signifies a delapidated . . ." E. E. Cummings, *Selected Letters of E. E. Cummings*, edited by F. W. Dupee and George Stade (New York: Harcourt, Brace & World, 1969), p. 184.

77 "About nine o'clock . . ." Burton Rascoe, *A Bookman's Daybook*, edited with an introduction by C. Hartley Grattan (New York: Horace Liveright, 1929), p. 28.

"There appeared a slight . . ." Dos Passos, *The Best Times*, p. 139.

78 "accompanied by a wispy . . ." Matthew Josephson, *Life Among the Surrealists* (New York: Holt, Rinehart & Winston, 1962), p. 252.

"disenchanted with the . . ." John L. Stewart, *The Burden of Time: The Fugitives and Agrarians* (Princeton: Princeton University Press, 1965), p. 85.

"We were all writing . . ." Cowley, *Exile's Return*, p. 222.

79 "a foot on the loud . . ." Susan Jenkins Brown, *Robber Rocks* (Middletown: Wesleyan University Press, 1969), p. 26.

80 "If there is a loonier . . ." *A Dial Miscellany*, edited with an introduction by William Wasserstrom (Syracuse: Syracuse University Press, 1963), p. xiv.

"there is far too much . . ." B. L. Reid, *The Man From New York: John Quinn and His Friends* (New York: Oxford University Press, 1968), p. 434.

"it was the best . . ." Wasserstrom, *A Dial Miscellany*, p. xv.

81 "I think of the . . ." Marianne Moore, "The Dial: Part I," *Life and Letters Today*, December 1940, quoted in Frederick J. Hoffman et al., *The Little Magazine: A History and Bibliography* (Princeton: Princeton University Press, 1947), p. 201.

"at the slightest excuse . . ." Dos Passos, *The Best Times*, p. 132.

"small square bleak . . ." John Dos Passos, *Manhattan Transfer* (Boston: Houghton Mifflin Co., 1925), p. 344.

82 "I am living . . ." *Thomas Wolfe's Letters to His Mother Julia Elizabeth Wolfe*, edited by John Skally Terry (New York: Charles Scribner's Sons, 1943), p. 138.

"the sag and lean . . ." Thomas Wolfe, *The Web and the Rock* (New York: Harper & Brothers, 1939), p. 387.

"It is a magnificent . . ." *Wolfe's Letters to His Mother*, pp. 150–51.

page

83 "He loved this old house . . ." Thomas Wolfe, *You Can't Go Home Again* (New York: Grosset & Dunlap, 1940), p. 26.

"The life of the great . . ." Thomas Wolfe, *The Story of a Novel* (New York: Charles Scribner's Sons, 1949), p. 28.

84 "About the year 1924 . . ." Cowley, *Exile's Return*, p. 210.

"Greenwich Village Too Costly . . ." Carolyn F. Ware, *Greenwich Village: 1920–1930* (New York: Harper & Row, 1965), p. 21.

"What in Washington . . ." Carl Van Doren, "Elinor Wylie," *Harper's Magazine*, September 1936, p. 360.

85 "the same imperious brows . . ." Louis Untermeyer, *From Another World* (New York: Harcourt, Brace & Co., 1939), p. 241.

"White faced . . . she . . ." Carl Van Doren, "Elinor Wylie," p. 360.

"then still one . . ." Nancy Hoyt, *Elinor Wylie: The Portrait of An Unknown Lady* (New York: Bobbs-Merrill, 1935), p. 69.

"That one room . . ." Hoyt, *Elinor Wylie*, p. 69.

86 "a tiny, cheerful apartment . . ." Hoyt, *Elinor Wylie*, p. 90.

"an enormous deal table . . ." Hoyt, *Elinor Wylie*, p. 90.

"in the largest of American . . ." Vincent Sheean, *Dorothy and Red* (Boston: Houghton Mifflin, 1963), p. 146.

"Red's hospitality was incorrigible . . ." Sheean, *Dorothy and Red*, p. 145.

87 "the most exclusive . . ." Churchill, *The Literary Decade*, p. 272.

"demolished back fences . . ." Mark Van Doren, *The Autobiography of Mark Van Doren* (New York: Harcourt, Brace & Co., 1958), p. 173.

"What first made me . . ." Carl Van Doren, *Three Worlds* (New York: Harper & Brothers, 1936), p. 208.

88 "I used to walk . . ." E. B. White, *Here Is New York* (New York: Harper & Brothers, 1949), p. 32.

"I signalized my solidarity . . ." Lionel Trilling, *A Gathering of Fugitives* (Boston: Beacon Press, 1956), p. 49.

After the Twenties

89 "There is too much . . ." Sherwood Anderson, *Letters of Sherwood Anderson,* selected and edited with an introduction and notes by Howard Mumford Jones in association with Walter B. Rideout (Boston: Little, Brown & Co., 1953), Letter to Roger Sergel, Dec. 21, 1937.

page
91 "a nice and unusually . . ." *Letters of James Agee to Father Flye* (New York: George Braziller, 1962), p. 65.

92 "so good a novel . . ." Djuna Barnes, *Nightwood* (Norfolk: New Directions, 1961), p. xii.

"I bought the simplest . . ." Anaïs Nin, *The Diary of Anaïs Nin,* 1939–1944, edited and with a preface by Gunther Stuhlmann, (New York: Harcourt Brace & World, 1969), p. 46.

93 "would tolerate no ill . . ." Constance Webb, *Richard Wright: A Biography* (New York: G. P. Putnam's Sons, 1968), p. 236.

"By the time . . ." Fern Marja Eckman, *The Furious Passage of James Baldwin* (New York: M. Evans & Co., 1966), p. 113.

94 "It was a period . . ." Doris Grumbach, *The Company She Kept* (New York: Coward McCann, 1967), p. 73.

"For some of us . . ." William Barrett, "The Truants: 'Partisan Review' in the 40's," *Commentary,* Vol. 57, No. 6, June 1974, p. 49.

"There was a ceaseless flow . . ." Interview with Elizabeth Hardwick, June 13, 1974.

95 "I found myself surrounded . . ." Simone de Beauvoir, *America Day by Day* (New York: Grove Press, 1953), p. 41.

"bad, yellowed paintings . . ." Michael Harrington, "We Few, We Happy Few, We Bohemians," *Esquire,* August 1972, p. 101.

"heterosexuals on the make . . ." Harrington, "We Few," p. 101.

"all it was was . . ." Interview with Gregory Corso, April 1971.

96 "I want you to . . ." Interview with Gregory Corso.

97 "Before the incident . . ." Interview with Ed Fancher, Spring 1971.

"a horrible single room . . ." Letter from William Styron, November 28, 1972.

"took your heart . . ." *Writers at Work: The Paris Review Interviews,* edited by Malcolm Cowley (New York: Viking Press, 1958), p. 78.

98 "a tiny but rather . . ." Letter from William Styron.

"on a wobbly table . . ." "The Talk of the Town," *New Yorker,* March 25, 1961, p. 31.

"I did a draft . . ." *New Yorker,* p. 31.

99 "There was a saloon . . ." *Writers at Work: The Paris Review Interviews,* Third Series, introduced by Alfred Kazin (New York: Viking Press, 1967), p. 333.

"Norman found that . . ." Interview with Dan Wolf, Spring 1971.

page

100 "every English major . . ." Harrington, "We Few," p. 103.

"As the people . . ." Harrington, "We Few," p. 162.

"they decided then . . ." Letter from Vance Bourjaily, December 14, 1972.

III. Lower East Side (pages 111–146)

The Immigrants' City

111 "the foul core . . ." Jacob Riis, *How the Other Half Lives* (New York: Charles Scribner's Sons, 1922), p. 55.

"with these hapless . . ." Riis, *How the Other Half Lives,* pp. 95–96.

"all that is loathsome . . ." Roi Ottley and William J. Weatherby, editors, *The Negro in New York: An Informal Social History* (New York: The New York Public Library, 1967), p. 77.

"picketed from end to end . . ." Riis, *How the Other Half Lives,* p. 58.

113 "We stand upon . . ." Riis, *How the Other Half Lives,* pp. 28–29.

"the region of Jews . . ." Joseph Jay Rubin and Charles H. Brown, *Walt Whitman of the New York Aurora* (State College, Pa.: Bald Eagle Press, 1950), p. 18.

114 "the wiping out . . ." Lincoln Steffens, *The Autobiography of Lincoln Steffens* (New York: Harcourt, Brace & Co., 1931), p. 203.

"It was on the Bowery . . ." Van Wyck Brooks and Otto L. Bettmann, *Our Literary Heritage: A Pictorial History of the Writer in America* (New York: E. P. Dutton & Co., 1956), p. 15.

115 "It is inevitable . . ." Stephen Crane, *The Red Badge of Courage and Selected Prose and Poetry,* edited with an introduction by William M. Gibson (New York: Rinehart & Co., 1958), p. vii.

"Eventually they entered . . ." Crane, *Maggie* in *The Red Badge of Courage,* pp. 4–5.

"the only interesting . . ." Van Wyck Brooks, *An Autobiography* (New York: E. P. Dutton & Co., 1965), p. 128.

116 "the best years . . ." Abraham Cahan, *The Education of Abraham Cahan* (Philadelphia: Jewish Publication Society of America, 1969), p. 264.

117 "In other languages . . ." Samuel Niger, "Yiddish Culture in the United States," *The Jewish People, Past and Present,* Vol. 4 (New York: Jewish Encyclopedic Handbooks, 1955), p. 288.

118 "before you have . . ." Riis, *How the Other Half Lives,* p. 108.

page

119 "Over steaming Russian . . ." Moses Rischin, *The Promised City: New York's Jews, 1870–1914* (Cambridge: Harvard University Press, 1962), pp. 141–42.

120 "the only Gentile . . ." Hutchins Hapgood, *The Spirit of the Ghetto*, edited by Moses Rischin (Cambridge: Belknap Press of Harvard University Press, 1967), p. xxviii.

"When my parents . . ." Jacob Epstein, *Let There Be Sculpture* (New York: G. P. Putnam's Sons, 1940), p. 4.

"The name was . . ." Riis, *How the Other Half Lives*, p. 115.

122 "I at that time . . ." Steffens, *The Autobiography of Lincoln Steffens*, p. 244.

"spent the whole . . ." Brooks, *An Autobiography*, p. 156.

"My eyes are fond . . ." E. E. Cummings, *Poems 1923–1954* (New York: Harcourt, Brace & Co., 1954), p. 81.

123 "a tenement canyon . . ." Michael Gold, *Jews Without Money* (New York: Horace Liveright, 1930), p. 13.

"Continuity was destroyed . . ." Henry Roth, "Henry Roth: No Longer At Home," *New York Times*, April 15, 1971.

The East Village

127 "New York was Charlie . . ." Interview with Allen Ginsberg, December 21, 1971.

"John Clellon Holmes . . ." Jack Kerouac, "The Origins of the Beat Generation," *Playboy*, June 1959, reprinted in *A Casebook on the Beat*, edited by Thomas Parkinson (New York: Thomas Y. Crowell Co., 1961), p. 70.

"being right down to it . . ." John Clellon Holmes, "The Philosophy of the Beat Generation" in *The Beats*, edited by Seymour Krim (Greenwich: Gold Medal Books, Fawcett Publications, 1960), p. 15.

128 "three full moon nights . . ." Bruce Cook, *The Beat Generation* (New York: Charles Scribner's Sons, 1971), p. 79.

"the Pierre-of Melville goof . . ." Jack Kerouac, *The Subterraneans* (New York: Grove Press, 1958), p. 15.

129 "Melville, armed with the manuscript . . ." quoted in Cook, *The Beat Generation*, p. 45.

"Like *The Subterraneans* . . ." Interview with Ginsberg, Winter 1971.

130 "the real thing to remember . . ." Cook, *The Beat Generation*, p. 51.

"Williams' precise real images . . ." Jane Kramer, *Allen Ginsberg in America* (New York: Random House, 1969), p. 174.

page

130 "transcribe the thought . . ." Kramer, *Allen Ginsberg in America,* p. 171.

"If I had a Green Automobile . . ." Allen Ginsberg, *Reality Sandwiches* (San Francisco: City Lights Books, 1963), p. 11.

131 "Who ate fire . . ." Allen Ginsberg, *Howl* (San Francisco: City Lights Books, 1965), p. 9.

"Way over on the lower . . ." Norman Mailer, *Advertisements for Myself* (New York: New American Library, A Signet Book, 1960), p. 139.

"hole in New York . . ." Norman Mailer, *The Deer Park* (New York: Berkley Publishing Corporation, A Berkley Medallion Book, December 1970), p. 300.

"There was a kosher brewery . . ." and subsequent quotations this paragraph, interview with Dan Wolf, Spring 1971.

132 "It was a very rough neighborhood . . ." Interview with Dan Wolf.

"The Beat Generation . . ." Mailer, *Advertisements for Myself,* p. 334.

133 "Tonite I got hi . . ." Ginsberg, *Reality Sandwiches,* p. 77.

134 "Who was there? . . ." Cook, *The Beat Generation,* p. 51.

"John Ashbery, Barbara Guest . . ." Frank O'Hara, "Larry Rivers: A Memoir," in *The Collected Poems of Frank O'Hara,* edited by Donald Allen, with an introduction by John Ashbery (New York: Alfred A. Knopf, 1971), p. 512.

"I live above a dyke bar . . ." Allen, *The Collected Poems of Frank O'Hara,* p. 286.

136 "a tenement dump . . ." and subsequent quotations this paragraph, interview with Patsy Southgate, April 29, 1971.

"The apartment was . . ." Interview with Patsy Southgate.

"LeRoi turned up . . ." Interview with Patsy Southgate.

137 "The people in San Francisco . . ." Interview with Hettie Jones, May 17, 1971.

"You just go on your nerve . . ." Allen, *The Collected Poems of Frank O'Hara,* p. 498.

"A poem is energy . . ." Cook, *The Beat Generation,* p. 121.

138 "It was huge, baronial . . ." Interview with Hettie Jones.

"then I go back . . ." Allen, *The Collected Poems of Frank O'Hara,* p. 325.

"cold-water flophouse . . ." Interview with Hettie Jones.

page
139 "Auden writes on a new . . ." Judson Hand, *The New York Daily News,* January 13, 1971.

141 "rundown smelly . . ." Interview with Jack Gelber, September 18, 1974.

"right in the heart . . ." Interview with Gregory Corso, April 1971.

IV. Gramercy Park (pages 147–164)

147 "the pioneers of the younger set . . ." Edith Wharton, *Old New York* (New York: Charles Scribner's Sons, 1924) , p. 80.

148 "If I wrote the Gospels . . ." quoted in Alfred Kazin, "Melville the New Yorker," *New York Review of Books,* April 5, 1973, p. 5.

"a most inglorious one . . ." Lewis Mumford, *Herman Melville* (New York: The Literary Guild of America, 1929) , p. 307.

"Our home . . ." Frances Thomas Osborne, *Bulletin of the New York Public Library,* Vol. 69, No. 10, December 1965, p. 656.

149 "a quiet interior of its own . . ." Mumford, *Herman Melville,* p. 326.

"Grandpa would walk . . ." Osborne, *Bulletin,* p. 660.

150 "the variety . . ." William Dean Howells, *A Hazard of New Fortunes* (New York: New American Library, Signet edition, 1965) , p. 158.

"New York is still . . ." Howells, *A Hazard of New Fortunes,* p. 159.

151 "There's only one city . . ." Howells, *A Hazard of New Fortunes,* p. 12.

"If a novel flatters the passions . . ." Clara M. Kirk and Rudolph Kirk, *William Dean Howells* (New York: Twayne Publishers, 1962) , p. 124.

"We must ask ourselves . . ." William Dean Howells, *The Rise of Silas Lapham* (New York: Bantam Books, 1971) , p. ix.

153 "Occasionally one could hear . . ." Stephen Crane, *The Complete Novels of Stephen Crane,* edited with an introduction by Thomas A. Gullason (New York: Doubleday & Co., 1967) , p. 394.

"The flood of orange light . . ." Crane, *The Complete Novels,* p. 394.

"Every incident and phase . . ." John Berryman, *Stephen Crane* (New York: William Sloane Associates, 1950) , p. 73.

154 "The big hall . . ." William S. Porter, *The Complete Works of O. Henry* (New York: Doubleday & Co., 1953) , p. 529.

page

154 "three doors from . . ." William Wash Williams, *The Quiet Lodger of Irving Place* (New York: E. P. Dutton & Co., 1936), p. 49.

155 When Washington Irving visited . . . This is well documented in Stanley T. Williams's biography of Irving. Williams quotes a letter from the writer's grandnephew John Irving: "The third-story front room in my father's house was set apart for my uncle, who had his books and papers there and could work undisturbed. He came and went as he pleased, sometimes staying a week or a month; and once he stayed nearly all winter . . . I can say positively that he never lived at the corner of Irving Place and Seventeenth Street . . . We lived in East Twenty-first Street when my uncle stayed with us."

"Fourth Avenue — born and bred . . ." Porter, *Complete Works of O. Henry*, pp. 1569–70.

156 "an interior that might . . ." *Paul Rosenfeld: Voyage in the Arts,* edited by Jerome Mellquist and Lucie Wiese (New York: Creative Age Press, 1948), p. 20.

"poets read their poetry . . ." Mellquist and Wiese, *Paul Rosenfeld,* p. 9.

"beneath his little collection . . ." Mellquist and Wiese, *Paul Rosenfeld,* p. 11.

157 "The really important thing . . ." Mellquist and Wiese, *Paul Rosenfeld,* p. 95.

158 "Someone gathered Zelda up . . ." Van Wyck Brooks, *An Autobiography* (New York, E. P. Dutton & Co., 1965), p. 361.

"Badly designed, with small rooms . . ." Jay Martin, *Nathanael West: The Art of His Life* (New York: Farrar, Straus & Giroux, 1970), pp. 121–22.

" 'Register him under . . .' " James F. Light, *Nathanael West: An Interpretive Study* (Evanston: Northwestern University Press, 1971), p. 70.

V. Chelsea (pages 165–183)

165 "One of the most depressing . . ." Edith Wharton, *A Backward Glance: The Autobiography of Edith Wharton* (New York: Charles Scribner's Sons, 1962), p. 54.

166 "cultivated ferns . . ." Edith Wharton, *The Age of Innocence* (New York: Random House, Modern Library, 1948), p. 31.

167 "one of those ancient . . ." Stephen Crane, *The Complete Short Stories and Sketches of Stephen Crane,* edited by Thomas A. Gullason (New York: Doubleday & Co., 1963), p. 197.

page
167   "where from the streams . . ." Crane, *Complete Short Stories*, p. 311.

"He was my father's . . ." *Writers at Work: The Paris Review Interviews*, Second Series, edited by Malcolm Cowley (New York: Viking Press, 1963) , p. 142.

168   "Silent, grim, colossal . . ." William S. Porter, *The Complete Works of O. Henry* (New York: Doubleday & Co., 1953) , p. 17.

"Invoke your consideration . . ." Porter, *Complete Works of O. Henry,* p. 11.

169   "New York City is . . ." James Weldon Johnson, *Autobiography of an Ex-Coloured Man* (New York: Alfred A. Knopf, 1970) , p. 89.

170   "This is not a bourgeois . . ." Interview with Virgil Thomson, June 24, 1974.

171   "Then who will know . . ." Edgar Lee Masters, "The Hotel Chelsea," *The Chelsean,* Vol. 1., No. 6, April 1940, p. 1.

"The rooms were dark . . ." Elizabeth Nowell, *Thomas Wolfe: A Biography* (New York: Doubleday & Co., 1960) , p. 400.

172   "I would hope . . ." Brendan Behan, *Brendan Behan's New York* (New York: Bernard Geis, 1964) , p. 78.

"It is the only hotel . . ." Arthur Miller, quoted in Marshall Smith, "A Room With Ghost $4 and Up," *Life,* September 18, 1964.

174   "he had been no more . . ." Samuel French Morse, *Wallace Stevens: Poetry As Life* (New York: Pegasus, 1970) , p. 65.

"I got a cheap . . ." Sherwood Anderson, *Sherwood Anderson's Memoirs,* edited by Ray Lewis White (Chapel Hill: University of North Carolina Press, 1942) , p. 407.

175   "And so there . . ." Sherwood Anderson, *A Story Teller's Story,* edited by Ray Lewis White (Cleveland: The Press of Case Western Reserve University, 1968) , p. 286.

"There were three big trees . . ." Van Wyck Brooks, *An Autobiography* (New York: E. P. Dutton & Co., 1965) , p. 153.

176   "who invariably, when asked . . ." Conrad Aiken, *Ushant: An Essay* (New York: Oxford University Press, 1971) , p. 71.

177   "abounded in recollections . . ." Brooks, *An Autobiography,* pp. 176–77.

"The lead review . . ." Alfred Kazin, *Starting out in the Thirties* (Boston: Atlantic Monthly Press, Little, Brown & Co., 1965) , p. 18.

VI. Midtown (pages 184–221)

page

184 "While New York . . ." Van Wyck Brooks, *The Times of Melville and Whitman* (New York, E. P. Dutton & Co., 1947), p. 324.

186 "put the crowning . . ." Edith Wharton, *The Age of Innocence* (New York: Random House, Modern Library, 1948), p. 10.

"He goes into . . ." Van Wyck Brooks, "Mr. Howells at Work at Seventy-Two," *The World's Work*, May 1909, p. 11548.

"He was a short . . ." Franklin Walker, *Frank Norris, A Biography* (New York: Russell & Russell, 1963), p. 170.

188 "About eleven o'clock . . ." Vachel Lindsay in Edgar Lee Masters, *Vachel Lindsay: A Poet in America* (New York: Charles Scribner's Sons, 1935), pp. 124, 126, 127–28.

"New York society . . ." William Dean Howells, *Literature and Life* (New York: Harper & Brothers, 1902), p. 179.

189 "I thoroughly detest . . ." H. L. Mencken, *Letters of H. L. Mencken,* selected and annotated by Guy J. Forgue (New York: Alfred A. Knopf, 1961), p. 134.

190 "Don't ever if . . ." Allen Churchill, *The Literary Decade* (Englewood Cliffs: Prentice-Hall, 1971), p. 157.

191 "*The Smart Set* . . ." Mencken, *Letters,* p. 269.

"Under you and Nathan . . ." Mencken, *Letters,* p. 65.

193 "one cubic foot . . ." Nathaniel Benchley, *Robert Benchley, A Biography* (New York: McGraw-Hill, 1955), p. 70.

194 "a cheaply furnished . . ." John Keats, *You Might As Well Live: The Life and Times of Dorothy Parker* (New York: Simon & Schuster, 1970), p. 70.

"Oh, so they . . ." Benchley, *Robert Benchley,* p. 183.

195 "As a result . . ." Benchley, *Robert Benchley,* p. 135.

"leadership in the group . . ." Samuel Hopkins Adams, *A. Woollcott, His Life and His World* (New York: Reynal & Hitchcock, 1945), p. 120.

196 "Their standards were . . ." quoted in Adams, *A. Woollcott,* p. 123.

"People romanticize . . ." Keats, *You Might As Well Live,* p. 295.

197 "It had been made . . ." "The New Yorker," *Fortune,* August 1934, p. 82.

198 "No restaurant keeps . . ." Brendan Gill, *Here at the New Yorker* (New York: Random House, 1975), p. 193.

page

199 "The new magazine . . ." James Thurber, *Credos and Curios* (New York, Harper & Row, 1962) , p. 27.

"The *New Yorker* . . ." Dwight Macdonald, "Lie Down and Laugh," *Partisan Review,* December 1937, p. 46.

200 "The different temperaments . . ." Dwight Macdonald, "Para-journalism II: Wolfe and the New Yorker," *New York Review of Books,* February 3, 1966, p. 23.

"At her untidy . . ." Edna Ferber, *A Peculiar Treasure* (New York: Doubleday, Doran & Co., 1939) , p. 293.

201 "The population is . . ." Edwin P. Hoyt, *Alexander Woollcott: The Man Who Came to Dinner* (New York: Abelard-Schuman, 1968) , p. 160.

202 "a small and disordered . . ." Adams, *A. Woollcott,* p. 110.

"a large room . . ." Carl Van Vechten, *Sacred and Profane Memories* (New York: Alfred A. Knopf, 1932) , p. 226.

203 "as exotic as pomegranates," Bruce Kellner, *Carl Van Vechten and the Irreverent Decades* (Norman: University of Oklahoma Press, 1968) , p. 45.

"full of silver . . ." Langston Hughes, *The Big Sea* (New York: Alfred A. Knopf, 1940) , p. 251.

"with George Gershwin . . ." Emily Clark, *Innocence Abroad* (New York: Alfred A. Knopf, 1931) , pp. 144–45.

204 "In the fifty . . ." Edward Lueders, "Mr. Van Vechten of New York City," *New Republic,* May 16, 1955, p. 36.

205 "the marble and gold . . ." Virgil Thomson, *Virgil Thomson* (New York: Alfred A. Knopf, 1966) , p. 135.

207 "I loved being . . ." William Saroyan, *Places Where I've Done Time* (New York: Praeger Publishers, 1972) , pp. 80–81.

208 "To this day . . ." Alfred Kazin, "The Writer and the City," *Harper's,* December 1968, p. 122.

"New York burst . . ." F. Scott Fitzgerald, *This Side of Paradise* (New York: Charles Scribner's Sons, Scribner Library Edition, n.d.) , pp. 29–30.

210 "When I went . . ." Walker Gilmer, *Horace Liveright, Publisher of the Twenties* (New York: David Lewis, 1970) , p. 235.

211 "a job with any . . ." Lillian Hellman, *An Unfinished Woman — A Memoir* (Boston: Little, Brown & Co., 1969) , p. 33.

VII.   East Side (pages 222–245)

page

222   "A day or two since . . ." Edgar Allan Poe, *Doings of Gotham*, collected by Jacob E. Spannuth, with preface, introduction and comments by Thomas O. Mabbott (Pottsville, Pa.: J. E. Spannuth, 1929), Letter III, p. 40.

223   "was located on eight . . ." Margaret Fuller, *The Love Letters of Margaret Fuller,* introduction by Julia Ward Howe (New York: D. Appleton and Co., 1903), p. 209.

   "I now know all . . ." Mason Wade, *Margaret Fuller, Whetstone of Genius* (New York: Viking Press, 1940), p. 72.

224   "Stopping on the Harlem . . ." Wade, *Margaret Fuller,* p. 141.

   "New York is the focus . . ." Margaret Fuller, in *Margaret Fuller, American Romantic,* edited by Perry Miller (New York: Cornell University Press, 1963), p. 251.

225   "We rented a furnished . . ." Mary Colum, *Life and the Dream* (New York: Doubleday & Co., 1947), p. 208.

226   "We heard Amy's voice . . ." Colum, *Life and Dream,* p. 216.

227   "bare as a bald . . ." *Dear Scott/Dear Max, The Fitzgerald-Perkins Correspondence,* edited by John Kuehl and Jackson Bryer (New York: Charles Scribner's Sons, 1971), p. 239.

   "I am sitting at the moment . . ." E. B. White, *Here Is New York* (New York: Harper & Brothers, 1949), pp. 10–11.

228   "circle of lemon-colored . . ." Louise Bogan, *What the Woman Lived: Selected Letters of Louise Bogan 1920–1970,* edited and with an introduction by Ruth Limmer (New York: Harcourt Brace Jovanovich, 1973), p. 258.

   "In Turtle Bay . . ." White, *Here Is New York,* p. 53.

   "Walls papered with maps . . ." Marion K. Sanders, *Dorothy Thompson: A Legend In Her Time* (Boston: Houghton Mifflin Co., 1973), p. 289.

230   "It did not matter . . ." John P. Marquand, *Point of No Return* (Boston: Little Brown & Co., 1949), p. 24.

   "Tawny wall-to-wall . . ." Curtis Cate, *Antoine de Saint-Exupéry* (New York: G. P. Putnam's Sons, 1970), p. 483.

231   "a dusty-plush . . ." Gloria Steinem, "A Visit with Truman Capote," *Glamour,* April 1966, p. 239.

   "As long as I live . . ." Edith Wharton, *A Backward Glance* (New York: Charles Scribner's Sons, 1964), p. 109.

page

231 "a bonbonnière of the last . . ." Leon Edel, *Henry James,* Vol. 5, *The Master: 1901–1916* (Philadelphia: Lippincott Co., 1972) , p. 262.

". . . She was charming . . ." Edel, *Henry James,* p. 262.

232 "I would go to . . ." Quentin Reynolds, *By Quentin Reynolds* (New York: McGraw-Hill, 1963) , p. 67.

"West's Disease" W. H. Auden, *The Dyer's Hand and Other Essays* (New York: Random House, 1962) , p. 241.

233 "a continuing, well-organized . . ." John Houseman, *Run-Through: A Memoir* (New York: Simon & Schuster, 1972) , p. 97.

"looks like something . . ." Charles A. Fenton, *Stephen Vincent Benét: The Life and Times of an American Man of Letters, 1898–1943* (New Haven: Yale University Press, 1958) , p. 247.

234 "I shall miss this tiny . . ." André Maurois, *From My Journal* (New York: Harper & Brothers, 1948) , pp. 3–4.

235 "the city had beaten . . ." John Steinbeck, "Making of a New Yorker," *New York Times Magazine,* February 1, 1953, p. 27.

"My new home consisted . . ." Steinbeck, "Making of a New Yorker," p. 66.

"New York is an ugly . . ." Steinbeck, "Making of a New Yorker," p. 66.

237 "There's the whole story . . ." Eugene O'Neill in Hamilton Basso, "Profile," *New Yorker,* February 28, 1948, p. 34.

"A street lined . . ." Anaïs Nin, *The Diary of Anaïs Nin, 1944–1947,* edited and with a preface by Gunther Stuhlmann (New York: Harcourt Brace Jovanovich, 1971) , p. 83.

". . . It reminded me . . ." Sylvia Plath, *The Bell Jar* (New York: Bantam, 1972) , p. 3.

238 "stark, bare, colorless . . ." John Keats, *You Might As Well Live: The Life and Times of Dorothy Parker* (New York: Simon & Schuster, 1970) , p. 274.

239 "He brought writers . . ." Norman Podhoretz, *Making It* (New York: Random House, 1967) , p. 237.

240 "It was one room . . ." Truman Capote, *Breakfast at Tiffany's: A Short Novel and Three Stories* (New York: Random House, 1958) , p. 3.

"God, to think . . ." Finis Farr, *O'Hara, A Biography* (Boston: Little, Brown & Co., 1973) , p. 150.

241 "No writer today . . ." Interview with Louis Auchincloss, April 11, 1973.

VIII. The West Side (pages 246–268)

page

246 "signalized [his] solidarity with . . ." Lionel Trilling, *A Gathering of Fugitives* (Boston: Beacon Press, 1956), p. 49.

247 "a sweet rural valley . . ." quoted in Harmon H. Goldstone and Martha Dalrymple, *History Preserved: A Guide to New York City Landmarks and Historic Districts* (New York: Simon & Schuster, 1974), p. 294.

249 John Hall Wheelock recalls . . . Interview with John Hall Wheelock, January 21, 1974.

250 "I have taken . . ." Mark Schorer, *Sinclair Lewis, An American Life* (New York: McGraw-Hill, 1961), p. 699.

"Baronial living room . . ." Fannie Hurst, *Anatomy of Me* (New York: Doubleday & Co., 1958), p. 287.

251 "2 boston . . ." E. E. Cummings, *Poems 1923–1954* (New York: Harcourt, Brace & Co., 1954), p. 229.

"I simply rejoiced . . ." Gertrude Stein, *Fernhurst, Q. E. D., and Other Early Writings* (New York: Liveright, 1971), p. 101.

252 "two separate lives" Interview with Louis Untermeyer, November 11, 1970.

"the upper-class . . ." Interview with Louis Untermeyer.

"Frost read with just . . ." Interview with Louis Untermeyer.

"one hundred and twenty-two rejection slips . . ." Arthur Mizener, *The Far Side of Paradise* (Boston: Houghton Mifflin Co., 1965), p. 86.

253 "one slice in a long . . ." F. Scott Fitzgerald, *The Great Gatsby* (New York: Charles Scribner's Sons, 1953), p. 28.

"The Newhouse apartment . . ." Lillian Hellman, *An Unfinished Woman — A Memoir* (Boston: Little, Brown & Co., 1969), pp. 3–4.

254 "As we played . . ." J. D. Salinger, *Raise High the Roof Beam, Carpenters and Seymour, An Introduction* (New York: Bantam, 1971), p. 198.

"at 108th and Broadway . . ." Salinger, *Raise High the Roof Beam*, p. 162.

"luxurious Manhattan apartment . . ." Letter from Herman Wouk, October 29, 1974.

"furnished the milieu . . ." Letter from Herman Wouk.

255 "The Village was . . ." Interview with Elizabeth Hardwick, June 13, 1974.

page
255 "I was rehabilitating . . ." Meyer Levin in Frederic Morton, "Bohemia, Such As It Is, On the West Side," *New York Times Magazine*, May 9, 1971, p. 72.

"the mass migration . . ." Morton, "Bohemia, Such As It Is, On the West Side," p. 92.

"If you're interested . . ." Interview with Alfred Kazin, September 6, 1974.

"They are, or until . . ." Irving Howe, "The New York Intellectuals, A Chronicle and A Critique," *Commentary*, October 1968, p. 29.

257 "but its characteristic . . ." Norman Podhoretz, *Making It* (New York: Bantam, 1969), p. 197.

"the last gasp . . ." Robert Lowell, *Notebook 1967–68* (New York: Farrar, Straus & Giroux, 1969), p. 155.

258 "The reason there are no . . ." Victor Navasky, "Notes on Cult; or, How to Join the Intellectual Establishment," *New York Times Magazine*, March 27, 1966, p. 128.

"until recently . . ." Alfred Kazin, "The Writer and the City," *Harper's*, December 1968, p. 111.

"On some nights . . ." Saul Bellow, *The Victim* (New York: Viking Press, Compass Books edition, 1961), p. 3.

259 "like a baroque . . ." Saul Bellow, *Seize the Day* (New York: Viking Press, 1961), p. 5.

"Unless the weather . . ." Bellow, *Seize the Day*, p. 4.

"Brownstones, balustrades, bay windows . . ." Saul Bellow, *Mr. Sammler's Planet* (New York: Fawcett, 1970), p. 12.

"It was aware . . ." Bellow, *Mr. Sammler's Planet*, p. 134.

"New York makes . . ." Bellow, *Mr. Sammler's Planet*, p. 277.

"By a convergence . . ." Bellow, *Mr. Sammler's Planet*, p. 255.

260 "Most of the interaction . . ." Interview with Jack Gelber, September 18, 1974.

"as long as I lived . . ." Isaac Bashevis Singer, *A Friend of Kafka, and Other Stories* (New York: Farrar, Straus & Giroux, 1970), p. 78.

262 "Carl Van Doren . . ." Interview with Alfred Kazin.

"taught Kerouac Shakespeare . . ." Obituary in *New York Times*, December 12, 1972.

264 "This," said Ginsberg . . . and subsequent quotations, interview with Allen Ginsberg, December 22, 1971.

page

265 "He seemed in his own . . ." Trilling, *Gathering of Fugitives,*
p. 50.

268 "the buildings looked . . ." Langston Hughes, *The Big Sea* (New
York: Alfred A. Knopf, 1940), p. 83.

"a high, horrible apartment-house . . ." Mizener, *The Far Side of
Paradise,* p. 86.

IX. Harlem (pages 269–311)

271 "one of the most . . ." James Weldon Johnson, *Black Manhattan*
(New York: Alfred A. Knopf, 1930), p. 146.

274 "It was a period when . . ." Langston Hughes, *The Big Sea* (New
York: Alfred A. Knopf, 1940), pp. 227–28.

"Jessie Fauset at the *Crisis* . . ." Hughes, *The Big Sea,* p. 218.

275 "He wrote me . . ." Zora Neale Hurston, *Dust Tracks on a Road*
(New York: Arno Press and the *New York Times,* 1969), p. 176.

"Mr. Johnson, I believe . . ." Hughes, *The Big Sea,* p. 218.

276 "there was always quite . . ." Hughes, *The Big Sea,* p. 247.

277 "Mr. Johnson's appearance . . ." Blanche E. Ferguson, *Countee
Cullen and the Negro Renaissance* (New York: Dodd, Mead & Co.,
1966), p. 86.

"We often speak . . ." Wayne Cooper, "Claude McKay and the
New Negro of the 1920's," *Phylon, The Atlanta University Review
of Race and Culture,* Vol. 25, No. 3, Fall 1964, p. 305.

278 "Nigger Heaven! That's . . ." Carl Van Vechten, *Nigger Heaven*
(New York: Alfred A. Knopf, 1926), p. 149.

279 "Like a flock . . ." Claude McKay, *Harlem: Negro Metropolis*
(New York: E. P. Dutton & Co., 1940), p. 16.

283 "$1.50, no job . . ." Hurston, *Dust Tracks on a Road,* p. 176.

"she went about Harlem . . ." Hughes, *The Big Sea,* p. 236.

284 ". . . 99 and 99/100 per cent . . ." Wallace Thurman, *Infants of
the Spring* (New York: Macaulay Co., 1932), p. 140.

"the only Negro reader . . ." Hughes, *The Big Sea,* p. 234.

285 "I know of only one . . ." Thurman, *Infants of the Spring,* p. 221.

286 "shortly left his . . ." Hughes, *The Big Sea,* p. 242.

"My family is from . . ." Jean Toomer, *Cane,* with an introduction
by Arna Bontemps (New York: Harper & Row, Perennial Classic
edition, 1969), pp. viii–ix.

page

286 ". . . I have not lived . . ." Harper & Row press release, 1969.

287 "Harlem's Broadway . . ." Rudolph Fisher, *The Walls of Jericho* (New York: Alfred A. Knopf, 1928), p. 189.

"They say . . . that if . . ." Nella Larsen, *Quicksand* (New York: Collier Books, 1971), p. 169.

288 "big-hearted, night-dark . . ." Hughes, *The Big Sea*, p. 244.

"a one-woman foundation" Interview with Ted Poston, January 1971.

"She saw a real need . . ." Roi Ottley and William J. Weatherby, editors, *The Negro in New York: An Informal Social History* (New York: The New York Public Library, 1967), pp. 257–58.

289 "the Negro intelligentsia . . ." Ottley and Weatherby, *The Negro in New York,* p. 259.

291 "Everybody dropped in . . ." Interview with Arna Bontemps, November 25, 1970.

292 "Ride back! . . ." Claude McKay, *A Long Way from Home* (New York: Arno Press and the *New York Times,* 1969), p. 132.

"the most galling thing . . ." Lena Horne and Richard Schickel, *Lena* (New York: Doubleday & Co., 1965), p. 55.

293 "I care for nothing . . ." quoted in Larry Neal, "Eatonville's Zora Neale Hurston: A Profile," *Black Review No. 2* (New York: William Morrow & Co., 1972), pp. 23–24.

294 "You know white folks . . ." Milton Meltzer, *Langston Hughes, A Biography* (New York: Thomas Y. Crowell Co., 1968), p. 241.

"More than Paris . . ." Nathan Irvin Huggins, *Harlem Renaissance* (New York: Oxford University Press, 1971), p. 24.

295 "Had I been a rich . . ." Langston Hughes, "My Early Days in Harlem," in *Harlem: A Community in Transition,* edited by John Henrik Clarke (New York: Citadel Press, 1964), p. 62.

296 "It's a nice place . . ." The Schomburg Collection, vertical file on Langston Hughes.

"What happens . . ." Langston Hughes, *Montage of a Dream Deferred* (New York: Henry Holt & Co., 1951), p. 71.

297 "Layers and layers . . ." Ann Petry, *The Street* (New York: Pyramid, 1971), p. 17.

298 "[He] had just come . . ." Ralph Ellison, *Shadow and Act* (New York: Random House, 1964), p. 14.

" 'You must learn how . . .' " Ellison, *Shadow and Act,* p. 15.

page

299 "I did *not* come . . ." "A Very Stern Discipline, An Interview with Ralph Ellison," *Harper's Magazine,* Vol. 234, No. 1402, March 1967, p. 84.

"who shared, night after . . ." Ellison, *Shadow and Act,* p. 199.

"Harlem is a ruin . . ." Ellison, *Shadow and Act,* pp. 295–96.

300 "In my novel . . ." Ellison, *Shadow and Act,* p. 173.

"Here," he writes . . . Ellison, *Shadow and Act,* pp. 296–97.

301 "he and other children . . ." James Baldwin, *Another Country* (New York: Dell, 1963), p. 20.

"These streets hadn't . . ." James Baldwin, *Going to Meet the Man* (New York: Dial Press, 1965), p. 112.

"cloudy, and far away . . ." James Baldwin, *Go Tell It on the Mountain* (New York: New American Library, Signet, 1963), p. 30.

302 "since I was not stupid . . ." Fern Marja Eckman, *The Furious Passage of James Baldwin* (New York: M. Evans & Co., 1966), p. 113.

"the only human part . . ." Eckman, *The Furious Passage,* p. 39.

"where people know . . ." Interview with James Baldwin by John Hall, *Transatlantic Review,* Nos. 37 and 38, Autumn–Winter 1970–71, London, New York, p. 14.

304 "The strip is practically . . ." Tom Wolfe, "A Harlem Writer Who Makes James Baldwin Look Like A Tourist, *New York Herald Tribune, New York,* July 18, 1965, p. 4.

305 "perhaps the first . . ." Interview with Larry Neal, Fall 1972.

"hip, bourgeois . . ." Interview with Larry Neal.

"Folks are trying . . ." Interview with Larry Neal.

"in and around . . ." Interview with Larry Neal.

X. The Bronx, Queens and Staten Island (pages 312–327)

The Bronx

312 "I am living . . ." Edgar Allan Poe, *The Letters of Edgar Allan Poe,* edited by John Ward Ostrom (New York: Gordian Press, 1966), Vol. 2, p. 325.

314 "We drifted from room . . ." Albert Bigelow Paine, *Mark Twain, A Biography* (New York: Harper & Brothers, 1912), pp. 1141–42.

"Please tell him . . ." Marie Waife-Goldberg, *My Father, Sholom Aleichem* (New York: Simon & Schuster, 1968), p. 187.

page

314 "We rented an apartment . . ." Leon Trotsky, *My Life: An Attempt at an Autobiography* (New York: Charles Scribner's Sons, 1930), p. 271.

315 "a brick cliff . . ." Herman Wouk, *The City Boy: The Adventures of Herbie Bookbinder* (New York: Doubleday & Co., 1952), p. 16.

"The Bronx? No thonx . . ." Ogden Nash, *The Bronx County Historical Society Journal*, Vol. 1, No. 2, July 1964, pp. 67–68.

Queens

316 "This is a valley . . ." F. Scott Fitzgerald, *The Great Gatsby* (New York: Charles Scribner's Sons, 1953), p. 23.

"Over the great bridge . . ." Fitzgerald, *The Great Gatsby*, p. 69.

Staten Island

317 "nearly blinded me . . ." Robert L. Gale, *Francis Parkman* (New York: Twayne Publishers, 1973), p. 57.

"I have to say . . ." Max Cosman, "Thoreau and Staten Island," *Staten Island Historian*, January–March 1943, p. 2.

319 "The cedar seems . . ." Cosman, "Thoreau," p. 2.

"I want a whole continent . . ." Henry G. Steinmeyer, *Staten Island 1524–1898* (Staten Island: Staten Island Historical Society, 1950), p. 48.

"he has naturalized and . . ." Walter Harding, *The Days of Henry Thoreau* (New York: Alfred A. Knopf, 1965), p. 150.

320 "I seem more or less . . ." Henry James, *A Small Boy and Others* (New York: Charles Scribner's Sons, 1913), p. 28.

"to childish retrospect . . ." James, *A Small Boy*, p. 28.

"God might have made . . ." Vernon B. Hampton, *Staten Island's Claim to Fame, "The Garden Spot of New York Harbor"* (Staten Island: Richmond Borough Publishing & Printing Co., n.d.), p. 69.

321 "It was evident . . ." Virgil Markham, "Literary Tradition on Staten Island," *Staten Island Historian*, January–March 1957, p. 3.

"When we had guests . . ." Markham, "Literary Tradition," p. 3.

XI. Brooklyn and Brooklyn Heights (pages 328–366)

Brooklyn

328 "From 1824–'28 our family . . ." Walt Whitman, *The Viking Portable Library Walt Whitman*, selected and with notes by Mark Van Doren (New York: Viking Press, 1960), pp. 486–87.

page

329 "We were both walkers . . ." Gay Wilson Allen, *Walt Whitman* (Detroit: Wayne State University Press, 1969), p. 85.

330 "Living in Brooklyn . . ." Van Doren, *The Viking Whitman*, pp. 489-90.

331 "In my dreams . . ." Henry Miller, *Black Spring* (New York: Grove Press, 1963), p. 5.

"Soon the street . . ." Henry Miller, *Tropic of Capricorn* (New York: Grove Press, 1961), p. 216.

332 "the street of early sorrows," Henry Miller, *My Life and Times*, abridged from the original edition (Chicago: Playboy Press, 1973), p. 110.

"I recall some wonderful . . ." Miller, *My Life and Times*, p. 111.

"It had pointed leaves . . ." Betty Smith, *A Tree Grows in Brooklyn* (New York: Harper & Brothers, 1947), p. 3.

333 "Every time I go . . ." Alfred Kazin, *A Walker in the City* (New York: Harcourt, Brace & Co., 1951), pp. 5-6.

"On the block itself . . ." Kazin, *A Walker in the City*, p. 84.

"One of the longest . . ." Norman Podhoretz, *Making It* (New York: Bantam Books, 1969), p. 3.

"am on right . . ." and "Piles of books . . ." George Plimpton, "The World Series with Marianne Moore," *Harper's Magazine*, October 1964, p. 51.

336 "My turf is mostly . . ." John Oliver Killens, *New York Times*, October 3, 1971.

337 "the version ten years later . . ." Interview with Arthur Miller, Spring 1970.

"My mother didn't . . ." Interview with Arthur Miller.

"gives a sense of hierarchy . . ." Interview with Arthur Miller.

338 "Once one gets off . . ." L. J. Davis, *New York Times*, September 26, 1971.

Brooklyn Heights

339 "a beautiful growth . . ." Henry R. Stiles, *The History of the City of Brooklyn*, published by subscription, Brooklyn, 1867-70, Vol. 2, p. 35.

340 "Families who . . ." Christopher Tunnard and Henry Hope Reed, *American Skyline* (Boston: Houghton Mifflin Co., 1955), p. 70.

"in a quiet . . ." James H. Callender, *Yesterdays on Brooklyn Heights* (New York: Dorland Press, 1927), p. 60.

page

342 "In a bare shed . . ." David McCullough, *The Great Bridge* (New York: Simon & Schuster, 1972) , p. 302.

"A stunning act . . ." Lewis Mumford, *The Brown Decades* (New York: Dover Publications, 1931) , pp. 96–97.

344 "Everytime one looks . . ." John Unterecker, *Voyager, A Life of Hart Crane* (New York: Farrar, Straus & Giroux, 1969) , p. 364.

"O harp and altar . . ." Hart Crane, *The Bridge, A Poem* (New York: Liveright, 1970) , p. 2.

345 "Brooklyn Bridge . . ." Marianne Moore, "The Plums of Curiosity," *Vogue*, August 1, 1960, p. 83.

346 "It was so esthetically . . ." Interview with Arthur Miller, Spring 1970.

"The place may seem . . . " Thomas Wolfe, *You Can't Go Home Again* (New York: Dell, 1934) , p. 369.

"an entire floor . . ." Thomas Wolfe, *Thomas Wolfe's Letters to His Mother Julia Elizabeth Wolfe,* edited by John Skally Terry (New York: Charles Scribner's Sons, 1943) , p. 217.

"very nice rooms . . ." Wolfe, *Letters,* pp. 233–34.

348 "The chief piece . . ." Wolfe, *Letters,* p. ix.

350 "as George Davis was . . ." Letter from W. H. Auden, April 20, 1970.
"Then there were those . . ." Letter from W. H. Auden.

"When he . . ." Anaïs Nin, *The Diary of Anaïs Nin, 1939–1944,* edited and with a preface by Gunther Stuhlmann (New York: Harcourt, Brace & World, 1969) , p. 281.

"This is not . . ." Constance Webb, *Richard Wright: A Biography* (New York: G. P. Putnam's, 1968) , p. 195.

"An amazing house . . ." Nin, *Diary,* p. 270.

351 "The street where . . ." Carson McCullers, "Brooklyn Is My Neighborhood," *Vogue*, March 1941, p. 62.

"At three o'clock . . ." McCullers, "Brooklyn," p. 138.

352 "It was just a nice . . ." Letter from Paul Bowles, May 19, 1970.

"Something from the lobby . . ." Letter from Paul Bowles.

"I remember having measles . . ." Letter from Paul Bowles.

"Benjamin Britten . . ." Letter from Paul Bowles.

353 "We lived there . . ." Interview with Arthur Miller.

"I used to sit . . ." Arthur Miller, "A Boy Grew In Brooklyn," *Holiday,* March 1955, p. 54.

page

354 "the rooms were . . ." Interview with Arthur Miller.

"We couldn't have . . ." *Brooklyn Heights Press*, March 6, 1958.
"never gravitated . . ." Interview with Arthur Miller.

355 "Everybody tried . . ." Interview with Norman Rosten, May 15, 1970.

"where I refused to . . ." Henry Miller, *Henry Miller Letters to Anaïs Nin,* edited by Gunther Stuhlmann (New York: G. P. Putnam's, 1965) , p. 104.

"At No. 27 . . ." Moore, "The Plums of Curiosity," p. 140.

356 "I was most impressed . . ." Truman Capote, "Brooklyn Heights: A Personal Memoir," *Holiday,* February 1959, p. 66.

357 "In aggravated moments . . ." Capote, "Brooklyn Heights," p. 113.

"silent miles . . ." Capote, "Brooklyn Heights," p. 114.

"Every kind of sailor . . ." Capote, "Brooklyn Heights," p. 114.

359 "Writing about FBI . . ." *Writers At Work: The Paris Review Interviews,* Third Series, introduced by Alfred Kazin (New York: Viking Press, 1967) , p. 268.

"lofty, tenting . . ." Brock Brower, "Always the Challenge," *Life,* September 24, 1965, p. 105.

"is tucked away . . ." Brower, "Always the Challenger," p. 105.

361 "Comparing the Brooklyn . . ." McCullers, "Brooklyn," p. 63.

Index